MODERN SAINTS

THEIR LIVES AND FACES

Book Two

The canonization of St. Vincent Mary Strambi by Pope Pius XII, June 11, 1950.

MODERN SAINTS

THEIR LIVES AND FACES

Book Two

By

Ann Ball

"After this I saw a great multitude, which no man could number, of all nations, and tribes, and peoples and tongues, standing before the throne, and in sight of the Lamb, clothed with white robes, and palms in their hands: And they cried with a loud voice, saying: Salvation to our God, who sitteth upon the throne, and to the Lamb."
Apoc. *7:9-10*

TAN BOOKS AND PUBLISHERS, INC.
Rockford, Illinois 61105

Nihil Obstat: Rev. Drew Wood
                     Censor Deputatus

Imprimatur: ✠ Joseph A. Fiorenza
                     Bishop of Galveston-Houston
                     April 18, 1986

Library of Congress Catalog Card No.: 82-50357

ISBN: 0-89555-221-3 The Set
ISBN: 0-89555-222-1 Volume 1
ISBN: 0-89555-223-X Volume 2

Further volumes in preparation.

Printed and bound in the United States of America.

TAN BOOKS AND PUBLISHERS, INC.
P. O. Box 424
Rockford, Illinois 61105

1990

DEDICATION

For Our Lady of Atocha
and her beloved Santo Niño:
May You take great joy in the lives of
these faithful friends.

For my children—Joanna, Sam, and the
"A.K.'s":
May you pattern your lives in joy on
the lives of these saints who showed
such love for the Holy Child and His
Blessed Mother.

DECLARATION OF OBEDIENCE

In loving obedience to the decrees of several Roman Pontiffs, in particular those of Pope Urban VIII, I declare that I in no way intend to prejudge Holy Mother Church in the matter of saints, sanctity, miracles, and so forth. Final authority in such matters rests with the See of Rome, to whose judgement I willingly submit.

—the Author

ABOUT THE AUTHOR

Ann Ball credits St. Christopher with beginning her interest in Catholic saints, as his was the first saint's biography she read. While sitting with a third-grade class during library period in Austin, Texas in 1964, she noticed a series of saints books for children on the shelves. Her father had carried a key chain with St. Christopher's image on it, so she began by reading his biography to find out why he was known as a patron of travelers. Later, it was a photograph of St. Therese of Lisieux in a wheelchair, and the startled reactions of her fifth-grade students at seeing a photograph—as opposed to a painting—of a saint, which led Ann into her hobby of collecting photographs of modern saints. She wanted to display these modern-day heroes and heroines as real people in order that they might be more believable examples to her students.

Ann Ball studied journalism at the University of Texas and holds a B.S. degree in education from the University of Houston. She taught school for many years, teaching almost all grades from first through twelfth. She has worked as a private investigator and is currently a corporate officer and manager for a private security company in Houston. Writing is her hobby. She writes poetry for herself and her friends. A convert to the Catholic Faith, she enjoys writing Catholic books—which she jokingly says are necessary in order to explain her religion to her large, extended, mostly Protestant family.

Ann has two children. Additionally, she considers herself blessed to have a large number of "A.K.'s"—"Adopted Kids." These are former students, friends of her children, and other young people who sometimes consider Ann as "another mother."

TABLE OF CONTENTS

ACKNOWLEDGEMENTS

Since I began "saint collecting" in the late 1960's, there have been many persons who have approved of and assisted in my research on modern saints—research which has resulted in this second volume. A complete list of all those who helped make this book possible would fill a book itself. Those persons listed in the bibliography pages under "Correspondence" have all contributed information or photographs. In order to locate these people, however, I have had recourse to many others who have directed me to the proper addresses.

Postulators and Vice Postulators of individual causes and of entire orders have been generous in taking time to answer questions and make suggestions. Never has anyone refused me help. From the archivist of the Sacred Congregation for the Causes of Saints to my next-door neighbors, from bishop to postulant, from well-known authors to previously unknown friends and correspondents, assistance in my project has poured in through my mail slot.

In particular, I would like to thank all those in the Chancery Office of the Diocese of Galveston-Houston for their assistance and advice. Mrs. Joan Carroll Cruz, Fr. Salvator Fink, O.F.M., Fr. Richard Flores, Fr. Boniface Hanley, O.F.M., Mr. Leo Knowles, Professor John McAleer, and Fr. John Rubba, O.P.—all "saint collecting" friends and authors—have sent books, leads, addresses and other valuable information. Numerous members of the Dominicans, the Passionists and the Salesians have sent encouragement and support. A number of the Basilian priests here in Houston have answered countless theological questions for me—in particular, Fr. James Gaunt, C.S.B., and Fr. John Boscoe, C.S.B.

Last, but most assuredly not least, I owe a large debt of gratitude to Mr. Tom Nelson, the publisher of this volume, who feels much as I do about the need to disseminate the stories of the modern heroes of the Catholic Church, and to Mary Frances Lester, the editor on this book. And for all those I have not specifically named but who have been so much a part of the preparation of this book, I leave your thanks in the hands of Our Blessed Mother.

AUTHOR'S PREFACE

My work in hagiography or lives of the saints ("saint collecting") is actually a hobby that got out of hand. As I related in the first book of *Modern Saints,* the idea for this book was conceived because of the reactions of a group of my students to a photograph of St. Therese the Little Flower. After making many references throughout the year to her and to her "little way," I brought to class a photo of St. Therese in her wheelchair. Comments ranged from "Where are the roses?" to "You mean she was real?"

I had been speaking of Therese Martin, a real person, but the children had visualized only a statue of a nun holding a bunch of roses. After questioning them, I discovered that these otherwise intelligent students had no concept of what sanctity was. And how could I expect them to be interested in or to imitate a plaster statue? Immediately I began to search for more photographs to "prove" that the saints were real.

Thus in the late 1960's I began collecting photographs of saints, beati (blesseds) and servants of God. Instead of romanticized portraits, I wanted to show my students real flesh and blood people who have lived the sort of lives that made them fit candidates for canonization—modern heroes well suited to imitation by all the faithful. I wanted my students to know that we all have the opportunity to become saints. Eventually I realized that my collection had grown to the scope of a book—or rather, more than one book—which, if published, might give this same message of hope to more than just the few children I taught. The first book of *Modern Saints* was published in 1983.

The response to the book was outstanding. One of the many pleasures I have derived from it has been receiving the letters people have written me; even today I still receive a number each year. Usually the writers are seeking more information about a particular saint or servant of God. This makes me happy, for I wrote *Modern Saints* as I would invite people to a party: Come and meet new friends; enjoy all, and make special friends of some. The servants of God are just that, very special friends of God.

One letter which I recently received asks a question that I have

xiii

been asked repeatedly: "How come there are so few married saints or single lay people canonized? It would really be nice for those of us serving God as married people and single people to know about some of our own." This is a good point, since one of the main purposes of canonization is to give an example of holiness for imitation by the faithful.

So why, one might ask, are there so few lay persons canonized? The answer has much to do with the complications of the canonization process itself. It is the most careful investigative process in the world and, prior to the 1969 procedural changes, was extremely long and involved, requiring much collecting and compiling of information and records. Even today it requires much investigation and compiling of information. The investigation still takes many years, but not as many years as formerly. Members of religious orders have often been the ones to promote the causes of their deceased members, keeping them progressing on the road to canonization. But Pope Paul VI streamlined the process somewhat, and today more and more causes for lay persons are being entered.

The same correspondent asked if I had ever considered writing a book specifically about lay saints. My own field of research covers those saints and servants of God—priestly, religious and lay—who have lived from 1800 to date. He will be pleased to know, however, that my friend Joan Carroll Cruz has written just such a book. The book is called *Secular Saints: 250 Canonized and Beatified Lay Men, Women and Children* and has also been published by TAN Books and Publishers. In that book he will find many examples of persons in the married and single states (plus widows and widowers) who have been canonized or beatified.

A final point I would like to address with regard to the persons in Book Two of *Modern Saints* is the great number of founders and foundresses of religious orders. Why are there so many? A brief look at the history of the Church and the world from the late 1700's to date will provide an answer. The French Revolution, the Industrial Revolution, the slave trade, the emigration to America and the various European wars all caused many new needs in the Church, creating new and different fields of endeavor. Thus the Church in the 19th century saw a multitude of persons inspired by God to combat the spiritual and temporal evils of the day and to bring in a rich harvest of souls.

To provide laborers for such works, a number of new religious orders were established in the Church. The specific charisms of their founders and foundresses were given to them by God and were used by them to combat the prevailing problems and strengthen the Church Militant.

My prayer is that each Christian today will follow the blessed example given us by these modern heroes and heroines and will use his or her God-given gifts to combat the specific problems and evils of our own times.

INTRODUCTION

What Is A Saint? A saint is any person who has died and gone to Heaven. All such persons, both known and unknown, are venerated on All Saints Day, November 1. But usually the word "saint" is used in reference to a Catholic who has lived a life of such exemplary holiness that the Church has officially proclaimed him a saint. This official declaration is called "canonization."

In the title of this book, the word "saints" is used loosely. In the case of those who have not been canonized, the word is to be taken simply as a description, rather than as an official title.

It is permissible to pray to and request the intercession of anyone believed to be in Heaven. However, official public honor in the liturgy is reserved for those whom the Church has recognized.

Who Can Become A Saint? Any Catholic who sincerely desires it can become a saint. God calls all the faithful to sanctity, and gives His grace to each one. The essence of holiness is the carrying out of God's Will each day through the practice of the virtues—especially faith, hope and charity—to an heroic degree. Extraordinary deeds and extraordinary mystical gifts are not necessary. Contemplative prayer is a very great help in bringing about deep love of God, though it is not absolutely necessary. All have an obligation to pray, and if a person perseveres in meditation and practice of the virtues, it is not unlikely that God will grant the gift of contemplative prayer, even to an "ordinary" person.

There is a great variety of personalities among the saints. Some have been witty and entertaining; others have been quiet by nature. Some have been rich, some poor, some beautiful, and some homely.

There are saints from countries not mentioned in this book. Those from countries which are today controlled by anti-religious governments are not represented here in the numbers in which they surely exist. Information on these is very scanty. There are, however, no geographic boundaries to holiness; saints can come from any place in the world.

Can Only Priests And Nuns Become Saints? Definitely not! Although the majority of the people in this book were priests or members of religious orders, all should strive for sanctity.

One reason there are so many religious in this book is that their orders were most helpful in supplying the information. In addition, the process of canonization is long and involved, and the members of religious orders have often been the ones to keep the causes of their deceased members progressing on the road to canonization; this involves much collecting and compiling of information and records. But there are also canonized saints like Gemma Galgani, who was refused admittance to the convent, or Maria Goretti, who preferred to die at an early age rather than commit a mortal sin. Many of the martyrs of all centuries were lay people. Not one of the twenty-two martyrs of Uganda was a priest or member of a religious order.

Do Catholics Adore Saints? No. God alone is worthy of adoration. Catholics venerate, or honor, the saints; the saints are accorded a veneration technically called *dulia.* To Our Lady is given a higher form of veneration called *hyperdulia,* but to God alone is reserved the supreme form of veneration known as *latria,* or adoration. God is glorified in His saints; the last of the Divine Praises is "Blessed be God in His angels and in His saints."

Why Does The Catholic Church Canonize Saints? Saints are canonized to honor them, to implore their intercession (prayers to God for men), and to give an example of holiness for imitation by the faithful. Canonization does not *make* anyone a saint; it is an official declaration by the Church that a person *is* a saint.

The Mystical Body of Christ is composed of the saints in Heaven, who form the Church Triumphant, of the faithful on earth, who form the Church Militant, and of the souls in Purgatory, who form the Church Suffering. The saints intercede for the faithful on earth and for the souls in Purgatory; the faithful on earth honor the saints in Heaven, ask for their intercession, and imitate their virtues.

Some saints, of course, did things which one ordinarily could not or should not attempt to imitate. For example, Padre Pio received the stigmata, the wounds of Our Lord. This is not something which a person should ask to imitate; certainly, however, a Christian should follow Padre Pio's example of devotion to Our Lord. Imitating the saints will not make anyone into a carbon copy of anyone else. Even though each virtue—humility, for example—is essentially the same from saint to saint, it will take on a somewhat different form in each individual, depending on God's will in each life.

A priest in Houston once remarked that saints often "come in clumps." As the reader will discover, many of the saints in this book did indeed know and influence each other.

Are Saints A Modern Idea? No. From early Christian times a special honor was paid to the martyrs, and intercessory prayer has a biblical basis. As early as the fourth century, exemplary Christians who were not martyrs were also being honored. The early Christians believed that those who had died for the Faith must be especially close to God, and priests began to offer Mass by the tombs of the martyrs. Later, the remains were removed from tombs to altars in churches named in honor of these martyrs. From this grew the term "raised to the honors of the altar."

At first, there was no official canonization procedure. Those who had died a martyr's death, or who had defended the Faith (confessors), or who had led an outstanding Christian life excelling especially in penance, teaching the Faith, or great charity, became revered as saints by popular acclaim. Local Christian communities spontaneously began to venerate these people. Even in the earliest days the bishops attempted to put some form of official order into this veneration, but inevitably abuses arose. The need for a definite standard of spiritual perfection was felt.

Up to the end of the first thousand years of Christian history, the Apostolic See gave its consent to the veneration of saints only tacitly, and no formal act is preserved in which the pope recommends or prescribes the veneration of any particular saint. In 993, Pope John XV undertook what can technically be called the first canonization, declaring by papal bull that Bishop Ulric of Augsburg was a saint. The first laws concerning papal dominion in the cases of canonization were promulgated by Innocent III (1199-1216), but a brief of Urban VIII in 1634 unequivocally reserved all matters pertaining to the saints to the Roman See. The provisions of this papal brief were further developed by successive popes and were codified in 1918 in the Code of Canon Law. Alexander VII instituted the solemn consummation of the process of beatification through the ceremony in St. Peter's Basilica. St. Francis de Sales was the first person to receive this honor, which was conferred in 1662.

How Does The Church Canonize Saints? The process of canonization by which Holy Mother Church declares a person a saint
is long and involved. The procedure is the most careful and thor-
ough investigative process to be found anywhere in the world. Until
the 1969 reforms of Pope Paul VI, which consolidated a number
of the steps, the canonization procedure involved 20 separate and
well-documented steps. Even after these reforms the procedure is
still long and complicated. Following is a brief sketch.

If a person has lived a most exemplary life, or died a martyr,
his cause may be begun. The cause may be requested by the faithful or may be begun by the bishop or by Rome. There is a series
of investigations and trials in the diocese, known as the Ordinary
Process. If the Congregation for the Causes of Saints (formerly
the Congregation of Rites) decides that the person truly died a
martyr's death or practiced virtue to an heroic degree, a detailed
examination of his life, writings, reputation and at least two miracles attributed to his intercession is made. This is called the Apostolic
Process, or Papal Process, and it signals the Introduction of the
cause for beatification. The Servant of God is declared Venerable,
and study continues. Martyrs do not need the same proof of miracles in this part of the process as do non-martyrs.

In order to insure accuracy and fairness, a Promoter of the Faith,
popularly called the "Devil's Advocate," is appointed to raise any
objections to the cause. If the Congregation's findings are positive,
the person is beatified, that is, he is declared Blessed. Persons
who have been declared Blessed, known as "beati," are honored
locally or in specific religious communities or dioceses.

After beatification, the process continues. There is a re-examina-
tion of the evidence, and there must be proof of two new miracles
through the intercession of the beatus (or beata). From earliest
times, miracles have been considered proof of God's approval of
the life of a candidate for canonization. There are numerous and
specific regulations dealing with miracles. Usually the cures accepted
as proofs of sanctity must be of an organic nature and must be
instantaneous. Although in most cases two miracles are required
for beatification and two for canonization, as many as four may
be required for each step in some cases where eyewitness testimony
to sanctity is not available.

If this part of the process is carried out successfully, the beatus
is canonized. In a magnificent solemn ceremony in St. Peter's Basil-

ica, the Pope declares to all the Church that this person is a saint in Heaven. The saint's veneration is extended to the entire Church. He may be named in the public prayers of the Church, including the Mass and Divine Office, and churches may be dedicated to him. His feast is incorporated into the liturgical calendar, usually on the day of his death, which is his birthday into Heaven.

The type of canonization outlined above is known as "ordinary," or "non-cultus." Most canonizations are carried out in this manner according to the ideas outlined by Pope Urban. In some cases, known as "extraordinary," the purpose of the Church's investigation is to prove that there is a long-standing history of veneration of a certain person. In this form of canonization, the requirement of miracles as proofs of the person's sanctity is dispensed with. The person's heroic virtue must be credible in light of what is known about him. In such cases, the Pope may dispense with the solemn canonization, and instead, after due investigation, he will "confirm the cult." This is called an "equivalent" canonization. Such was the case with the beatification of Kateri Tekakwitha, the first American lay person to be beatified.

How Many Saints Are There? Of all the holy persons who have ever lived—the sanctity of many of whom may never even have been suspected—only a few begin the long canonization process, much less complete it. Many Christian martyrs throughout history were not even buried with the information of their names. Many causes are dropped before completion. Most of the saints are known to God alone.

The revision of the Church calendar after Vatican II led to much speculation that some saints had been "demoted." This is inaccurate. No canonized saint has ever suffered a loss of status. Many of the saints removed from the calendar had never been formally canonized to begin with, but even these may still be honored privately, and in some areas, publicly.

Although one unofficial listing of recognized saints shows 2,565 entries, it is not possible to compute the exact number of saints acclaimed locally before the year 1000. Some estimates range to over 4,000. Between the year 1000 and August of 1980, only 423 persons were officially canonized by Rome. (Up to 1634, only 125 had been canonized.) When you consider that this small number includes several groups of martyrs, such as the Twenty-two Martyrs

of Uganda and the Forty English and Welsh Martyrs, it is obvious
that the Church has canonized only a few saints. Between 1665
and August of 1980, the Church declared 1,224 persons Blessed,
and causes for well over 1,000 other Servants of God are currently
under investigation in Rome. Hopefully the reforms made in the
process by Pope Paul VI will help to speed up the procedure so
that the Church may soon have saintly examples from all states
of life and all parts of the world.

Explanation Of The Information In The Chapter Headings

The title of the chapter is the name by which the person is commonly known. The first of the two names in smaller type is the
person's complete name and current title, and the second name
is his baptismal name. In a few chapters there is only one name
in smaller type; this is the baptismal name. In these cases the
popular name and the complete name are the same.

The letters after some of the names indicate a particular religious order. For example, the letters D.C. after St. Elizabeth Seton's
name indicate that she was a member of the Daughters of Charity.
(Often these initials refer to the Order's name in Latin.) The dates
given are the years of the saint's birth and death. The country
is the country where the saint was born and died; if a second
country is listed, *that* is the country in which he died. Finally,
the saint's age at the time of his death is given.

In the preparation of this book I have made every effort to be
accurate, especially with regard to the status of each cause. Any
error of fact in the text is unintentional.

ANN BALL

MODERN SAINTS

THEIR LIVES AND FACES

Book Two

— 1 —

SAINT ELIZABETH SETON

Saint Elizabeth Ann Seton, D.C.
Elizabeth Ann Bayley
1774 - 1821
United States
Died Age 46

Although she embarked on a career of public charity soon after her marriage, no one dreamed that the young Episcopal society matron, Elizabeth Bayley Seton, would one day be the first native-born American to be canonized by the Catholic Church.

Born two years before the American Revolution, Elizabeth grew up in the "cream" of New York society. She loved dancing and the theater. Elizabeth inherited a hot temper, though she would learn to control it well. A prolific reader, she read everything from the Bible to contemporary novels.

In spite of her high society background, Elizabeth's early life was quiet, simple, and often lonely. Her mother died when she was only three. Her stepmother was indifferent to Elizabeth and her sister; and her father, a physician, was often away from home. A warm, affectionate, outgoing child, Elizabeth showed an early inclination for contemplation of God, especially in her examination of His natural wonders. Her greatest pleasure was "reading prayers." As she grew a little older the Bible was to become her continual instruction, support and comfort; she would continue to love the Scriptures for the rest of her life.

In 1794, Elizabeth married the wealthy young William Seton, with whom she was deeply in love. The first years of their marriage were happy and prosperous. Elizabeth wrote in her diary that first autumn, "My own home at 20—the world—that and heaven too—quite impossible."

This time of Elizabeth's life was to be a brief moment of earthly happiness before the many deaths and partings she was to suffer. Within four years Will's father died, leaving the young couple in charge of Will's seven half brothers and sisters, as well as the family's importing business. It was also about this time that Elizabeth and two of her friends began charitably ministering to the poor and needy, earning the nickname of "Protestant Sisters of Charity." At this time Catholic sisters had not yet become well-known in the United States.

Now events began to move fast—and with devastating effect. Both Will's business and his health failed. He was finally forced to file a petition of bankruptcy. In 1802, when Elizabeth was 28 years old, the couple's fifth child was born, adding to the cares of an already large household on a frugal budget.

In a final attempt to save Will's health, the Setons sailed for Italy, where Will had business friends—the Filicchis. They took their eight-year-old daughter Anna with them for company, and left the other four children with Will's half sisters.

Things turned out badly there also, for the authorities of Tuscany had heard reports of the dread yellow fever in New York, and therefore kept the Setons for a month in a cold, damp quarantine building at the port. Will survived this, only to die eight days later of tuberculosis.

Although Elizabeth had lost the man she "loved. . .more than anyone could love on earth," she was consoled that Will had recently awakened to the things of God. This seemed an answer to her tireless prayers for him, and she was comforted that his last words were for herself, their children, and Christ Jesus.

It seems that the illnesses and deaths of family members and friends would form the fabric of Elizabeth's life. The many enforced separations from dear ones by death and distance served to draw Elizabeth's heart to God and eternity. The accepting and embracing of God's will—"The Will," as she called it—would be a keynote in her spiritual life.

Elizabeth was always very concerned about the eternal destiny of her many loved ones, and she would try to direct the attention of dying friends to the next life. Fear and concern for her own and her children's eternal destiny, and desire for eternity, were always before her mind; these motives would eventually lead her into the Catholic Church.

At this time in her life Elizabeth was assisted by the Filicchi brothers, who were impressed by the young widow's beautiful soul.

The Catholic Filicchis—Antonio and Filippo (and his wife

Amabilia)—were the embodiment of kindness and consideration for Elizabeth. She wrote to a friend, "Oh, my! the patience and more than human kindness of these dear Filicchis for us! You would say it was our Saviour Himself they received in His poor and sick strangers."

In Italy, Elizabeth captivated everyone by her own kindness, patience, good sense, wit and courtesy. Neighbors there were so impressed by her courage and by her devotion to her dying husband that they said, "If she were not a heretic she would be a saint."

During this time Elizabeth became interested in the Catholic Faith, and over a period of months the Filicchis guided her in Catholic instructions. One of the brothers accompanied her back to New York, for ocean travel in those days would not have been safe for a young widow alone. The brothers never abandoned her, giving her a regular allotment of money for the support of herself and her family. They became lifelong friends of Elizabeth.

When her friends in New York realized that Elizabeth meant to convert to Catholicism, they rushed to re-instruct her in the Episcopalian faith. Especially poignant were the conversations she had with the minister Mr. Hobart, a forceful and intelligent man, eloquent preacher and friend of Elizabeth, who used many arguments to dissuade her from conversion. Filippo Filicchi, on the other hand, gave her Catholic books to read and tried to impress on Elizabeth her obligation of making a serious investigation and search for the true religion. A year of uncertainty and inner anguish for Elizabeth followed.

Elizabeth's desire for the Bread of Life was to be a strong force leading her to the Catholic Church. To her dear sister-in-law Rebecca, her "Soul's Sister," she wrote, "How happy would we be, if we believed what these dear souls believe: that they *possess God* in the Sacrament, and that He remains in their churches and is carried to them when they are sick!. . .The other day, in a moment of excessive distress, I fell on my knees without thinking when the Blessed Sacrament passed by, and cried in an agony to God *to bless me,* if He was *there*—that my whole soul desired only Him."

Having lost her mother at an early age, Elizabeth felt great comfort in the idea that the Blessed Virgin was truly her mother. She asked the Blessed Virgin to guide her to the True Faith. Elizabeth was also attracted to the Catholic teaching that suffering can expiate sins. In the Anglican church the prayerbook's Ash Wednesday reference to "fasting, weeping and mourning" had been explained as being simply an old custom; but Elizabeth noted that the Catholic Mrs. Filicchi did not eat until three p.m. during Lent, offering the sacrifice for her sins in union with the Saviour's sufferings. Elizabeth was deeply impressed.

Elizabeth also noticed the difference between Catholic and non-Catholic deathbeds. She wrote to Mrs. Filicchi that in assisting at non-Catholic deaths, "I go through an agony never to be described," while a Catholic dying person is consoled and strengthened by every help of religion, and the priest, "the one you call *Father* of your soul, attends and watches it in the weakness and trials of parting nature with the same care you and I watch our little infant's body in its first struggles. . .on its entrance into life."

In her agony of soul over the crucial decisions she was called upon to make, Elizabeth lost weight and became almost a skeleton. The thought of her responsibility for her children's faith on Judgment Day weighed heavily on her. Seeing her distress, the children exclaimed, "Poor Mama!"

Finally, after much interior anguish, Elizabeth decided, "I will go peaceably and firmly to the Catholic Church: for if faith is so important to our salvation, I will seek it where true Faith first began, seek it among those who received it from *God Himself*." She looked forward with great anticipation to receiving the Sacraments for the first time, saying she would even be ready to make her confession "on the housetops" in return for absolution. After her First Communion she wrote, "At last. . .at last, *GOD IS MINE AND I AM HIS! Now, let all go its round—I Have Received Him*."

Thus Elizabeth finally joined the Catholic Church in 1805. When her sister-in-law converted to Catholicism, Elizabeth became the object of suspicion and distrust, so it became very difficult for her to remain in New York; this city, like most places in the young American nation, was decidedly prejudiced against Catholicism. During her few remaining years in New York Elizabeth tried to establish several ventures in order to become self-supporting, but they all failed.

The president of St. Mary's College in Baltimore suggested that Elizabeth come and start a school in that city. A natural teacher, Elizabeth gladly accepted the chance to educate and to spread the Faith. She added religion to the curriculum at St. Mary's, and soon two other young women came to help with her work. They began plans for a sisterhood. A wealthy convert donated $10,000.00 to the project, and the group moved to Emmitsburg, Maryland, where they established the first free Catholic school in America. When the young community adopted their rule, they made provision for Elizabeth to continue raising her children.

On March 25, 1809, Elizabeth Seton pronounced her vows of poverty, chastity and obedience, binding for one year, in the presence of Archbishop John Carroll of Baltimore. From that time, she was called Mother Seton. The sisters adopted a formal religious habit that same year.

As with all fledgling communities, there were periods of trouble and setbacks. Additionally, Mother Seton suffered personal hurts and losses; two of her sisters-in-law died, and her daughter Annina made a foolish engagement. Further suffering (though also relief) came when the young man broke the engagement. This daughter died an early and painful death of consumption at age 16. Guided by her mother, she attained to great virtue and holy dispositions during her last year and was received into the new sisterhood before she died. Elizabeth's sense of loss at the death of her daughter was profound, but she completely submitted herself to God's Will in this, as in all matters. "Never by a free act of the mind will I ever regret His Will," she stated.

Although Mother Seton was now afflicted with tuberculosis, she continued to guide her children. Elizabeth's sons were a constant source of heartbreak. She said they were her "greatest anxiety in life." At one point she wrote to her favorite child, William, "To lose you here a few years of so embittered a life is but the common lot; but to love as I love you, and lose you forever—oh, unutterable anguish!" But although she did not live to see it, their lives turned out well in the end, through the prayers and perseverance of their saintly mother. One son died at sea while charitably nursing a companion. The other died a good death and was the father of an archbishop and a nun.

The rule of the Sisterhood was formally ratified in 1812. It was based upon the rule St. Vincent de Paul had written for his Daughters of Charity in France. Despite the hardships of poverty and the tragedy of a number of early deaths, the number of applicants to join the sisters in their work increased steadily from the beginning. Today six groups of sisters trace their origins to Mother Seton's initial foundation.

The frail little mother was a perfect pattern for her sisters. Outwardly, she retained her composure, even through the pain of another daughter's death in 1816. Calmly she guided and directed the sisters in their growth. By 1818, in addition to their first school, the sisters had established two orphanages and another school.

As a teacher and an administrator, Mother Seton was most capable. She visited the classrooms daily and hired competent lay teachers to instruct the children in fields where she felt her sisters were not properly prepared. The children under her care, as well as the sisters, admired and loved her.

Mother Seton was full of the kindness and tenderness of a mother toward her spiritual daughters and her pupils. She guided them with practical advice, making sure they realized how serious they must be about their souls. "You must be in right earnest, or you will do little or nothing." She told the sisters, "...the first end I propose in our daily work is to do the will of God; secondly, to do it in the manner He wills it; and, thirdly, to do it because it is His will."

Mother Seton firmly believed that the essential purpose of an education was to bring the pupils to lead good Catholic lives with their sights clearly set on eternity, the purpose of all human existence. She warned them that it was wise to avoid balls, the theatre, and the gay life in general in order to avoid "singeing their wings" like the butterfly on the candle. Yet she was not trying to turn the girls into nuns. She told them that she wanted to prepare most of them to become good mothers of families.

Mother Seton was full of maternal tenderness for "her girls." She wrote frequent little spiritual notes to them; one of these reads, "Mother begs Our Lord to bless her dear Eliza that she may be an ever-blooming rose in His paradise. Come under the shawl this morning and love and bless Our Jesus.—your poor, affectionate Mother." Even after they left school the girls would often write to Mother Seton for advice.

Elizabeth with her loving heart had many friends during her life. Her many letters to them, as well as her diary, show the sweetness and deep affections of her heart. Always, she was concerned above all for the person's spiritual welfare and salvation.

For the last three years of her life Elizabeth felt that God was getting ready to call her, and this gave her joy. She did feel some fear over her sins, but she said she had a greater fear of living and daily adding to her life of sins. She wrote, *"The thought of going home,* called out by *His Will*—what a transport."

Mother Seton died in 1821 at the age of 46, only 16 years after becoming a Catholic. Her spiritual director, Father Simon Gabriel Brute, wrote a glowing tribute to her character. In a letter to her long-time friend and benefactor, Antonio Filicchi, he wrote: "Her distinguishing characteristic was compassion and indulgence for poor sinners. Her charity made her watchful never to speak evil of others, always to find excuses or to keep silence. Her other special virtues were her attachment to her friends and her gratitude, her religious respect for the ministers of the Lord, and for everything pertaining to religion. Her heart was compassionate, religious, lavish of every good in her possession, disinterested in regard to all other things. O Mother, excellent Mother, I trust you are now in the enjoyment of bliss!"

St. Elizabeth Seton was canonized on September 14, 1975.

Sisters of Charity of Mount Saint Vincent-on-Hudson

Elizabeth Bayley Seton about the time of her marriage at age 20. The groom was the wealthy young William Seton, with whom Elizabeth was deeply in love. *(Artist unknown.)*

Above and below: St. Elizabeth Ann Seton sometime before age 30. After a time her husband Will's health and business began to fail, and by age 29 Elizabeth was left a widow with five children. A new phase of life would soon begin for her. *(Miniatures by C. B. Fevret de St.-Mémin.)*

After a long, anguished search for the truth, Elizabeth embraced the Catholic Faith. She founded the Sisters of Charity in the United States and undertook the work of educating children, while raising her own at the same time. Elizabeth's heart was always full of love for her children; she was especially concerned about their eternal salvation. She died at age 46, only 16 years after becoming a Catholic. Elizabeth Seton is the first American-born canonized saint.

2

SAINT JOAN ANTIDA THOURET

Joan Antida Thouret
1765 - 1826
France - Italy
Died Age 60

France was suffering the agonies of the French Revolution. The commissioner spoke: "As a school mistress, you must take the oath of hatred of royalty." The sturdy young Frenchwoman replied, "I hate nobody. And although I teach children, I do so freely and without charge. I am sufficiently rewarded by serving God in serving my neighbor."

The commissioner reminded her that the oath would wipe out the stain of emigration (it was against the law to leave France), a crime of which she stood accused (she had gone across to Switzerland for a while) and that there was a special military commission charged with the duty of shooting emigres.

Unmoved, the young woman refused. She replied that she would not be very sorry to die in front of a firing squad.

"But that would be suicide!"

"No," came the calm reply, "it would be the soldiers who killed my body; I myself will not kill my soul!" The commissioner left to consult with the central administration.

The young woman went immediately to seek advice from her confessor, who told her that in order to avoid blaming herself for imprudence she would have to go into hiding, once more becoming a refugee for the love of God.

Thus St. Joan Antida Thouret lived and suffered through the Reign of Terror. All that she experienced served to prepare her for the magnificent works of charity she was to begin, after the Revolution, in the minds and hearts of the Sisters of Charity (of St. Joan Antida)—sisters who even today carry on her apostolate and her spirit.

Joan was born on November 27, 1765 in Sancey, a parish in

the rural district of Baume-les-Dames in Franche-Comte. She was one of the seven surviving children of John Francis and Joan Claudia Thouret. John was a farmer and a merchant tanner. Joan was the joy of her frail and sickly mother. From her mother and her godmother, Joan learned her catechism and her devotion to God. It was at the bedside of her mother that she learned the job of serving the sick.

Joan's father was undoubtedly a good and faithful man. However, he was somewhat weak in character, and his sister Oudette, who lived with the family, often seemed to be the real head of the household.

When Joan was seven, there was talk of sending her to school. Although her aunt made some objections, she finally gave in, saying that perhaps it would be a good thing for a Thouret girl to be able to read. Joan's mother considered it unthinkable for such an obviously intelligent child not to receive all the elementary education which the village school could provide.

In one brief winter, Joan quickly learned reading, spelling and her catechism. But in the spring, when the children were returned to their families, as was the custom, her aunt declared that she had no need of writing; that was sufficient for working on a farm. Joan's father protested only weakly. So instead of returning to school Joan took on the duty of shepherding the family sheep and cattle.

One of her childhood companions testified that as a shepherdess Joan was quick to go and head off the cattle from danger or from causing damage, and she also assisted her companions with their flocks. Willingly, and as often as she was asked, Joan kept watch over all the animals while her companions slipped off to play. She loved to be alone and so took this opportunity to pray, never complaining.

At last, when she was nearly 13, Joan made her First Communion. From this time on she was sent less frequently to the fields and instead worked in the house and the stable under the orders of her Aunt Oudette.

In 1781 Joan's mother, who had suffered so uncomplainingly as her health grew weaker, finally passed away. She breathed her last in the arms of her daughter Joan, full of resignation, and anxious only for those whom she was leaving on earth. These she confided to God.

On his return from the funeral, Joan's father shocked his sister and the rest of the family by turning to Joan and saying, "Joan Antida, you must take the place of your dead mother and do what she was unable to do." Thus the young girl of 16 was charged with the responsibility of managing the household for the large family, which included Joan's six brothers.

In spite of her busy workload, Joan often found time to slip away and take food to the poor. Her father was happy to give an alms to every beggar who came to the door, but he would have scolded his daughter had he known that she sometimes fasted in order to feed one more hungry person.

Joan suffered from a servant girl who tried to corrupt her, but this trial only proved an occasion for Joan to increase her diligence in practices of piety, finally making a vow of chastity. When her brothers left home to join the army, Joan never failed to give them salutary warning of the dangers to body and soul which awaited them.

Joan began to feel a distinct call to the religious life. She was greatly attracted to the idea of entering a cloister, but from time to time she was so filled with compassion for the sick and poor whom she met that she thought she should perhaps become a nursing sister. Her godmother advised her to consult her confessor, who told her that her place was still, for a time, at home. She began to assist him in the parish by teaching catechism classes. From time to time he listened at the door of her classroom and later remarked: "[She] must have an angel's patience to go on repeating the same word 20 times to these illiterate children!"

At 21, Joan determined to follow her vocation. Her godmother consulted a nursing order, and the reply came that they would be happy to receive her. Then the blow fell. Her father refused his permission, and her aunt threatened to find a husband for her. Indeed, a willing young man was found.

Strengthened by prayer, Joan remained determined to become a sister. Finally, she obtained her father's grudging consent. Her aunt, however, refused to allow any of the family money to be spent on a dowry, so in July of 1787, Joan left home—without hope of return—to go and enter the Sisters of Charity, the order founded by St. Vincent de Paul. Greatly loved and esteemed in her village, Joan slipped away during the night in order to avoid an outcry from the villagers. Her godmother and the parish priest had persuaded some of the richer parishioners to make up a small dowry for her.

After a three-month postulancy, Joan arrived in Paris in 1787 to become a novice with the Sisters of Charity. At her reception, the superior asked her, "What can you do?" Joan's sincere reply was, "Nothing." Later, the novice mistress told Joan, "You are always saying that you can do nothing; you must say that you can do everything, for you do well everything which is given to you."

For a time, Joan suffered a period of ill health and it was feared that she would not be physically able to stay. Then, as always, she went to God in prayer with her plea. There was no miracle, but an elderly sister who worked in the dispensary begged to be allowed to try a cure that the others had not used—and Joan was returned to health.

Joan stayed with the sisters for five years, humble and hidden. With them she studied and learned the rule which had been so wisely written by St. Vincent. She learned more and more about nursing, and she worked to serve God in His poor and sick.

Joan was a pretty girl; for this reason, and also because of her serenity and inner beauty, she was attractive to all. More than once she received a proposal from one or another of her patients; these usually began: "As you have not yet taken your vows. . ."

Joan was well-loved by the other sisters, and were it not for the political upheaval which then struck France and all of Europe, it is quite likely that she would have lived the rest of her life as a Sister of Charity of St. Vincent de Paul. Instead, on her last assignment, that with the sisters in Sceaux, the blow fell. The Reign of Terror had begun, with its pitiless religious persecution. Joan was recalled to Paris, where she served as a nurse with 44 other sisters at the Hospital of the Incurables.

When religious orders were ordered to cease religious practices, each sister managed as best she could. Refusing to accept "Juror" priests (those who had taken the oath of the Civil Constitutions), the sisters made Holy Communions of desire and assisted at Mass in thought and desire. The ingenious Joan transformed a coal nook on one of the floors in the hospital into an oratory for her own use, and slipped away to pray in the black dust, or to do the spiritual reading prescribed by her rule.

Finally the sisters were summoned to take the oath of loyalty to the revolutionary government, and when they refused they were brutally expelled by the soldiers. They returned to the mother-house in Paris to wait. There the novice mistress told Joan that she should learn to write. She was given a few short lessons. Her first letter was to the priest who had been her confessor when she was in the Hospital of the Incurables. She wrote, "I am a sinner and I consider myself very fortunate to suffer something for the name of Jesus Christ."

By April of 1792, Joan had been transferred to the hospital at Bray. One day toward the middle of the month, the civil authorities of the town presented themselves at the hospital and summoned the sisters to the chapel. One sister alone could not be found—Joan Antida, who, scenting the blow, had climbed over the garden wall!

The president of the committee read decrees which forbad the sisters to wear religious dress. The men then threatened the sisters into making an oath of fidelity to the new revolutionary laws. The soldiers then began escorting the sisters out. At this time, Joan was discovered in her hiding place in the enclosure; while the soldiers dragged her out, they taunted her that she wanted martyrdom. Bravely, Joan answered, "I should be glad of it." Thereupon a soldier struck Joan on the chest with the butt of his rifle, knocking her unconscious. As there were no witnesses to this scene, Joan concealed the incident. Later it was found that two of her ribs had been broken; they remained crossed over each other.

In a circular letter the superior instructed the sisters not to wear their habits but to dress simply and modestly. In order that they might continue to serve the poor, she instructed the sisters to fall in with every civil law that they could honorably obey, provided that it was not against religion, the Church, or conscience.

The Church in France began to be watered, and then flooded, with the blood of martyrs. Joan, at 28, was still a novice; ordinarily she would have been preparing for first vows, but there were no religious services, no chaplain—only sadness and persecution. All that remained possible was for very small groups to go secretly to Mass in houses where a priest celebrated Mass in secret.

At this time Joan had a unique task—which was also an exceptional honor. She frequently carried the Mass vestments, by wearing them under her dress, to the priests hidden in Paris. She went on these errands alone, trusting only in God. Had she been discovered, she would have been put to death either on the scaffold or by being flogged, as were three of her sisters.

At last, in October of 1793, the order was legally dissolved and scattered, most of the sisters departing to find refuge with their own families. Traveling on foot, Joan sadly began to retrace her steps to her family in Besancon.

Although Joan was entitled to receive a sum of money, as her dowry had been confiscated, she refused this for it meant taking an oath which she could not in conscience take. "I will not sell my soul for money," she said. Instead, penniless, she wandered and suffered, laboring for God's glory. Joan once said, "I would cross the oceans, I would go to the end of the world, if I knew that God wanted it for His glory."

The complete account of her years during the Terror makes thrilling and inspiring reading. She secretly taught the Faith, she nursed the sick, she assisted priests in hiding and she attended executions to pray for strength for those to be martyred. Time after time there were narrow escapes, some of which Joan effected by her quick wit and logic, while some were made only by flight. At one point, while living with a group of religious persons, she was expelled from the country. The group traveled to Switzerland and to a number of other places before returning to France. Always, God provided.

At last the Terror abated, and religion began to trickle back into France. In 1799 Joan returned to Besancon to fulfill a promise to establish, with the help of God, an organization for the instruction of children and for assisting the sick poor.

At age 34, Joan began her work by opening a small school. This was the mustard seed from which the giant tree of the Sisters of Charity of Besancon would grow; this institute was eventually to become known as the Sisters of Charity under the Protection of St. Vincent de Paul—popularly known as the Sisters of Charity of St. Joan Antida. Politically, France was still in upheaval at this time. It would be some time yet before the Sisters of Charity of St. Vincent de Paul would be regrouped.

"This is the origin of our Institute," she wrote. "On April 11, 1799, with the consent and approval of [the administrative bishop of the diocese of Besancon], I opened a free school for the education of girls in the rue des Martelots, and in a few days I had a large number of pupils. I was alone, but God in His goodness gave up His blessing. . .I received two aspirants, then a third and a fourth. I instructed them how to teach the pupils, making them watch how I did it myself."

As the little group grew, they began to be called the "Sisters of the Soup Kitchens and Little Schools," from their practice of taking soup to the sick poor. At first they had no religious habit, although each wore a similar headdress. Each wore a crucifix which she had received when she promised to serve God in His sick and poor, but this was worn only inside the house.

When Joan learned that the Sisters of Charity in Paris had been reorganized, she went to her confessor and asked his advice on what to do if she were recalled by them. He instructed her to remain where she was and to continue with the new work she had begun.

The little community grew rapidly. Joan wrote the rule for her sisters herself, basing it on the rule of St. Vincent de Paul. It was fortunate that she was blessed with an excellent memory, as no written copy of his rule could be obtained. The foundress modified and adapted the rule to provide a practical plan for her sisters—a plan which remains basically unchanged today, as it covered not only the needs of her time but also took into account the needs of the future. Joan's work was so complete that when it was given papal approbation, only a few minor points were amended; none was greatly changed. One beautiful passage which explains the spirit of the community reads: "The sisters usually have a temporary room as their cell, and only the streets of the city and the wards of the hospitals as their cloister, only obedience as their enclosure, and only the fear of God as their grille." Joan became known as Mother Thouret.

Perhaps one of the most impressive foundations of Mother Thouret and her sisters was that made in 1802, when they were asked to take charge of the prison of Belleveaux. This was a criminal and debtors' prison for both men and women which contained approximately 500 inmates; Joan and six of her sisters were given complete charge of it. With regard to the hygiene, order and morals prevailing there, the prison had been described as a "cesspool," a "den of wild beasts" and an "antechamber of Hell."

Upon arrival, Mother Thouret was shocked by the filth and saddened by the despondence and apathy which afflicted most of the inmates. She realized that only through much work could the prisoners be rehabilitated, and that—before all else—cleanliness and order must be established. The sisters set to work at once, and in spite of the danger and wretched conditions, the prison became a model establishment. Mother Thouret bought cotton and yarn and began a program in which the prisoners spun and wove cloth and made garments. For the first time, they were paid a portion of the price received for their labor; the rest of the money went to the maintenance of the facility, to pay for nourishing soups rather than the bread and water the prisoners had been living on. Even the most hardened and dangerous of the prisoners came to treat these humble sisters with love, respect and awe.

With the advent of Napoleon and the re-establishment of order in France, the Sisters of Charity grew and spread. During his reign, Joan's order was approved and commended. And at the request of Napoleon's mother, Joan traveled to Italy to begin foundations there.

Was Mother Thouret, the lover of the Cross, finally to be allowed to relax in comfort? Most decidedly not. Her greatest trial was yet to come. Due to political and religious factors, the Bishop of Besancon refused to accept the directives of Rome, and he claimed that the sisters in his diocese must recognize him as their superior; Joan would no longer be Mother General. The bishop went so far as to issue an official interdict that forbad her entrance into any of her houses in his diocese, and he even calumniated her publicly.

Although for years Mother Thouret had considered these sisters her daughters, by this ruling they became a separate order. On her last trip through the area Joan knocked at the door of the motherhouse she had founded and nourished, and was refused admittance by the portress, who told her sadly, "We have orders about you." When the door was closed, Joan kissed it, and then burst into tears.

Joan tried to straighten out this situation, but the split continued. She would spend the rest of her life opening houses in Italy.

Mother Thouret's motto was "Forward always, and for God alone!" She told her sisters, "I am a daughter of the Church; imitate me in this."

Although Joan had never allowed her ill health to slow her down, her harsh life took its toll. Moreover, she had suffered from diabetes for years. Mother Thouret died in Rome on August 24, 1826, after suffering a stroke. She was nearly 61 years old.

She who had suffered so on earth at the division of her order must have smiled with joy in Heaven when her sisters, both those in Besancon and those of her other houses, united to request that their foundress' cause for canonization be opened. And in one body they attended the canonization ceremony in Rome in 1934 when Pope Pius XI declared to the entire Church that the humble and courageous Mother Joan Antida Thouret was a saint in Heaven. At the time of Joan's beatification there had been 997 houses of her order and 7,500 sisters.

St. Joan Antida Thouret, whose life with the Sisters of Charity was disrupted by the Reign of Terror during the French Revolution and who was thus led to found a new order and open many new houses. Her motto was "Forward always, and for God alone!" Joan had been given the task of managing the family household—which included six brothers—at age 16 when her mother died. She learned to write when in her 20's.

3

BLESSED MAGDALEN OF CANOSSA

Magdalen Gabriella of Canossa
1774 - 1835
Italy
Died Age 61

In the little cell where Mother Magdalen of Canossa had died on her knees, praying to Our Lady, her body now lay on her poor bed. For months, doubled over with asthma, Mother Magdalen had preferred to sit in her chair, rather than lie on her bed to take her few brief periods of rest. Now, her crumpled body was so bent that the Mother Superior despaired of fitting it into the coffin. Additionally, the strong smell of the bitumen used in the varnish for the coffin had made Mother Christina so sick that she herself felt ready to die.

With tears in her eyes and sorrow in her heart, the superior remembered Magdalen's great obedience to established authority, and how diffident and humble she had been—she, who had been born in a castle, and had held the rank of Marchioness. She recalled the kindness and charity of the beloved foundress of the Canossian Daughters of Charity.

Kneeling before the body, the superior prayed, "Marchioness, you were always obedient during your lifetime; be so even after your death—stretch yourself out. And please, will you not stop this awful smell!" The superior then left the room. Upon her return, the body was stretched full length so that the lid of the coffin could be nailed down, and the offending odor had disappeared.

Those who read the above anecdote may try to find some scientific explanation of the facts. Most who knew Blessed Magdalen of Canossa, however, would simply find it to be one more example of her humility and charity. On Palm Sunday of 1835, Magdalen was buried in a marble sepulcher in St. Joseph's Church in Verona. On the beautiful marble sepulcher, a gift of her brother Boniface, one may still read the words she had written to all of her daughters shortly before her death: "Dear Sisters, choose the shortest cut to Paradise, the way of holy obedience. Obey with a generous heart, unmindful of the sacrifices obedience asks of you...Love charity...Love humility."

Magdalen Gabriella of Canossa was born at Verona, Italy, on March 1, 1774. She was the second of the five children of the Marquis Octavius of Canossa and Marchioness Maria Teresa Szlugh. A member of an old and aristocratic family, Octavius was also an ardent naturalist and amateur geologist. Maria Teresa was a lady in waiting at Empress Maria Theresa's court in Vienna.

Magdalen was a bright, attractive, precocious youngster. Her family was loving and close, and the parents made it a point to emphasize the importance of the Faith. Magdalen was her father's pet, and whenever she was with him she wanted to see, to understand, and to know all that he could teach her. From him, she learned early to see God's beauty in nature.

Sadly, when Magdalen was about five, her father died suddenly and unexpectedly. For two years Magdalen lived, along with her mother, at her father's ancestral home. Then Maria Teresa remarried and the children were left at the Canossa palace with their grandfather, and with their Uncle Jerome as guardian.

A governess was found for the children, but she did not understand Magdalen, and thus caused her much suffering. All the riches of the beautiful palace and the most favored way of life could not console the little girl for the loss of her parents.

Magdalen began to suffer through a number of serious and painful illnesses, some of which could not be properly diagnosed or treated. Of one attempted treatment, she remarked, with her native sense of humor, "Is the remedy effective? At this rate it will wear off not only the pain, but my skin as well. I will share with St. Bartholomew the glory of being flayed alive!"

Somehow, during her growth and adolescence, Magdalen determined to belong to God alone. When she was struck with the dreaded smallpox, she answered her uncle's worried questions with the words, "The Bridegroom I have chosen will not worry about my face. No one needs to admire me, because I will become a nun."

At 17, Magdalen was beautiful, intelligent and rich—a most attractive and desirable young lady. Sincere and honest admiration came easily her way, and she could not help but feel the worldliness with which she was surrounded. In the midst of the preparations for her older sister's wedding, Magdalen felt a need for seclusion. Therefore, with the permission of her uncle, and on the advice of her spiritual director, she went to stay for a time with the Sisters of St. Teresa, Carmelites. There she was filled with a true joy in being alone with her Divine Lover, but she also felt a yearning to relieve the sufferings she saw in the world. She wanted to make God's love known to all; she wanted to help the sick and the poor. She saw much evil in the world, but analyzing the problems which she noticed, she began more and more to feel that many of the evils were caused by ignorance.

The prioress was a holy nun, and to her Magdalen unburdened her soul. This wise nun advised her to follow the advice of her spiritual director and stay at home until she saw God's plan made clear for her. At age 19 Magdalen again attempted to enter a Carmelite convent; but although she was attracted to the vocation of a Carmelite, she was again told that the cloister was not her vocation. She returned home, and for a number of years held the responsibility of running the family home of Canossa.

As the lady of the house, Magdalen used her considerable talent for organization to run things smoothly. Even after her uncle's late marriage, she remained in charge by the wishes of her new aunt, a young and sickly woman. Magdalen was known as a wise and just administrator. She treated all with Christian charity, but was not foolishly sentimental. Magdalen greatly impressed all by her sincere piety and her abhorrence of everything that could in the least endanger her chastity. When Napoleon was on his Italian campaign he lodged at the Canossa castle. Eyewitnesses relate that the dignity and grace of Magdalen greatly impressed him. On one occasion she had the misfortune of falling down some steps while he was present. An officer hastened to lift her up, but she refused assistance, and it is said that Napoleon cried out, "Leave her alone! Do not dare to touch her; she is an angel."

As time went on, the health of Uncle Jerome's wife grew worse. As she lay on her deathbed, she extracted from Magdalen a promise to care for her son Charles, Magdalen's nephew. Magdalen carried out this responsibility, as well as that of the female head of the family, until her brother Boniface married an intelligent and competent young woman who could run the household almost as well as Magdalen herself and who would love and raise the little boy as though he were her own.

At last Magdalen felt herself free to follow whatever path God should direct her to. Her future vocation was first made known to her by the Blessed Virgin Mary in a vision at St. Mark's in Venice.

Magdalen had realized deeply, through her work with a deaf and dumb boy, that all children were loved by God. A special ideal of Magdalen's would be the "specialness" of those who had not been favored with sight, hearing, intelligence or voice. Another of God's graces to Magdalen was her realization of the blessings of nursing the sick. And as she saw the appalling ignorance of God's love among the poor, she understood that the teaching of Christian doctrine was a favored work of her Divine Spouse.

The core of Magdalen's apostolate was to be the education and training of girls, especially those of the lower classes—many of them to go on to become teachers. Magdalen believed that education should be for all. She prayed, "Dear Lord, if it be Thy wish, let me carry out the training of girls to make them teachers; so that everybody, without any distinction of rank or class, may receive an education."

Magdalen opened her first school in 1803. In 1805, in a daring request to the conqueror Napoleon Bonaparte, she asked for and obtained the rights to an abandoned Augustinian monastery near San Zeno. In spite of the political upheavals of the time, Magdalen, with her forceful personality, began to carry out the designs Our Lord had for her soul and she expanded her works of charity and education. Magdalen and her companions became known as the Canossian Daughters of Charity. The Institute grew, and Magdalen was able to open houses and schools in Venice, Milan, Bergamo and Trent.

The special protection of God was evident in Magdalen's work, which often faced great difficulties due to the circumstances of the times. Magdalen's great sanctity and prudence gave internal strength to her congregation. Moreover, people knew what she had left in the world; they knew the innocence of her life and saw the noble example of her humility and extreme poverty. God granted her extraordinary graces, and even during her lifetime she was revered as a saint. Magdalen said, "Charity is a fire that spreads and aims at encompassing the whole world."

As with many of God's favorites, Magdalen lived through poverty, calumny, change and a number of other daily crosses. Also, special mystical graces became commonplace with her. Although her biographers have not made a great point of presenting this aspect of her life, it is true that Magdalen of Canossa experienced visions, ecstasies and levitations. In her humility, she took great pains to disregard, or cover up, all supernatural manifestations when she could. Nevertheless, before many of her greatest triumphs, there have been occurrences which defied human explanation.

Once, when Magdalen and a sister were in a room writing some letters, the sister heard scuffling, as of the feet of some animal on the floor. Looking at Magdalen, the sister noticed that she was making gestures as if to drive away an unruly animal. Nothing else could be seen, however. When questioned, Magdalen evaded the issue, taking the sister's hand and leading her around the room to reassure her that nothing was there.

On another occasion, Magdalen went to her room to get some papers and received a violent blow which sent her rolling under the bed. When she tried to get up, some hidden power pinned her to the floor. Mother Christina, who had heard the fall, rushed in to see what had happened and tried to help Magdalen get up. Finally, she had to ask a servant to assist her to move the bed. As the foundress finally regained her footing, her face bore a strange smile of victory. In both these instances she had been the object of an attack by the devil.

One phenomenon which was evident in Magdalen's life was her ability to foresee and predict future events. The sister who assisted Magdalen in her last moments recalled that back in her childhood, upon meeting Magdalen, the latter had predicted that she would eventually become a Canossian and that she would help Magdalen at her death.

In 1831 Magdalen of Canossa also founded the Sons of Charity, who share the same apostolic aim as the Daughters of Charity. In addition, a number of other works of charity owe their beginnings to her. Magdalen often encouraged those who shared her love of God but felt attracted to a different apostolic aim, to follow God's Will for them by traveling along a different path.

Today, the Canossian Daughters of Charity have spread worldwide. In speaking of the saintly Foundress, Pope Pius XII summed up her virtues in the words, "Humility in charity, charity in humility." Magdalen of Canossa was beatified on December 7, 1941.

Bl. Magdalen of Canossa, who founded the Canossian Daughters of Charity for the teaching of girls, especially of the lower classes. She was granted extraordinary mystical gifts and was revered as a saint in her own lifetime. In her youth Napoleon Bonaparte was greatly inspired by her dignity and grace when he saw her at her father's castle.

4

SAINT ANDREW KIM AND COMPANIONS

The 103 Martyrs of Korea
Died in Korea
Died 1839 - 1846 and 1862 - 1867

In 1984 the Catholic Church in Korea celebrated its bicentennial. Two hundred years had passed since a young Korean scholar, Lee Sung-hoon, had traveled to Peking in 1784, where he was baptized into the Catholic Church, and then returned to his homeland with a number of religious books and articles and a spark of faith which was to ignite the fires of Christianity in the land of Korea.

On May 6th of 1984, in Seoul, Korea, in the first canonization to take place outside of Rome since the thirteenth century, Pope John Paul II named 103 new saints on what he called the "happiest day, the greatest feast, in the whole history of the Church in Korea." These 103 martyrs are representative of the approximately 10,000 Christians martyred in Korea over a period lasting almost 100 years. Included in the group of 103 are 92 lay persons from nearly every walk of life—45 men and 47 women. Also included are the first native Korean priest, Andrew Kim Tai Kun, and 10 French missionaries. Of the total of 103 martyrs, 79 had been beatified in 1925—victims of the earlier persecution, and 24 had been beatified in 1968—victims of the later persecution.

Korea is the only country in the history of the Church to begin evangelizing itself via trade contacts with China. This work began with the efforts of a group of Korean scholars who studied the Christian Faith from the books that Lee Sung-hoon had brought back from China. These lay Koreans began catechizing others and baptizing them.

This original group of lay Catholics became convinced, through their reading, that they needed a priest, and an envoy was sent to Peking with this request. The bishop there readily agreed, and in 1795 Father Chu Mun-mo, a priest of the Peking diocese, became the first missionary priest to Korea.

Father Chu Mun-mo was martyred after six years of labor in Korea. The persecution associated with his death, that of 1801 - 1802, is said to have cost the lives of over 300 of the converts. Anti-Christian propaganda had branded the Catholic Faith as something which denied the authority of parents and the king and claimed that the Christians planned to bring in European troops to conquer the country.

Repeated appeals were made to Peking and to Rome, and at last, in 1831, a deeply impressed Vatican responded by committing priests of the Paris Foreign Mission Society to work in the Church in Korea.

Bishop Barthelemy Bruguiere and Father Pierre Philibert Maubant set out on the long and difficult journey across China to Korea. Bishop Bruguiere died before reaching Korea, but Father Maubant arrived there in 1836 and went to the capital, Seoul. From a position of hiding, he began ministering to the Christians.

Bishop Laurent Joseph Marie Imbert was appointed vicar apostolic and arrived in Korea in 1837. Then a third missionary arrived, but in 1839 a fresh persecution arose. Bishop Imbert and his two foreign colleagues surrendered themselves to the authorities, hoping that this might avert some of the official wrath from the faithful. The three were tortured and executed, along with numbers of Korean Christians, both men and women. Others were imprisoned or exiled. In contrast to the persecution of 1801 - 1802, when many of the martyrs were from prominent families, in the storm of 1839 most of the victims were of more humble estate. A total of 70 Christians are said to have been beheaded, and 60 were strangled, beaten to death or died of their wounds.

Two examples will serve to illustrate the faith and courage of the martyrs. A factory worker named Protasius Chong earned his daily living by weaving ropes from straw. He was baptized around the age of 30 and took an active part in promoting the Christian Faith by providing housing for Catholics in rural areas when they came to receive the Sacraments. He was arrested in 1839, put in jail and tortured. Giving in to the torture, Chong agreed to renounce his faith, and was released from jail. Later, however, he reconsidered and returned to tell the judge that he wished to retract his renunciation. Once again he was imprisoned and beaten. He died from his injuries at the age of 41.

A 17-year-old girl named Agatha Yi, along with her younger brother, was falsely told that her parents had betrayed their faith.

Agatha replied, "Whether or not my parents betrayed is their affair. As for us, we cannot betray the Lord of Heaven, whom we have always served." Agatha was then executed along with her parents and her brother, all four thus winning the palm of martyrdom.

In 1845 Bishop Jean Joseph Ferreol, after several attempts to enter the country, was at last successful. In the meantime, contact had been established between the Christians and the outer world by a young Korean student for the priesthood, Andrew Kim, who went back and forth between the Christian groups and his ecclesiastical superiors. He was ordained in 1845. Shortly thereafter Father Kim became a victim of the anti-Christian policy of his government; he was beheaded in 1846. His execution was precipitated by a letter which a French admiral had written to the Korean authorities threatening reprisals for the deaths of the three missionaries who had been killed in 1839.

Immediately prior to his martyrdom, Father Andrew Kim had written a letter to the faithful, urging them to accept persecution as an act of God's providence. He told his flock that the Church in Korea could be no exception in a Church founded on the sufferings of Our Lord and spread by the sufferings of the Apostles.

The decade following Bishop Ferreol's arrival (1845) marked a period of rapid growth for the Church in Korea. A second native priest, Thomas Choi Yang-op, was ordained. Korea now had 12 priests and 23,000 believers.

In 1866 a final violent persecution broke out, again threatening the Church in Korea with extinction. Two Bishops and seven other missionaries were executed. Three missionaries escaped by fleeing the country. By September of 1868, 2,000 of the Christians had perished. From among these come the additional martyrs adding up to 103.

Despite the fact that 10,000 Korean Christians had been martyred, the Foreign Mission Society of Paris would not be discouraged. Again and again attempts were made to place missionaries in the hostile country. In 1876, two French priests were led into the country by Korean guides. In 1877, a new bishop entered the country. He was Felix Clair Ridel, one of the priests who had escaped the persecution of 1866. Bishop Ridel was arrested, but French pressure on China and Japan obtained his release.

A new anti-Christian law was issued in 1881, but it was not strictly enforced. And in 1882, the persecutions were formally ended by treaty with the United States. A treaty with France in 1886 gave protection, and even a somewhat favored status, to both missionaries and their converts. Thus the persecutions of the Christian missionaries became a thing of the past. In 1886 there were in Korea five priests and 12,500 Catholics.

The Church in Korea had experienced persecution for close to 100 years, a period marked by some 10 persecutions of varying degrees of severity. Finally the "seed of Christians," that is, the blood of countless known and unknown Christian Korean martyrs, began to yield its harvest.

Today the Catholics of South Korea number well over one and a half million. In North Korea, now suffering the persecution of Communism, there are no recent statistics available on the number of Catholics; the last reported estimate (1969) was 100,000. Those North Korean Catholics who are holding onto their faith are doubtless suffering terribly for it. There may well be further stories of Christian heroism there, which may eventually become known. In the meantime those suffering Christians have most urgent need of prayers.

성인 김대건(안드레아) 신부

Father Andrew Kim, the first native Korean priest and one of the 103 Martyrs of Korea beatified in Seoul, Korea in 1984.

Mural depicting the 103 Korean Martyrs. The group of 103 includes 92 lay persons—45 men and 47 women. (Mural at Heihwadong Church, Seoul.)

Above and following page: Actual scenes of torture.

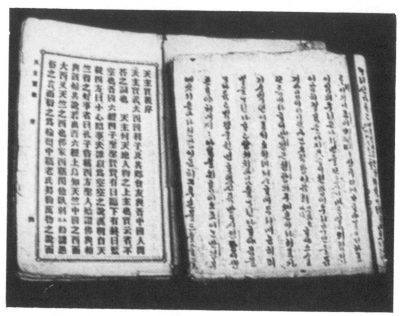

Upper: Matteo Ricci's *The True Doctrine of God.*
Lower: First catechism, produced by Chong Yak-chong.

5

SAINT VINCENT MARY STRAMBI

Saint Vincent Mary Strambi, C.P.
1745 - 1824
Italy
Died Age 79

"Within the current month of June, no later than July 15, you will...place in the hands of the Viceroy the oath of loyalty which you must give to His Majesty Napoleon, Emperor of France and King of Italy, your new Sovereign. In addition, you must declare your submission in a pastoral letter to the people."

Bishop Vincent Strambi of Macerata laid aside the letter containing the latest French demands and had recourse to his constant source of strength—prayer. Then, pen in hand, he wrote his reply: "My conscience and that of the Supreme Pontiff resolutely condemn the oath. I'll not be a traitor to my sacred duty!"

The saintly bishop then penned another note. He wrote to Pope Pius VII that he was determined to suffer imprisonment, exile and even death in defense of the rights of the Church.

A few days later, the chief of police called on the Bishop and, handing him a document, bluntly demanded that he sign it.

"I know what those pages contain and I will not sign them," replied Bishop Strambi.

"If you do not sign them, I have orders to confiscate all your episcopal revenues," the officer said.

"Do so," was the reply.

"Bishop, you will be banished from your diocese."

"I am ready. I am willing to suffer everything rather than betray the sovereign rights of the Church by taking an oath forbidden by the Vicar of Christ."

The bishop was placed under house arrest. On the day he was to leave, September 28, 1808, troops with fixed bayonets surrounded his house to keep the people from causing an insurrection.

When the door opened, the Bishop walked out with only a breviary and a walking stick, the only personal possessions he was taking with him. When the mayor asked where his carriage was, the Bishop replied that he had no carriage and that all of his income had been distributed to the poor. The mayor objected to his making the long 400-mile journey to Milan on foot, and ordered a carriage. With a Passionist lay brother as a companion and a soldier for a guard, the Bishop began his journey into exile.

As Bishop Strambi gave the crowd his blessing, one man expressed the fear that the Bishop would never come back.

"Don't worry, the tempest will be short-lived," replied Bishop Strambi. "In five years it will be over and I shall return to Macerata."

This prediction came true, as did many others made by St. Vincent. In five years he returned in triumph to his diocese.

Vincent Strambi was born on January 1, 1745 in the little town of Civita Vecchia, on the west coast of Italy. He was the only child of Joseph and Eleanora Strambi to survive infancy. Mr. Strambi was a well-to-do druggist. Both of Vincent's parents were good Christians, and he learned much of his charity from their influence.

As a youngster, Vincent had a tendency to be quick-tempered and stubborn. He was full of life and mischief and sometimes hard to manage. His parents gave him affection but did not spoil him; when necessary, they administered firm correction. Vincent learned reading, writing and catechism at home, and he mastered his catechism so well that he was confirmed at the age of seven.

Vincent enjoyed activity, and loved to play a type of football called *pallone*. With his active imagination, he also enjoyed games of make-believe. Two of his favorite "Let's pretend" games were playing pirate and playing priest. He was expert with a slingshot, and with his mischievous nature this sometimes got him into trouble. In those days, drinking water was brought from a public well in large earthen pitchers carried on the shoulders of housewives. On one occasion Vincent simply could not resist taking aim and cracking a pitcher—to the sudden anger of a drenched local housewife.

Vincent learned his thoughtfulness for the poor from his parents, who gave him many examples of charity. They gave generously, and soon the boy began to imitate them. More than once, he gave away his coat to some poorly dressed child. Once he went too far. He saw a little boy who was so ragged as to be almost naked, so he took off his entire suit, gave it to the child, and ran home in his underclothes! After this, Vincent's father gave him a stern talk explaining the imprudence of his actions and forbidding him to give away any of his clothes in the future without consulting his parents.

At age 12, Vincent knew his catechism so well that the local pastor appointed him to teach the younger children. He would walk through the streets ringing a little bell. The children would come and gather in the public square before the church and listen to Vincent explain the lesson. Even as a child, Vincent displayed the zeal and talent which would make him one of the most noted preachers of his time.

When Vincent was fifteen, he asked his parents to allow him to study for the priesthood. Although his parents would have preferred that he marry and continue the family, they gave their consent.

At the seminary, Vincent began to feel a call to the religious life. He applied for admission with the Capuchin Fathers, but the superior advised him to wait. He then went to Rome to take a course in sacred eloquence, and while there made a spiritual retreat with the Vincentian Fathers. Their missionary spirit appealed to him and he asked to be accepted by this order, but again his application was denied. The superior thought Vincent looked too frail to withstand the missionary life. This surprised Vincent for, although he did not look robust, he was healthy and had never been sick. He continued his studies at Viterbo and then at Montefiascone, where he was appointed prefect. Because of his outstanding qualities, Vincent was appointed in 1767 as acting rector of the seminary, an office he held for about five months. At this time he was only 22 years old and not yet ordained!

Prior to Vincent's ordination in 1767, he made a retreat with the Passionists, where he was met by their saintly founder, St. Paul of the Cross. During the 10 days of the retreat, Vincent observed the life of the community and became convinced that his vocation was to be a Passionist. Going to Father Paul, he begged for admittance. The founder did not believe that Vincent had the physical strength to live up to the Passionist Rule and kindly, but firmly, refused.

Vincent was ordained, and was employed by the bishop in preaching in the diocese. He still felt the call to enter a missionary order and return to Rome for further studies. During this time, he made several trips to plead with St. Paul of the Cross to let him become a Passionist, and at last the holy Founder gave in and accepted him.

Vincent entered the novitiate at Monte Argentaro in 1768. Here he was given a new name—Father Vincent Mary of St. Paul.

Peace was not yet to be his, however, for Vincent's father was incensed by his son's entrance and sent a bitter letter to St. Paul of the Cross demanding that Vincent be dismissed. The Founder, of course, refused to dismiss Vincent, and he wrote Mr. Strambi that it was solely up to the young man whether or not he stayed. Vincent's father appealed to the bishop, who sent a priest to interview the novice. The report was successful and Vincent was then left to spend his novitiate in peace. He made his vows as a Passionist in 1769. After his profession, he was transferred to the monastery at Sant Angelo, and in 1771 he began to give missions.

Father Vincent seemed untiring on missions, both in preaching and in hearing confessions. He became one of the greatest preachers of Rome, whither he was transferred in 1773. Before every sermon he prayed before the Crucified Christ because, as he said, "The preacher who possesses the knowledge of Jesus from the crucifix is able to make all Hell tremble." St. Vincent Strambi was one of the great Italian missionary preachers—like St. Alphonsus Liguori, St. Leonard of Port Maurice and St. Paul of the Cross—who by their lives and preaching won innumerable souls for the Faith despite the growing unbelief of the "Enlightenment."

In Rome Fr. Vincent also taught theology and sacred eloquence at Sts. John and Paul, the Passionist monastery. There he was particularly noted for the care he gave to the sick brethren, one of whom was the saintly Founder.

In 1780, Father Vincent was made rector of the Roman monastery, and the next year was elected provincial. From this time until 1801, when he was made a bishop, he served the community in a number of offices, wrote the life of St. Paul of the Cross, and fulfilled the apostolate of confessor and director of souls.

In July of 1801, Father Vincent was informed by the Holy See that he had been named Bishop of the united sees of Macerata and Tolentino. The news was unexpected, and the humble priest feared the honor might be a great misfortune for his soul. He went to speak with Pope Pius VII and told him that he felt incompetent for such a grave responsibility. He pleaded his love for the monastery and his preference for life as a missionary. The Pope, however, told Vincent that he had not been proposed by anyone as an honor, but rather that he himself had appointed him in accord with his own knowledge and divine inspiration, and that Vincent must accept.

Bishop Vincent took over the diocese on August 14, 1801. He furnished his room in his new home with the same simplicity as in the one he had occupied in the monastery. He kept the same motto: *Passio Domini Nostri Jesu Christi* (The Passion of Our Lord Jesus Christ). A window was cut through the wall to the adjoining chapel so that he could constantly be in the presence of Our Lord in the Holy Eucharist.

Because of the politically troubled times, Vincent felt that the diocese needed a great deal of spiritual improvement. He arranged for missions to be conducted throughout the diocese, and he himself assisted in preaching and hearing confessions. He stressed the need for better knowledge of the Faith and organized groups of laity to teach catechism. He also pioneered in fostering frequent reception of Holy Communion as a return to the ancient practice of the Church and as a source of life and strength in everyday life.

Knowing that the welfare of souls depends so much on the clergy, Vincent did all he could to foster the best possible training for the priesthood. He screened the applicants himself, and his extraordinary discernment became legendary.

In addition to St. Paul of the Cross, Vincent was acquainted with another Passionist saint, Gaspar del Bufalo, promoter of devotion to the Precious Blood of Jesus. As a young man studying for the priesthood Gaspar del Bufalo had received the diaconate when he was struck by an unsettling uneasiness and indecision regarding the great dignity of the priesthood. Bishop Strambi was able to banish his fears; Gaspar del Bufalo was ordained and eventually canonized.

As bishop, Vincent stayed very busy—he built churches, homes for the aged, orphan asylums and many other charitable enterprises. More and more, however, the secular powers began to encroach upon the rights of the Church.

In 1809, Pope Pius VII was arrested and placed in captivity. The conditions of his captivity were severe. His correspondence was inspected and he could not receive visitors without witnesses. Even his signet ring was demanded of him. This "ring of the fisherman" is used to seal the official documents known as papal briefs. In a gesture of bravery, the Holy Father surrendered the ring only after he had broken it in two.

The year before, Bishop Strambi had been sent into exile. It was only when Napoleon was defeated by the Allies in 1814 that the saintly Bishop went back to his diocese. The Pope, too, was able to return to Rome.

Now, at age 69, the Bishop tried to bring his diocese back to normal. His own residence had been left in such a condition as to be unfit for habitation; finding the cost for the repairs so high he said, "That is far too much. The needs of the poor are so pressing that I will not deprive them of the help that money would enable me to give them. The repairs can wait and my successor can rebuild the episcopal house." He then moved into the seminary, where he occupied two small rooms.

The work of reconstruction was menaced by another war. Napoleon had escaped to Paris and would once more attempt to create an empire. Although in the end Napoleon was defeated and exiled to the Island of St. Helena, his attempt to reconquer the Papal States brought hardships to the people.

On one occasion a vastly outnumbered Austrian army under General Bianchi battled the French forces under Marshal Murat outside the city of Macerata. If the French were victorious, they would occupy the city—with fearful consequences.

The leading citizens went to seek the Bishop's advice and prayers. He summoned the seminarians to the chapel and urged them to ask Our Lord, through the intercession of the Blessed Mother, to spare the city. After himself kneeling in prayer for half an hour, Vincent stood up and said, "My sons, Macerata is saved! Give thanks to the Giver of all blessings and to the loving Mother of Mercy." He then instructed the vicar general to circulate among the people and reassure them. The people later learned that the French had indeed been defeated.

Another grave danger then presented itself. Since Macerata favored the Austrians, it was feared that the French troops, in their retreat, might pass through and sack and burn the city in revenge.

To the great surprise of the people, Bishop Strambi left the city and went out into the field of battle toward the French Army. He at once approached Marshal Murat and pleaded with him to prevent any trouble. Murat promised that his troops would be detoured away from Macerata.

Then the Bishop went back to the city, borrowed a carriage and had himself driven toward the Austrian troops. General Bianchi saw the vehicle coming and galloped out to see who it was. When he saw Bishop Strambi, he was concerned for his safety and told him to return to the city. Vincent only smiled, telling the General that he had come on a mission of mercy. He expressed the joy of the people over the victory and then begged the General to cease slaughtering the fleeing soldiers. General Bianchi agreed to this appeal to Christian charity, and he later attributed the victory solely to the prayers of Bishop Strambi. The Bishop, of course, laid the victory at the feet of the true victors—God and the Blessed Virgin Mary.

Bishop Strambi continued his strenuous activities, but time and again he begged to be allowed to retire and finish his life in one of the Passionist monasteries. This retirement was not permitted by Pope Pius VII. After the Pope's death, Vincent made the same appeal to his successor, Pope Leo XII. After some hesitation, the Pope accepted Vincent's resignation (in 1823), but directed that he live in the papal residence and act as the Pope's confidential adviser.

As Vincent left his diocese, giving a final blessing, he slipped off his episcopal ring. Handing it to a priest, he instructed him to sell it and use the money for the poor.

Pope Leo fell ill in December of 1823. On December 23 the doctors told Vincent that the Pope's condition was critical and that they judged the case to be hopeless. But the aged Bishop approached the bedside and, after praying with the Pope, assured him that he would not die. Nevertheless, the Last Sacraments were administered.

"Have courage, Holy Father, there is somebody who will offer his life for Your Holiness," Vincent told the Pope. He then left to say Mass in the Pope's private chapel. Little did his assistants realize that a twofold sacrifice was being offered that day at the altar—the Sacrifice of Calvary for the salvation of all men, and that of the elderly Bishop for the temporal life of the Pope.

After Mass, word was brought to Vincent that the Pope had suddenly taken a turn for the better. "Thanks be to God, He has accepted the sacrifice," was the puzzling reply of the Bishop.

At dawn, when Vincent visited the Pope, he informed the Pontiff of a secret which God had made known to him. He told the Pope that his pontificate would continue for another five years and a short time longer. This prediction, like many others made by the saintly Bishop, came to pass in due course.

On December 28, Bishop Strambi suffered an apoplectic stroke which paralyzed his entire body. He was able to make his last confession, and immediately afterward lost the power of speech. His jaws became tightly locked and he could not receive Holy Communion.

On December 30, a priest mentioned the Bishop's condition to one of Vincent's penitents, Blessed Anna Maria Taigi, who told him to have Mass said for the Bishop at dawn, at which time Vincent would be able to receive Holy Communion, enjoy a half hour of thanksgiving, and would then lapse into his former condition and die.

The next morning Vincent regained his speech, received Holy Communion and spent some time in recollection. He kissed his crucifix slowly and then sank into a coma which lasted until his peaceful death the next morning, January 1, 1824. This was Vincent's 79th birthday, as well as the day of his birth to eternal life.

Vincent Mary Strambi was canonized by Pope Pius XII in 1950.

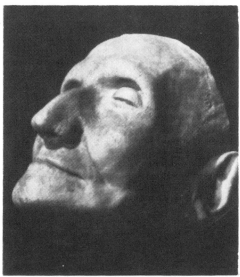

Anon./Schamoni/Christiana Verlag, Stein am Rhein

Death mask of St. Vincent Mary Strambi, saintly bishop who was deported and exiled from his diocese for 5 years for refusing to take an anti-Catholic political oath demanded by Napoleon Bonaparte.

Bishop Strambi, one of the greatest Italian missionary preachers. He said, "The preacher who possesses the knowledge of Jesus from the crucifix is able to make all Hell tremble." He offered his life to God in exchange for that of the critically ill Pope Leo XII. A few days later Vincent was struck with a sudden illness and died soon after, on his 79th birthday. The Pope recovered and lived another five years.

— 6 —

SAINT VINCENT PALLOTTI

Vincent Aloysius Francis Pallotti
1795 - 1850
Italy
Died Age 54

"The love of Christ impels us." Inspired by this scriptural passage, Vincent Pallotti became one of the most active priests of the 19th century. He was a man of an amazing variety of apostolic activities, of unusually austere penances, and of exceptional mystical gifts.

One of his most remarkable gifts was the ability to convert hardened sinners. Moreover, very often miraculous circumstances would enable him to be in the right place at the right time to prepare a soul for death. Vincent could often tell whether a sick person was going to die or recover. At times, through his intervention and prayer, the sick person would be cured. Sometimes, also, Vincent seemed to have supernatural knowledge.

Vincent Pallotti was born on April 21, 1795 at Rome, one of four surviving children of a wealthy grocer. Both of his parents were noted for their piety and charity.

As a child Vincent exhibited early signs of the piety, the gentleness and the loving nature for which he would be known all his life. At school he was a great favorite with his teachers because of his obedience and industry.

At first, however, in spite of his application, Vincent made little progress in his studies. His mother suggested that he make a novena to the Holy Spirit for greater success—and to the wonder of all he soon took first place in his class. He later followed the course of studies at the Roman College, receiving many scholastic awards in the process. Instead of being vain about these awards, his comment was that the ability to gain them was given to him in order that he might do more for the glory of God. He believed that humility was the foundation of all virtue, and he attributed any

44

success to God alone.

Though Vincent was economical in matters concerning his own person and preferred the simplest clothes, his charity, even as a youngster, was unbounded. He would save part of his dinner or dessert to give to the poor. Once when Vincent was arriving home in a carriage, a poor barefooted beggar came up to ask for an alms. Vincent instantly took off his own shoes and gave them to the beggar. When scolded by his father for impetuous acts such as this, he would either take the reproach in silence or else simply say that he had given the article to someone who needed it more than he did.

At age 16 Vincent wanted to enter the Capuchin Order, but his confessor dissuaded him because of his delicate health. Instead, he obtained his father's consent to prepare for the diocesan priesthood. He was ordained a priest on May 16, 1818, at age 23.

As Vincent's parents were quite wealthy, he lived first with his family as a private chaplain while he continued his studies. After attaining the doctorates, he became a private tutor in the department of dogma in the Roman University, an office he filled for 10 years. Whenever and wherever there was an opportunity to do apostolic work, Vincent joyfully accepted it.

In 1829 he resigned his post as teacher and accepted the rectorship of a poor church called the Church of the Holy Ghost. He had previously been offered the rectorship of a wealthy parish, but he refused. Soon he had attained a reputation as a divinely favored confessor and director and was obliged to stay many hours in the confessional. He entered a life of continual activity as a confessor, director of spiritual exercises, missionary to the people, and preacher.

At Vincent's beatification process everyone affirmed that his greatest ministry had been as a confessor, and that the good he did in this way was incalculable. Often he would be in the confessional all day and up to about midnight. He was extremely kind and patient, but also firm when necessary. He could read hearts and he often converted the most obdurate sinners.

Father Pallotti wished to bring the blessings of religion to the people of all lands and to enkindle the fires of faith and love in the hearts of all men. His goal was universal: he wanted to make everyone in the world a Catholic, to make every Catholic a good Catholic, and to make every good Catholic an apostle. A group of close friends, cleric and lay, were accustomed to gather in his room to discuss ways of increasing faith and fostering love. They decided to translate into Arabic and print some copies of a book by St. Alphonsus Liguori and have it sent to the missions in the Near East. As this would cost a goodly amount of money, and they wanted to prevent any talk of abuse of funds, Father Pallotti decided to form a society to administer the work. This became the beginning of his religious establishment; in 1835, he obtained approbation from the Church for the Society of the Catholic Apostleship, for both priests and lay people. The priests and brothers of this society are now known as the Pallottine Fathers and Brothers. In accord with the same rules as those set up for this society, Father Pallotti also organized a congregation of women for the religious training of young girls, and finally a kind of third order to which persons of all conditions might belong.

The poor and working classes held a special claim on Father Pallotti's compassion. He used his organizational skills to found and influence a number of permanent works for their spiritual and temporal needs. He formed guilds for the various avocations and established schools dedicated to improving agricultural methods. Also, he established country savings banks to protect small farmers.

Saints seem to come in "clumps," and a number of holy people who today are headed toward the honors of the altar were friends of Father Pallotti. One of his good friends was Blessed Bernard Mary Clausi, and for nearly 20 years he was the spiritual director of the Venerable Elizabeth Sanna. St. Gaspar del Bufalo died in Vincent's arms.

Soldiers and prisoners, especially prisoners condemned to death, were particular loves of Vincent. As soon as he was summoned to one of those unhappy condemned felons, he hastened to his cell and remained with him until the moment of his execution, realizing that eternal salvation often depended on the man's last moments. He spared neither labor, tears nor prayers to bring him to repentance. Vincent even instituted a special branch of his society to prepare these poor men for a happy death.

In Rome it was the custom to kiss the hand of a priest. In his humility, Vincent found this custom intolerable, so up his sleeve he wore a little reliquary, on the back of which was painted a picture of the Blessed Virgin and Child; with wonderful dexterity he always managed to substitute this pious image for his hand so that people found themselves kissing a portrait of Our Lady.

Vincent had a hatred of waste—whether of time or of material things. He used to carry a book with him so as not to waste time while waiting for anything. On one occasion a young priest had received a letter and was about to crumple it and throw it into the fire. Father Pallotti stopped him and had him tear off the portions of the paper which were not written on and put them into a basket. The young priest obeyed unwillingly, thinking that the effort was really a waste of time. When he had finished, Father Pallotti noted that the basket was full of paper—as indeed it was—and he asked the young priest to find one of the men who collected such scraps. The man came and paid about 10 cents for the basket of scraps.

Then Father Pallotti and the young priest went to pay a visit to the Hospital of the Holy Spirit. On the way, Father Pallotti stopped and bought a box of crackers with the coin. At the hospital, there was a great sinner in bed 15 of one of the large wards; he was dying. Whenever a priest would come near him, he would foam at the mouth and utter all manner of blasphemies. On being told of this man, the two priests first went to the chapel to pray for the man's soul, for, as our saint said, "God is all-powerful and wishes the salvation of this man more than we do ourselves."

On entering the ward, Father Pallotti went first and visited with a number of other patients. When the man in bed 15 began to rave and blaspheme, he noticed that no one was paying any attention to him, so he closed his eyes. Quickly, Father Vincent went to stand by his bed. When the man opened his eyes, he saw the priest in the act of blessing him. He opened his mouth and began to curse again, but before he was well-started Father Vincent slipped one of the crackers into his mouth, saying gently, "Eat, my son, it will do you good."

The man had to stop to chew the cracker and swallow it, giving the priest time to say a few words. When he began again to curse, the priest repeated the same maneuver, time and again.

At last divine grace conquered and the man began to weep. He made an act of contrition and Father Pallotti heard his confession. As the young priest held the candle for Extreme Unction, he heard the dying man say over and over, "My Jesus, mercy! Jesus, Mary and Joseph, assist me in my last agony!" And so he died with expressions of the deepest penance. Father Pallotti then turned to the young priest and said, "There is a soul saved and gone to Purgatory. . .you see, my friend, of what use were those little scraps of paper."

Vincent was gifted with a number of supernatural gifts. Several of these were introduced into the process of his beatification and thus examined closely. He possessed to a high degree the gift of knowing the spiritual state of souls that came to him for advice.

He also had an extraordinary insight into the future. During his last illness, he assisted St. Gaspar del Bufalo, going to see him every day. Taking leave of him one morning as usual, he promised to return the next day. A few hours later, while busy with some ministerial work a long way from Gaspar's house, he suddenly broke off and left immediately, hurrying to the bedside of the Saint. Vincent had hardly entered the room when Gaspar's agony began; he died in Vincent's arms a few minutes later. Vincent exclaimed, "Oh beautiful soul, oh beautiful soul!" He had seen the Saint's soul entering Paradise. On another occasion Vincent told a priest that the soul of Pope Gregory had just gone to Paradise. When the priest expressed astonishment that the holy Pope had spent so many months in Purgatory, Vincent replied that great holiness was necessary if one were not to dread God's judgment.

Another time he and another priest were headed for a certain destination when Vincent suddenly insisted that they take another street. The priest objected, saying that it would be the long way to where they were going. Father Vincent only urged him to hurry, and then almost broke into a run. In a few moments they met a woman who rushed up to Vincent and begged him to come into an adjoining house to help a dying woman. There Vincent blessed her with his Madonna image and exhorted her to have confidence in the intercession of the Blessed Virgin; she was instantly cured.

A number of people have testified to seeing him lifted off the ground in ecstasy while saying Mass. Another special gift was that of bilocation. Once Vincent was hearing the confession of a young man when, in the middle of the confession, Vincent seemed unconscious. The young man thought he was asleep and shook the door of the confessional, asking what was the matter. In a few minutes Vincent replied that nothing was wrong and took up the confession where the young man had left off. When the young man arrived home, he learned that another young man who lodged with him had just died, and that he had been assisted at the end by Father Pallotti!

One time Father Vincent interrupted a boy watching a game and persuaded him to make his confession. Then he said to him, "My dear boy, if by chance you should ever need my ministry, do not hesitate to send for me, no matter at what hour." That night the boy awoke with a severe pain; when the doctor could do nothing, he sent for Vincent. Vincent prepared him for death and the boy died in his arms before morning.

Vincent's miraculous influence over the most hardened sinners was well noted. Vincent had unbounded confidence in God, and God answered his confidence by granting remarkable conversions. He also had great power over the devil and was sought after as an exorcist.

Once a young man who had led a thoroughly wicked life and was bitterly anticlerical threatened to shoot any priest who came near him, and he kept a gun by the side of his sickbed. When Vincent came to the house, the parents even warned Vincent against their son. Vincent asked for a disguise; dressed in a woman's gown with a veil to cover his head, he entered the young man's room. The young man's mother announced that the visitor was going to stay with him so that she might get a little rest. Under pretext of arranging the young man's pillows, Vincent slipped his little Madonna picture under the fellow's head. Vincent spent the night on his knees praying that the devils would leave the man, and in the morning when he threw off his disguise, the young man had been converted.

In 1847 Vincent drew up his will, leaving the bulk of his fortune to various works of charity, the foreign missions, and for the diffusion of good books. He wrote a number of letters, and in several he predicted his death. It has been said that Vincent offered his life to appease the justice of God provoked by the scandals currently going on in Rome. Our Lord revealed to him the exact day of his death through Blessed Clausi who, on leaving for Paola, wished Vincent good-bye with these words: "Vincent! Let us leave this filthy world. Ah! One month and three days after!" Vincent died one month and three days after Father Clausi.

In January of 1850 Vincent developed a bad case of pleurisy, accompanied by fever. On his deathbed he manifested every virtue which could adorn a priest. His last words were spoken to Don Vaccari, who had implored him to pray for a recovery: "...for the sake of charity, let me go where God will have me." Vincent breathed his last without the slightest struggle.

During life Vincent had attained the reputation of working miracles, and he did not stop after death. Moreover, there are on record at least six appearances of this saint after his death. A sweet fragrance was noted for one month in the room where he had died.

The process of beatification was begun in 1852. In 1906 and again in 1949, his tomb was opened and his body was found incorrupt. Vincent Pallotti was beatified on the 100th anniversary of his death and was canonized by Pope John XXIII in 1963.

Stab. L. Salomone, Rome

Sarcophagus containing the body of St. Vincent Pallotti, with the face and hands covered in silver. (Church of St. Salvatore, Onda, Italy.)

St. Vincent Pallotti, Founder of the Pallottines, who had a remarkable gift for converting hardened sinners; he would often spend all day and a good deal of the night in the confessional. At his beatification process all affirmed that his greatest ministry had been that of hearing confessions and that the good he did in that way was incalculable. (*Painting by A. Gottwald.*)

St. Vincent Pallotti experienced levitations, bilocation, ecstasy, reading of hearts and other forms of supernatural knowledge.

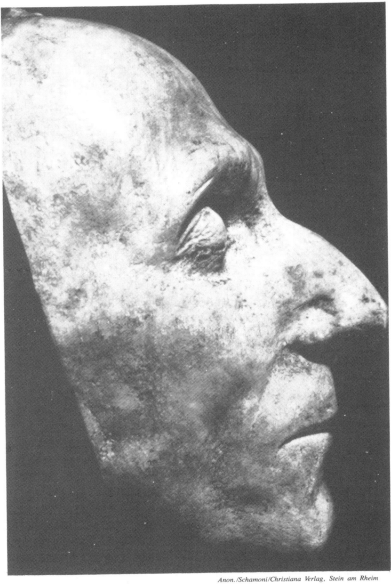

Anon./Schamoni/Christiana Verlag, Stein am Rheim

Death mask of St. Vincent Pallotti, in the Pallottine Generalate, Rome. St. Vincent was born, lived his life and died in Rome, but his ideal was a universal one: he wanted to make everyone Catholic, to make every Catholic a good Catholic, and to make every good Catholic an apostle.

7

MOTHER THEODORE GUERIN

Servant of God Mother Theodore Guerin, S.P.
Anne-Therese Guerin
1798 - 1856
France - United States
Died Age 58

"It is impossible to have any idea of the extravagance of the Americans without having seen it. We did not see one woman who was not wearing a bonnet. Even the milkmaids wear them while milking the cows. Milk is carted around in quite a stylish conveyance drawn by two horses, and the men who distribute it are dressed as if for a wedding."

So wrote Mother Theodore Guerin, a 41-year-old French sister, in 1849 upon her arrival in New York. She was the leader of a group of six Sisters of Providence traveling from their motherhouse in France to found a new congregation in Indiana at the request of the Bishop of Vincennes.

Anne-Therese Guerin was born in Brittany, at Etables, a small town in western France. Her father was a naval officer who supported his family very well.

There was not much opportunity for an education in Etables, for the Revolution had destroyed the schools there. Therefore Anne-Therese's mother, who was well-educated and had been a member of the French nobility, taught her two daughters herself. When a young woman opened a school in town, Anne-Therese attended for only one year. She often skipped class to roam the beach or the hills.

Later a young cousin who was a theological student came to live with the family, and learning of Anne-Therese's indifference to learning, he offered to teach her himself. In the year that he stayed with the family, she learned a great deal from him.

Because of her studies with her cousin, Anne-Therese became proficient in catechism and was therefore allowed to make her First

Communion at the early age of 10. On the day of her First Communion she told the priest that she wanted to be a nun when she was grown up.

When Anne-Therese was nearly 15 her father was killed. He was ambushed and slain by robbers as he was returning home on leave. His death left his wife with very little money and two children to bring up. Mrs. Guerin grew more and more to depend on her oldest daughter. Anne-Therese took up her duties cheerfully and courageously, nursing her mother through a severe illness, taking care of her younger sister and running the house. For a number of years she continued in this manner.

One day when some girls were talking, as girls do, about the type of man they would marry, they asked Anne-Therese about her future husband. Anne-Therese did not answer right away, but finally she said, "I shall marry a king," and left it at that. When her mother heard the story later and asked about her meaning, Anne-Therese spoke for the first time of her desire to enter the convent.

At first her mother opposed the idea, and in an effort to persuade Anne-Therese to stay at home she invited young men to the house to meet her pretty daughter. She also saw to it that Anne-Therese went to parties. One young man who proposed to Anne-Therese asked her why she wanted to become a nun. She replied that she felt she must do something for God and for souls.

Finally, when Anne-Therese was 25 years old, her mother relented and gave her permission; Anne-Therese would be able to enter a convent with her mother's blessing.

After hearing of the Sisters of Providence, with their small but inspiring work and their need for new members, especially those who could teach, Anne-Therese entered with them as a postulant in August of 1823. Here she received the new name of Sister St. Theodore.

During her first year in the convent Sister Theodore had a severe illness. Because the medical treatment was poor and the medicine harsh, she was left with impaired health. For the rest of her life she was never able to eat solid food, and she was never completely well, but her condition did not impair her ability to work hard.

For eight years Sister Theodore was superior at the house and school in Rennes. On her arrival there she had been treated with rudeness and distrust by the girls at the school. Instead of using the stern and strict punishments common in schools in those days, Sister Theodore used reason and love and thus won over her pupils.

Sister Theodore spent the next six years with a group of her sisters in Soulaines. Here again, the people loved her and grew to depend on her aid in many matters, in addition to that of the education of their children.

In 1839 a messenger from Bishop Brute of Vincennes, Indiana, came to France seeking religious to work in the mission fields of America. The superior of the order asked Sister Theodore to lead a group of Sisters of Providence in this undertaking. Sister Theodore had her doubts—she was already 41 and her health had not been good for some time. She knew that if she failed, the whole mission would fail. But finally, after much prayer, she agreed. In July of 1840 the sisters set sail for America. The voyage, by sailing ship, took a little over a month. At last, after many days of seasickness, the sturdy little band reached New York.

From New York the sisters traveled to Philadelphia by train. The train went at the unheard-of speed of 20 miles per hour. Far from being frightened, the sisters enjoyed the new experience, for this was the first train they had ever seen. In Philadelphia they stayed for a brief time with the Sisters of Charity. In spite of the fact that neither group spoke the same language as the other, they met in the chapel on common ground. Many French settlers visited the Sisters of Providence there. They then traveled to Baltimore by boat and train. Finally, on September 18, the sisters set out on the last lap of their journey to Indiana. They traveled by railroad, steamboat, stagecoach and canal. At last they reached their destination—St. Mary-of-the-Woods, Indiana.

The sisters had made a promise not to speak upon their arrival until they had made a visit to the Blessed Sacrament. The local priest led them to a small, single-room log cabin. They did not realize that it was a church until they saw the little pyx which held the Host resting on an altar of three boards laid across two stakes driven into the ground. Covering the altar was a blue cotton cloth—there was no tabernacle. At Mass the next morning, the sisters realized that this tiny room served not only as the church, but also as rectory and workroom for the priest.

At first the sisters' house was not ready, and they stayed with a Catholic family. They were joined by four postulants, increasing the small community to 10. Because of the crowded conditions in the small farmhouse where they were staying, Mother Theodore requested that the bishop buy the house outright for them—and he did. One of the postulants began teaching English to the French sisters.

For many years poverty was the lot of the sisters. Complaints were few, though, for they knew how important their apostolate was. Mother Theodore's belief in the providence of God was communicated to all of the sisters. "I always find a new sacrifice to make when I think I have reached the end. May God be blest for it! In eternity it will not be too much."

Mother Theodore and her group had come to help the bishop in his work of educating the children of the diocese. The sisters followed the French custom of operating a boarding school, where the students paid tuition which helped pay for a free school. But in the beginning most of the Catholic families in the diocese were too poor to be able to afford tuition. At this time there were no public schools outside of the eastern part of the United States, so the majority of the first pupils at the sisters' academy were Protestant. There was a great deal of anti-Catholic feeling during this period of American history, and these first Protestant boarders were helpful in dispelling some of the strange myths that the people believed about Catholics. Later, as the sisters' work grew, so did the affluence among the Catholic community, and the schools filled with young Catholics.

Many of the children that the sisters taught had come to them with very little religious training. Their pioneer parents were too busy to talk to them of religion, and the children did not receive much religious training at all. The Catholic families were happy to have the sisters provide this education for their children.

An excellent teacher herself, Mother Theodore insisted on this excellence for all her sisters. "To teach children," she told them, "two virtues are necessary—justice and kindness." In her daily instructions to her sisters, she often reminded them of the spiritual beauty of their vocation as teachers. "Have you ever thought, dear Sisters, that you are privileged to do on earth what Our Lord did? He instructed, and you instruct. He was often surrounded by little children, and you spend your lives among them; it is truly sublime to be devoted to the service of our neighbor. But we must not think it an easy task. We must possess all the virtues before we attempt to teach them to others."

A number of times the community had to face difficulties and misunderstandings with one of the ecclesiastical authorities. Mother Theodore cautioned her sisters to remain obedient and to accept any hardships as tests from God: "Let us submit to the will of God. He has always protected us; if we love Him, He will never abandon us."

Despite her almost constant ill health, Mother Theodore always radiated enthusiasm and confidence in God. She was fond of giving little conferences, or talks, to both her pupils and her sisters. Once the order began to grow, Mother Theodore was frequently too busy to write often to the sisters in the other houses. She said, "Prayer is our postal service, our telegraph, our surest means of communication." The sisters knew she used this method of communication on their behalf frequently.

Mother Theodore was a practical woman. Although funds were never in excess, she told the sisters, "All we teach our children must be for the glory of God and for the love of the children. The profit that the community derives from its school is a secondary consideration. Believe me, there will always be money enough at St. Mary's if the religious are good religious."

Mother Theodore was a builder. In spite of difficulties with ecclesiastical authorities, poverty and ill health, she—a pioneer herself—built a congregation which brought the knowledge of Christ to the hardy pioneers of America.

After a lengthy final illness, Mother Theodore died quietly on May 14, 1856, after having received the Last Sacraments. Her death had been foretold to her only a few months before by Sister St. Francis who, two days before her own death, had received the special favor of seeing Heaven for a moment, and of having Christ call her by name and tell her of her own and Mother Theodore's impending death.

A cause for Mother Theodore was introduced in 1956.

Ven. Mother Theodore Guerin, who at 41, in precarious health, left France to open Catholic schools in the pioneer territory of St. Mary-of-the-Woods, Indiana. Life was primitive. Mother Guerin said, "I always find a new sacrifice to make when I think I have reached the end. May God be blest for it! In eternity it will not be too much."

8

SAINT JOHN VIANNEY
The Curé of Ars

John-Marie-Baptiste Vianney
1786 - 1859
France
Died Age 73

St. John Vianney often experienced the physical presence of the devil. He was kept awake by loud terrifying noises, assailed by threatening words, and sometimes dragged across the room. The holy Curé (parish priest) of Ars suffered from these diabolical visitations over a period of 30 years. He came to accept them as a matter of course and often even spoke of them in a bantering manner.

John-Marie-Baptiste Vianney was born on May 8, 1786, in Dardilly, France. His parents, Matthieu and Marie Vianney, had six children, of whom John was the fourth. The family were farmers, and the children learned early to accompany their parents to their work in the fields. The sturdy country folk were staunch Catholics, and Marie brought up all of her children with a love of God. John was a lively child and precocious in all matters of religion.

From the time he was about seven, it was John's chore to tend the flocks. He was usually accompanied by his younger sister. While they sat looking after the cattle and sheep they knitted stockings of wool. Sometimes John would talk his sister into knitting his stocking so that he could pray or build a shrine for a small wooden statue of Our Lady or mold miniature saints from clay. When the other shepherd children would come to see what the Vianney children were doing, John would talk to them about religion. In effect he became their catechist, as many of the children had had no religious training at home.

During the time when the horrors of the French Revolution had closed the churches and forced religious into hiding, the Vianney family often sheltered some of these holy refugees. Their charity to the poor, too, was well known. In spite of the many chances they took, the family was never betrayed.

In 1795, when he was nine, John attended school for the first time. He was loved by his teacher for his excellent conduct and his application to work. He was not a dull boy, but he had great difficulty in learning anything much beyond his catechism. In 1797, at the age of 11, John made his first confession to a missionary priest in hiding. He lived briefly with an aunt in order to be near some sisters who secretly prepared him for his First Holy Communion, which he made when he was 13.

When the years of his childhood had ended, he went to work on the farm. His piety and constant praying, his frankness and his courtesy, endeared him to all.

"If I were a priest, I should gain many souls to God," the young man said. His father, however, objected. John was a good worker and was needed at home, and there was not enough money for the necessary education. For a number of years the struggle went on. At last a small presbytery school was opened nearby, and John's father relented. The 19-year-old John left with a happy heart.

At the school John tried his hardest, but Latin grammar was all but incomprehensible to this young man who had spent so many years working in the fields rather than studying in school. The other students, who noticed his prayers, fasting and diligence, attempted to help. At their age (about 12), however, it was easy to lose patience with one who seemed so stupid. One impetuous boy, Mathias Loras, once lost his patience with John and boxed his ears in front of the others. John knelt and humbly asked forgiveness of this boy who had treated him so outrageously. At that point Mathias, who had a heart of gold and a loving nature, was suddenly smitten with grief; with a face full of tears he threw himself into the arms of John, who was still on his knees. This marked the beginning of a long friendship. Mathias Loras became a missionary bishop to the United States and eventually the first Bishop of Dubuque, Iowa. He emulated the holiness of his friend so well that many persons consider him worthy of canonization.

For a while John became very discouraged, even telling the good Father Balley, his teacher, that he wanted to return home. This priest recalled to John's mind the thought of the priesthood and of laboring for souls and thus persuaded him to persevere. John made a pilgrimage to the shrine of St. Francis Regis for the grace to learn enough Latin to enable him to do his theology, and on his return his progress was slowly but surely better. At the age of 21 John finally received the Sacrament of Confirmation.

Through a series of clerical errors, John was conscripted into the army and then, through illness and some other circumstances, found himself for a time in the position of hiding out as what we would call a "deserter." Eventually deserters were pardoned.

At last, at the age of 24, John was back in school with Father Balley. His report read: "Application, conduct, and character...Good. General knowledge...Very weak."

Eventually John Vianney would be dismissed from the Grand Seminaire at Lyons, an event that he considered one of the greatest sadnesses of his life. Yet his humility kept him silent, and his faith kept him from defeat. Convinced that he could never become a priest, as he felt he would never know enough Latin, he spoke to a friend about becoming a brother. But Father Balley persuaded him to try again for ordination.

At age 29, John stood for the examination before a group of seminary authorities. They knew Father Balley's reputation and realized he must have had some reason to recommend this student who seemed so stupid. Should they reject the poor aspiring seminarist, so full of good will, or simply keep him waiting? They decided that if John Vianney could find a bishop willing to accept him, he was to be free to seek admission in another diocese. This was their way of declining all responsibility in the matter.

John Vianney's good teacher, however, realized the danger in this decision and persuaded the examiners to come and see the unhappy aspirant in his familiar surroundings. There John was able to give good and satisfactory answers. The Vicar General, Father Courbon, a simple and unsophisticated man, asked, "Is the Abbé Vianney pious? Has he a devotion to Our Lady? Does he know how to say his Rosary?...Very well, I summon him to come up for ordination. The grace of God will do the rest."

At long last, in August of 1815 at the age of 29, John Vianney was finally ordained. He was assigned to the parish of Ars as its Curé, or pastor. The Vicar General told him, "There is not much love for God in that parish; you will bring some into it." Like many French villages, Ars was feeling the evil effects of the French Revolution. Drinking, dancing and attendant sins, profanation of Sunday and neglect of religious obligations were rife; faith was weak and religious ignorance was common. John set out to win back these souls.

At Ars, especially during his first years there, the Saint performed the most severe penances, disciplines and self-denials—thus drawing down graces from God upon his flock. Bloodstains were left on his wall where he had collapsed after scourging himself for long periods of time. For six years he lived exclusively on boiled potatoes, and he always lived in the utmost poverty. Later he tempered his rigorous penances somewhat, though they continued to be terrifyingly severe. The Curé's desire was to convert his parish. His simple life and complete humility endeared him to his people. He gave catechism instructions regularly; his favorite topic was love for Jesus in the Blessed Sacrament. The parish began to change for the better.

John Vianney felt a great attraction toward both prayer and fasting. In 1839 he revealed to a young priest, "My friend, the devil is not greatly afraid of the discipline [whip or scourge] and other instruments of penance. That which beats him is the curtailment of one's food, drink and sleep. There is nothing the devil fears more, consequently, nothing is more pleasing to God. Oh! how often have I experienced it! [In my early years at Ars] it happened at times that I refrained from food for entire days. On those occasions I obtained, both for myself and for others, whatsoever I asked of Almighty God." Tears were streaming down the Saint's cheeks as he spoke. After a while he continued: "Now things are not quite the same. I cannot do without food for so long a time—if I attempt it, I lose the power even of speech. But how happy I was whilst I lived alone! I bought from the poor the morsels of bread that were given them; I spent a good part of the night in the church; there were not many people to confess, and the good God granted me extraordinary graces." In this way the period of his most severe penances was for John Vianney also the time of his greatest consolations.

The love of God and the love of souls provided the motivating power for the Curé of Ars. Although his severe penances and self-denials weakened his health, and although he suffered also from an intermittent fever which was supposedly due to the unhealthful climate, John would not rest. His zeal spurred him to action in his desire to save souls. He scolded the fallen, fed the hungry, instituted a "providence" (school and home) for orphans and poor children, administered the Sacraments, catechized and, in all, loved his parishioners. This love was felt, and slowly Ars responded.

St. John Vianney possessed the ability to read the hearts of his penitents. He had the gifts which mystical theologians call intuition and prophecy. There are literally hundreds of well-documented examples of his use of these gifts.

Once, the mother of two sons traveled to Ars to seek the counsel of the Curé. Her youngest son, only 18, had fallen in love with a girl of 15 and, in spite of his mother's advice to the contrary, intended to marry her. When the woman arrived at the church, it was full; she took the only seat available, which was at the back of the church. Having only a little time, she realized that the wait would be too long and so decided to leave. At the moment she made this decision, she noticed a white-haired priest come out of the confessional and walk directly to her. He bent and whispered in her ear, "Let them marry. They will be very happy." She was amazed, as she had never seen the Curé before and he had never seen her, not did he have any way of knowing that she was coming.

Another time, a father of three sons, who longed for a daughter, met Father Vianney on the street. Father Vianney gave him four rosaries, saying they were for the man's children. "But Father, I have only three boys," the man replied. Father Vianney told him that the fourth rosary was for his daughter. Sure enough, a daughter was born within a year.

To a mother of a large family distressed because she was expecting yet another child he had encouraging words, then added that there were many women in Hell because they did not accept the children God wished to send them.

Soon, the fame of this humble priest spread over France, attracting hordes of troubled souls. At last, he was spending from 13 to 17 hours per day in the stifling, cramped confessional. From 1827-1859, the church at Ars was never empty. Over the years the number of pilgrims increased steadily until in 1845 there were 300-400 arrivals daily. In the last year of the Saint's life there were 80,000 recorded pilgrims who traveled by public conveyance. Counting those who came by private transport, the total number of pilgrims was between 100,000-120,000 that year. One year he admitted that he had converted 700 "big sinners" that year.

From time to time God permits a favored soul to do battle with the devil. The devil, of course, tempts all men, but he usually keeps himself hidden. In other, much rarer, cases, the presence of the devil is revealed by terrifying manifestations. Such was the case with the humble Curé. Loud noises, transportations, smashing of objects, occasional physical attacks and other disturbances were endured by St. John Vianney for years. These phenomena became a familiar part of his life, and he referred to the devil by a nickname: the *grappin* (griffin).

When his confessor asked John Vianney how he repelled the attacks of the devil, he replied, "I turn to God; I make the Sign of the Cross; I address a few contemptuous words to the devil. I have noticed, moreover, that the tumult is greater and the assaults more numerous if, on the following day, some big sinner is due to come." "At the beginning I felt afraid. I did not then know what it was, but now I am quite happy. It is a good sign: there is always a good haul of fish the next day."

Sometimes the Curé would say, "The devil gave me a good shaking last night, so we shall have a great number of people tomorrow. The *grappin* is very stupid; he himself tells me of the arrival of big sinners... He is angry. So much the better!" It was this knowledge, the malice of the devil and the pleasure of God, that gave the frail priest the stamina for the superhuman toil of hours in the confessional after spending nights in sleeplessness. Saving souls, always saving souls. St. John Vianney never allowed diabolical vexations to deter him from his priestly duties. Even after having endured hours of sleeplessness, he would report to the parish church to hear confessions at the appointed hour of midnight. People waited for hours. One penitent was observed awaiting his turn from 5 a.m. to 5 p.m.

Many of the pilgrims who came to Ars were afflicted with physical as well as spiritual ills, and some were cured there. The stir caused by these happenings disturbed John Marie, since he worried that people would attribute the cures and miracles to him instead of to their real author, God. After receiving a relic of St. Philomena[1] from the saintly Pauline Jaricot, John Vianney developed a great devotion to and mystical affiliation with St. Philomena which was to last until his death. When people came to him seeking cures, he would tell them to ask St. Philomena—and to this saint's intercession he gave all the credit for the resulting cures. John Vianney said he had never failed to receive anything he asked of her. He wanted her to perform spiritual rather than physical cures in his parish, but she sometimes performed physical cures too.

There is good evidence of many miraculous happenings in the

life of St. John Vianney. For instance, around 1830, corn and flour were miraculously multiplied to feed the children of the Providence.

St. John Vianney felt the greatest attraction toward prayer, yet the time for much prayer was denied to him because of the long hours he spent hearing confessions, consoling the afflicted, visiting the sick, counseling those in doubt and attending to his other priestly duties. When a friend asked him for his advice on mental prayer, the Saint's answer was, "I no longer have time for regular prayer, but at the very first moment of the day I endeavor to unite myself closely to Jesus Christ, and I then perform my task with the thought of this union in mind." His friend concluded that, in spite of his sadness at being denied the time for his attraction, John Vianney's entire life was one long prayer.

John Vianney had a great longing for solitude, and one of his greatest desires in his old age was to be allowed to retire to a monastery and thus have time for prayer and penance before his death. Time after time he requested this of his superiors, and time after time his request was denied. Three times he even tried to run away to a monastery or another parish. St. John Vianney was destined to die a parish priest. In spite of weariness, illness and old age, he continued to labor for those souls entrusted to him. People knew he was a saint; they would snip off pieces of his soutaine and even wisps of hair as relics; also, pages were taken from his breviary. Publications praising the Curé provided a stream of unwanted publicity; to one author he complained, "Before long you people will be putting me up for sale at the fair."

Toward the end of his life, John Vianney collapsed four times in one day on the way to the church, and it was with extreme difficulty that he got up again. When a friend told him that he looked very tired, he replied with a smile, "Oh, the sinners will end by killing the poor sinner."

Completely worn out with exhaustion, the elderly Curé fell ill in July of 1859. He never stopped his efforts to save souls, even at this point, although his words during catechism instructions could not be understood and he often passed out briefly in the confessional. At last, on the night of July 29, he knocked on the wall of his room and whispered, "It is my poor end." He asked for his confessor, and when told that the doctor would also be summoned, he replied that the doctor could do nothing—but for the first time ever he made no objection to those ministering to him.

The only objection he made was when a sister of St. Joseph, who was tending him, began to brush away the flies which had settled on his face. He made a gesture and whispered, "Leave me with my poor flies. . . .The only vexatious thing is sin!"

With tears streaming down their faces, his parishioners begged for the privilege of visiting their saintly pastor a last time, or of being allowed to kneel at the door to his room. Pilgrims who arrived and begged to be allowed to see the confessor were told to kneel down outside, and at stated times a little bell was rung to signal that the Curé would bless them from his bed. As for John Vianney, he did not seem to belong any longer to the earth. He seemed constantly lost in contemplation, and he spoke few words.

John Vianney received the Last Sacraments on August 2. He murmured, "How kind the good God is. When we are no longer able to go to Him, He Himself comes to us." At two in the morning on August 4, 1859, supported by the arms of Brother Jerome, John Marie Baptiste Vianney "gave up his soul to God without agony" and fell asleep like the laborer whose task has been well done.

The cause for the canonization of John Vianney was begun in 1862. In 1904 at the ritual exhumation preceding beatification, the body of the Saint was found to be dried and darkened but perfectly entire. Only his face, though still recognizable, had suffered a little from the effects of death. His heart was perfectly preserved. The body was dressed again and a wax mask was made for the relic; today it is preserved in a beautiful reliquary above an altar in the basilica which was annexed to the old parish church of Ars.

John Vianney was canonized by Pope Pius XI on Pentecost Sunday, May 31, 1925 and proclaimed Patron of Parish Priests by the same Pontiff in 1929.

---

[1]On May 24, 1802, as a workman was clearing a gallery in the catacomb of St. Priscilla in Rome, he discovered a loculus, or cavity, previously unknown. In the tomb were the bones of a young female and a shattered glass phial which indicated that the young woman was a martyr. From an inscription on the bricks sealing her tomb was derived the name "Philomena." In 1805 the remains were moved to the church of Mugnano del Cardinale near Nola, Italy. Devotion to St. Philomena became widespread and various apparitions of her were reported. Her cult was authorized by Pope Gregory XVI in 1837, with a feast day of August 11. In 1961 St. Philomena's name was removed from the calendar of saints because of lack of historical information about her. She may of course still be invoked and honored, even though she is no longer mentioned in the liturgy.

Lithography print of St. John Vianney made in 1845 by Jules Meunier, at which time the Saint would have been 59 years old. It is considered one of the best portraits of the Curé of Ars.

The Curé of Ars, who converted thousands of souls in his lifetime. He suffered much from physical attacks of the devil, as well as demonic noises to frighten him at night, so that he often got little sleep. The Curé noted that when the devil had given him a particularly hard time it was a sign that a big sinner—"a big fish"—was on his way to confess the next day.

Statue of St. John Vianney, the Curé of Ars, sculpted by Cabuchet and purchased by the parish priests of France for this monument. The poor and humble Curé spent from 13-17 hours per day in the confessional, attracting people from all over France. Over a period of 20 years, 100,000 people came annually to the little village of Ars. In his lifetime the Curé converted thousands of sinners. Pope Pius XI proclaimed St. John Vianney the Patron Saint of Parish priests.

70

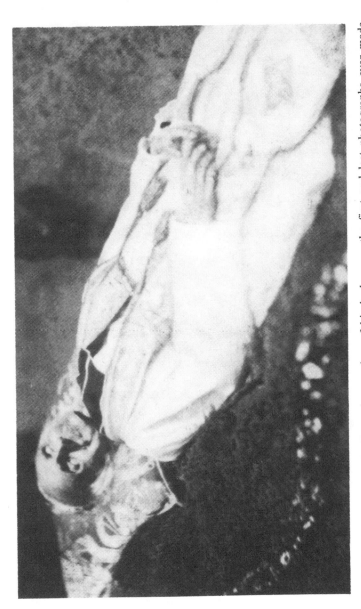

The Curé of Ars in death. Four photos taken of his body were the first and last photographs ever made of the Curé. The body was brought outside, and someone held an umbrella to keep off the sun's rays while the pictures were taken. Two days later the funeral was held, attended by five or six thousand persons.

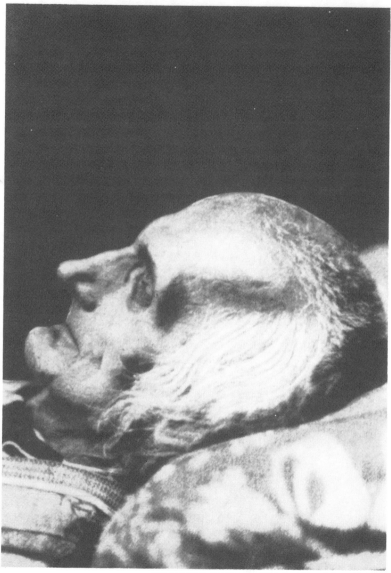

Foto M. Bernard, Belley/Schamoni/Christiana Verlag, Stein am Rheim

Another view of the holy Curé of Ars in death. Before he died, when it was time to bring him Holy Viaticum, he murmured, "How kind the good God is! When we are no longer able to go to Him, He Himself comes to us." News of the Curé's death spread like wildfire, and crowds of pilgrims began arriving to pay their last respects.

9

VENERABLE PAULINE JARICOT

Venerable Mother Pauline Jaricot
Marie-Pauline Jaricot
1799 - 1862
France
Died Age 62

Pauline looked down at her pauper's certificate. Written in French were the words: "Pauline-Marie Jaricot, living on the hill of St. Barthelemy, is in need and is receiving relief." Bankrupt and deeply in debt, she now had an official certificate of poverty and a license to beg on the streets of Lyons.

Pauline had once been a wealthy woman, having been born into the family of a rich industrialist. A pioneer of Catholic lay action, she had used her leadership talents to set up religious associations on an organized foundation, becoming famous in her own day. She had received great praise from two Popes and from several members of the hierarchy. But in her last charitable project she had fallen victim to a swindle, which left her deeply in debt, a debt she spent the last 10 years of her life struggling in vain to pay off. Yet Pauline died embracing her cross out of love for Jesus Christ. The Curé of Ars once stated in a sermon, "I know one person who knows how to accept crosses, very heavy crosses, and who bears them with great love—Pauline-Marie Jaricot of Lyons."

Marie-Pauline Jaricot was born on July 22, 1799, the youngest and favorite of the seven children of Antoine and Jeanne Jaricot, in Lyons, an industrial center in east-central France. Antoine, the 13th son of a poor shepherd, had survived the bloody revolutions of France to become a wealthy silk merchant by means of his intelligence, wit, courage and hard work. His youngest daughter seems to have inherited his great abilities as an organizer.

The pampered and precocious Pauline was a true child of the Napoleonic times—spirited and impetuous. She prayed, "Lord, show me what You want me to do—in a hurry."

At age 14 Pauline was beautiful, vain and worldly. At 15 she was the belle of every ball, and she admitted to having a new boyfriend every month. At 16 she came close to being formally engaged to a wealthy young man to whom she was secretly engaged and whom her father approved of, but another circumstance intervened.

Pauline suffered an accident in which she fell off a chair and apparently suffered some form of concussion, or brain damage, causing a semi-paralysis that defied the medical knowledge of the time. The nature of her condition has been argued by historians, but the results were clear and dramatic. For months Pauline had to be watched so that she did not hurt herself. Her speech was erratic, her walk unbalanced, her limbs uncontrolled and her pain unbearable. The death of her beloved mother was not reported to her for fear that she would become irretrievably unbalanced.

Thus at 16 Pauline was the epitome of the "poor little rich girl." Added to her physical condition was what one might call an "identity crisis." By the evidence, she was a physical and emotional wreck. But one day, after making a confession and receiving Holy Communion, peace came over her. She began to recover.

One Sunday during Lent of 1816, Pauline heard a sermon by an outspoken priest named Abbé Würtz who preached on the sin of vanity. Dressed in the latest Parisian fashion, as usual, Pauline listened, and for perhaps the first time really understood what was meant by the "vanity" and "emptiness" of the world. In accord with the Abbé's advice she undertook a characteristic reversal of her previous life. She freely gave away her possessions until her father intervened, she began to work in the hospital's incurable ward—to the great consternation of those who knew her—and in place of her beautiful clothes she now dressed as a peasant, and in purple, a color she despised. Some people were of the opinion that Pauline had lost her mind. Later, commenting on her course of extreme action, Pauline said, "I went to the extreme limit, for if I had not broken off everything at the same time, I would never have gained anything. I was so overcome at appearing in public in the sorry purple dress that I trembled in every limb. A middle way would have been insufficient to make my resolution unshakable." The Abbé also advised Pauline to receive Holy Communion daily; this was almost 100 years before the practice became common.

One of Pauline's brothers told her, "Pauline, you are taking your soup too hot; let it cool a bit." The "folly of the Cross," however, had grabbed this fervent soul. From that time on Pauline did not waver, but persevered in her determination to follow the Will of God as she knew it.

In 1817, on the eve of Palm Sunday, Pauline was kneeling before the Tabernacle, lost in prayer for the conversion of sinners and the salvation of France, when suddenly she became aware of the presence of Christ. He asked her, "Will you suffer and die for Me?" Although terrified, Pauline replied, "Yes." She never took this back.

Pauline undertook an apostolate of helping poor factory girls. Then, when only 19, she organized a group of these girls to offer prayers in reparation for the sins of the world and to win France back to the Faith. They were called "Reparatrices of the Heart of Jesus." At her young age Pauline showed an amazing talent for leadership, organization and the ability to inspire others. She then asked the girls for "prayers and pennies," in that order, to support the French missions in the Orient. She had been inspired by a priest's statement that 180 francs a year would maintain a catechist in China and enable more than 2,000 babies, exposed on the seashore or elsewhere, to be baptized. Very soon there were groups of Pauline's Reparatrices in several other cities and towns.

Pauline saw the need for a central organization for the effort, so she set up a pyramid-type structure to collect the funds on a weekly basis; the basic unit was a group of 10 girls, with one being assigned to collect a *sou* (about five cents) from each girl every week. To spread the work, each girl was to find nine more. By the end of 1819, when Pauline was still only 20, this organization, now known as the Society for the Propagation of the Faith, had made a very solid beginning, giving valuable support to the missions—and not only in the East. In fact, a plaque in the Cathedral of St. Louis in New Orleans, Louisiana states that that diocese "was among the first to benefit from her apostolic zeal."

Nevertheless, Pauline faced a great deal of opposition and criticism, especially from those who felt she was transgressing on the work of the clergy or of established missionary organizations. Thus, only three years after founding the Society for the Propagation of the Faith, Pauline willingly turned over her work to others. It was to grow and prosper greatly.

Three years later, in 1825, Pauline was to lay the foundation

for a second great Catholic work. Convinced that good works without
prayers are ineffective, and understanding the benefits of the Rosary as a meditation on the spiritual depths of the life of Christ,
she thought of a plan that was as practical as it was spiritually
beneficial—a "living Rosary" which consisted of groups of 15 persons who would each be assigned one of the 15 mysteries to pray
(not just "say") every day. As Pauline wrote to her brother Phileas,
who was a priest, "It will be an army of good, and besides, one
month of dwelling daily on the life of Our Lord makes a half
hour a month of meditation." On at least one occasion an uprising
of soldiers was averted through prayers of the Living Rosary, and
Pauline was asked to organize several sections of the Living Rosary
in the army. As one soldier said of this devotion, "It counts a
lot and it's done soon." One bishop wrote to Pauline, "It is remarkable that this year many more went to the Sacraments at Easter.
It was attributed to the Living Rosary."

Each member was also to contribute a very small payment of
dues each year for the purchase of literature to counteract the atheistic
and anti-Christian type of literature which was flooding France during that time. The Living Rosary spread very rapidly, with most
French bishops happy to have it in their dioceses, so by 1827 there
were 150 groups established in France. Nevertheless, as with the
Society for the Propagation of the Faith (though to a lesser extent),
there were still a number of detractors. But in 1827 Pope Leo XII
gave the association his official blessing. It soon spread to many
other countries and became affiliated with the Dominican Order.
Pope Gregory XVI also was to issue a brief solemnly approving
the Association of the Living Rosary. After only 10 years, more
than 2,000,000 Frenchmen declared themselves united in the Living
Rosary. In a few more years the Association had 3,000,000 members.

Pauline's brother Phileas, who was ordained as a Sulpician priest
in 1823, was a great influence in her life. Assigned as chaplain
at the charity hospital in Lyons, he attempted to bring about justice
and social reform in his province. He also attempted to organize
some of the religious sisters who had been disbanded and dispersed
during the French Revolution. He was assisted in this by Pauline
and a small, loosely organized religious group she had founded
to serve the poor. Sadly, Father Phileas was murdered, by poison-
ing, for his principles.

Pauline bought a house, which she named "Lorette," and established a small, loosely structured community of women who wore no habit except the regular peasant dress and devoted themselves to the poor and sick. The group, called the Daughters of Mary, pursued a life of prayer and work for the salvation of sinners. Pauline had wanted the group to be contemplatives, but the others desired a more active life. Pauline became known as "Mother Jaricot." She taught the sisters to have a childlike, perfect obedience, seeing themselves like blocks of wood to be carved.

In 1834 Pauline inherited a large sum from her father, giving her the means to support any charity she desired. But by that time her labors had told heavily on her and her health was in ruins; she had a growth on her lungs, a serious heart disorder, and she was barely able to walk.

Nevertheless, at this time Pauline determined to travel to Rome to request authority from Pope Gregory XVI to continue the Living Rosary apostolate. Some of its detractors were still quite vocal in their criticism. But by the time she reached Rome, where she stayed with St. Madeleine Sophie Barat at the Convent of the Sacred Heart, Pauline was unable to get out of bed. On hearing of Pauline's illness, the Pope came to see her at the convent.

After this meeting, the Pope remarked on leaving that Pauline was so ill that he did not expect to see her alive again. Overhearing his remarks, Pauline told him that she planned to go to the shrine of the holy maiden Philomena and pray for a cure, and she asked that, if she returned on foot, he would proceed without delay to the final inquiry into Philomena's cause for sainthood. The Pope agreed.

Five weeks later, friends carried Pauline into the church at Mugnano to pray before Philomena's shrine. Two days after that, during Benediction, she felt a new surge of life, stood up, and walked unassisted out of the church. A few days later, Pauline knelt before the Holy Father in the Vatican; Pope Gregory kept his promise regarding the cause of Philomena, and he gave Pauline permission to build a chapel in her honor in Lyons. Within a year, on January 13, 1837, the Pope had authorized the cult of St. Philomena. August 11, the day of Pauline's cure, was assigned as St. Philomena's feast day. It should also be noted here that Pauline gave the Curé of Ars a relic of St. Philomena, for which he was very grateful; the Curé was to become St. Philomena's most famous devotee.

In 1839 Pauline responded to the pleas of the missionary bishop

Charles de Forbin-Janson. He had told her that he had thousands of abandoned babies in his diocese each year, and he begged her for help. Pauline's brilliant response was to ask the children of France to sacrifice what they could, very small amounts, to save the souls of the abandoned and unwanted children of the rest of the world. She established a regular plan of tiny contributions to carry out large enterprises. Were it not for the money contributed to the missions in this way, many of these abandoned children would have remained on the streets, rather than being fed and spiritually nourished in Catholic orphanages and schools. This organization became known as the Association of the Holy Childhood.

The France of Pauline's time was in a constant turmoil. Following on the Industrial Revolution, social conflicts and grave injustices to laborers were common, with industry being built up at the cost of the workers' lives being torn down through low wages and inhuman working conditions. After much thought and having received encouragement from the Bishop of La Rochelle and the Curé of Ars, Pauline attempted to establish a model factory town which would follow the principles of Catholic social justice and charity. She borrowed money from many creditors, some big and some small, and contracted to purchase a property which contained an iron foundry. It also boasted a stream, a flour mill and a beautiful chapel.

But without Pauline's knowledge, one of her advisors used moneys set aside for the project to pay his own personal debts and to live in luxury. The project fell through, and Pauline was held accountable for the purchase price, interest and the other debts which the man had contracted. Thus, due to faith in dishonest associates, Pauline failed in her largest and grandest religious enterprise. In this project, too, voices were raised against Pauline, saying that it was her pride which had led to this disaster.

Pauline was to spend the rest of her life attempting to collect the funds necessary to pay this debt—430,000 francs. These last 10 years she spent as a pauper, as she cut down on expenses, begged, and lived primarily on bread and cheese, saving every possible *sou* and attempting somehow to pay off the huge debt before she died. She was not to succeed in this, however; the debt was paid off only after her death.

At this time of her need the Society for the Propagation of the Faith refused to come to her aid. And when the Pope himself asked the society to help their foundress, who was responsible for so much good in the Church, they denied that she was the foundress. They went so far as to say to her, "You never laid claim to the title of foundress of this movement until you found yourself in financial difficulty. Our money is for the missions, not for you." Pauline, who knew well the purpose of the society, never held this rejection against them. Instead, she prayed constantly for those who had oppressed and spoken against her. She once wrote to friends, "Charity is the greatest of all treasures; everything should be sacrificed to preserve it unblemished."

To the end of her life Pauline attempted to uphold her honor and her ideas of justice and truth, begging and constantly denying herself in order to pay off creditors. With each denial of aid she prayed for those who denied her. But being human, she also cried. On one occasion when a poor woman sick in bed attacked Pauline with insults and the accusation that she had never cared about anything but money, Pauline turned to a faithful companion and said, "It's too much...it's more than I can bear." Yet Pauline found that it was the poor rather than the rich who would give generously. Of her beloved poor she remembered, "They cried for me!" She thought of a time when a little old lady had approached her at a railroad station and handed her a rolled-up handkerchief containing 200 francs with the words, "It is all I have, Pauline, but it is yours." Calumniated, rejected, and officially a pauper, Pauline Jaricot prayed, "Father, if I cannot pay my debts before I die, grant me the same grace that the good thief had."

One day near the end of her life, feeling that she was at the end of her strength, Pauline had her companion take her to see her beloved friend St. John Vianney, the Curé of Ars. When he saw how dreadfully cold she was upon arrival, he attempted to make a fire, but the damp wood and straw he used only created smoke. The Curé consoled Pauline and urged her to have confidence in God regarding the burden of her debts and the calumnies of those who were against her. Presently footsteps were heard, and the Curé had to leave, saying, "It is the people from the church. They have been waiting to make their confessions—perhaps four hours now, and they are coming to find me." He gave Pauline a small wooden cross, pointing out the inscription on it: "God is my witness, Jesus Christ is my model, Mary is my support. I ask nothing but love and sacrifice."

In her last will and testament the valiant Pauline wrote, "My only treasure is the cross and my heritage is most precious to me...What difference does it make to me...that You take away from me earthly goods, reputation, honor, health, life, so that You lead me to descend through humiliation into the deepest pit of the abyss...for it is in this deep abyss that I find the hidden fire of Your love. I accept Your chalice. I know I am not worthy of it and I am afraid of it, but it is through this suffering that You will strengthen me, transform me, bring me to union with You."

At the end of her life, broken and defeated on a human plane, Pauline was still able to offer herself willingly as a sacrifice for the preservation of the Faith and in reparation for crimes against the Church. In chronic poor health, she had developed edema and "dropsy," gaining weight.

Pauline said that her greatest consolation was to have always submitted to the Holy Catholic Church and the Chair of Peter. She said, "I dare hope that, carrying to the foot of the Tribunal the blessing of the Vicar of Christ, I shall there receive that of my supreme Judge." She forgave all who had injured her, hoping to receive the same forgiveness of her own sins. She made her companion and nurse, who alone knew what Pauline had suffered from many persons, promise never to tell anything that would harm anyone's reputation or offend against charity. Calling together her spiritual daughters one day, Pauline gave them a final message. "Before every action, consider if it is pleasing to God. And never go to bed without asking pardon for the small injuries you have done during the day. It is a practice I began in my youth and which I have always continued...And don't forget to thank God for having called you to His service. Oh, I know that for me there has been nothing but great good fortune since I vowed to consecrate myself to the service of God."

As her death approached, Pauline was sometimes heard to murmur to herself. One time she said, "Paradise, how lovely you are. Light without shadow. Beauty ancient and ever new. Oh, what a union of hearts."

Early in the morning of January 9, 1862, Pauline cried out her last words: "Mary, my Mother, I am all yours!" At her death her face, which had borne the marks of age and illness, became calm and young-looking, and she appeared to smile. Three days later, in a pauper's coffin, her body was carried to the family crypt.

Pope Leo XIII stated that Pauline's work "brought her rebuff, blame, calumnies, contempt and whatever could cast down the most steadfast soul.... By her faith, hope, fortitude, meekness and ready acceptance of every trial, she proved herself to be the true disciple of Christ." In June of 1930 Pope Pius XI officially opened the cause for the beatification of Pauline Jaricot. A decree on her virtues was issued in 1963.

Photo Jean-Loup Charmet, Missi.

Venerable Pauline Jaricot, Foundress of the Society for the Propagation of the Faith and the Living Rosary. She also became a friend of the Curé of Ars and was to be perhaps the main influence in making St. Philomena known to the Catholic world. As a young girl she was vain, worldly and much admired. But an illness and emotional breakdown at age 16 led to a striking conversion at age 17; thenceforth Pauline was a different person, soon to be launched on her remarkable career of organizing Catholic works of prayer and charity.

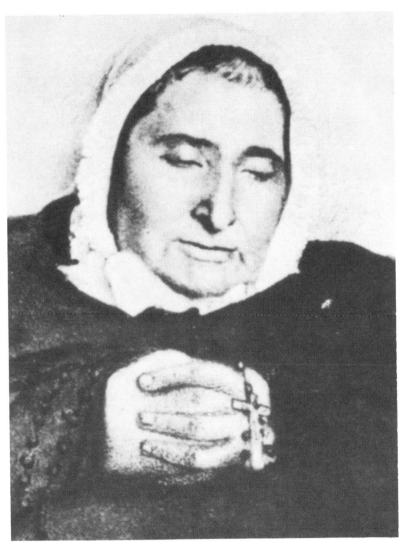

Pauline shortly before she died. The vain and worldly girl had become a saintly woman. Pauline was afflicted with edema, which caused her tissues to swell. Though she had once been wealthy, she died deeply in debt, due to misplaced trust in a financial backer. Her last years were spent as a pauper as she cut down on expenses, begged and lived mainly on bread and cheese in order to save money. Yet at the end of her life she said, "Oh, I know that for me there has been nothing but great good fortune since I vowed to consecrate myself to the service of God."

10

SAINT JOSEPH CAFASSO

Joseph Cafasso
1811 - 1860
Italy
Died Age 49

Father Joseph Cafasso had spent a whole week preparing the prisoners for confession, using a large prison room in which there were 45 of the most noted criminals. Almost all had promised to go to confession on the vigil of the feast of Our Lady, but now that the vigil had arrived, none would go. What was Don (Father) Cafasso to do?

With the ingenuity of charity he walked over to the biggest, strongest prisoner and took hold of his luxuriant long beard. Thinking this was a jest, the prisoner protested, but Don Cafasso replied, "I will not let you go until you go to confession."

"But I don't want to go to confession," replied the criminal.

"You may say what you like, but you will not escape from me; I will not let you go until you have made your confession."

"I am not prepared."

"I will prepare you."

Certainly the burly prisoner could easily have freed himself, but instead he allowed the priest to lead him to a corner of the room for confession.

Presently a commotion was heard from that corner of the room. Moved by Don Cafasso's words, the man was so overcome by sighs and tears that he was almost unable to tell his sins.

Then, afterward, appeared a great marvel. This man who had previously been most vehement in his refusal went to his companions and told them he had never been so happy in his life. He became so eloquent in exhorting them that he succeeded in persuading them all to confess. Don Cafasso heard confessions until late that night.

Joseph Cafasso was born on January 15, 1811 at Castelnuovo

d'Asti in the Province of Piedmont in the north of Italy, about 20 miles from Turin. From earliest childhood his docility, obedience, recollection and love for study and pious exercises endeared him to his parents and his teachers alike. Joseph Cafasso was slight of stature and had a weak constitution, along with a deformity of the spine. Yet this was never to hold him back from the most rigorous penances and the most strenuous apostolic labors.

At age 15, Joseph decided to become a priest. He studied at the seminary at Chieri, where he is remembered for his extreme charity toward his companions, his submission to his superiors, his patience, and for many other virtues. He was also noted for his ability in listening to and advising his companions. Those who knew Joseph Cafasso could not explain how a clerical student so young could have arrived at such a high degree of virtue, and they sometimes expressed their amazement by stating that he had never been affected by Original Sin. Testimonies after his holy death confirmed that no one had ever noticed in him any sin, however small.

At the beginning of his priestly life, Joseph wrote down a resolution which he kept until the end of his life. He knelt one day before a crucifix and said, "O Lord, Thou art my inheritance. . . .This is the choice which I have made voluntarily on the memorable day of my ordination. . .But not only, O my God, do I wish to be all Thine; I wish to become a saint, and as I do not know whether my life will be long or short, I protest to Thee that I wish to make myself a saint soon. Let the people of the world seek the vanity and pleasures and dignities of this earth; I wish and desire and seek only to become a saint, and I shall be the happiest of men if I make myself a saint soon—a great saint."

In 1827, when Joseph Cafasso was a first-year theology student, there occurred the first meeting between himself and John Bosco, three years his junior. Joseph Cafasso was to become a very great influence on John Bosco; the latter was also to become a canonized saint.

At the time of their first meeting John Bosco was only 12 years old; noticing Cafasso standing by the church door, he offered to show the young cleric the sights of the feast that was being celebrated that day. Joseph Cafasso declined, stating that he was waiting for the church to be opened. John Bosco then remarked that "there is a time for everything—a time to go to church and a time to amuse oneself." Joseph Cafasso began to laugh, and then he responded with the following words which summed up his entire program of life: "He who embraces the clerical state sells himself to the Lord, and must henceforth set his heart on nothing in the world except what can redound to the greater glory of God and the advantage of souls." Don Cafasso later became John Bosco's confessor, spiritual director and most trusted friend. It is from John Bosco's testimony that we have taken most of the information in this chapter.

In his priestly ministry, Don Cafasso displayed great zeal in explaining the word of God, and he was such a popular preacher that he was often invited to give missions and preach retreats in various districts. Moreover, he spent several hours daily in the confessional and was able to bring great help and consolation to his penitents. He had a most special aptitude for saying the right thing. From his learning, experience, and also a special gift from God, he was able to understand just what a penitent needed and to give clear, exact advice, theologically correct and marvelously adapted to the needs of each penitent.

Don Cafasso had a wonderful gift of touching hearts. Catholics who trembled at the mention of death would experience a complete change of heart after speaking about it with him. They would even exclaim: "I no longer fear death; I even desire that it come soon, provided that I have Don Cafasso somewhere near at that moment." Don Bosco says that "a single word from him—a look, a smile, his very presence—sufficed to dispel melancholy, drive away temptation and produce holy resolution in the soul." He had the rare gift of being able to inspire confidence in those whose cases appeared desperate. Sometimes condemned criminals who in desperation wanted to kill themselves would experience an amazing change of heart after speaking with him, and they would become filled with joy and the desire to offer up their execution in penance for their sins. Obstinate sinners who refused to receive the Sacraments on their deathbeds would be conquered at the word of Don Cafasso. Anyone speaking with this holy priest felt arising within himself the love of God and the desire for Heaven. All these wonderful transformations of soul came about because "the heart of Don Cafasso was like a furnace filled with the fire of divine love, lively faith, firm hope and ardent charity."

Joseph Cafasso became assistant at the ecclesiastical college attached to the Church of St. Francis of Assisi. Here he performed most valuable work for many years in training young men for a fruitful apostolate as priests. His conferences on moral theology revealed his ability to solve difficult cases with ease; he was consulted on these even by bishops. He was indefatigable in studying Sacred Scripture, Church history, the writings of the Fathers and moral, dogmatic, ascetical and mystical theology. Going beyond abstract studies, he passed on his own experience, learning, prudence and zeal for the salvation of souls, inspiring the students with the sublime sentiments which enflamed his own soul.

Don Cafasso supplied books and money to students in poor circumstances in order to help them finish their studies. He had an active apostolate among the poor boys of the city, providing them with clothes, jobs, and often food until they were able to earn their own living. After their temporal needs were attended to, he taught them the truths of their religion.

Don Cafasso also had a particular mission to prisoners. He spent a great deal of time with these poor unfortunate men and women, hearing their confessions and helping them in any way possible. It is difficult to say which was greater, his courage or his charity, as even the most hardened criminals did not frighten him. Many priests did not have the necessary qualities for this difficult work, but Joseph Cafasso devoted himself tirelessly to the care of these souls—and with the most wonderful results.

Don Cafasso had once been called to Candia Canavese to attend three men condemned to death, one of whom died impenitent. (Don Cafasso had not had an opportunity to prepare this man for death.) When he returned to the college, he went to the church and, kneeling before the Blessed Sacrament, made the following prayer: "Merciful Jesus, if it be Thy will to call me to assist these unfortunate men, most willingly I offer myself for this work, and I ask Thee for the grace that all those whom I shall accompany to the gallows will be converted." At the gallows in Turin, Don Cafasso attended 68 men; not one of them died without leaving well-founded hope of his eternal salvation.

When Don Cafasso learned of a sentence of execution, he visited the condemned man often and as far as possible spent his last night with him. He would spend the remainder of the night before the execution prostrate on the floor in adoration before the Blessed Sacrament, and he scourged himself to blood in order to secure the eternal salvation of the condemned. On the day of the execution, after saying Mass for the prisoner and giving him Holy Communion, Don Cafasso would make his thanksgiving along with him and then entertain him. He laughed and grieved with the prisoners, and he would willingly have died with them in order to secure their eternal salvation.

Then Don Cafasso would ride in the cart with the criminal to the place of execution. Seated beside the condemned man, with crucifix in hand he would wipe away the tears, encourage the prisoner and console him with the hope of an eternal reward. Showing the prisoner the crucifix, he would say, "This is a Friend who will not terrify you, who will not abandon you. Hope in Him and Heaven is yours!" Don Cafasso would even promise the condemned an immediate entrance into Heaven, bypassing Purgatory, if they would offer up their execution as an act of penance. As a little service in return, he would give the prisoner messages to deliver for him in Heaven.

Once the obstinacy of a well-known criminal caused Don Cafasso great anxiety. But after experiencing the priest's great goodness and charity, the malefactor asked him, "Don Cafasso, do you think that with so many crimes on my head I can still save my soul?"

Cafasso answered, "I believe it is certain, for who is it that will be able to take you out of my hands? Even if you were in the vestibule of Hell, and if there remained outside but one hair of your head, that would be sufficient for me to drag you from the claws of the devil and transport you to Heaven."

The condemned man replied, "Oh, if that is so I will die willingly and let this life of mine be sacrificed to God in penance for my sins." He met his death with these sentiments.

In spite of his weak constitution, Don Cafasso remained continually available in his own room to counsel any who needed his help or advice. He understood and constantly preached that every moment of time is a great treasure, and so he took advantage of every occasion to do good.

In his private life, he took every occasion to practice mortifications and penance, especially that of self-denial. As superior of the ecclesiastical institute of St. Francis, he could have dispensed himself from many things. Instead, he set his own personal example by fulfilling his duties and being exact in the observance of the rules. He was like a machine which the sound of the bell brought instantaneously to the fulfillment of the duty of the moment.

St. John Bosco recalled one occasion when he brought Don Cafasso a glass of water. The latter had it in his hand when the bell for the Rosary rang. He drank no more but put it down and was going immediately to pray the Rosary. John Bosco said to him, "Drink it, and you will have time afterward to go to prayer." Joseph Cafasso answered, "Do you wish me to prefer a glass of water to a prayer so precious as the Rosary, which we say in honor of Our Blessed Lady?"

St. Joseph Cafasso had a great love for the Blessed Virgin Mary and constantly promoted devotion to her. He continually remembered her by his ejaculatory prayers and pious practices, dedicating every Saturday to her completely by rigorous fasting and by giving her everything she demanded of him for that day. He often expressed the desire to die on a Saturday, and this request was granted.

After spending many hours in the confessional, Don Cafasso was observed more than once leaning on a bench to prevent himself from falling. To all offers of comfort, he replied, "The body is insatiable; the more we give in to it the more it demands." Also: "Our rest will be in Heaven. O Heaven, whoever thinks on you will not suffer from weariness."

Don Cafasso lived a strenuous life of penance, prayer, charity and labor. In spite of his many infirmities, he refused to allow himself more than his regular five hours of sleep per night, and he took practically no other rest. A favorite saying of his was, "Fortunate is that priest who spends his life for the good of souls; most fortunate is he who dies laboring for the glory of God. He will certainly receive a great reward from that Supreme Master for whom he labors." John Bosco affirms that St. Joseph Cafasso had never during the whole course of his life spent a cent to satisfy a taste or provide amusement for himself.

John Bosco expressed his amazement at the amount St. Joseph Cafasso accomplished; he called this "the most marvelous" thing about this priest. That is, Joseph Cafasso seemed to be always occupied with his clerical students, training them to preach and to hear confessions, yet it also seemed that his whole life was devoted to instructing poor boys and to visiting and hearing the confessions of those in prison. Then again, he appeared to be always preaching, always in his room giving audiences, or praying, or hearing confessions. But he was also found in adoration in any church where Forty Hours adoration was in progress, as well as bringing concord to families, visiting and hearing the confessions of any of his penitents who happened to be in the hospital and of the sick and those on their deathbeds, as well as fulfilling other duties. Furthermore, he left enough writings to have been a full-time writer. John Bosco concluded that this marvelously active life shows how much can be accomplished by the charity of a priest aided by divine grace. "Such a priest may in a certain sense be omnipotent, according to the expression of St. Paul: 'I can do all things in Him who strengthens me.'"

There are strong reasons to believe that Don Cafasso received a special revelation from God regarding the day of his death. He put his affairs in order, giving directions for the proper functioning of the college, answering letters, adding a few things to his will and making the spiritual exercise for a good death that he usually made at the end of each month. He spent the last three days before his final illness almost completely shut up in his room while he made these arrangements.

On the morning of June 9 he made his way, with a painful effort, to the confessional and spent several hours hearing confessions. When he returned to his room, he went to bed. Although from that moment and for the last 13 days of his life he must have been in great pain—suffering, among other ailments, from a stomach hemorrhage—he issued no complaint. He went to confession and received Holy Communion many times during his last illness.

On his last day he received Extreme Unction and the papal blessing with plenary indulgence, which he wished for so ardently. He was gracious to all who came to visit him, but after a few moments made a sign for them to leave so that he could converse with his Divine Lord and His Blessed Mother.

Joseph Cafasso passed away quietly and peacefully on June 23, at the age of 49, after having spent his entire substance for the glory of God and the salvation of souls. He was very much mourned and sorely missed, as very many had benefited from his great charity and zeal. Joseph Cafasso was canonized in 1947.

St. Joseph Cafasso, who obtained from God the grace of converting all of the condemned criminals he prepared for the gallows (68). One obstinate and well-known criminal questioned whether it was still possible for him to be saved. Don Cafasso replied, "I believe it is certain, for who is it that will be able to take you out of my hands? Even if you were in the vestibule of Hell, and if there remained outside but one hair of your head, that would be sufficient for me to drag you from the claws of the devil and transport you to Heaven."

Despite his weak constitution St. Joseph Cafasso accomplished an enormous amount of work for souls in his 27 years of priesthood; one of his favorite sayings was, "Fortunate is that priest who spends his life for the good of souls." He considered every moment of time to be a great treasure. St. Joseph Cafasso would also say, "Our rest will be in Heaven. O Heaven, whoever thinks on you will not suffer from weariness."

11

SAINT MADELEINE SOPHIE BARAT

Madeleine Sophie Barat
1779 - 1865
France
Died Age 85

The Reign of Terror had recently ended in France, with its whole-
sale murder of priests and religious. Nearly the entire system of
Catholic education had been destroyed. In 1789 France had had
60,000 religious men and women and 4,000 convents and monasteries, many of these including schools. But the guillotine and the
severe deprivations and miseries of the times had claimed the lives
of innumerable religious, and the rest had been scattered and their
houses pillaged or burned. Thus the children of France were growing up without knowledge of the fundamental truths of the Faith,
and the love of God was dying out in the hearts of the French people.

It was in these times that Divine Love called to Sophie Barat,
and Sophie answered. Although she had never even seen a nun,
at age 20 she banded together with two other young women to
found a society dedicated to the Sacred Heart for the purpose of
educating young girls, with the particular object of teaching them
to know and love God. The Society of the Sacred Heart was to
be one of the major instruments in bringing Christian education
and love for Jesus Christ back to France. But the Society was to
spread way beyond France. Before her death at age 85, Madeleine
Sophie Barat saw 111 houses of the Society established in many
countries of Europe and even in America, with nearly 4,000 sisters
calling themselves her daughters.

Madeleine Sophie Barat was born to a cooper and his wife on
December 12, 1779 at Joigny in Burgundy, France. She had a brother,
Louis, and a sister, Marie-Louise, both several years older than
she. Her father was kind-hearted and a hard worker, full of common sense; her mother, Madeleine, was better educated than he,
sensitive, deeply religious and very loving. Madeleine Sophie—

who was called Sophie, probably to avoid confusion with her mother—seems to have inherited the best qualities of both her parents.

As a young child Sophie was charming, and she won the hearts of her family members with her playful gaiety, intelligence and loving nature. As a young girl she was the center of admiration among her friends, who were attracted by her beauty, graciousness and the music of her gentle voice. Madeleine's older brother Louis, who was also her godfather and a clerical student, undertook to channel and discipline his sister's affectionate nature by rigorous advanced studies; although these were difficult, Sophie felt her mind and heart greatly expand through them.

The Reign of Terror brought bitter grief to the Barat family. Louis, then a deacon preparing for the priesthood, was thrown into prison and was saved from the guillotine only by the fall of Robespierre. After his ordination, Louis brought Sophie to Paris and helped her to continue her education. He took upon himself her spiritual guidance, imposing upon her the strictest penances and disciplines. Louis foresaw a valorous future for his sister. "Can you be satisfied with mediocrity when heroism is within your grasp?" he asked. Sophie longed to do "great things for God." With her generous soul, she prayed, "Give me grace in proportion to the work...*All* grace to save *all* sinners."

Sophie felt attracted to the cloister of Carmel, but Louis introduced her to a Father Joseph Varin, who told her that God wanted her to lead the mixed life of prayer and teaching. He felt it to be God's Will that she found an order devoted to the Sacred Heart for the work of educating women—a counterpart to the Jesuit Order, which educated young men; he pointed out the great need of the Church and the misery of so many souls who did not love Our Lord, who alone is able to give them happiness. This priest fired Sophie with a zeal for souls that was to last throughout her life, surviving a great flood of bitter trials. Fr. Varin once wrote to Sophie, "You promised me that Our Lord should find in you one according to His Heart, a great and generous soul, a soul always ready to enter into His designs, without being astounded at their difficulty." He also wrote to her, "You must learn to know the mind and heart of Jesus, and give yourself up entirely to His guidance." These two goals were to become central to the rule of the society Sophie would found.

On November 21, 1800, Sophie Barat and two companions solemnly consecrated themselves to the Sacred Heart. Looking back on that act years later Sophie said, "I knew nothing, I foresaw nothing, I accepted all that was given me." Two years later these women took their vows in the Society of the Sacred Heart of Jesus. They agreed that generosity should be the keynote of the society: "To love without measure in the labor of winning souls to Our Lord."

The next year they opened a school in a little house in Amiens. One of Sophie's companions described that first foundation: "We were like people feeling their way in the dark; it was God's way with us, He always acted thus, just lifting the veil that we might see our path step by step, but not beyond." Each subsequent foundation, too, seemed to begin with nothing but bare walls. Sophie saw her own role as simply that of a defective instrument of God, and she instilled this attitude of humility into the other sisters also.

Father Varin wrote to Sophie, "I know that you will have a great deal to suffer before the Society is solidly established, but nothing alarms me, because I know also that Our Lord will give you a heart larger than all that you will suffer, and such a heart can obtain all things from Him. I congratulate you on having entered on your present path, and I congratulate myself on having helped to direct you to it. In no other course of life would you have the thousandth part to bear of what awaits you here, only remember that your courage and faith must be steeped in tender and loving confidence in Our Lord."

In December of 1802, Father Varin visited the young sisters. To 23-year-old Madeleine Sophie Barat he put the question, "Why did God make you?" When she answered, "To know Him, to love Him, and to serve Him," he then asked what it meant to serve God. She answered that it meant to do His Will. Then he told Sophie that it was God's Will that she become the superior of the little group. Madeleine Sophie wept and begged that she not be given this responsibility—but as in all else, she obeyed the Will of God. Madeleine Sophie was to fill this office for 62 years. Years later she commented, "I smile with pity when anyone calls me foundress...We were the rubble, the rough stones that are thrown into a foundation...Our Lord is the cornerstone of this building."

The sisters felt great affection for their mother superior and were extremely attached to her, despite Mother Barat's attempts to teach them detachment from creatures. Mother Barat also emphasized the essential importance of maintaining the union of charity "at the cost of any sacrifice." She wrote, "It is easy to agree when each one seeks God's interests and not her own. Personal pretensions spoil everything. If we cling to humility, all will be well."

In 1804 the new society received from Blessed Philippine Duchesne a convent located north of Grenoble, and Philippine herself entered the Society of the Sacred Heart. At this time Mother Barat was 25; Philippine was 10 years older and had already had much experience of charitable work and of the religious life. The two women became close friends at first meeting. Mother Barat's spirituality and gentle charm calmed the impetuous nature of Philippine. With humor, kindness and firmness, the Foundress urged Philippine on to sanctity. Twelve years later Philippine and four companions obtained permission to set out for the mission lands in America.

St. Madeleine's motto was "To suffer myself, and not to make others suffer." God permitted the Society of the Sacred Heart to be very severely tried for many years, with others trying to take over and rewrite its constitutions, seeming to destroy the work Sophie had been bidden to undertake, and even threatening her with excommunication (the document bearing this message turned out to be a fraud). Madeleine Sophie responded to these many storms with patience, meekness and confidence in God, believing this was what God wanted of her. The Archbishop of Besancon advised her, "You will gain nothing by command, but all will come right by kindness, compliance and forbearance. So if there must be excess, let it be in leaning toward Our Lord's way of acting. He always meets us more than half-way in spite of our faults." Eventually the problems and opposition were resolved and the society spread and grew. The Archbishop of Paris, who had been one of Sophie's most adamant opponents, wrote of her after the storms had cleared, "She is a true religious of the meek and humble Heart of Jesus; she did not open her mouth to defend or excuse herself."

Seeing that many among the ranks of the wealthy are alienated from God at an early age, Mother Barat made it a chief aim of her society to educate wealthy young women. On the other hand, she also wanted the poor to have the advantages of a Catholic education, so she used the profit from the boarding schools to fund free schools for the poor. With regard to passing on the holy Catholic Faith, Mother Barat taught her sisters, "Fill your hearts with love of God, and then you will be able to instill it into them. If we are united to God . . .we shall be able to do wonders for them."

And: "The Creator alone can work in souls. The less we put of ourselves, the more Our Lord works. That is why He generally chooses those who are of little worth, mere nothings, as His most precious instruments." Mother Barat also wrote that when we are chosen for the service of our neighbors' souls, "we shall never again find rest on earth..."

Mother Barat showed remarkable enlightenment, prudence and a far-sighted understanding of her times. Having witnessed the French Revolution, she well understood to what depths the world sinks when it is ruled by "Reason" rather than by God's law. She set a very high value on the possibilities of influence of good Christian women. She wrote: "How rare it is to find a valiant woman! It is perhaps necessarily so, since Scripture says that they are more precious than pearls and diamonds...Let us however work to train a few. ...For in this century we must no longer count on men to preserve the Faith. The grain of faith that will be saved will hide itself among women. How different are God's thoughts from ours!" She also wrote, "The world exerts all its power to gain women, to rob them of their faith and ruin them." To a gathering of the Children of Mary at Lyons she said, "Between women and God is often arranged the eternal salvation of husbands and sons. But for this she must be the valiant woman—strong to uphold purity of life; strong to keep inviolate the treasure of faith; strong in every battle of life; great-souled in the face of calumny, persecution and death...and remember, sorrow is the training ground of strong souls." She also wrote, "A woman cannot remain neutral in the world; she too is set for the fall and resurrection of many." Thus Mother Barat trained the girls under her charge for their life's work—which was seen as chiefly being the work of being wives and mothers.

In education Mother Barat strove to "unite the useful with the agreeable." She stressed the teaching of language—French first, and then Latin—including grammar and the ability to read and write well. She considered this the fundamental basis of all learning. She also stated that education must extend to the smallest detail and embrace both physical and moral education. Moreover: "Children's minds need the marvelous; let us give it to them in all the wonders that their faith reveals."

Mother Barat stressed the importance of memory: "The wealth or the poverty of our intellectual life depends chiefly on our memory." Yet more importantly, she wanted the girls to learn how to think well. Mother Barat recognized and adapted to the changes of the times with regard to education, though she would not compromise on religious principles: "When it is a question of souls, what does the pen or pencil, the ruler or the paper matter to God?"

Madeleine Sophie said that children were her life, her rest, the dew of her soul. She wrote, "I would have founded the society for the soul of one child." And looking back at the end of her life she was to say, "To give the children to Our Lord and wrest them from Hell—that it is which has kept up my life for 85 years."

Mother Barat longed for solitude, yet she realized that God's Will was for her to be a superior. She wrote, "The life of a superior ought to be one of continual self-sacrifice. This will become sweet to them through humility and the inner life of the soul." On another occasion she wrote, "God alone and His Cross. That heart is too covetous for which this treasure is not enough." Despite her many time-consuming and difficult duties as superior, Mother Barat was noted for always being a patient and gracious listener.

Because of her strong spirit of faith, Madeleine Sophie Barat was endowed by God with the gift of miracles. Extraordinary favors from Heaven were numerous in her lifetime, and she had marvelous success in converting obstinate sinners.

At the time of Mother Barat's death there would be 93 houses and schools of her society in operation in 12 countries; there had been 111, but several had been closed in revolutionary upheavals or because of other problems. Several houses had been established in America in the states of Louisiana and Missouri. In a reference to political exile, Mother Barat revealed the magnanimity of her heart when she stated, "If we are banished from France, there is plenty of room in the Sacred Heart, and the whole world is ours. America, the Burmese Empire, and even China are asking for us, and we shall go further afield to found new colonies." On another occasion she said that "the Society is for all times and for the whole world." One of her followers wrote of her, "She wished and even hoped to succeed in setting the whole world on fire with the love of God."

In 1864, at the age of 84, Mother Barat begged to be allowed to step down from the post of superior general of the society, but she was unanimously re-elected—although she was given an assistant. Around that same time she said, "Strength and voice are failing me, even my eyesight is going, but what matter if the soul can gather all its energy and work more vigorously as the body weakens."

On Sunday, May 21, Mother Barat announced to the community at recreation, "I was most anxious to see you today, for on Thursday we are going to Heaven." Four days later, on Ascension Thursday, she passed from this life. Years before she had said, "If God hears my prayer, there will be no last words of mine to repeat, for I shall say nothing at all." Her prayer was granted, for in the last few days of her life she lost the power of speech, having been struck by a paralysis.

Thus Madeleine Sophie Barat died at the motherhouse of the Society of the Sacred Heart of Jesus in Paris. At the ritual exhumation of her body in 1893, her coffin was found to be falling to pieces because of the dampness of the vault. The Saint's body, however, was still entire, with the features recognizable and the slender fingers still clasping a small crucifix.

In 1904, during the suppression and expulsion of religious orders from France, the body of Mother Barat was taken for safekeeping to Jette, Belgium, where it is still enshrined. Madeleine Sophie Barat was beatified in 1908 and canonized in 1925.

St. Madeleine Sophie Barat, who founded the Society of the Sacred Heart, a counterpart to the Jesuits; she began this society to educate girls who were growing up like heathens in France after the turmoil of the French Revolution. She wrote, "To give the children to Our Lord and wrest them from Hell—that it is which has kept up my life for 85 years." She wanted to train valiant women: "For in this century we must no longer count on men to preserve the Faith. The grain of faith that will be saved will hide itself among women." Mother Barat saw the opening of 111 houses and schools of the Order she had founded.

12

SAINT EUPHRASIA PELLETIER

Saint Mary of St. Euphrasia Pelletier, R.G.S.
Rose Virginie Pelletier
1796 - 1868
France
Died Age 71

In exasperation the teacher looked at the high-spirited 10-year-old Rose Virginie Pelletier. "Virginie," she said, "pay attention, for you will surely become an angel or a demon!" The little girl replied, "I shall be a nun. I know I shall have to be thoroughly broken in, but I shall be a nun someday."

Virginie did, indeed, become a nun. With her natural leadership abilities and her organizational skills, this remarkable foundress of the Institute of the Good Shepherd was to see the opening of 110 houses of the Institute—14 of them in the United States. She set for her sisters a major goal to save souls, especially those of young girls and women who had fallen into sinful ways of life either through seduction, other tragic experiences, or by willfully following their own evil inclinations. St. Euphrasia was to become a fighter for souls, a woman who told her sisters: "If they [religious] want to be quiet and to attend exclusively to prayer, tell them to go to Carmel or to the Visitation. Here there are combats awaiting them, and they must learn to fight as well as to pray."

Rose Virginie was born on July 21, 1796, the eighth child of Dr. Julian Pelletier and his wife, Ann Mourain, in Vendee, France. Dr. Pelletier baptized his infant daughter at home because of the anti-Catholic persecution then raging. The Pelletier family was staunchly Catholic, and they continued the practice of their religion and of their works of charity among the poor and the sick of the district even amidst the dangers and persecutions of the French Revolution.

The family was eventually forced to flee to the island of Noirmoutier. On the island they hoped for safety and freedom. But the Revolution followed them, and for many years Catholics were forced

to keep the Faith in the spirit of the catacombs. It was a very difficult time for the Church; in 1809 Pope Pius VII would be taken
prisoner by Napoleon.

Although the times were dangerous, Virginie's family was stable
and secure in the Faith. As a child there is no doubt that she was
very good and genuinely pious. She was also lively, impetuous and
strong-willed.

In 1808 some Catholic sisters came to Noirmoutier to open a
school, and Rose began to study there. But after the death of three
of Rose's sisters and her much-loved father, her mother decided
to return to Soullans. Madame Pelletier then decided it was for
Rose's good that she go to boarding school, and so she was sent
to Tours.

The young girl was very unhappy there for the next four years.
She was never able to go home for the holidays, and her mother
died before she finished her schooling. Rose was lonely, homesick,
and had difficulty in adapting herself to this way of life. She was
further bothered by an attack of scrupulosity and an unsympathetic
confessor. Yet Rose did not give way to self-pity and resentment,
but remained strong in her religion and in her efforts to control
her own nature. One of the teachers became her beloved and lifelong friend. This woman was able to sense the unusual quality of
Rose's character, and she fostered her native intelligence in her studies
and gave her wise guidance in her spiritual life.

Only those who themselves have suffered deeply can truly understand the sufferings of others. Doubtless God permitted Rose to
know from her own experience what it was like to be uprooted
from home and parents and assailed by difficulties so that later
on she could have a deeper and fuller understanding of the problems of those with whom it would be her destiny to work.

Rose had no doubt that she had a religious vocation and that
she wanted to save souls. The reading of the life and writings of
St. Teresa of Avila inspired in her a fervent enthusiasm for everything ideal, and especially for the saving of souls. She had heard
stories of African children sold as slaves, and the memory remained
with her. She said, "I cannot forget them. I dream about them at
night. Little black girls coming to me, putting their arms about
my neck and saying to me: 'Come to us, come and help us. Come
and teach us how to know Jesus and to love Him.'" Yet despite
Rose's desire to save souls, she did not know which order to join.

In Tours there was a re-established house of Refuge. In 1641 St. John Eudes had established the Congregation of Our Lady of Charity of the Refuge to reclaim women and girls who had been the victims of seduction or of tragic home circumstances and who had thus fallen into sin, putting their immortal souls in grave danger. St. John Eudes had a profound perception of the value of souls; he said, "Remember, my daughters, that a soul is worth more than a world, and that consequently to lend one a hand to withdraw her from the abyss of sin is a greater thing than to create an entire world and to draw it from nothingness into being." Nevertheless, the congregation of the Refuge had never flourished, and when the French Revolution came, both the sisters and the penitents were scattered.

A few of these women managed to come together again after the Terror, and it was there in Tours that Rose Pelletier first saw the sisters and learned about their work. After visiting with the superior, she became convinced that this was the work God wished her to do. Rose's guardian, however, flatly refused to permit her entrance to this congregation—but relented when her schooling was over, and on the condition that she make no vows until she came of age.

Thus in 1814, at the age of 18, Rose entered the Congregation of Our Lady of Charity of the Refuge. At her clothing she took the names of Mary and Euphrasia. She had very much wanted to take the name Sister St. Teresa of Avila, but the superior felt this presumptuous, so Rose humbly researched until she found an obscure Greek saint whose life she desired to emulate.

Rose was professed in 1817. The sisters all took the three vows of poverty, chastity and obedience, plus a fourth vow which had been prescribed by St. John Eudes: to labor for the salvation of souls. In addition, Sister Euphrasia voluntarily added another vow: to give up the indulgences she might gain during her life or which others might gain for her after her death. She put all these indulgences into the hands of the Blessed Virgin Mary to apply to the souls in Purgatory as she saw fit. This act of renunciation tested Sister Euphrasia sorely when her sister soon died unexpectedly, yet her offering remained a willing sacrifice.

Earlier, Sister Euphrasia had been struck by a supernatural insight that the virtue of obedience is the best means to sanctity, and she had obtained permission to make her vow of obedience a year before profession. In years to come she exclaimed, "Oh, I really believe, my dear daughters, that perseverance in my vocation is due solely to the virtue of obedience. Attach yourselves, then, very much to this virtue, if you wish to persevere. Always obey whatever you may be told to do. Obey simply like children." She also would tell them to follow the Rule so perfectly that if all the Order's documents were destroyed by fire it would be possible to reconstitute it by observing the lives of the sisters. "Dig deep into the Rule as you would into a mine of gold. As little children are nourished by milk, so should you draw your strength from your Constitutions. They are the star that will lead you to Heaven . . ."

From the beginning Sister Euphrasia showed a particular ability to deal with the girls and young women entrusted to them, even though these were very often difficult and sometimes even abusive. With truth and humility she realized: "If we had been plunged into misery, had we belonged to bad parents, perhaps we would have been wicked as many others." Sister Euphrasia seemed able to win the confidence of even the most wayward. She understood that she had to win the confidence and love of the girls, to make them happy and comfortable, and to catch their interest. "It is better not to preach too much; it only wearies them," she said. "It is better to keep them interested and to try to be very just and always kind." She believed that these girls must be shown the beauty of virtue, so that they would almost unconsciously grow to love it. Instinctively Sister Euphrasia seemed to understand that one of the most powerful influences on the girls was the lives of the religious, especially their purity.

The great driving force of Sister Euphrasia's life was love for souls and the desire to save them. She said, "I have a burning, consuming longing to save souls." Her great secret for winning wayward girls back to God was love and kindness; later, as Mother Superior, she would always guide the other sisters to be very kind to the girls under their care. She told them that the girls who had fallen into sin were to be treated like Veronica treated Our Lord, wiping His disfigured face with her veil. She expressed her program thus: "Love them, love them very much. Console and strengthen these wounded sheep; make them happy, very happy, by God's grace; this is your duty. Do not forget that you will win hearts to Our Lord only by charity." She would emphasize the following fundamental principle: "Do not imagine that letting them suffer is going to convert them."

Without lessening proper authority or offending against justice, Mother Euphrasia constantly practiced the charity of Christ toward wayward girls. She taught the other sisters to have compassion on girls struggling to turn away from habits of sin: "These poor souls have to do great violence to themselves, and have many passions to root out of their souls. Do you think that it is easy for them to obey, or to work?" (Constructive work was one of the important elements of the program.) "The more spiritually sick our girls are, the greater should be our interest in them. The stronger their inclination to evil, the deeper should be our compassion for them." "A cup of milk," she said, "given at the right moment to one of your children, will do more to bring her back to right dispositions than would acts of severity." The type of love Mother Euphrasia taught was "love of appreciation": "The Saints *appreciated* the soul of a poor child in rags and full of faults, the soul of a sinful man or woman, because God loves these souls and because the Precious Blood was shed for their ransom. . ." Looking back, Mother Euphrasia could say, "I always loved the girls—and I always loved them with all the strength of my soul." The strength for this type of love—often difficult and discouraging—was to come from mental prayer.

Sister Euphrasia was convinced that the chief cause of serious misdeeds, in addition to starvation for love, was ignorance of religion. Knowing nothing of the restraints of God's commandments, these girls saw no reason to obey human rules either. After seeing that they were fed and clothed, Sister Euphrasia's first concern was to teach the girls the tenets of their neglected Faith, as she felt that "Nothing else is as helpful or as lasting."

Explaining the crucial importance of religious instruction in bringing back to God those who had fallen into a life of sin, Sister Euphrasia said, "The great means of laboring for the salvation of souls and the conversion of sinners is to instruct them in the truths of their Faith. . . .Teach the catechism; explain the maxims of the Gospel to them, for these are the only roads to Christian sanctity. . . .I cannot recommend the study of the catechism too strongly. . . .Frequently read also Sacred History and Church History; such reading should form the foundation of many of your lessons. It may be said that there is more danger for the salvation of an ignorant person than for one who knows her religion. A person who is instructed may finally listen to the voice of conscience and yield to remorse. But what hope is there of converting a poor ignorant creature who has never heard of God, who does not know how to distinguish between vice and virtue? You know, my dear daughters, that there are seven Spiritual Works of Mercy, of which one of the most important is to instruct the ignorant. Therefore, instruct the young persons and children confided to your care thoroughly and solidly."

Yet Sister Euphrasia knew that much good judgment is required in order to speak of spiritual things opportunely. For instance, "It would not be timely to speak to the girls of penance on a day when they had been given a dinner they did not like. On the contrary, it would be better to say to them: 'Poor children, I am so sorry you had that dinner today. I was really vexed about it.'. . .On some other occasion tell them what a great evil sin is."

In 1825 Sister Euphrasia was elected superior at the early age of 29. In line with her inspired vision, she immediately began to branch out in the work.

Some of the penitents were so sincerely converted that they wanted to make religious vows. For these Mother Euphrasia established the Sisters Magdalen where, in a separate establishment but still under the care of the Refuge sisters, these penitents could live a fully religious life of contemplation and penance. She opened a boarding school for girls from good families, and a house for orphans. This young superior had a genius for organization, as well as the ability to carry through new projects and to attract more and more vocations.

Mother Euphrasia had once explained her priorities thus: "Our chief concern is for the wayward girls and the Sisters Magdalen. With us they will always come first." Mother Euphrasia's own sanctity and love for souls helped enkindle in the other sisters the necessary zeal and spirit of self-denial. "After listening to our Mother," said one sister, "one would go to the end of the world to save only one soul."

It seems that souls and the Eucharist were Mother Euphrasia's two loves. She said, "With the Blessed Sacrament and souls to save I would willingly consent to be deprived of the eternal reward for many long years." She was deeply distressed one day when the ciborium containing consecrated Hosts was stolen from a church; she exclaimed, "If the Sacred Hosts were found even in a gutter, how happy I would be to consume them immediately, if I were allowed!" She begged the sisters to pray that the Hosts would be found.

Soon the Bishop of Angers wanted a Refuge opened in his city. After obtaining permission from the council, Mother Euphrasia established the requested Refuge. Then after her term of office at Tours expired, she became the superior of Angers. In spite of primitive and poor conditions, the house prospered and more and more bishops began to ask for foundations. Four more were begun, and still the bishops requested more help in caring for their strayed sheep.

At last it became evident to Mother Euphrasia that there was need of a central government and a superior general, so that the various houses could coordinate their work and give each other mutual help. The old Refuge houses had all been autonomous, and this seemed to be one of the main reasons why they had expanded so little. After much prayer Mother Euphrasia decided to put the matter before Rome and ask for a clause in the constitutions which would put all the new houses under a central government. The older Refuge houses were to be allowed to choose whether or not they would remain autonomous.

At this time a great deal of calumny began to be spread concerning Mother Euphrasia, with charges that she was self-seeking and only a restless innovator who wished to depart from the wishes of the Founder, St. John Eudes. All this and more that was worse was said of her. Even the Bishop of Tours humiliated her.

At the beginning of this opposition, God had given to Mother Euphrasia, in prayer, this command: "Wait, be silent, pray, suffer, hope!" These words became her motto.

One day at Vespers Mother Euphrasia decided to write to Rome herself. In her cell, on her knees and in tears, she began the letter: "Behold the handmaid of the Lord; be it done unto me according to Thy word." This letter pleaded the cause of the generalate, or centralized government. In the letter was not one word of blame against any of those who had accused her.

In 1835 Pope Gregory XVI asked: "How many letters have been written against Mother Euphrasia?"

"Thirteen," was the answer.

"And what has she said in her own defense?"

"Not a single word."

"Then, she is in the right." With this statement, the Pope signed a decree establishing the Angers convent as the motherhouse of the Congregation, now to be known as the Institute of Our Lady of Charity of the Good Shepherd—or, more popularly, the "Good Shepherd Sisters." It would have a superior general residing at Angers. Mother Euphrasia was unanimously elected.

Mother Euphrasia said to the members of the Institute, "You will now go forth, my daughters, and pitch your tents from one end of the earth to the other. Your zeal must comprise all lands and all peoples. I do not wish any longer to be called French. I am Italian, English, German, Spanish; I am American, African, Indian; every country is my own where there are souls to be saved."

True to this prediction, the Institute began to spread worldwide. The works were widely varied, but had a single aim—the salvation of the souls of girls and women who had either fallen into sin or else were in serious danger of doing so.

Mother Euphrasia's one motive was always the salvation of souls. In fact, the Good Shepherd Sisters take a fourth vow, zeal for the salvation of souls, in addition to the usual vows of poverty, chastity and obedience. She was obsessed by the limitless possibilities for saving souls in contrast with the present limitations of the congregation. But in all her works of expansion her trust was in God's grace, not in herself: "If I gave in to human prudence, this very evening I would dispatch ten letters to stop ten projects. But no, they will be done in spite of me. When all seems lost according to human prudence, it is then that all is gained."

Mother Euphrasia urged her daughters on to greater love for the souls under their care: "Enlarge your hearts; the mistress of a class should be like a pelican who feeds her young with her blood. My dear daughters, if you have not sufficient room to receive all the poor girls who knock at your door, beg the angels to come and push back the walls so that not one of these dear sheep may remain outside the fold."

Before each foundation and during its early stages, Mother Euphrasia would suffer severe interior trials and have many exterior crosses to bear. It was almost as if these sufferings were the labor before the birth. Soon after the establishment of the generalate, Mother Euphrasia offered her life for the Institute.

The Foundress expressed her attitude toward suffering in these words: "We need crosses and humiliations; if they were wanting we should perish. When we truly love God, nothing seems hard to us where His glory is concerned." And on the 50th jubilee of her profession, Mother Euphrasia recalled the poverty of the Institute's beginnings—a poverty "the most utter, the most absolute. And the greater the poverty, the crosses and the humiliations our monasteries meet with, the more sure they will be to receive graces. I love that saying, 'Grace is a fruit of the Cross.' "

By 1868 Mother Euphrasia was seriously ill. For more than 20 years she had had a cancerous growth in her side, and the malignancy had now reached very serious proportions. She was physically worn out, and she developed a bad case of pneumonia. Yet when she was urged to take some extra rest in the mornings, she answered, "Would you deprive me of my only consolation? I have so often told you, Holy Communion is my very life. . . .What would have become of me during these last two years without the Bread of the Strong?" At the end Mother Euphrasia lingered for six weeks in severe physical and mental suffering—at one point suffering uninterruptedly from nausea for a period of 12 days—yet she did not utter a word of complaint.

Despite her great pain Mother Euphrasia said, "My soul is in the deepest peace. I feel that God is with me. I impress the Will of God upon my heart." And regarding her heavenly Mother: "O how happy I am under the protection of the Most Holy Virgin. What would I have become without her? My poor little boat has so often been tossed to and fro, and I have been so opposed, my dear daughters, but the Mother of God has well protected it."

Mother Euphrasia also rejoiced on her deathbed that she had always maintained a deep attachment to Rome, although this loyalty had cost her "many sorrows, many crosses, and the greatest difficulties." She said to those around her deathbed, "Oh, love Rome! There is the light. There is the column of fire which enlightens the world." The saintly Foundress also said: "What a comfort St. Mary Magdalen has always been to me. She is my patroness."

Mother Euphrasia died on April 24 of 1868. Her life had exemplified her words: "What are we in this world for, if not to love God and help to save souls?" "My dear daughters, as my last will and testament I bequeath to you two things: love of the cross and zeal for the salvation of souls."

At the time of Mother Euphrasia's death there were almost 3,000 Good Shepherd sisters in foundations all over the world. The saintly Foundress was canonized by Pope Pius XII in 1940.

Rose-Virginie Pelletier at age 18, shortly before she joined the convent. In her youth she suffered the death of her father, mother and three of her sisters, in addition to a difficult four-year period at a boarding school.

Sister Mary of St. Euphrasia Pelletier in the white veil of a novice. At her profession two years later, she took a fourth vow, which had been prescribed by St. John Eudes—to labor for the salvation of souls—plus an additional vow: to give up the indulgences she might gain during her life or which others might offer up for her after her death, placing these in Our Lady's hands to apply to the Poor Souls as she saw fit.

111

A painting of Sister Mary of St. Euphrasia Pelletier, Foundress of the Good Shepherd Sisters to care for and educate wayward girls and those in moral danger. She believed that the chief causes of serious misdeeds were ignorance of religion and starvation for love. She placed a high value on catechism instruction, saying, "Nothing else is as helpful or as lasting."

Mother Euphrasia's great motivation was the saving of souls; one of the sisters said, "After listening to our Mother, one would go to the end of the earth to save only one soul."

13

FATHER JOHN JOSEPH LATASTE

Servant of God Father John Joseph Lataste, O.P.
Alcide Lataste
1832 - 1869
France
Died Age 36

In the pre-dawn of a fresh September morning in 1864, a young Dominican priest trudged toward the melancholy prison of Cadillac. He had been assigned by his superiors to give a retreat to the women prisoners at this depressing house of correction.

In spite of his predilection for the sinful and suffering, the young priest went with a heavy heart and a sense of hopelessness. What would he say? How many would come to hear him? Would they come only out of curiosity or to see a new face? Would they listen? How could he inspire these women, who had fallen so far, with a sense of God's love?

Kneeling before the crucifix in the small sacristy, Father Lataste heard his retreatants filing into the chapel. Some of them stumbled over the chairs because it was 4 a.m. and they were so sleepy. Permission for the retreat had been given by the authorities, but as the prisoners' work could not be stopped, the conference had to be held early in the morning and after the work was finished in the evening. One could hardly imagine a congregation less inspiring, less prepared to receive the word than these women. With a last desperate prayer, Father Lataste entered the chapel.

Describing his feelings later in a letter to a friend, Father Lataste wrote, "I cannot tell you the impression they made on me. There were about 400 of them, in their rough prison clothes and with a sort of handkerchief tied tightly around their heads, giving them a most singular appearance. They looked really repulsive—at least to me. But that was because, in spite of myself, I had been influenced by popular prejudice."

The young Dominican looked at the rows of faces—hopeless, bitter, defiant, marked by sin and suffering. And as he looked, he seemed to recognize them. Here were those he had always wanted to help—the poorest, the most afflicted, tempted, and neglected. In them, he recognized the person of his beloved St. Mary Magdalen. When he began to speak, it was from the heart: "My dear sisters..."

Father Lataste began by pointing out to these women that God had a purpose in bringing them there. "Ah, if He had not loved you so much, if He had wanted you to be lost, He had only to let you go on as you were. But you see how very much He loves you since He has taken the trouble to stop you in the midst of your course, on the very edge of the abyss. He has also given you this retreat so that you may come to recognize your faults, confess them, and receive pardon. 'Those whom I love I chastise.' [*Prov.* 3:11]. You see how very true that is?"

Father Lataste went on to compare the inmates' lives with the lives of cloistered religious who had voluntarily chosen to be shut in by walls. "And what is it that makes them happy in such an austere life? The love of God! To love God and to know that one is loved by Him...that is the only real happiness on earth; with that, even suffering becomes a joy . . . One of the greatest and sweetest joys of this life is to suffer for someone we love. Those of you who have ever really loved will understand that. And you too can experience this joy! Yes, these walls...all the hard things which you are obliged to accept, you can make these voluntary and meritorious before God."

The women listened, spellbound. The young priest preached nothing that they had heard before; he preached hope, and he showed them a way to transform their lives—to become saints—simply by loving. Eyes that had long ago forgotten how to cry filled with healing tears.

On that day was born a brilliant and radical idea for a new and most needed apostolate in the Church.

Alcide Lataste was born at Cadillac, France on September 5, 1832, almost in the shadow of the great women's prison. His father professed to be an atheist, although he was a man of much natural goodness and a high moral sense. He was in the textile business and owned a few vineyards. Madame Lataste was a devout Catholic and a good mother who brought her children up with a strong faith and a special devotion to the Blessed Virgin Mary. They were a happy and united family, and although they were not rich, they lived in comfortable circumstances.

Alcide was the youngest of seven children. While he was still a small baby he became very ill, and the doctors suggested the fresh air of the country as a cure. Alcide, therefore, went to live with a foster mother until he was four, when he became well enough to return home.

At seven Alcide began school with the Brothers of the Holy Spirit, and it was then that he first expressed the desire to become a priest. Two years later he attended the Junior Seminary at Bordeaux, where in 1843 he made his First Communion. A year later he was confirmed. At that time Alcide began to realize what it means to be a priest, and he began to speak less and less of his vocation to his parents. In those days, if a young man did not remain in the seminary after his entrance, it was considered something of a family disgrace. Alcide's parents, therefore, not understanding his silence and wondering if his vocation had only been a childish dream, decided to send him to another school.

Thus in 1846, Alcide was sent to the college of Pons, north of Bordeaux. When he arrived he spoke to the head of the college about his aspirations and his difficulties with wondering whether he would be able to stand up to the requirements of the priestly life. The decision was made to put Alcide in the special section reserved for those students who were going on to be priests. However, when his father heard of this plan he objected, stating his wish that his son be with the ordinary students, mixing with all types. He thought this would prove once and for all whether or not there was a solid vocation. When the head of the college informed Alcide of his father's request, he warned the young man to choose his companions carefully. Sadly, this advice was not followed, and Alcide began to drift about carelessly with the most light-hearted of companions.

At the end of that first year Alcide still vaguely cherished the idea of one day becoming a priest. But as time slipped by, he drifted more and more into worldly ways. In spite of the prayers and reproaches of his older sister (his godmother), he gradually seemed to lose all thought of a vocation. During a period of about three years he suffered such violent temptations and scruples that he began to wonder if he would be able to remain faithful even as an ordinary Christian. He said he seemed to hear two voices, one telling him to be a priest and the other saying "No."

When Alcide was 18 he finished school and went home to his family. He stayed there for a year, and then in 1851 took the entrance examination for the civil service. He left to begin his career at the treasury office in Bordeaux, and later was transferred to Privas. In both cities he met friends who interested him in working with the Society of St. Vincent de Paul. His evenings were passed in long visits to the sick and the poor. Alcide gave his whole heart to this work. He really loved Christ's poor, and because they realized this, they accepted him as their friend. His life was full and happy, and there was no time to feel lonely.

Then, quite unexpectedly, Alcide fell in love. Cecile was 16 and he was 21. Alcide decided to ask her to become engaged, but there was a certain procedure to be followed. First he spoke with his confessor, and then he talked the matter over with his parents. They refused their consent. He was too young, he did not make enough to support a wife, and financially it was not considered a good match. Although Cecile's family was a good one, they were not rich. Cecile was fond of Alcide, and her family would have welcomed him. However, the decision of his parents would have to stand, at least for the time.

Mr. Lataste was convinced that this love had been only a passing attraction. Feeling that a few months' separation would end the affair, he requested that his son be transferred. The request was granted, and Alcide was transferred to Pau. As his parting gift to his beloved Cecile, he gave her a small statue of Our Lady.

One evening on his way home from work in Pau, Alcide entered a church and went up to pray in front of Our Lady's altar. His prayer was that Our Lady would understand that he would not ask for the happiness of marriage with Cecile if it was not God's Will. At the same time, he urgently requested that Our Lady make known to them God's Will, asking that if the union was not approved they would receive some sign. The sign was to be given, although not immediately.

In 1855 Alcide's favorite sister, his foster mother, and his beloved Cecile all died within the space of a month. Swiftly he had lost three women whom he had loved and who had loved him, each in her own different way. Alcide began to understand that his happiness would not come through creatures, but through God alone. By the road of suffering he was coming back to his vocation.

In 1857 Alcide wrote to the Dominican Order requesting

admittance. Cecile's letters were burned, and he resigned his post with the treasury office. On November 4, 1857 he entered the Dominican novitiate at Flavigny, becoming Brother John Joseph.

Within two months of his entrance he had an accident in which his finger was badly crushed. The surgeon who operated did not do a good job, and for a time it was feared that two of his fingers might have to be amputated. This would have finished his dream of the priesthood. Had this happened, he planned to ask to stay in the order as a lay brother. Fortunately, the finger finally healed.

Shortly after this Brother John Joseph developed a bone malady in his hip which caused severe pain, and while his leg was paralyzed he was obliged to stay in the infirmary. There his prayer life deepened. Gradually he regained the use of his leg and was able to take up the normal life of the community.

After his profession, Brother John Joseph was transferred to St. Maximin. There, in 1860, he was present at the translation of the relic of St. Mary Magdalen to the basilica. He was permitted to kiss the relic before it was placed above the altar. There he realized clearly that the most degraded sinner has within him the possibility of becoming a great saint.

This grace of understanding was the final preparation for Brother John Joseph's great work. For four years he remained at St. Maximin, and during that time he developed a profound devotion to the great penitent saint, Mary Magdalen. He asked her to teach him something of the depths of God's merciful love.

Brother John Joseph made his solemn profession in 1862 and was ordained in 1863. Less than a year later, he was sent to preach that first retreat in Cadillac.

The young Dominican priest left his first prison retreatants with two great thoughts: (1) What God loves more than all else is to be loved, and (2) God does not ask us what we were; He is only interested in what we are today.

Over and over during the retreat, Father Lataste had asked himself what would happen to these women when they were at last released from prison. Most of them did not want to go back to their old way of life, but who would help them? Some of them had even expressed a desire to consecrate the rest of their lives to God, if that were possible, but no existing order would accept them. Because they would be marked and stigmatized as former prisoners, many of them would again be pushed down into the gutter.

Father Lataste could not bear leaving these women without any hope for the future. In front of the Blessed Sacrament in the prison chapel, from the union of love and sorrow in the priest's heart, the idea for Bethany was born. The prisoners must have a home to go to on their release—not a hostel or a refuge, but a real home. He must find other women of strong faith and purity of character to make a home for them, to form the beginning of a community which would receive them as sisters. There they would live, work and pray together as a family united in their love of God and their desire to make reparation for sin.

Although many people thought Father Lataste was crazy, there were others who had experienced prison work and were all in favor of his idea. Father Lataste presented his idea to his superiors; they approved of it and gave him permission to write a pamphlet about the work.

In this pamphlet he explained the need for this work and the reason for its name, "Bethany." Father Lataste explained that this name had been chosen "because the Gospel tells us that at Bethany lived Martha, of inviolable virtue, and Magdalen, the sinner. And Jesus loved to come and rest in their home. When Jesus looks at souls He does not look at what they were, but at what they are—not at their faults, but at how much they love. He judges them as they are, by the strength of their love."

With the founding of the Dominican Sisters of Bethany, as with the beginning of most other orders in the Church, there were setbacks and trials. However, as Father Lataste said, it was "God's work," and it prospered and grew. A Sister of Charity of Tours, the former Victorine Berthier, came to help Father Lataste in beginning this work. This devoted woman, Sister Henry Dominic, became the first superior and is known as the co-foundress of the order. The Dominican Sisters of Bethany are a contemplative order, although two or more of the sisters from each convent are allowed to visit women's prisons to console and give spiritual encouragement to the women there.

In 1867 Father Lataste requested of his superiors, and was given, two years to complete the formation of the infant congregation. He did not know that a greater Superior had given him just that length of time to live. Earlier, in a letter to Pope Pius IX, Father Lataste had offered his life for the intention of having St. Joseph named as Patron of the Church, and of having the Saint's name inserted in the Canon of the Mass.

In 1868 Father Lataste came to Bethany to stay. He had become a sick man, and his constant efforts on behalf of the sisters were too much for his already strained health. His last illness began in December, and he was to remain an invalid until his death in March.

On the morning of March 10 it was obvious that the end was near. The sisters gathered around his bed and, following an old Dominican custom, sang the *Salve Regina*. Father Lataste seemed to try to pronounce the words with them, although he could do no more than whisper. At the words *"Mater Misericordiae,"* "Mother of Mercy," his lips ceased to move and his gaze was lost to eternity.

Father Lataste had given instructions for his grave: a large cross was to be made from two pieces of the branch of a tree with the bark left on them. This has become a custom in all the cemeteries of Bethany, where each grave has continued to be marked this way. At the last, Sister Henry Dominic exchanged her rosary for that of Father Lataste. To this day, the Superior General of Bethany wears the rosary of the Founder.

A cause for the beatification of Father Lataste was entered in 1937.

Today the Dominican Sisters of Bethany have a number of houses in Europe and two in America. There, where each sister's past is a closed book, "Marthas" and "Magdalens" live together in the love and service of God.

Fr. John Joseph Lataste as a young man. In his late teens he drifted away from his ideal of becoming a priest, and at age 21 he fell in love. One evening he asked Our Lady for a sign as to what he and his fiancée Cecile should do, saying he would accept the will of God. A few months later his beloved Cecile died, along with his foster mother and his favorite sister—all within the space of a month. The young man came to realize that his happiness would come not through creatures but from God alone.

Fr. Lataste, who founded the Dominican Sisters of Bethany for women who were former prisoners and who wanted to dedicate the rest of their lives to love and reparation. Two points Fr. Lataste stressed with these women were: 1) what God desires above all else is to be loved; and 2) God asks not what we were but what we are now—which is measured by how much we love Him.

14

BLESSED MARY OF PROVIDENCE

Eugenie Smet
1825 - 1871
France
Died Age 45

At age 45 Mother Mary of Providence, Foundress of the Helpers of the Holy Souls, was hovering between life and death, and the doctors had notified her confessor that she might die at any moment. For years she had been suffering intensely, both physically and interiorly, in a mysterious participation with the sufferings of the souls in Purgatory. Her confessor wrote to her: "The good God gave you the thought of sacrificing yourself for them [the souls in Purgatory]. See how well He does all that He does! You are a prisoner and the souls in Purgatory are prisoners. You are bound by your pain, and they are held captive. . .You are on fire, and they are in flames . . . You are like the burning bush which burns without being consumed; everything that you suffer is for the greater glory of God."

On her fiery bed of pain, suffering from cancer in one of its most virulent and painful forms, Mary of Providence understood her confessor's advice. She even took delight in being "the providence of Providence" and in offering her sufferings for the souls in Purgatory that God loves so well.

Mary of Providence was born into the Smet family in Lille, France on March 25, 1825; she was named Eugenie. Her parents were wealthy, and Eugenie and her four sisters and one brother were brought up in a period of ease and tranquillity. The family was a close one, and devout. In Lille, Eugenie began her education as a day boarder in a private Catholic school directed by ladies of good family.

Around 1835, the family moved to their country home in Loos. Eugenie loved the beauty of this estate and often played outside with her little friends.

123

Once when she was about seven, a group of children were chasing butterflies over the wide lawns and brilliant flowerbeds of the Smet estate. Suddenly, Eugenie stopped and asked her companions, "Do you know what I am thinking? If one of our companions were in a prison of fire and we had the power to let her out by saying one word, we'd do it right away, wouldn't we?"

The other children, puzzled, looked at Eugenie. She continued, "That's Purgatory. The souls are in a prison of fire, but the good God asks us only for a prayer to let them out and we don't say it!"

Even as a young child Eugenie's original mind was beginning to link Divine Providence with Purgatory. Later, at about 12 years of age, she began to be pulled by an overwhelming zeal for God's glory. "My God," she prayed, "You are my Providence. If I could but someday be Yours! . . . You give me everything; if only I could give You something!"

With her ingenuity and creative thinking, Eugenie thought of a way. She told herself, "I know how I can be the providence of God. He loves the souls in Purgatory so much, and He cannot deliver them because of His justice. I will give Him these souls whom He loves, and I shall ask others to give them to Him by prayers and little sacrifices. I will tell them to be the providence of the dear Lord, since He is our Providence. We can give something to Him who gives us everything." Thus Eugenie was not only moved by compassion for these poor captive souls themselves; she also desired to give *to God* these souls that He loved.

When she was 12, Eugenie was sent along with her sister Maria to boarding school at the Convent of the Sacred Heart in the rue Royal at Lille. At first the brilliant, warm and mischievous little girl was very homesick. Later she realized that in many ways she was "at home" with the sisters in this atmosphere of tranquillity, and one day she announced: "My parents have sent me here for five years, but I shall ask for two years more and then I shall become a nun." Her companions shared a good laugh at this remark, for they well knew all the mischief there was in Eugenie, and they could not imagine her as a sister.

Popular and a real leader, Eugenie kindled enthusiasm within her friends; she moved them to offer prayers and sacrifices for her beloved souls in Purgatory. Mother Madeleine Sophie Barat, the Foundress of the Society of the Sacred Heart, came to the convent for a visit. On meeting Eugenie, Mother Barat remarked to the Mistress

General with saintly intuition, "Who is that girl with the appealing eyes and the strong, intelligent face? She is a child of great promise. Watch her carefully."

During a retreat in 1842, Eugenie promised Our Lord that she would refuse Him no sacrifice. For the rest of her life she was to celebrate this date as that of her conversion.

Eugenie felt she had a vocation to the religious life, but for some time she suffered from questions about it.

After Eugenie left school at 18, she went home to her family in Loos. She studied art and music, shared the duties of the household, spent pleasant hours at the fireside with her embroidery and attended all the social gatherings. Her mother enjoyed introducing her daughters into society, and Eugenie enjoyed the endless round of parties. After returning home, however, she went to her room upstairs and returned to deeper thoughts. At last she told her parents that she wanted to enter the Convent of the Sacred Heart. They refused, saying that her health was too delicate for them to allow her to take such a step.

Although Eugenie appeared to be robust, her health was always poor. The reasons for her chronic ill health have not been determined, but she suffered often from neuralgic pains and frequent attacks of "grippe," or influenza. Eugenie went to speak with a priest, asking him whether her health would prevent her from being a religious; he reassured her.

The Smet family had always been concerned about the poor, and Eugenie found the beginnings of an apostolate at home. With her mother and sisters she mended and sewed garments for the poor. She received donations for those in need, and when packing up parcels for them she added her own touch by writing "Pray for the poor souls in Purgatory" under the name of the recipient. She made soup and took it to the poor. Additionally, she assisted in raising funds for the restoration of a church, for the missions and for the poor. She had a remarkable ability to set religious projects in motion—and a particular talent for fundraising. But with all of her many-faceted activities, Eugenie still did not give up her idea of a religious vocation.

During Eugenie's time at home, two of her charities of note were her work with the Society of the Holy Childhood, which had been established for the rescue of discarded Chinese infants, and her promotion of devotion to Our Lady of La Salette, a devotion which was not well known at the time.

On the Feast of All Saints in 1853, Eugenie received an inspiration to found a religious congregation which would offer prayers and sacrifices for the souls in Purgatory. She thought to herself, "There are communities that supply the various needs of the Church Militant, but there is none consecrated entirely to the relief of the Church Suffering." With her childlike faith in God's Providence, she asked for five signs to be given her, so as to insure that her imagination was not leading her toward something that God did not really want. All of the signs were given to her—yet she found herself plunged in confusion and uncertainty about how she should begin the foundation. A group already established for the Poor Souls urged her to join with them. Advice came from every direction, throwing her into doubt and confusion. Even the attraction she had felt for the work deserted her, while her attachment to her family became stronger than ever. She said, "If one were to imagine a blind person pushed by an irresistible force toward an abyss, one would have an exact picture of my dispositions at the moment of sacrifice."

One person who encouraged Eugenie—although the two never met in person—was the Curé of Ars, St. John Vianney. Through correspondence, this saint provided guidance and strength when Eugenie was suffering these terrible uncertainties and interior struggles. When he heard of her idea he said, after deep prayer, "Here is the work for which God has been asking for so long a time." Other advice followed. The Curé's encouragement also sustained Eugenie later when she wanted to escape and return home. Eventually the Curé of Ars would have great admiration for Eugenie and her work; on one occasion he said, "I should rather have a visit from her than from a queen." And when people spoke of the Foundress, he would say, "I know her."

The new congregation was to be called the Sisters, Helpers of the Holy Souls. Eugenie herself would receive the name Mary of Providence.

The foundation began in Paris in 1856. The little group at first shared an apartment and later found a suitable house. To earn their daily bread the sisters depended on charity and their own work. One of the occupations in which they were employed at first was stringing beads, receiving payment from a contractor. The house of the congregation was sometimes itself called "Purgatory" because of the Institute's aim—which Mary of Providence would sum up in the words: "Pray, suffer, work for the Souls in Purgatory."

As with the beginnings of any religious order in the Church, the community suffered through many trials and hardships. Poverty and misunderstanding were the common lot of Mother Mary of Providence and her first companions. In addition, Eugenie suffered throughout her life from poor health and from serious interior trials. She has left a written diary, never meant for any eyes but her own, of all that she suffered, especially in giving up her family. It is a mark of her sanctity that none who knew her suspected how she really felt, for with her gaiety, charm, and her unfailing trust in Divine Providence, she always seemed to be the popular magnet which drew others. Once in a letter written to her mother, Mary of Providence displayed her native humor when referring to her own health: "My sufferings are as hidden as my virtues." She managed to conceal her spiritual sufferings in the same manner.

When the community became more established, the sisters began to care for the sick poor as a temporal work, often bringing souls back to the Sacraments after years of absence, arranging for valid marriages for unwed couples who had been living together, and helping the dying to pass from this life in the grace of God. A rule based upon that of St. Ignatius was adopted in 1859. The rule does not impose any habit on the sisters, so that they may carry out their apostolate without hindrance. In future years they sent missionaries to China, with many Chinese women becoming cooperators with them, and they also began to branch out to other parts of the world.

Mary of Providence possessed a burning soul, yet she had the coolness of patience. Slowly the congregation began to achieve its purpose—which was, as Mary of Providence expressed it, "To devote ourselves to the most desolate of this world and the next." "I would like to empty Purgatory with one hand, and with the other to fill it with souls snatched from the brink of Hell." "We must help souls to reach the end for which they were created." Also: "One can accomplish nothing except through love."

Mary of Providence's diary gives evidence of mysterious sufferings which she underwent: "I seem to have a fire running through my veins." Her confessor said to her, "Your perpetual sufferings seem as much supernatural as natural to me; God wills them with a special design over you." He also told her, "It is your vocation that places you in that state. It is the torture of the Souls in Purgatory."

For eight years Mary of Providence endured a very painful aridity. She said to Our Lord, "Lord, there is a void in my heart and You do not come to fill it!. . .You have set my heart on fire yet You always remain away from me!. . .Jesus, where are You?. . .That is my constant cry by day and by night!" She said that physical and moral sufferings enveloped her "like a winding sheet." "I am a soul in torment—but no one suspects it." "If you would know how I see myself before God, I am always deaf, dumb, blind." The devil even tempted her against faith in the existence of Purgatory, making her feel that all her sufferings for the souls there were useless. Yet she persevered in faith, realizing that her sufferings were like those of Purgatory. "A soul in Purgatory lives without light because it cannot see God, without joy because it cannot possess Him; but it is fully and always obedient to Him. My life must be a continual Purgatory: that is the path along which God wills to lead me."

In spite of her chronic poor health, Mary of Providence did not slow down her prodigious activity until her last illness. She said, "One must know how to do everything, above all to bear everything laughing. When we arrive in Heaven we shall take a chair and sit down, we shall be tired enough." Despite her own deep sufferings, others saw Mary of Providence as "the life and joy of the house, always calm, serene, the gayest one at recreation. She disseminates confidence and peace. She is made to console in every pain." And though her health was greatly deteriorating, she appeared rosy and healthy.

By 1870, it was apparent that Mary of Providence had at last achieved the total abandonment to God's Will for which she had so long striven. When asked by one of the sisters what she intended to do about some decision to be made, she replied, "Never ask me what I intend to do. I myself never know. I do what God wishes me to do. I have no project other than to accomplish His Will, and it is remarkable that the dear Lord nearly always makes me do the opposite of that which, according to my heart, I would naturally desire." She told her confessor, "I no longer have any other desire than to do the Will of God." Daily she recited the Rosary on her most precious possession, a rosary given to her by the Curé of Ars. She called this devotion her "chloroform," referring thus to its calming effect.

In July of 1870 war was declared between France and Prussia. Mary of Providence was destined to hear the roar of cannon tearing apart the stillness of her religious life, to see her daughters broken-hearted at the loss of loved ones, and to see her country torn and bleeding.

Thus the new year of 1871 dawned drearily. Mary of Providence commented, "We begin the new year as we ended the last, on the cross." She told her sisters, "Let us attach ourselves to the cross; it is our only hope. Life is so short, and eternity will never end."

Mary of Providence died peacefully on February 7, 1871, at age 45, sitting in her chair and clutching her rosary from the Curé of Ars. She passed to eternity late in the afternoon on the day in which the Church commemorated the prayer of Christ in the Garden of Gethsemane.

Today the spiritual daughters of the saintly Foundress labor in a number of countries. In 1957 Mary of Providence was declared Blessed.

Eugenie Smet, Bl. Mary of Providence, who began the Sisters, Helpers of the Holy Souls, devoted to the relief of the Souls in Purgatory—though the sisters also did other work. Even in her childhood Eugenie had been haunted by the thought of the Poor Souls suffering in their "prison of fire" and by the desire to free these souls for Heaven as a gift to God.

Bl. Mary of Providence said, "I would like to empty Purgatory with one hand, and with the other to fill it with souls snatched from the brink of Hell." Yet she had great difficulty in finding her vocation. The Curé of Ars encouraged her in her uncertainty and inner struggles; he came to have great admiration for her and her work, saying on one occasion, "I should rather have a visit from her than from a queen."

15

SAINT CATHERINE LABOURÉ

Saint Catherine Labouré, D.C.
Zoé Catherine Labouré
1806 - 1876
France
Died Age 70

Sister Catherine Labouré appeared no different from the other Sisters of Charity. She was silent and obedient, humbly serving the old men in the Hospice of Enghien. Yet God had set her apart from her sisters and entrusted her with a mission which was to become known throughout the Catholic world. In the days of her novitiate Catherine had been privileged with visions of the Blessed Virgin Mary and of the Miraculous Medal—a devotion which was to spread far and wide even during her lifetime, with the Miraculous Medal soon becoming one of the most loved popular devotions in the Church.

Within a few years millions of people all over the world were wearing the Miraculous Medal. It can also be said that it was the visions of St. Catherine Labouré that ushered in the Marian Age, for since then the Blessed Virgin has appeared on earth many times, and the Popes have made two *ex cathedra* statements on her privileges. Yet despite Catherine's momentous mystical experiences, it was not until the time of her death that people learned she was "the sister of the apparitions." Years later, at her canonization, Pope Pius XII was to call Catherine Labouré the "saint of silence."

Zoé Catherine Labouré was born at Fain-les-Moutiers, France, on May 2, 1806. She was the ninth of 11 children. Their parents were well-to-do peasant farmers. Madame Labouré was a devout and valiant woman who taught Catherine the elements of holiness. When this good mother died, Catherine experienced a deep emptiness. One day shortly after the burial, the nine-year-old Catherine went into her parents' bedroom, where on a shelf stood a statue of Our Lady. Climbing up on a chair, she threw her arms around the statue and spoke aloud to the Blessed Virgin Mary: "Now, dear blessed Mother, you will be my mother." Far from being the result of a momentary sentiment, this was an act which was to set the direction for Catherine's entire life.

When Catherine's older sister left home to follow a religious vocation, Catherine, at age 12, took over the management of the whole household, which included five family members and 13 hired men. This was a tremendous responsibility for a young girl, as it included cooking, serving, and calculating and seeing to the provisions, the laundry, the dishes and the housecleaning, in addition to caring for her invalid brother. But Catherine dedicated herself to these duties as to the Will of God and proved herself most capable of managing the domestic responsibilities very well.

A steady, serious, quiet girl, Catherine attracted a number of suitors, but she unfailingly declined all proposals of marriage. Even at this age she had begun to think of entering a convent.

At 19, Zoé had a dream in which, while she was praying in church, an elderly priest beckoned to her. She was afraid and ran away. Later in the dream, as Catherine was visiting a sick person, the old priest appeared again. He said to Catherine, "My child, it is good to care for the sick. You run away from me now, but one day you will be glad to come to me. God has designs on you. Do not forget it." Later, visiting a hospice run by the Sisters of Charity, Catherine's gaze was to be riveted by a portrait on the wall—a portrait of this same venerable priest, who turned out to be the Order's founder, St. Vincent de Paul. Upon hearing about these experiences, Catherine's confessor concluded: "St. Vincent de Paul calls you. He wants you to be a Sister of Charity."

When Catherine was 22 years of age, after serving her father and the household faithfully and diligently for 10 years, she asked her father's permission to follow her vocation. He refused. Instead, he sent Catherine to live for a time with her brother Charles in Paris, where she was to work as a waitress in Charles' lunchroom. But after a year Catherine was so unhappy that her brother sent her on to her sister-in-law, Madame Hubert Labouré. This woman begged Catherine's father to allow his daughter to carry out what she believed to be God's Will in the matter of her vocation. At last Catherine's father relented and gave his consent.

Catherine did her postulancy, a three-month period, with the Sisters of Charity of St. Vincent de Paul in the house of Chatillon-sur-Seine. It was there that she first learned to read. In April of 1830 she moved to the motherhouse, on rue du Bac in Paris, to begin her nine-month novitiate, or "seminary" time. Catherine later said that upon entering she was so happy that she felt she was "no longer on the earth."

In the novitiate, Catherine began to have a number of extraordinary visions. During a novena in honor of the translation of the relics of St. Vincent de Paul, she had a vision of the Founder's heart on eight or nine successive days. Through these visions Catherine was shown St. Vincent's desires for his two orders, the Vincentian Fathers (or Lazarists) and the Sisters of Charity, with special reference to the coming turmoil in France. Moreover, Catherine saw Our Lord daily. She later wrote, "I was favored with a great grace; it was to see Our Lord in the Blessed Sacrament. I saw Him all the days of my seminary. . .except the days when I doubted [the vision]."

On Trinity Sunday of 1830 Catherine saw Our Lord in the Blessed Sacrament as Christ the King. Then suddenly, as she looked upon Him, all His kingly ornaments fell to the ground. This was a prophecy of the coming fall of King Charles X, signalling the end of the French monarchy and the approach of many miseries in France.

Catherine reported each of these mystical experiences to her confessor, a young Lazarist priest named Father Aladel. Father Aladel heard her words skeptically, privately believing that the young novice had an over-active imagination. He advised her to keep silent and continue her novitiate peacefully and humbly. This is exactly what she did. Catherine was a model of humility and holy obedience.

On the night of July 18-19, July 19 being the feast of St. Vincent de Paul, Sister Labouré was again to experience a most remarkable vision; it was on this night that she was to see her first apparition of the Mother of God. Catherine had been sleeping when she was awakened by a young child, who told her to go to the chapel, as the Blessed Virgin was waiting for her. She dressed hurriedly and followed the child to the chapel.

The lamps in the convent seemed to be burning everywhere, and the chapel was brightly lit as if for midnight Mass. Catherine was led to the sanctuary, and she knelt there to wait. About midnight, the child said, "Here is the Blessed Virgin." Later, when

Catherine was told to write down the facts of this night, she wrote, "I heard a noise like the rustle of a silk dress—a very beautiful lady sat down in Father Director's chair. The child repeated in a strong voice, 'Here is the Blessed Virgin.' I flung myself at her feet on the steps of the altar and put my hands on her knees." Catherine looked up into her Mother's eyes. Years later she was to write that this was the sweetest moment of her life.

Our Lady gave Catherine several messages, some of them for herself personally. She said, "The good God, my child, wishes to entrust you with a mission. It will be the cause of much suffering to you, but you will overcome this, knowing that what you do is for the glory of God....You will be contradicted, but do not fear, you will have grace....Have confidence. Do not be afraid. You will see certain things; give an account of what you see and hear. You will be inspired in your prayers: give an account of what I tell you and of what you will understand in your prayers." Catherine was also assured that she would always have unerring certainty of God's Will.

Our Lady went on: "The times are very evil. Sorrows will come upon France; the throne will be overturned. The whole world will be upset by miseries of every kind." There was pain on Our Lady's face. But she continued: "Come to the foot of the altar. There graces will be shed upon all, great and little, who ask for them. Graces will be especially shed upon those who ask for them." Our Lady then gave Catherine several messages and prophecies regarding the Vincentian Fathers and the Sisters of Charity. She went on to say that numerous sufferings would befall France and the whole world, yet she urged confidence and gave the assurance that "I will be with you." Our Lady then began to name various terrible sorrows to come, especially in France: "My child, the cross will be treated with contempt; they will hurl it to the ground. Blood will flow; they will open up again the side of Our Lord. The streets will stream with blood. Monseigneur the Archbishop will be stripped of his garments...." The Blessed Virgin could not finish speaking for weeping. She concluded with the words, "My child, the whole world will be in sadness." Catherine was given to understand that these sorrows would arrive in 40 years' time. Then the Blessed Virgin disappeared like a "light that is extinguished."

One week later, in a brief and unexpected revolution called "The

Glorious Three Days," King Charles X was deposed, the Archbishop's palace was sacked, churches were desecrated, the cross was trampled underfoot and priests and bishops were beaten and killed. In 1870-71 there would be another outbreak of this terrible anti-religious frenzy in an uprising known as the *Commune*. And aside from these revolts, France suffered and was yet to suffer for many, many years from the often brutal anti-religious forces let loose in the days of the French Revolution (1789).

In spite of the momentous revelations she had received, Catherine still kept silent to all but her confessor. She continued to work daily at the chores assigned to her.

The revelation of the great mission which Our Lady had foretold came soon—on November 27, 1830. Catherine was praying in the chapel with the community when the Blessed Virgin again appeared to her "in all her perfect beauty," resplendent with light, and holding a globe in her hands, while brilliant rays radiated from rings on her fingers. A voice spoke to Catherine interiorly with the explanation of the vision. The globe represented the entire world, especially France, and each person in particular. The rays represented the graces which Our Lady sheds on those who ask for them. Some of the gems on Our Lady's fingers gave no light; these represented the graces for which people forget to ask her.

Suddenly the globe in her hands disappeared and she lowered her hands. She was seen standing on a white globe onto which rays of light streamed from her jeweled hands, and an oval frame formed around her with the words: "O Mary, conceived without sin, pray for us who have recourse to thee."

Catherine heard interiorly the direction to have a medal made on this model. Those who would wear it would receive great graces. Our Lady said, "They should wear it around the neck." She reiterated, "Graces will abound for persons who wear it with confidence."

Then the oval turned, and Catherine saw what was to be put on the back of the medal. The medal was to bear an M through which was woven a bar, which in turn was surmounted by a cross. Underneath the M were the hearts of Jesus and Mary—the one crowned with thorns, and the other pierced by a sword. Twelve stars encircled the whole.

Again Catherine described to Father Aladel her visions and the instructions she had received regarding the medal. Again he doubted. Finally, when Catherine kept insisting that she was told interiorly at prayer that the Virgin was not satisfied, Father Aladel went to the Archbishop of Paris to lay the matter before him. After consideration, the Archbishop gave permission for the medal to be struck and distributed.

In May of 1832, the first medals were distributed. Soon there were many cures and conversions through it, perhaps the most famous being the sudden conversion of the Jewish Alphonse Ratisbonne, who became a Catholic, a priest, and then spent over 30 years in the Holy Land as a missionary to the Jewish people. The medal soon came to be called the "Miraculous Medal," and it signalled a great renewal of devotion to the Blessed Virgin Mary. Favors granted through the medal have continued to this day, and are numbered in the millions. Many of these have been reported to the national Shrine of the Miraculous Medal in Germantown, Pennsylvania.

After the apparitions and on receiving the habit of the Order, Catherine was transferred to the hospice for old men at Enghien; she remained there for the rest of her life. She worked quietly and humbly until her death. No religious life could have seemed more ordinary, simple or commonplace. Catherine worked at the hospice for many years with a number of assigned duties: first kitchen work, then for more than 40 years she was in charge of the hospice—preparing the old men's meals, repairing their clothes, seeing to their Mass attendance and their recreations, providing them with tobacco, nursing them when they were sick, bringing them into line when they disobeyed her wise regulations, seeing that they received the Sacraments before death and having Masses said for the repose of their souls. In all Catherine's 40 years fulfilling these tasks, not one of her beloved old men died without receiving the Last Sacraments.

Catherine was also in charge of the chicken yard for a time, and in her old age she was the portress. Thus she lived out a statement she had once made to another of the sisters: "The Blessed Virgin wishes that the sister who saw her live in humility." And in response to the question of whether she were not bored with her life of daily routine, Catherine answered, "One is never bored with doing the Will of God." At the time of Catherine's beatification, Pope Pius XII declared that she was the "saint of silence and of the duties of her state."

There were some suspicions among the sisters that Catherine

was "the sister of the apparitions," but she just laughed at such suggestions if they were brought up. But on one occasion, in her last year of life, when a young sister scoffingly remarked that the seer had seen only a picture, Catherine fixed her eyes on the doubter and stated firmly, "Sister, the sister who saw the Blessed Virgin saw her in flesh and bone, even as you and I see each other now."

Catherine did not neglect her family after she entered the convent. She prayed for them and kept in touch with them, taking particular care that they fulfilled their religious obligations. Special objects of her concern were her older sister—who left the convent for about 12 years before returning in humility; one of her brothers, who did not practice his religion; and her brother-in-law, who also was indifferent to his faith. Catherine also arranged for a niece to keep an eye on her brother so that if he fell ill he would not die without the Sacraments. The brother-in-law used to joke, "Zoé wishes to convert me, but she hasn't managed it yet. A fine girl, all the same." But during an illness he surrendered to God, and he died peacefully a year later, having received the Sacraments.

Catherine lived much of her life in recollection. Of her prayer life, she wrote, "When I go to the chapel, I put myself before the good God and say to Him, 'Lord, here I am, give me what You wish.' If He gives me something, I am happy and I thank Him. If He gives me nothing, I thank Him still, because I do not deserve anything more. Then I tell Him all that comes into my mind. I tell Him my sorrows and my joys—and I listen." Catherine also had the lifelong gift of being able to receive a reply when she spoke to Our Lady. This fulfilled the promise Our Lady had made to Catherine at her last apparition; the voice had said: "You will see me no more, but you will hear my voice in your prayers."

In 1876, a few months before her death, Catherine knew that her time had come and that she would not live past the year. For the first time she confided her secret to someone other than her confessor; following the instructions of the Blessed Virgin, she revealed to her superior, Sister Dufés, that she was the sister of the apparitions.

After receiving the Last Sacraments, Catherine died peacefully on December 31, 1876. She was buried in a small chapel of the house that had been the place of her work for so many years.

On March 21, 1933 the ritual examination and exhumation of Catherine's body was made as part of the regular process for beatification. At that time the body was found to be incorrupt. Some sisters still living in 1987 could recall the exhumation and the fact that Catherine's limbs were still lifelike and flexible and could be moved as if she were alive. Today St. Catherine's body, still beautifully preserved, can be seen and venerated in the chapel of the Sisters of Charity at rue du Bac, Paris. Thousands of pilgrims visit this shrine every year.

Catherine Labouré was canonized by Pope Pius XII on July 27, 1947.

Central Assoc. of Mirac. Medal, Philadelphia

The Miraculous Medal. The very first medals were struck in 1832. The medal had originally been called the Medal of the Immaculate Conception, but because of the flood of miracles and conversions which hit the Catholic world right after the Medal was introduced, it became known as "the Miraculous Medal." Our Lady said, "Graces will abound for those who wear it with confidence."

St. Catherine Labouré, who as a novice in the Sisters of Charity saw the Blessed Mother and received the Miraculous Medal apparitions in 1830, beginning what is often called "the Marian age."

The only authentic unretouched photograph of St. Catherine Labouré taken while she was alive; it was taken in 1876, the year of her death at age 70.

Above: A photograph of St. Catherine Labouré in death. She had died peacefully, at age 70, with no struggle and with scarcely a sigh, after fulfilling her duty quietly for all the years of her life. The superior immediately revealed to the other sisters that Catherine had been "the sister of the apparitions." News spread quickly through Paris, and clergy and laity alike lined up on the sidewalk to pay their last respects. Catherine had kept her secret all her life, spending 40 years hiding from any glory as she faithfully and lovingly fulfilled her assignment of caring for the old men in the Hospice of Enghien.

Facing page: The incorrupt body of St. Catherine enshrined in the chapel of the motherhouse of the Sisters of Charity at 140, rue du Bac, Paris. (The hands are made of wax.)

16

BLESSED MARIA OF JESUS CRUCIFIED
The Little Arab

Blessed Maria of Jesus Crucified, O.C.D.
Maria Baouardy
1846 - 1878
˙ Israel
Died Age 32

"I love ants because they are little. I wish I could be like them. I love onions and potatoes because they grow unnoticed and do good things. When you want to be big, make yourself little." In these words Sister Mariam—or Maria—of Jesus Crucified expressed the program of her whole life.

"The Little Nothing" is the name by which this humble Palestinian Carmelite preferred to be called. The zig-zag path of her existence was filled with extraordinary mystical phenomena. Blessed Maria of Jesus Crucified was an ardent promoter of devotion to the Holy Spirit, and the Holy Spirit filled her nothingness with His special mystical gifts. He made her a living synthesis of these gifts—ecstasies, stigmatas, knowledge of hearts, prophecies, levitations, bilocations. Not a day passed without her experiencing the splendor of these marvels. Maria's lifespan coincided with the reign of Pope Pius IX, and a number of her prophecies went to him. Yet her secret was simplicity, and she remained simple in everything.

Maria Baouardy was born in Abellin near Galilee on January 5, 1846. She was born in poverty and was the only one of 13 children who survived infancy. Ten days after her birth she was baptized and confirmed in the Greco-Melkite rite of the Roman Catholic Church.

In 1849, when Maria was three years old, both of her parents died within a few days of one another. She was adopted by a paternal uncle with whom she moved to Alexandria, Egypt when she was eight years old. Here she made her first confession and First Holy Communion.

A fanatical Muslim once struck at Maria with his scimitar, causing a severe throat wound. But Maria was cured through the intercession of Our Lady.

After refusing an arranged marriage, Maria went into service with the Nadjar family. She worked as a servant girl in Egypt, Jerusalem and Beirut. When the Nadjar family moved to France, Maria accompanied them.

At the age of 19 Maria became a postulant with the Sisters of St. Joseph of the Apparition at Marseilles. But because of misunderstandings surrounding her mystical gifts, she was dismissed from the congregation less than two years later.

Then Maria and her former novice mistress, Mother Veronica, entered the Carmel of Pau, France. Maria received the Carmelite habit and began her novitiate. Soon she began to experience more ecstasies and revelations. In his hatred of her total trust in the Holy Spirit, the devil tortured her.

In 1870 Maria travelled to India with a group of Carmelites. There, at Mangalore, they founded the first Indian Carmel. Maria was professed there as a lay sister in 1871—the first Carmelite to be professed on Indian soil. Her name in religion was Sister Maria of Jesus Crucified. When the sisters later encouraged Maria to become a choir sister, she declined and begged to stay unnoticed.

In 1872, because of serious difficulties and confusion regarding her mystical phenomena, Maria returned to the Carmel of Pau in France.

As a child Maria had never attended school, and she remained almost totally illiterate. The sisters tried to teach her to read and write at the convent, but they had to give up. There is only one page extant which was scribbled in her own handwriting. But in spite of her lack of formal education Sister Maria was able to give sound and sublime theological counsel. Her spiritual knowledge had its source in union with God.

Maria had special gifts of participating in the mysteries of Jesus, of understanding the mission of the Holy Spirit, and of a profound love for the Church and the Pope. She ardently promoted devotion to the Holy Spirit.

In 1875 Sister Maria of Jesus Crucified became inspired to found a Carmel in Bethlehem. She in turn inspired a generous benefactor, Miss Berthe Dartigaux, to help in making the new foundation. Maria herself chose the site, and she eventually became architect as well as director of the work.

Maria's three years in the budding Carmel of Bethlehem were to be a long and difficult Way of the Cross. Illness, work, direction of the building project, mystical "nights" and voluntary expiations made her days a long martyrdom of love. To the end, she remained "The Little Nothing."

In 1878 Maria went to Nazareth to look for some land for a second Carmel. On the way, through spiritual intuition, she recognized the true site of the town of Emmaus of the Gospels. With Miss Dartigaux's help, the sisters were able to buy the property. Twenty-three years later, in 1910, the foundation was to become a reality.

On August 21, 1878 Maria suffered a bad fall in the monastery garden at Bethlehem, where she was helping the workers. She broke her left arm, and the fracture quickly turned into incurable gangrene. Maria died in the late hours of August 26. Her last words were, "Oh, yes, mercy."

The body of this little mystical flower of the Holy Land is buried at the Carmel of Bethlehem beneath a stone on which is carved a lovely tribute from her sisters: "J.M.J.T. Here, in the peace of the Lord, lies Sister Maria of Jesus Crucified, a white-veiled professed religious. A grace-filled soul of exemplary virtue, she was outstanding for her humility, her obedience and her charity. Jesus, the only love of her soul, called her to Himself in the 33rd year of her life and the 12th of her religious life. Bethlehem, August 26, 1878. May she rest in peace!"

The length of this inscription, very unusual for a Carmelite, shows how much Maria's sisters loved the one they called *La Petite Arabe—* "The Little Arab."

At her beatification in November of 1983, Pope John Paul II expressed his confidence that Blessed Maria of Jesus Crucified would intercede for the cause of peace in the Near East, the troubled land of her birth.

Blessed Maria (Mariam) of Jesus Crucified, born near Galilee and known to her sisters as "the Little Arab." Sister Maria's life was filled with mystical gifts—ecstasies, stigmatas, knowledge of hearts, prophecies, levitations, bilocations. Not a day passed without her experiencing mystical phenomena. This picture was taken while she was in ecstasy.

Bl. Maria of Jesus Crucified founded the Carmel of Mangalore, India and
the Carmel of Bethlehem, and she obtained land where the Carmel of
Nazareth would be built. Bl. Maria had received a mystical intuition that
the Gospel town of Emmaus had been located on this property. This picture is from a group photo of sisters coming to Bethlehem for the founding
of the new Carmel.

17

CORNELIA CONNELLY

Servant of God Mother Cornelia Connelly, S.H.C.J.
Cornelia Augusta Peacock
1809 - 1879
United States - England
Died Age 70

In May of 1849, in highly anti-Catholic England, a Roman Catholic priest (formerly an Anglican minister) sued his separated wife, now a Roman Catholic nun, for restitution of conjugal rights.

At the vortex of this whirlwind of controversy and public scandal stood the nun, Mother Cornelia Connelly—mother of four children and now the founder of a religious order. She was accused of deserting her children (in reality, their father had taken them away from her), of deserting her husband (although it was he who had initiated the separation), and of several other actions inexplicable by human standards.

The Protestant court ruled in favor of the plaintiff, Rev. Pierce Connelly. However, Cornelia's lawyers immediately appealed, and the judgment was reversed in 1851. But while the initial trial lasted, the scandal provided daily fuel for the sensational press. The facts of the case were so strange that even today many Catholics have difficulty appreciating the sanctity of Mother Connelly when they first learn about her life. Yet Cornelia had done her utmost to carry out God's Will—and that not capriciously or willfully but with the most careful of advice.

Cornelia was the seventh child of a prominent Philadelphia businessman, Ralph Peacock, and of Mary Swope Bowen, formerly a widow, and a woman wealthy in her own right. As a child, Cornelia was happy, somewhat untidy, and strong-willed. She was also considered to be quite a beauty. Cornelia was well-educated by private tutors at home. She had a high intelligence, spoke several languages, was an artist and musician and had been trained in voice. Her father died when she was nine, and her mother died when she was 14. Cornelia then went to live with her half-sister.

Of Cornelia's religious formation before her marriage we know very little. Neither she nor her six brothers and sisters were baptized in infancy. At 22 Cornelia was baptized in the Episcopal church. Later, three of her four surviving brothers and sisters were to follow her into the Catholic Church. The other professed and practiced Unitarianism.

In December of 1831 Cornelia married the Rev. Pierce Connelly, an Episcopal minister. Pierce was a graduate of the University of Pennsylvania and a member of the bar of that state; he had given up law to serve the church.

The young couple were transferred to Natchez, Mississippi, far from the Anglican society they had been used to. Many of their new friends were Catholics, and after a while, both of the Connellys felt drawn to the Catholic Church. They decided to convert. This would mean many sacrifices—their home, some of their friends, Pierce's job and a promising future. However, both were determined since they were convinced this was the Will of God. Fortunately, they had made a number of good investments so that they had a sufficient amount of money not to have to worry about the loss of employment. At this point Pierce and Cornelia had two children.

At this time the Connellys made an extended visit to Rome. Before their passage, Cornelia was received into the Catholic Church. In Rome, Pierce petitioned to be admitted to the Catholic Church, confirmed, and received as a candidate for Holy Orders; he presented these petitions in a private audience with Pope Gregory XVI. The Pope later remarked that the petition had moved him to tears. There seemed to be no doubt as to the sincerity of Pierce's vocation; nevertheless, the Pope advised him first to be received into the Church and then to give himself plenty of time before considering the possibility of ordination. After Pierce's reception into the Church, the young family extended their European tour, making many high society friends and entering gaily into the social whirl.

When the American financial panic struck in 1837, the Connellys hurried home to rescue what was left of their investments. There was not much left. Fortunately the Jesuits offered Pierce a teaching position at St. Charles College at Grand Cocteau, Louisiana. Cornelia gave music lessons at the school to help make ends meet.

In spite of the deprivations of an almost frontier-like existence, Cornelia was supremely happy. She loved her husband and her children, and from the beginning of her marriage she had considered the love and care of them as her way of serving God.

A presentiment of tragedy seemed to begin to haunt Cornelia at this time. After making a retreat at which she was introduced to the Spiritual Exercises of St. Ignatius, she was one day inspired to pray, "My God, if all this happiness is not to Thy greater glory and the good of my soul, take it from me. I make the sacrifice." Soon she was to learn exactly how great was the sacrifice that would be asked of her.

Twenty-four hours later a big dog playing with Cornelia's beautiful little two-and-a-half-year-old son knocked the child into a vat of boiling maple sugar. As there was no good medical treatment available at the time, all Cornelia could do was hold her dying baby in her arms for the next two days until he died.

Then, several months after the baby's death, when Cornelia was expecting her fourth and last child, Pierce seemed to have something on his mind. On the way home from Mass one day he told her what it was. He felt that he was being called to the priesthood, and he wanted to return to Rome to petition the Pope again. He asked her to help him take the necessary steps.

Although she felt she would die of sorrow, Cornelia responded that she would follow God's Will explicitly. She knew that the Church would only permit Pierce's ordination on condition that she make a solemn vow of chastity. From that time the couple decided to practice mutual celibacy in order to test their sincerity in the matter. Nonetheless, Cornelia did not expect Pierce to leave until they had fulfilled their parental obligations to the children. A prayer in her spiritual notebook reveals her frame of mind at this time: "O my God, trim Thy vine, cut it to the quick, but in Thy great mercy root it not yet up. My God, help me in my great weakness. Help me to serve Thee with new fervor."

In December of 1843, after another audience with the Pope, Pierce brought his family to Rome. After consultation with Cornelia, the Pope gave his permission for the marital separation. Cornelia and the baby were to go to a convent of the Sacred Heart Sisters in Rome, where Cornelia would be considered a postulant as long as the baby needed her. The older children were to be placed in boarding schools.

In 1844 Cornelia made a retreat in which she endeavored to impress upon her soul the fundamental truths of life. She wrote, "Without reserve fly from what the world loves. Seek to be despised, but not to merit it. It is for the glory of God that we should be saints. God wills what is for His glory; therefore God wills us to be saints. God wills me to be a saint. I will to be a saint. *Therefore I shall be a saint.* Live for Eternity. Eternity, Eternity, Eternity." Then, in accord with the Spiritual Exercises of St. Ignatius, she made these notes: "The three degrees of perfection: 1st. To avoid mortal sin. 2nd. To avoid any venial sin or even voluntary defect. 3rd. To *suffer* purely to be more like our Divine Model. My offering given in the Mass." Then she added, "I renounce the world, the flesh and the devil, and give myself all to Thee, to know Thee, to love Thee and to serve Thee. Amen."

Pierce undertook his preparatory studies, completed them, and was ordained to the priesthood. Cornelia brought their daughter Adeline to receive her First Holy Communion from her father on the day of his ordination. Cornelia's response to Pierce's ordination was: "I have given him to God; this thought gives me much consolation."

Cornelia's life, too, was moving toward a new beginning. At the age of 36, at the urging of Bishop (later Cardinal) Wiseman, Cornelia embarked on what was to become the great work of the rest of her life, founding the Society of the Holy Child Jesus, a congregation to educate young girls in England. Bishop Wiseman had recognized the great need for such a group and had wanted Cornelia to begin one. Taking her two youngest children, whom she planned to keep with her (the oldest boy was already in boarding school in England), Cornelia moved to England. She first began her foundation in Birmingham, but a short time later it was moved to Derby.

The young community's rule was based on that of the Society of Jesus. The first foundation was called St. Leonard's.

Cornelia proved to be a superb religious superior, as well as a good businesswoman and a clear-headed educator. Her own children remained constantly in her thoughts and in her heart, yet she became a most devoted mother to this new family. Testimonies abound as to her great love for the young sisters in the community and the children they cared for. One stated, "My impression when I first saw her was that I had found a mother." Another said: "She inspired me with absolute confidence. I felt I could say anything to her." Cornelia remained in all things a mother, and her influence over little children was especially marked.

Pierce had obtained a chaplaincy on an English estate, and within only a year of his ordination, he too was in England. But without Cornelia's loving and cheerful presence and approval, and when his advancement in the hierarchy seemed thwarted, Pierce began to change. He developed an almost pathological jealousy of Cornelia and of Bishop Wiseman, her helper in founding her order. At first Pierce had seemed to be proud of her success, but when he realized that she now paid more attention to her spiritual director than to him—who had completely dominated her for 15 years—he began to meddle, attempting to change the rule of the Society of the Holy Child Jesus and even claiming to be its founder.

Then suddenly, with no warning and for no apparent reason, Pierce took the children away from Cornelia. The baby was not yet six, and Cornelia felt his loss greatly. However, Pierce was the children's legal guardian and Cornelia had no say in the matter.

Then, in 1849, after realizing that he could not interfere in the foundation Mother Connelly had made, Pierce had her served with a writ to appear before the Protestant Court of Arches, suing her for the restitution of conjugal rights. In the anti-Catholic England of this time, this was a real treat for scandal. It seemed that all Pierce's thoughts for the Catholic Church had vanished. It created a national scandal and was a source of great suffering for Mother Connelly. Her response was to cling ever closer to the Will of God.

Pierce won the case, but as Cornelia's counsel immediately appealed, no legal action could yet be taken. Therefore, Pierce threatened in a rage to use illegal force. Cornelia had to be on her guard lest he come to the convent and bodily kidnap her.

Not wishing to worry the young sisters, Cornelia told them nothing about her worries. The convent had a beautiful view of the sea, and one day a young novice remarked on a pretty yacht lying off the coast. Cornelia looked at the yacht and calmly replied, "Yes, it is a lovely sight. I often thank God for our view of the sea." She did not voice her silent thanks that He also provided warnings of danger—she had recognized the boat as belonging to Pierce's friends.

In spite of expectations to the contrary, Cornelia won her case on appeal, through a decision of the Privy Council. Pierce was now out of money to continue any legal battle, but Cornelia paid his court costs to keep him out of jail. Naturally, in the political climate of the day, this final act of generosity on her part did not receive public acclaim.

Cornelia's winning of the court case seems to have robbed Pierce of his last few bits of sanity and self-control. He began to rant against the Church. In a pamphlet entitled *Reasons for Abjuring Allegiance to the See of Rome,* which was printed in 20 editions, he told anti-Catholic lies such as that Bishop Wiseman had instructed Catholics to burn heretics and that the King would be shot if the Catholics were allowed to overrun England.

Finally Pierce seemed to tire of it all and left England. He was re-accepted as an Anglican clergyman. His resentment toward Cornelia gradually died down and he wrote kindly to her convent upon her death. Pierce would finish his days as pastor of a small church in Rome.

When he left England Pierce took the children with him. In the years to come Cornelia would have little contact with her children. Pierce had a most convincing way about him and henceforth the children's attachment to their mother was broken. The boys, Frank and Mercer, both died outside the Church. It is significant that one day the tower bell was heard tolling all by itself at an unaccustomed hour; when this was brought to Mother Connelly's attention, she said, "We should look upon this as a call to prayer. Let us pray for whatever soul may be in need." Later, word was received that Cornelia's son Mercer had died; as far as could be determined, his passing had coincided with the bell's unexplained tolling.

The Connelly daughter, Adeline, returned to the practice of the Catholic Faith after the deaths of her parents. She offered her life for her brother's conversion and died holding her mother's crucifix.

To Mother Connelly the loss of her children and their defection from the Faith was the deepest sorrow of her life. "I would willingly give them up if only their souls were safe," she said. Yet her personal sufferings were always kept beneath the surface. One of the young sisters once asked her, "Mother, do you ever cry?" "Why, child," she replied with a bright smile, "the tears are *always pouring down the back of my nose.*" On another occasion Mother Connelly remarked, "The thought of my children never leaves me"; then she added quickly, "but I would not be without this precious jewel of the cross." The Archbishop of New Orleans was to write to Mother Connelly, "The new family you have adopted should be as dear to you as your own, since it is such in the eyes of God."

Thus Cornelia's sacrifice was complete. She had given up her husband and children not once, but twice—first when she had sacrificed her family in order that her husband might realize his vocation, and finally when he went against the Church and drew their children away also.

Cornelia's life was by no means all made up of negatives, however. She wholeheartedly embraced the second vocation which God had given to her, becoming a woman of great holiness and a mother to many souls. Many people remarked on an indescribable appearance of sanctity which seemed to radiate from her eyes and her smile. This was especially noticed by children. She used to say that it was "a waste of time and a waste of grace" to dream of the future or brood over the past. She was totally devoted to the Will of God. People also used to remark on Mother Connelly's great tranquillity and on her childlike gaiety. She taught that even in sickness and sorrow there should always be joy in the heart, and that a smile should show the sunshine of the soul.

Mother Connelly had this maxim placed in a conspicuous place on the walls: "The hand at work, the eye on the tomb, the heart in Heaven." Her constant habit was to abandon herself into God's hands, endeavoring—as she expressed it in a prayer to the Child Jesus— "to depend in all things on Thee, as Thou didst depend on Thy Mother and St. Joseph."

Mother Connelly often made lists of prayer intentions. Her list for 3:00 on Good Friday of 1857 reveals many desires of her heart:

1. Conversion of Pierce, Adeline and Frank, and of all friends and relations.
2. The affairs of Rupert House to be settled for our good.
3. All the general intentions of the past year.
4. That all in our Society may become Saints.
5. That our children may also be holy.
6. That no one connected with us may ever be lost.
7. That our number in the Novitiate may increase sevenfold, and also the Boarding-Schools in each house.
8. Friendship and holy peace with our neighbor [*A property dispute was in progress*].
9. Several conversions [*specified*].

10. Freedom from infectious diseases in the communities and schools [*They were recovering from an epidemic of scarlet fever at St. Leonard's*].

In addition to motherly sensitivity and kindness, Mother Connelly also had great firmness, so that strangers often judged her to be obstinate and self-opinionated. She was a woman of great intelligence; architects, financiers, lawyers and educators all found that she was able to meet them on their own ground. Mother Connelly was especially good at mathematics, and at the early death of her son she dealt with her sorrow by making herself work through a number of geometry problems every day.

The Society of the Holy Child Jesus was a precious godsend for many young girls. At the time Cornelia began the society, education for girls was at a low ebb in England. Moreover, many Irish refugees from the potato famine needed the type of education that she provided. Cornelia trained girls in the practice of their holy faith and also expanded their minds in many fields, including philosophy, logic, astronomy and architecture. She believed in a liberal education rather than a specialized curriculum, and she always tried to make school so interesting that temptations to laziness and disobedience in large part disappeared. She aimed to develop character and initiative in the girls, saying, "We have to learn to make strong women who, while they lose nothing of their gentleness and sweetness, should yet have a masculine force of character and will." To this end Mother Connelly allowed the girls a fair amount of freedom and gave them her trust.

Mother Connelly made great efforts to draw the girls under her care to Our Lord. She would tell the sisters not to become too attached to them, saying, "Be careful not to steal their young hearts from Our Lord." The children in turn were inspired to real piety and virtue. Four of her girls are known to have asked Our Lord at their First Communion that if in the world they would ever commit a mortal sin, they might never leave the convent. Two of these young girls were suddenly taken ill and died, and the other two became nuns.

At the time of Mother Connelly's death in 1879, there were convents of her order with schools following the design she had mapped out in six English cities, as well as four in America and one in France. Today the Order has spread throughout the world.

Cornelia had written, "Give me the grace to know Thy Will, and the strength to do it." God had surely answered this prayer.

Mother Connelly died on April 18, 1879, at the age of 70. Her years of anguish and her other sufferings had taken their toll: her body was filled with rheumatic pain, her body and face were marred with eczema, which gave her an appearance of being scalded, her beautiful eyes sunk in and her body was shrunken. Yet to the end she was full of fervor and trust in God, and her death was peaceful. At the last hour the disfigurement caused by her illness passed from her face, which took on a look of peace and spiritual beauty.

By her own wish, Cornelia was buried in the convent cemetery at Mayfield. On Easter Friday, 1935, her body was exhumed for reburial in a place prepared as a memorial to her in the convent church at Mayfield. When the grave was opened, the body was seen to be very well preserved. The Bishop of Southwark appointed an historical commission to do the necessary exhaustive research for a cause for beatification; this research material was taken to Rome in the early 1980's.

Cornelia Connelly at the time of her marriage in Philadelphia (1831). Both Cornelia and her husband Pierce were Anglicans (*he* was a clergyman) at the time of their marriage, but both became Catholics a few years later. Cornelia would bear four children before agreeing to her husband's request for a separation so that he could become a priest. She was an affectionate mother, and her children loved her deeply.

Cornelia Connelly in Rome, 1846, after her separation from her husband. It was during this year that Bishop Wiseman called Cornelia to England to persuade her to found the Society of the Holy Child Jesus to educate young girls in England.

159

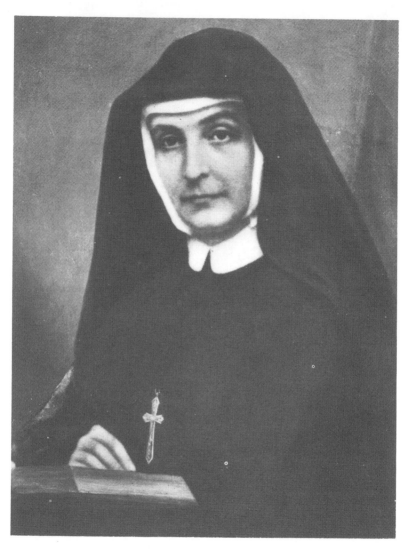

Mother Cornelia Connelly in the habit of the Society of the Holy Child Jesus, an order which she founded at age 36 to care for and educate young girls in England. Cornelia suffered a great deal from her husband Pierce, who after ordination had begun interfering with her new Society, then abandoned the priesthood and sued Cornelia for restitution of conjugal rights. Pierce won, then lost on appeal; he went back to being an Anglican minister. He took away their young children from Cornelia, alienating them from their mother and from the Catholic Faith. Cornelia said, "I would willingly give them up if only their souls were safe."

Though pictures depict her with a somber expression, Mother Connelly's habit was always to keep her sorrows to herself and even to maintain a joyous heart. A young sister once asked her, "Mother, do you ever cry?" She replied with a bright smile, "Why, child, the tears are always pouring down the back of my nose." Yet people would remark on Mother Connelly's great tranquility and childlike gaiety.

161

Mother Connelly in 1874, at around age 65. She had an especially marked
influence over little children, and they in turn were very attracted to her.
Mother Connelly told the sisters, "Be careful not to steal their young hearts
from Our Lord."

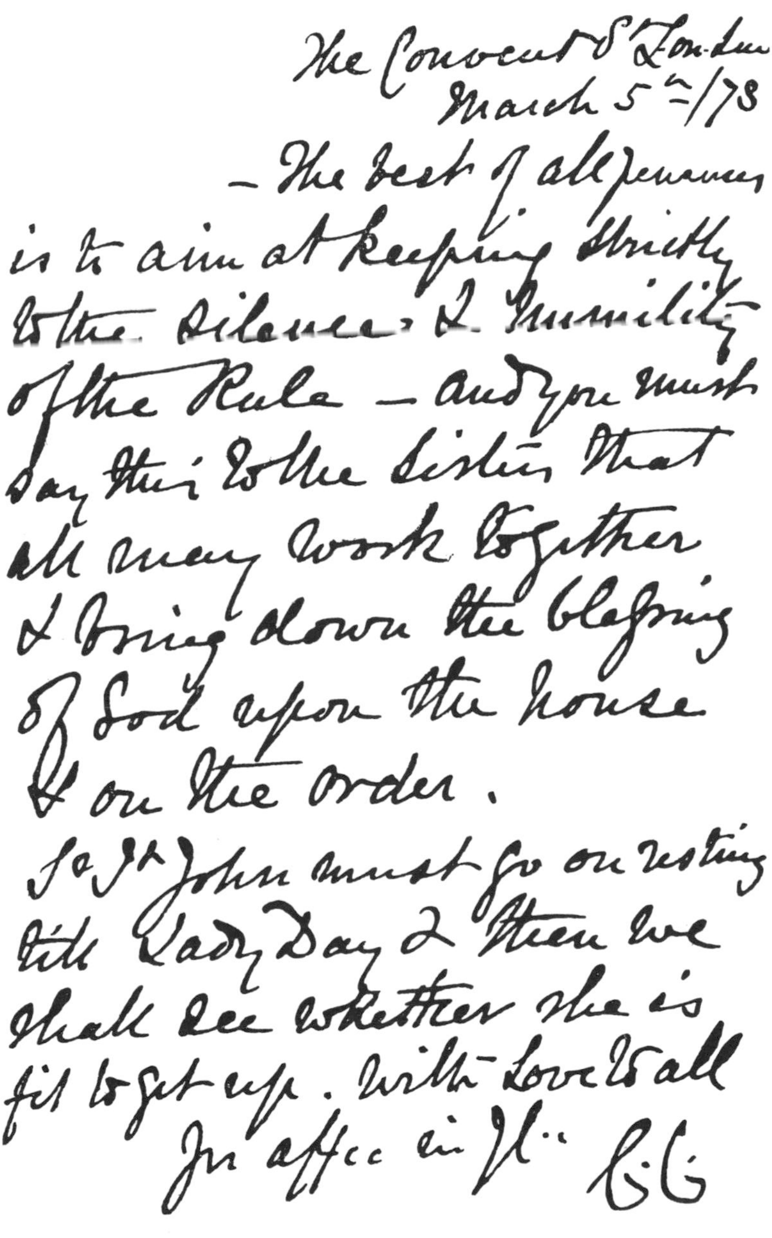

The Convent St Leonards
March 5th/78

— The best of all penances
is to aim at keeping strictly
to the Silence & humility
of the Rule — and you must
say this to the sisters that
all may work together
& bring down the blessing
of God upon the house
& on the order.

So Sr John must go on resting
till Lady Day & then we
shall see whether she is
fit to get up. With love to all
In affec in Jm.· C.C.

Part of a letter written by Mother Connelly, showing her wise guidance
of the sisters. ("Lady Day" is the traditional British name for the Feast
of the Annunciation, March 25.)

163

Mother Cornelia Connelly around 1877, at about age 68, two years before she died. Her motto, which she had put up in a conspicuous place, was "The hand at work, the eye on the tomb, the heart in Heaven."

164

18

BLESSED JEANNE JUGAN

Blessed Mary of the Cross
Jeanne Jugan
1792 - 1879
France
Died Age 87

"Little Sisters, take good care of the aged, for in them you are caring for Christ Himself." So spoke Jeanne Jugan, who against all human prudence and armed with only faith and courage founded the Little Sisters of the Poor when she was nearly 50 years old.

Jeanne Jugan was born on October 25, 1792 in a small fishing village of Brittany, France. She was the sixth of the eight children of Joseph and Marie Jugan. When she was three and a half, her father was lost at sea. Her mother struggled for years to keep the family together in their one-room, earthen-floored cottage.

Revolution and war made the France of Jeanne's childhood an anticlerical nightmare. Nonetheless, Jeanne and her family, like most Bretons, remained devout Catholics. In spite of laws forbidding religious practices, Jeanne and her family took part in morning devotions in the tiny chapel of Our Lady of the Orchard. Jeanne received her knowledge of the Catholic Faith from her mother and from a group of sisters of the Third Order of the Heart of the Admirable Mother (founded by St. John Eudes), called the "trotting sisters." Convents had been suppressed by the government, but works of charity were still being carried on by these women who lived at home but went here and there, helping wherever they were needed. These sisters all had a price on their head, but despite the laws and prohibitions of the regime, they continued their work of teaching catechism to the French children.

When Jeanne was about 16 she became the kitchen maid of the Viscountess de la Choue, a kind-hearted Christian woman. This woman took Jeanne with her on her visits to the sick and the poor on and around her estate. From her Jeanne learned, by example, the meaning of truly Christian charity and a refinement of manners not customary among those of the peasant class.

A young sailor fell in love with Jeanne and begged her to marry him. She declined, telling him that she had decided to dedicate herself to the service of God and had decided not to marry.

When she was about 25, Jeanne sorted through her clothes and gave her sisters "everything that was smart or pretty" and set out to serve the poor in the town of Saint Servan. To this end and in order to support herself, she took a job in the crowded hospital there, where she prepared dressings, applied bandages and performed other services to relieve the miseries of the 300 patients and 35 foundlings there. It is recorded that some of the patients suffered from "scurvy, itch and venereal diseases." Jeanne also joined the Third Order of the Heart of the Admirable Mother. After six years of devoted toil at the hospital, Jeanne was so worn out that she had to leave this work.

She went to work for a good Christian woman named Mlle. Lecoq. Jeanne was so exhausted that, in a reversal of roles, the lady spent more time waiting on the maid than the maid on the lady! Mlle. Lecoq insisted that Jeanne receive proper food, medicine and rest. Daily the two women spent hours in prayer, and they assisted at Mass. They also instructed the town's children in their catechism. Additionally, the two labored to care for the poor and other unfortunates. At last, worn out from the strain, the elderly Mlle. Lecoq died.

In 1837, the 45-year-old Jeanne and a 72-year-old woman named Francoise Aubert rented part of a humble cottage. There Francoise earned a small amount by spinning, and Jeanne continued to hire out as a domestic laborer. They were joined by Virginie Tredaniel, a 17-year-old orphan who worked as a dressmaker. The three formed a community of prayer. They taught catechism and assisted the poor. Whatever they had left over from their earnings, they gave to the poor.

And there were *many* poor. In the social chaos following the French Revolution, beggars were everywhere and misery was rife. At one point half the population of Saint Servan was on the welfare rolls. The suffering seemed overwhelming.

At age 47, while in the hire of a man named Monsieur Leroy, Jeanne determined to dedicate the rest of her life to the poor. When she told her employer of her decision to leave, he at first tried to argue her out of her decision. He told her she had been a good servant and offered her higher wages and shorter hours to stay with his family. But Jeanne declined the offer. She told him she had decided to work for the poor of her town and that she intended to collect from door to door and to offer shelter to all she could, particularly the aged poor. When Monsieur Leroy sarcastically asked her how she, who was poor, would find means to feed those who were starving, she answered softly, "From people like you, Monsieur Leroy. You are a kind man. I know you will help me."

Realizing that Jeanne's love and logic had won the argument, Monsieur Leroy said, "Mademoiselle, God has given you the grace of asking." With a hearty laugh, he presented her with 3,000 francs, a very substantial sum, which would purchase a large amount of food. "Take these, and God bless you."

With the approval of Francoise and Virginie, Jeanne turned her attention to the most pitiful of the poor—abandoned old ladies. In 1839 she brought home a blind widow named Anne Chauvin. Until then, this woman had been cared for by her own sister, but the sister had fallen ill and been taken to the hospital. With no one to care for her, the widow was in desperate straits. In order to provide sleeping quarters for their guest, Jeanne gave up her own bed and climbed up to the loft to sleep. Furthermore, she adopted Anne "as her mother." This act held great significance in Jeanne's life. Henceforth she was to share intimately in the sufferings of the poor, even physically, considering herself one of them. This characteristic is expressed in the name that eventually developed for Jeanne's charitable work: The Little Sisters of the Poor.

Soon the little community had a second elderly guest. This was a servant woman who had spent her life as a faithful retainer for two wealthy people. When they lost all their money, the servant had spent her savings, and later begged, to provide for them. At their death, the faithful servant was left destitute and infirm. This time it was Virginie who gave up her bed; she moved into the loft with Jeanne.

Shortly thereafter two young women began visiting the little home and volunteering their services. Jeanne wrote a simple rule for them, Virginie, and herself. She based it on the rule followed by the Third Order of the Heart of the Admirable Mother. Francoise, at her age, was content just to spin and pray.

By the summer of 1841, Jeanne and her companions needed more room for themselves and their guests, so they rented an abandoned bar close to the harbor; this was referred to as "the big basement."

Encouraged by the Brothers of St. John of God, Jeanne began to beg in the town and the others earned wages to support the household. Soon even these quarters were too small. With the help of many who contributed amounts small and large, Jeanne purchased the former convent of the Daughters of the Cross, which had been confiscated by the government when religious orders were suppressed. The building was in good condition but needed a number of repairs; these were made by the volunteer labor of many of the townsfolk. By 1843 Jeanne and her sisters were caring for 44 elderly women and one abandoned sailor; soon other men came also. Jeanne called this home the Home of the Cross.

Many of Jeanne's elderly women had made their living by begging. Now, they would say to Jeanne, "Sister Jeanne, go out instead of us, beg for us." As she found the Will of God in the events of life, Jeanne begged for the old women. She would say to a benefactor, "Well, sir, the little old woman won't be coming anymore. I shall be coming instead. Please be so kind as to go on giving us your alms."

With a little basket over her arm, Jeanne went about her begging in the town to raise the funds needed to support the home. Rich and poor alike helped; the shipyard workers customarily gave her a penny or two each payday. A number of wealthy women helped by begging funds themselves. Although it was against her proud nature to ask for anything, Jeanne set aside personal considerations to provide for her beloved elderly.

In her old age, she recalled what a victory over herself she had had to win in becoming a beggar. "I used to go out with my basket, looking for something for our poor. . . it cost me a lot to do this, but I did it for God and for our dear poor." When she instructed the other sisters, she told them, "Little Sisters, let us knock in God's name." Jeanne firmly believed and taught that what is done for the poor is done for Our Lord. She told the sisters to do penance by accepting the cold and weariness experienced on their "collecting" rounds.

In her begging, Jeanne was quick to explain her motives. If asking for wood to construct a bed, she would say, "I should like a little wood to relieve a member of Jesus Christ." She had a charming manner, and that, along with her obvious faith and love for the elderly poor, often moved the hardest hearts. Once, when she returned a second day in a row to a man for another donation, he became angry. She turned aside his anger and got another donation by saying, "But Sir, my poor were hungry yesterday, they are hungry again today, and tomorrow they will be hungry too."

Another time, a cross old man struck her in reply to her request. Gently she replied, "Thank you; that was for me. Now please give me something for my poor."

Jeanne did not beg for money alone. She asked also for leftover food, clothes and other items needed to care for the elderly. Practical considerations prevented the elderly women from assisting in the begging. Had they gone out, they would have been subjected to many dangers on the streets—especially those with a temptation to alcohol. Instead, the residents sometimes did a little spinning or weaving to help out.

Jeanne was always ready to accept another person. She trusted in God and did her part diligently, and there was always enough. She even refused to accept any kind of regular income, believing that to do so would be to lose the right to receive charity. She wanted the sisters to depend on God daily. Her old people were happy and well cared for, and their number kept increasing.

Once Jeanne asked an officer of the Angers garrison to loan her some of his band members to entertain the old folks. The officer sent over the entire band.

On another occasion butter was in short supply and the old people were eating dry bread. Jeanne exclaimed, "But this is the land of butter!" and straightaway asked St. Joseph to provide them with butter, rounding up all the empty butter dishes and placing them before his statue. A few days later a donor showed up with a very large shipment of butter. To this day the Little Sisters of the Poor depend on St. Joseph with the same technique—and the same results.

But Jeanne was not solicitous only for bodies; it is said that "she *groaned* over the loss of souls—especially the souls of the aged." Later on, she would very often say to the novices and postulants, "Knock, knock at Heaven's gate for souls!" She would ask them to pray that a certain person or other would be converted. She had a special solicitude for "prisoners and those under sentence of death." Passing on some information regarding herbal drinks to a postulant, she said, "The aged are grateful for small attentions, and these are a way of winning them for God."

In 1842 Jeanne and her companions formed a religious association. They took vows and Jeanne was elected superior. The women adopted religious names for themselves. Jeanne's name was Mary of the Cross, but people continued to call her by her given name. In fact, her name became well-known throughout the region.

Later on a parish priest, Fr. Le Pailleur, on his own authority, made one of the other sisters, Marie Jamet, superior in place of Jeanne. Jeanne accepted this without complaint, though doubtless with suffering and misgivings. Fr. Le Pailleur probably felt that he could more easily control the young Marie Jamet, who was his penitent, and he had his own ideas of directing the group, which was by now well known.

In 1845 Jeanne was awarded the Montyon Prize by the French Academy. This award was made to "reward a poor French man or woman for outstanding meritorious activity." Jeanne applied the cash award toward the support of her apostolate. She was also honored with a gold medal presented by the Freemasons. Jeanne had the medal melted down and made into the cup of a chalice for use at Mass.

In 1846 Jeanne established a second home, in Rennes. There she and two of her companions once had to give up their own beds in order to accept three new invalids. Later, when asked where they had slept, she replied, "On the floor." When asked if this had not been hard, she answered, "We never noticed." Soon a third house was opened, at Dinan, in a former prison built into the city wall.

By the summer of 1851 there were over 100 sisters in the congregation, and 10 houses had been established for the aged poor. By the end of the same year there were 15 houses and 300 sisters. At this time, the sisters were caring for about 1,500 elderly and sick poor. Jeanne would travel around to the various houses, getting things done and getting people to donate, yet remaining in the background. The institute was given episcopal approval in 1852, with tentative papal approbation in 1854 and final papal approval in 1879. By then there would be 36 houses and about 4,000 old people. The sisters' rule was based on the spirituality of St. John of God.

In 1852 Fr. Le Pailleur called Jeanne to the motherhouse, at the time in Rennes. Jeanne obeyed without complaint and began her hidden life.

Many of the young sisters who lived with Jeanne in the last years of her life had no knowledge that the serene old sister whom they loved so well was in reality the foundress of their order.

In 1856 a new motherhouse and novitiate was opened at Saint

Pern. Jeanne was sent there with the postulants and novices.

Jeanne always maintained complete discretion about the wrongs that had been done to her. She never complained. She was always in good spirits, smiling and laughing. The young sisters loved her and loved to listen to her words of good advice. She had many deep insights into the spiritual life, insights which she expressed in simple words:

"You must be very little before God. When you pray, begin like this. Imagine yourself a little frog before God." "By the Ave Maria we shall get to Paradise." "Little ones, you must always be cheerful. Our little old folk do not like long faces." She told the sisters not to weary the old people with too many prayers of devotion: "You will weary your old folk; they will get bored and go off for a smoke...even during the Rosary!" Also: "You musn't begrudge your efforts in cooking for them any more than in looking after them when they are ill. Be like a mother to the grateful ones, and also to those who don't know how to be grateful for all the things you do for them. Say in your heart, 'I do it for You, my Jesus!' Look on the poor with compassion, and Jesus will look kindly on you in your last day." Jeanne said, "In all things, everywhere, in all circumstances, I repeat: 'Blessed be God.' "

Jeanne constantly lived in the presence of God. When she could not sleep at night she would unite herself to the Masses being offered in foreign lands. She said that the sisters should love the Holy Father above everyone else and that "All good things come to us from the Church."

Jeanne felt that her apostolate was a special gift from God. She would say enthusiastically, "We are blessed to be a *little sister of the poor!* Making the poor happy is everything...never causing suffering to anyone old and poor. We must *spoil* them all we can." For Jeanne, the aged were "God's mouthpiece."

She insisted on prayer for benefactors: "You are to say the Rosary for our benefactors. How grateful we ought to be for them. What could we do for our dear old people without them? We must pray, and pray hard!"

On rainy days Jeanne would look after the two postulants sent to the post office, saying to them, "Look, little ones, you must...not catch cold through your own fault, for your health is not your own. It belongs to God, who wants to employ you with the poor."

Telling the sisters to make a habit of turning to Our Lord in confidence, she said, "Go and find Jesus when your patience and strength give out and you feel alone and helpless. He is waiting for you in the chapel. Say to Him, 'Jesus, You know exactly what is going on. You are all I have, and You know all. Come to my help.' And then go, and don't worry about how you are going to manage. That you have told God about it is enough. He has a good memory." Words of counsel such as these endeared Jeanne to all who knew her. They also explain her own virtue, as she followed her own advice very well.

Often, pointing to a beautiful flower, she would say to a young sister, "Do you know who made that?" The sister would reply, "God." Jeanne would then look her in the eye and say with intense gratitude, "Our Bridegroom did!"

In her old age Jeanne suffered from an ulcerated leg. She used a walking stick to walk slowly and painfully to the loft of the chapel, where she would pray for hours before the Blessed Sacrament. She would often say, "How I long to die!" When someone would reply, "You mustn't die," Jeanne would say, "Yes, yes, I want to; I want to go and see God."

In 1879 Jeanne was 87. She was very thin and partially blind. Her eyelids were half-closed due to deterioration of the nerves, but she continued to reflect cheerfulness and love. At this time the community she had founded had 2,400 Little Sisters and had spread across Europe and across the Ocean. In the summer she became so weak that she was forced to remain in bed. Toward the end of August, she was given the Last Sacraments. Her last words were, "O Mary, my dear Mother, come to me. You know I love you and how I long to see you!"

After her peaceful death, Jeanne was buried in the graveyard at the motherhouse. Nothing at the site indicated her part in the history of the Little Sisters.

The truth concerning the beginnings of the Little Sisters of the Poor had been hidden for many years. During her life Jeanne herself would not claim the honor nor the title of foundress. She knew very well that it was not her own work, but God's; and if others wished to claim it for themselves, that was simply their own foolishness.

Gradually the truth prevailed and was brought to light. Further investigations were made into her life and virtues.

Jeanne Jugan was beatified in Rome on October 3, 1982.

Above: This is the only known photograph of Bl. Jeanne Jugan; it was taken when she was around 80 years old. At age 45 Jeanne began caring for homeless elderly people in her own home, which work soon grew into the Little Sisters of the Poor.

Following page: The beatification portrait of Bl. Jeanne Jugan, showing her with her "collecting" basket over her arm. Putting aside personal pride, the Little Sisters daily went out door to door asking for food, clothing and money. Jeanne dearly loved the old folks; she would exclaim, "We are blessed to be a *little sister of the poor!* Making the poor happy is everything. . . never causing suffering to anyone old and poor. We must *spoil* them all we can." (*Painting by Dina Bellotti.*)

174

19

SAINT MARY JOSEPH ROSSELLO

Geronima Benedetta Rossello
1811 - 1880
Italy
Died Age 69

As the sisters gathered around the bed of the dying foundress of the Daughters of Our Lady of Mercy, a child's broken weeping came from the corner of the room by the door. A little black girl stood there, crying for the friend who had been her mother and protectress. No one had the heart to send her away.

The little girl represented only one of the many acts of charity of St. Mary Joseph Rossello. Like many others, the child had been stolen from her real mother in Africa by slave traders—and then ransomed by the priest Don Verri.

This kindly priest often ransomed slave children who had been kidnapped from their homes in Africa. After he managed to raise the money to buy the children's freedom, he would travel about finding suitable homes for them. Many of the children had been brutalized and ill-treated by the Moslems and were frightened and in poor health by the time Don Verri managed to get them to Italy. He always left those who were in the worst condition with Mother Rossello.

Mother Rossello never regretted any of the work or money involved in assisting the rescue operation. Her only sadness was when one or another of the little slave children died, due to the fact that they had been sick, ill-treated and starved for so long that even the best of care could not save them. With a characteristic trust in Providence, however, she told her sisters that these little Negro children brought twin blessings to the House: Those who lived were a witness to Divine Providence; those who died, having been baptized, became heavenly protectors for the Order.

Known as Benedetta in her childhood, Mother Rossello had been born near Savona, Italy on May 27, 1811, the fourth of nine chil-

dren of Bartolomeo and Maria Rossello. The Rossellos were poor
pottery workers. Benedetta's parents gave their children as good an
education as possible, considering their means. The religious training came from the home, and the parents taught as much by example
as by words.

As soon as she was old enough, Benedetta, like all the Rossello
children, helped with the pottery making. She was known as a lively,
active youngster, but even at an early age she also showed a natural
inclination to be deeply spiritual.

At the local school, Benedetta earned a reputation for being a
bright child who did well in math and who could read and write
well. Stories from the Bible fascinated her, and after hearing them
in school, she went home and read them again. The pastor loaned
her a book of saints, and she was often seen retelling the stories
to her friends. Later, she told her parish priest that she wanted
to become a hermit in the desert, to pray and do penance—and
yet she also wanted to become a missionary to teach the pagan
children about God.

Benedetta often went with a group of her friends to visit the
shrine of Our Lady of Mercy at Savona, about two miles from
her home. Sometimes, a little lame girl named Pauline went with
them. Pauline would not have gone at all if it had not been for
Benedetta, who held her hand as they walked and lagged behind
when Pauline tired. Although Pauline was a spirited girl, two miles
is a long way for someone who has to limp. Sometimes, when
Pauline seemed too tired to walk further, Benedetta would pick
her up in her strong arms and carry her part of the way.

At 19, Benedetta was a healthy and charming girl. On one occasion, her cousin approached her on behalf of a young man who
wished to marry her. Benedetta told her she felt that her future
belonged entirely to God. Then, puzzled, she said that she was
not certain how she knew that, nor what shape her life would take,
but that she definitely did not want to marry.

Money at the Rossello home was never abundant, so to help out,
Benedetta took a job as a companion to a sick man and his wife,
the Monteleones. The couple had no children and became very
attached to Benedetta.

At the age of 16 Benedetta had become a member of the Third
Order of St. Francis; she tried to keep the Rule faithfully. In her
job as companion, she was allowed plenty of time for Mass, visits

to the Tabernacle and other religious practices. She also spent a great deal of time reading to her sick employer, and the books most often chosen were lives of the Saints. Benedetta particularly liked the common laborer saints. When Signor Monteleone teased her about already being on the road to sanctity, Benedetta laughed and said, "No, Signor, I am no saint material. I am just sinner material." Recalling the experience of St. Isidore the Farmer, he told her, "Don't laugh, just remember someday how I said that in the future the angels might come to help you with your own work in the fields!"

Benedetta stayed with the Monteleones for nine years, and then told them that she wanted to leave in order to enter a convent. They offered to adopt her and leave her their great wealth upon their death, but she declined.

Benedetta felt she had a religious vocation, and she applied at several convents, but everywhere she was turned down because she had no dowry. She made up her mind that should she herself ever found a religious order, she would require only the dowry of a heart that loved God and wished to serve Him.

By 1834, when she was 23, both her parents had died and there was no one left in her family who needed her. A short time later, her kind employer and benefactor also died. Benedetta stayed on with Signora Monteleone, however, until she overcame her grief at the loss of her husband.

During this time it happened that the Bishop of Savona was very sad. On his long walks through the city he noticed many homeless girls growing up with no religion and no education. He wished there were a group of sisters to help him provide a home and loving training for these girls.

When Benedetta heard of the Bishop's concern, she timidly went to him and told him that she had always wanted to do works of mercy such as this and that she was ready to help in any way. After reflecting, he told her that perhaps she was the one whom God had sent to assist him in this work, and he asked that she attempt to find some companions to work with her.

The parting from her friend and helper was a bitter one for Signora Monteleone, who had never believed that Benedetta would carry through with her idea of becoming a religious. When Benedetta left she told the old woman that she would always keep her in her prayers.

Benedetta then went to her hometown and found three childhood friends who were willing to band together with her in the work that the Bishop wanted started. The small group set up in a poor rented house and began by doing sewing and embroidery to get some independent funds for their work. They chose the name Daughters of Our Lady of Mercy, a name often abbreviated as the Daughters of Mercy. On October 22, 1837 the four were given a habit and a simple rule, and each took a new name. Because of her great devotion to the foster-father of Our Lord, Benedetta chose the name of Joseph; thus her full religious name was Sister Mary Joseph, though she was commonly called Sister Joseph—in Italian, Sister Josepha. Sister Joseph became the first novice mistress, and Sister Augustine became the tiny group's first superior.

Within eight days after the Bishop had blessed their house, they had already begun four projects. In order to secure funds for immediate needs, they opened a small day and boarding school for girls who could afford to pay tuition. They also opened a free day and boarding school for the poor. They made uniforms for the girls in this free school, as the girls who came to them were usually in rags when they arrived. A fifth project was the teaching of catechism classes in the city.

On August 2, 1839 the Daughters of Mercy took perpetual vows. Then the Institute began to grow, attained legal status, and soon spread to other cities. Sister Joseph's own sister became a postulant. In the elections for permanent positions, Sister Joseph was elected superior, a position she was to hold for the rest of her life. Later the congregation took on other responsibilities, such as the care of a leprosarium and the raising of ransomed Negro girls.

Mother Joseph talked often with the sisters, instructing them on how to treat the children. Some of the girls were difficult to handle when they first came. She said, "They have been unhappy. We must make them happy. We must be angels toward them." With her loving patience, the girls grew healthy and strong, secure in the love of God and happy in the home of Providence.

In 1859, a dream came true for Mother Joseph. She began a House of Providence in Savona where she could insure the safe future of many homeless girls too young to make a living for themselves. Some of the girls were brought there by kindhearted members of the laity; some were sent by judges. Each girl who came had her own story of degradation, poverty or cruel treatment.

At first, these girls went to Mass in two groups. Those who had shoes could walk to a church more distant; those who were barefoot went to the closer church of the Capuchins. Mother Joseph herself begged from friends and shopkeepers to make certain that all the girls were properly provided with enough clothing by winter.

At the House of Providence, funds were always short, though Mother Joseph trusted implicitly in her patron, St. Joseph, to provide. She said, "To St. Joseph, all children are images of the Child he reared."

One day, she found that there was no food at the Providence, and no money to buy any. At her suggestion, everyone in the house went into the chapel to pray. After a while, Mother Joseph sent one of the sisters to see if anything had been put into the almsbox while they had been praying. The sister returned with two small coins and two buttons.

Mother Joseph took one look and said, "We have prayed too briefly, or too poorly—we must pray more." After an hour, the sister went to check again, and there in the box she found the necessary money.

In 1869 Mother Joseph did something which, for a woman, was quite startling: she founded a seminary. This seminary accepted only boys who were too poor to carry out their vocation. In spite of a good deal of opposition, the seminary won the approval of the Bishop and thrived.

Mother Joseph urged her sisters always to practice patience, love and kindness to everyone. She said, "The world never leaves you in peace; that you must learn to accept as a fact. But you must have patience."

During the last years of her life Mother Joseph suffered from spiritual aridity. Along with the ills of her body, she suffered from doubts and a turbulent spirit. A prolonged illness began to take its toll on her, and by the spring of 1880 Mother Joseph had so little strength left that she spent nearly all her time in bed. She began to feel totally useless, and she cried to the sisters that her sins made her fear the final judgment. To no avail the sisters reminded her of her good work in the past. She was inconsolable. In desperation, the sisters asked a priest to come and talk with her in hopes he might bring her out of the darkness she was living in. When the sisters asked if he had been able to put Mother Joseph's fears to rest, he sadly replied, "Let us adore the plans of God." Yet,

Mother Joseph never stopped praying and receiving frequent Communion. At last, with the help of her friend Father Filomeno, a Capuchin priest, she came out of this dark night of her soul. In gratitude she told him, "Oh, the wonderful Providence of God, and how good that He made you His messenger."

During Mother Joseph's final illness, the infirmarian often heard her talking; she wondered if her patient's mind was wandering. One day she came into the room quietly and realized that Mother Joseph was praying to her beloved St. Joseph in familiar tones. "My sweet saint, keep my daughters under your protection. Be with the Institute always. Protect my little children."

On December 6, during a faint, Mother Joseph was given Extreme Unction. The next morning, a priest was praying beside her and suggesting short prayers for her to repeat. With a look of calm resignation on her face, she told him, "It is enough." It was obvious that she was at peace. She spoke only once again, that evening. Her last faint words were quite clear: "Lord, into Thy hands I commend my spirit." It was December 7.

At the time of Mother Joseph's death, the Daughters of Mercy had some 67 hospitals, schools and homes for wayward girls.

In 1913, the informative process in her cause was begun by the diocesan authorities of Savona. Her original burial place was in the town cemetery, but in 1917 the sisters received permission to transfer the body to the grounds of the motherhouse. When they exhumed the body, it was found to be entirely incorrupt. At the ritual exhumation before beatification, the body was again exhumed and was again found to be incorrupt.

A dispute arose regarding the final resting place of the beata. There was a new motherhouse, and those in charge wanted the body kept there. At the old motherhouse, however, the aged and infirm sisters begged that they at least be given a major relic. In accord with the suggestion of an old priest it was decided that a doctor would remove the heart, which was to be taken to the old motherhouse, the cradle of the Congregation.

When the delicate operation was completed, the heart, too, was found to be incorrupt. What is more—to the amazement of all who were observing, the heart of this woman who had been dead for 58 years still bled! It was immediately placed in a receptacle containing a fluid; this solution was changed several times, yet it still became reddened with blood. This precious relic of their foundress was greatly treasured by the elderly sisters.

St. Mary Joseph Rossello was canonized by Pope Pius XII on June 12, 1949.

The incorrupt body of St. Mary Joseph Rossello, who founded the Daughters of Our Lady of Mercy to care for homeless girls. At an exhumation 58 years after her death, witnesses noted that her heart was incorrupt and still gave off blood.

Mother Joseph Rossello with some of the little black girls she took in after a good priest ransomed them from the Moslem slave traders who had kidnapped them from their homes in Africa. Mother Joseph trusted implicitly in St. Joseph to provide the necessities of life for her children; she said, "To St. Joseph, all children are images of the Child he reared."

The girls whom Mother Joseph took in had their own individual stories of poverty, degradation or cruel treatment. Some were sent to her by judges. Some were difficult to handle. Mother Joseph said, "They have been unhappy. We must make them happy. We must be angels toward them."

Mother Joseph's last years were marked by illness and by spiritual aridity, feelings of uselessness and fear of the Final Judgment. Eventually, with the help of a good Capuchin priest, she emerged from these purifying trials. When she died at age 69 her last words were, "Lord, into Thy hands I commend my spirit."

20

BLESSED PAULINE VON MALLINCKRODT

Maria Bernardine Sophia Pauline von Mallinckrodt
1817 - 1881
Prussia - Germany
Died Age 64

Mother Pauline von Mallinckrodt was full of kindness for beggars and often brought them into the convent for a good meal and an alms. To control Mother Pauline's generosity, a daily amount per beggar had been set. When some of the other sisters were displeased that certain ones were coming twice in the same day, Mother Pauline's reply was, "Never mind. Give it to them if they ask it. And don't forget this—the giving of alms never made anyone poorer." She chided Sister Elizabeth, who was worried about having enough supplies to give to the poor, saying, "You are not up to the faith of your patron saint, child. Perhaps if you were you would receive much more for your poor."

Happiness and gratitude to God were hallmarks of the life of Mother Pauline von Mallinckrodt. Wealthy, well-educated and a member of the nobility, this attractive young woman felt impelled by the love of God to dedicate her life and her fortune to the service of the poor and the blind. Despite her many trials, Mother Pauline saw in each facet of her life something to be grateful to God for. She once remarked, "I can scarcely comprehend God's unspeakable goodness to me."

The daughter of a Lutheran father and a staunchly Catholic mother, Pauline was born on June 3, 1817 at Minden, Westphalia. She was the eldest of four children. Her parents' love for each other was so great that it transcended many conflicts over religion, normal in a mixed marriage. In addition, there was a law in Prussia that children were to follow the religion of their father. Being a government official, Pauline's father could have lost his appointment because of his disobedience to this law. Pauline's brothers were baptized in the Lutheran faith, but Mr. von Mallinckrodt allowed his wife to bring up all her children according to Catholic morals and principles.

Pauline began school at a private Catholic elementary school. Once she was tardy for several days in a row. The headmistress determined to find the cause, as Pauline would say nothing in her own defense. Finally, the headmistress noticed that Pauline's school-bag was bulging. On inspection the bag was found to be full of pieces of glass, which Pauline admitted she had picked up in the street on the way to school. Her explanation? "I don't want poor children who have no shoes to be hurt."

For such a young child, from a wealthy home, to have noticed and attempted to do something about this problem is an indication of her lifelong desire to serve the poor and the suffering. By this incident, however, she also learned a valuable lesson—that very often one's impulses to do good must be subjected to a higher law, called "duty."

Later, Pauline attended an academy in Aix-la-Chapelle, where she was influenced by the exceptional teacher Miss Luise Hensel, a friend of the mystic Anne Catherine Emmerich. There Pauline assisted in many student projects to assist the needy.

The social life enjoyed by Pauline's family was an active one, and Pauline took many trips to various countries in Europe. She attended a boarding school in Liege, Belgium for a time, where she was active in drama and dancing groups. She made her debut in 1833.

In June of 1834 Pauline's mother died after a brief illness. The 17-year-old girl was faced with the care of her young sister, who was just about to enter primary school, and of her two teenage brothers, as well as the responsibility for the household. She had servants to help her, but she was in charge of their direction. Pauline resolved to make the home as happy and well-run as it had been when her mother was alive. Also, she followed her mother's example of being a home nurse and took some training in nursing skills.

Although more than one suitor called on Pauline, she found only one of them difficult to refuse. She was extremely fond of him, but she decided not to marry him because he was not a Catholic. After the difficult act of informing him of her decision, Pauline felt a great peace; she found herself drawn to a religious vocation. "In refusing him, I had likewise severed the bond which attached me to the world. The Lord was pleased to reward the sacrifice with a peace of soul such as I had never known. I detached myself more and more from all that surrounded me, and my soul found complete satisfaction in God."

About this time, in company with a group of former classmates, Pauline began a life of charity and service to the poor of Aix-la-Chapelle, in addition to her duties at home. Pauline was primarily drawn to the old and the ill, often assisting during the night at the deathbed of one of her beloved poor and making arrangements for a decent funeral. In addition, she often brought orphans or neglected children to the hospital for a bath or a good meal.

Often, as her duty as the official hostess for her father demanded, Pauline attended or gave parties or dances. But no matter how late these lasted, she could be seen early the next morning attending daily Mass. When Pauline was 20, her confessor allowed her the rare privilege of receiving Holy Communion daily. She later told her spiritual director, "...I was living in the excitement of a noisy world, yet I knew that though I was engaged in friendly intercourse with others, my heart had to be reserved for Jesus, whom I would invite into my soul in the morning." Regarding Holy Communion, Pauline wrote to a friend, "This is indispensable to my happiness. To it I owe the grace of persevering in my faith even in the turmoil of the world. It is not, as some suggest, that I seek consolation there. No, I seek the Lord Himself..."

In the ballroom or the sickroom, at home or on the street, Pauline was always noted for her cheerfulness and her kindness. She was also known as one who made excuses for others' faults.

Even after his retirement, Pauline's father enjoyed entertaining. Pauline once wrote her former teacher, Miss Hensel, that the distraction resulting from this caused her to have little time to spend with the poor she loved. She added, "Of course, I know that God is served and glorified in any way, provided one acts out of pure love of Him."

Early each morning Pauline walked or rode to church for Mass. Often, on leaving the church, she would feel the tug of a little hand on her sleeve. One of her beloved poor children would be standing there with a request for her to visit a sick friend or relative. For this reason Pauline carried her little basket of home remedies to Mass with her each day.

Because many of the chronically sick poor could not be treated in the local hospital, Pauline worked with a non-denominational group of ladies to visit, nurse and feed the sick poor in their homes. One time, when leaving after a visit to several blind children, Pauline's tender heart was torn and there were tears in her eyes as she burst out to her companion, "They need me most of all, the little blind ones! Oh, Anna, if I could only take care of every neglected blind child in the city!"

Pauline's special concern began to focus on the small children of poor sick mothers—neglected children who had no supervised place to go to during the day. She established a nursery school similar to today's child-care centers. With tireless energy and personal charm, she raised funds for this project. The bishop allowed Pauline to use part of an almost empty Capuchin cloister, but the three elderly brothers there did not appreciate the children's noise. One brother became angry and even threw a stone at Pauline when the children ran over his celery bed. Pauline responded by sending the brothers tea and white bread each evening—which went a long way toward establishing harmony.

In 1842 Pauline's father died. All the von Mallinckrodt children began to live their own lives, apart from the former close family group. Pauline began to devote more and more of her time to the nursery school and the care of the sick. Feeling that she had a vocation to the religious life, she began to study which order she should enter.

One day Dr. Hermann Schmidt, the husband of a former classmate of Pauline's, found several blind children while on a tour in the country. He brought them to Pauline, asking, "May I entrust them to your care?" Pauline found a place for them, and soon other blind children were brought to her to be cared for and taught. Pauline learned the proper methods of teaching the blind at one of the civil institutes for the blind; she stayed up late molding letters and figures to aid in their instruction.

More and more blind children came, since Pauline could not turn away anyone who asked. She even resolved not to join any religious order that would not also accept her blind children. One New Year's Pauline planned a party at which the blind children at her school in Paderborn played host, entertaining the guests with music and dancing. One guest exclaimed, "I think that no children in the country are so happy as the blind children of Paderborn!" This happiness and good cheer would later become a point of

Pauline's rule for her sisters: To give to the blind, and all the ones entrusted to our care, a happy heart.

Once Pauline found a 23-year-old retarded girl named Margretchen in one of the worst slums of the city; her mother had kept her hidden for years. In addition to her other handicaps, the girl was half blind. In spite of warnings from all who knew of the situation, Pauline took her home, cleaned off the filth and vermin, and began lovingly to instruct her. Margretchen was obstinate and untaught and would respond to nobody but Pauline; she called Pauline *Die Gute,* "The Good One." Regarding this girl, Pauline asked, "Should an individual be regarded as a total imbecile because she has never been taught, or even been in contact with human kindness? [She] too has a soul, and I trust that grace can operate powerfully even in the soul of one who is retarded." Margretchen made her First Communion around age 29 and was to live at the school for 54 years.

Realizing that she needed more help, Pauline asked a former classmate, a young woman who had begun the Sisters of the Poor Child Jesus, to send her some sisters to staff her schools. But the classmate, Mother Clara, replied that her own order was too new and small for this; she counselled Pauline to ask the Auxiliary Bishop of Cologne for his advice. The Bishop told Pauline that he believed she should form her own order. He advised her, "Just go ahead calmly and discreetly, but with determination." With quiet, calm, discreet determination, Pauline von Mallinckrodt was to establish a new religious institute known as the Sisters of Christian Charity.

Pauline and three other young women received their habit in 1849. After the ceremony, Pauline's brothers and sisters were surveying the new habit. Her brother Hermann felt it needed something, and he playfully touched his cane to the white coif, bending it down. He said, "There it is; now our Pauline has a heart about her face." The other sisters approved the heart-shaped modification, and it was adopted as part of the habit of the Sisters of Christian Charity.

The following year, on the day of her profession, Pauline wrote in her diary, "You, my Beloved, shall be the one goal of my soul. With delight I toss away all I have accumulated in life's journey and instead I shall set forth to find in poverty and chastity and obedience the pearl of eternal life." Pauline was to lead and guide the new congregation as its superior until her death in 1881.

Pauline had once hesitated to enter the religious life for fear she would have to give up the privilege of daily Holy Communion.

She was allowed to receive daily in the convent, and Jesus in Holy Communion continued to be a daily necessity of her soul. In each new house she was to establish, her first concern was to have an oratory with the Blessed Sacrament reserved. Pauline said, "I am willing and ready to build house after house, and at no matter how great sacrifice, if only such a guest as Jesus deigns to take His abode there." She also said, "This Sacrament of Life is the life source of my congregation."

Mother Pauline's kindness to the poor was without reserve. One time when a half-blind beggar woman and ragged dirty little girl—her head crawling with vermin—came to the door, Mother Pauline spied them from the garden. She brought them in and gave them a good meal, then getting a pail of water and soap she proceeded to wash the little girl. Cutting off much of her matted hair, she carefully cleaned the child's scalp of blood and dirt and then gave her clean clothes. This mother and child came back a few more times and Mother Pauline never hesitated to attend to the little girl with the same care and motherly kindness.

When a former pupil broke into the house at one of the foundations, Mother Pauline heard out the whole story, then said to the sisters, "Poor lad, don't scold him so much. Think what a good thing it is that it was to us he came. Now we must help him. I'll see what I can do." The sisters learned later that the boy had returned to an honest life.

Complete trust in the Will and Providence of God carried Mother Pauline through the many ups and downs of the formation, growth and expansion of a new religious order in times of political upheaval. Her competent direction carried the sisters through war, lawsuits, deaths of loved ones and struggles with the government.

The Prussian government under Prime Minister Bismark was attempting to stamp out the Catholic Church. Convents were being closed and Catholic sisters were being prohibited from teaching. At this time the Sisters of Christian Charity were in charge of 15 public schools, nine private high schools, four orphanages with schools, day nurseries, boarding schools, the blind institute and a hospital. The sisters could have continued teaching if they had laid aside their habits and assumed secular dress, but Mother Pauline refused to consider this possibility. She replied to the government, "Nothing in this world will make my sisters faithless to their vows, and so I could not accept your offer at such a price." Finally, in

January of 1877, the decree of dissolution banning all teaching orders was announced, and thus the sisters were forced to leave the land of their founding. As the sisters were expelled, Mother Pauline had to find new places for them in other countries.

Over the succeeding years Mother Pauline was to accompany many groups of sisters to the wharf to see them off as they began missionary journeys westward to the Americas. By 1879 she had made foundations in North and South America and sent 150 sisters to labor there. During this year she herself paid a visit to the United States to check on the welfare of her sisters and plan for the future. One of her constant words of advice to her sisters was, "Become saints, my dear sisters." After attending a crowded and beautifully celebrated High Mass with 30 acolytes at the cathedral in Philadelphia, Mother Pauline commented, "And our little Bismark in his pretensions and his pride wants to destroy the Catholic Church! Let him come to America and see that what he suppresses in one country is blossoming and prospering in another." Seven years later Mother Pauline made a second trip to the United States.

Mother Pauline hated to be photographed, but her sisters found a way to get around her. For the 25th anniversary of the founding of the congregation they got the Bishop to order her to have her picture taken. She had to comply. When copies were sent around to the various houses, Mother Pauline accompanied them all with a form letter which said, "I cannot conceal the fact that I hold Sister Anna and Sister Augustine in suspicion as the instigators of this command." Then she added, "Since it is impossible for me to be in your midst personally on this day...I come to you at least in photograph."

On April 25, 1881 Mother Pauline became ill with pneumonia. By April 28 her condition had become critical. Despite that, she managed to attend to several important matters concerning the congregation. Her last official act was one of utter selflessness. She had reserved a sum of money from her personal fortune to be used for stipends for Masses to be said for the repose of her soul. But knowing the sisters had been worried about some money that they owed, she directed in her will that even this money be used to pay debts. On that same day she sent out her last, affectionate farewells. Six hours later she breathed her last.

The funeral procession of Mother Pauline von Mallinckrodt was led by some of the blind children she had so loved and cared for.

A priest friend, in writing to her temporary successor, aptly summed up the life of this generous soul: "Reverend Mother has fought a good fight; it was the combat of love, with love, for love."

Pauline von Mallinckrodt was beatified by Pope John Paul II on April 14, 1985.

Bl. Pauline von Mallinckrodt, who founded the Sisters of Christian Charity, sisters who cared for and educated blind children and poor children in schools, day nurseries, orphanages, boarding schools and a hospital. A point of Mother Pauline's rule for her sisters was this: To give to the blind, and all the ones entrusted to our care, a happy heart. Mother Pauline sought out and cared for neglected children with a true motherly heart, not hesitating to bathe them and clean off accumulated filth and vermin, all the while showing great love and kindness.

21

SAINT PAULA FRASSINETTI

Paula Angela Maria Frassinetti
1809 - 1882
Italy
Died Age 73

An angry mob surrounded the convent, shouting, "Death to the Dorotheans!" Between the years 1850 and 1859, the revolutionary spirit prevailed in Italy, with widespread political unrest. Religious orders were suppressed, and many religious and clerics were ordered to resume secular dress and leave their convents, schools and seminaries. Riots and mob violence were common.

Law and order were non-existent in Rome. When the fighting broke out there, the motherhouse of the Sisters of Saint Dorothy was caught between two fires. The streets were swept with bullets, and for days the nuns prayed and worked while shells passed over their convent and bullets spattered on the walls.

Inside the convent walls the courage, peace and obvious calm of the Superior of the Order, Mother Paula Frassinetti, was a constant reminder to the other sisters to have confidence in God. Like the patroness of the order, St. Dorothy, Mother Paula feared no man, believing that God would protect His own.

A friendly captain came secretly to the convent to inform Mother Paula that he had received orders to set fire to the convent before withdrawing his soldiers. Although he had argued against doing this, he feared that he would be obliged to carry out the command. In order to insure the sisters' safety should he be forced to burn the convent, he promised to send an ambulance down the street in front of the convent at full speed before the torches were lit. That would be the signal to escape immediately.

Without telling anyone of the burden weighing on her mind, Mother Paula waited and prayed. When the community retired for the night, Mother Paula, rosary in hand, began her long vigil. All through the night she wandered alone about the house, stopping frequently to peer from the windows on each side of the house. As the sky began to brighten with the freshness of dawn, Mother Paula's prayers changed from acts of supplication to acts of gratitude. The soldiers had withdrawn and the motherhouse was safe.

The future foundress of the Sisters of St. Dorothy was born on March 3, 1809 in Genoa, Italy. Although her parents were not poor, they were not wealthy either, except in the love of God. All the children of John and Angela Frassinetti were taught early that the only thing worth striving for in life was to please God. Of the five children, all four of the boys became priests; Paula (Paola in Italian), the only daughter, would become a religious. The children learned of the love of God from the example of the parents in their daily practice of faith and charity.

Paula, the middle of the five children, was a little queen, much adored by her four brothers. The older boys teased and played with her, and the younger ones constantly requested her help.

Paula was very close to her mother, from whom she learned sewing, knitting and all the fine arts of housekeeping. The first great grief in Paula's life was the death of her mother when she was nine years old. From this time, Paula considered Our Lady as the replacement for her earthly mother, and throughout her life she went to Mary with all her trials and troubles, as well as with her joys.

Paula's aunt came to live with the family to care for the children. Within three years, however, she too died, leaving Paula, at 12, the "little mother" of the family. Although she was shy and quiet by nature, Paula managed the home with an efficiency which astonished everyone.

Paula never attended a regular school, nor was the family able to afford a private tutor. The political situation in her part of Italy was not favorable to religion, so her father and her brothers served as teachers. She was a good pupil, with good intellectual abilities, and she soon surpassed in achievements those who attended the regular schools.

Paula kept house for her father and brothers for seven years. After attending daily Mass, she would return to her household chores. Here the first stirrings of a religious vocation began to make themselves felt in the soul of this quiet young woman, but she realized that she was still needed at home. She maintained recollection of soul as she worked, and interior prayer became a part of her life.

When Paula was about 20, she became seriously ill with a cough that seemed to portend an incurable disease, possibly tuberculosis. Her brother, who had already been ordained, was the pastor in Quinto, a small village in the beautiful countryside on the west coast of Genoa. It was felt that the bracing air and healthful country life might help Paula toward a recovery; although the parting caused the family much sorrow, a lengthy visit was arranged. After a few months, Paula's health was completely recovered.

In the months that she had been with her brother, Paula had begun performing a number of works of charity among the parishioners. When her father realized how much good she was doing, he agreed to allow her to remain in Quinto indefinitely.

On hearing this glad news, Paula's brother began a school for the poor girls of his parish, placing it under Paula's direction. Paula, for her part, was glad that she now had a chance to help the poor so loved by Our Lord.

Paula taught the girls all the traditional school subjects and household arts, and most of all she gave them religious instruction. More than just a teacher, Paula became the moral trainer for all the girls in her school. Her gentle nature and motherly love radiated joy to all who were near her. She was helpful and encouraging to her students, and she taught them the best form of discipline—self-discipline.

Paula's favorite theory of education was that children must love and be loved. She claimed that love would form students as nothing else could, drawing out the best in them and lifting them to God.

One time, a very spoiled and self-willed student in Paula's school created a "scene." Paula heard of the incident just as she was starting out on a short trip; she called the girl to accompany her. This girl knew that she deserved a good scolding and imagined that it would be given to her on the way. What was her surprise when Paula spoke only of God's goodness and of spiritual things! Not a word was said about her previous behavior. By the time their destination was reached, the girl's rebelliousness had given way to real penitence.

Paula loved the children because they were God's. Her aim was to foster noble-minded women whose strong faith would enable them to overcome any problems they would face.

Paula's first followers in the congregation she would found came when she was helping her brother in his parish. After Benediction on Sunday afternoons, Paula and a group of young women began taking walks in the woods near the church. When Paula spoke of the love of God, her face would light up and she would seem almost forgetful of those with her. As they listened, her companions began to realize the beauty of a life spent entirely for God. Inflamed by Paula's words, the young women began to long for a life of service of Our Lord and began to talk about a rule and vows.

Soon Paula felt that it was God's Will for a group of these young women to band together for the education of girls, as well as for their own personal sanctification. There were already a number of orders of cloistered nuns in Genoa where those with a vocation might apply, but Paula wanted a congregation which would mix an active apostolate with the contemplative form of prayer to which she was so drawn. Additionally, many of these first followers of Paula were poor girls who could not afford the dowry required to join the established orders.

Paula spoke of her idea to her brother, who spoke with other, more experienced priests. She received encouragement for her aspirations, and eventually founded the Congregation of the Sisters of St. Dorothy, also called the Dorotheans. Their apostolate was to be the education of girls. To implore God's blessing on her work, Paula spent whole nights before the Tabernacle and practiced severe penances. Thus the new congregation was begun.

To be certain, there were trials and periods of unrest in the new congregation. Just as with many new institutes in the Church, there were times of internal disagreements, and in the Europe of Paula's day there was also an antireligious political situation to deal with. But through all trials, the faith of the sisters kept them alive and growing. Within her lifetime Paula was to see her order spread to Portugal and then across the ocean to Brazil. No matter what hardships there were, postulants continued arriving to carry on the work begun by this courageous foundress.

As new houses began to spring up in Italy, Paula frequently made surprise visits to her sisters, much to their delight. Once she undertook a perilous trip to bring help and cheer to a convent located in an isolated valley which had experienced heavy rains, causing a nearby river to overflow its banks. Flash floods there had been a constant threat. Back in Genoa, Paula had received unfavorable weather reports about the area. The motherly heart of the Foundress demanded that she go to the sisters. Accompanied by a postulant who was fond of adventure and a cabman from the flooded town who wanted to return home to see if his family was safe,

Paula set out on the dangerous trip.

As the three neared the valley, rushing water at one point covered the wheels of the carriage. The frightened horse stalled, and the driver was in favor of turning back. Paula seemed to sense that it would be as dangerous to return as to push forward. She said, "Let us go on in the name of God. Our Lady will help us!" They started forward, then suddenly heard a dull roar. Looking back, they realized that the riverbank had caved in, carrying the road with it. Had they remained for only minutes longer they would have been washed to their deaths.

When Paula reached her destination the sisters were overjoyed at the arrival of their Mother. Her obvious spirit of faith and peacefulness calmed even the most frightened of the sisters. Soon the heavy rains stopped and the danger was past. The driver refused any payment, and he told others that he was grateful for his life. "That nun I brought from Genoa must be a real saint," he remarked.

In 1835 a dread epidemic of cholera broke out in northern Italy. The Sisters of St. Dorothy were angels of consolation to many who were stricken by this terrible disease. Paula and her sisters would go out and spend the entire day nursing and comforting the sufferers. As mentioned earlier, between 1850 and 1859 the political situation in Italy was antireligious. Yet during those times the good works of the Dorotheans did much to demonstrate the value of religious orders for society as a whole.

In 1886 the Order spread to Brazil and Portugal. In neither country did the sisters have an easy time. Mother Paula said, "I feel that the Congregation is destined to flourish and do an immense amount of good, and the more I see difficulties arising, the stronger grows my belief that this foundation is the Will of God." Slowly but surely, the seed which had taken root produced new little plants, providing a large harvest of souls.

From the founding of her congregation, Paula was a true mother to her sisters. She was never too busy to help, guide or counsel them. Her humility, however, was such that time after time she wished to resign the leadership of the Congregation. Time after time her request for retirement was not granted. For 48 years, Paula directed the Institute. Divine Providence blessed it by increasing its members and blessing its every undertaking with success.

In 1870, war and political strife shook all of Italy. In particular, Paula felt an agony of sympathy for the Holy Father. One of her letters from that period shows her great empathy for the Pope and indicates that she felt it was natural for her own congregation to suffer ill treatment since the entire Church, through the Holy Father, was suffering so much. She wrote, "It would be a torture for me if I were not having my share of troubles. What good times these are for accumulating great spiritual riches. Jesus, who has placed His holy cross on our shoulders, is with us; what is there to fear? Let us press on, following Him along the way to Calvary. We must not let ourselves be crushed, even by the spiritual miseries we see around us. Let us do what little we can to remedy them and then throw ourselves, with all that is ours, into the paternal arms of Divine Providence."

In 1876 a stroke paralyzed the right side of Paula's body. A second stroke in 1879 and a third in 1882 rendered her completely helpless. "God is only taking back what is His; may He be ever blessed," was Paula's response.

During her last illness, Paula was visited by Don Bosco. Already his reputation for miracles had spread throughout Italy, and the sisters were hopeful that his blessing might cure their beloved foundress. In answer to their anxious questions, the great Saint replied, "My children, your mother's crown of merits is completed." His words were prophetic, for shortly afterward Paula contracted pneumonia. After receiving the final Rites of the Church, she gathered her little remaining strength, turned to a picture of Our Lady and murmured, "My Mother! Remember I am your child." At last, on June 11, 1882, Paula went to her reward. After Paula's death, many visitors came to pay their last respects, taking the opportunity to touch their medals and rosaries to her body.

In 1906 Paula's body was exhumed and found to be incorrupt, the joints being as flexible as the joints of a living person. Today her body, still preserved, can be seen and venerated in Rome.

At St. Onofrio, the Dorothean Motherhouse in Rome, the remains of St. Paula Frassinetti rest in a silver and crystal casket, the gift of the sisters and pupils of the Brazilian Province. The casket is situated beneath the tabernacle of the main altar of that chapel where the Saint had prayed so many hours when her health prevented her from doing more active work. Paula had told her sisters, "I never tire of being near Jesus." Today, her remains rest in the shadow of the Blessed Sacrament.

Paula Frassinetti was beatified in 1930 and canonized in 1983.

St. Paula Frassinetti, who founded the Dorotheans for the teaching of girls. The girls were taught traditional school subjects, household arts and, most of all, were given religious instruction. St. Paula's favorite theory of education was that children must love and be loved; she felt that love would form children as nothing else would.

When Italy was rocked by war and political strife in 1870, with much suffering for the Holy Father, St. Paula wrote, "It would be a torture for me if I were not having my share of troubles. What good times these are for accumulating great spiritual riches..." St. Paula's body has been preserved incorrupt.

22

SAINT THERESE COUDERC

Marie-Victoire Couderc
1805 - 1885
France
Died Age 80

Although St. Therese Couderc is recognized today as the foundress of the Religious of the Cenacle, a congregation which made over a dozen new foundations in her lifetime, her own life was remarkably hidden. Therese's vocation seems to have been to plant and nurture the first seed, then retire to the background for most of the remaining 45 years of her life. As others opened house after house, Mother Therese watered the young plants with hidden sacrifices, privations, unjust exile, hard manual labor and, during her last decade of life, terrible mystical sufferings. Yet near the end of her long life Therese affirmed that all her sufferings had been utterly worthwhile: "What does it matter if my bare and cut feet filled my sabots with blood; I would willingly begin my journey again: I have found God so completely."

Marie-Victoire was born on Febuary 1, 1805 in Sablieres, France to Claude and Anne Mary Couderc, hard-working, very religious French country folk. One of two girls in a family of 10 children, Victoire became adept at household management at an early age. Following the example of her mother, she allowed plenty of time for attending Mass and making visits to the Blessed Sacrament. Prayer came naturally, and she prayed as she worked.

From her early teens, Victoire felt the call of a religious vocation, but her father resisted. She was needed at home to help with the work on the family farm.

At a retreat during Lent in 1825 she met Fr. Terme, a priest who lived near the shrine of St. John Francis Regis; Father Terme had founded a group of teaching sisters at Aps. During the retreat they met and held a lengthy discussion which ended with the priest's visit to Victoire's father, asking that Victoire be allowed to become one of his sisters. At the time, Monsieur Couderc refused, but in 1826, after receiving a letter of appeal from Fr. Terme, he relented. In January of 1826, shortly before her 21st birthday, Victoire Couderc left for Aps with her belongings tied in a large kerchief knotted at four corners. Her father had refused to provide any dowry for her entrance.

There was a problem near the shrine of St. Francis Regis which bothered Fr. Terme very much. The inns near the shrine were very crowded, so the innkeepers lodged men and women together indiscriminately in the same rooms. To solve this Fr. Terme built a hostel for women pilgrims and brought Victoire, now Sister Therese, and two other sisters to staff it. He moved the novices from Aps to this community and asked Therese to be their novice mistress. Within a year he needed the superior of the little group in another place, so he appointed Therese, then only 23 years old, as the new superior. She would hold this position for 10 years. As Mother Therese, she was charged with running the hostel during the warmer months, training the novices, arranging for the support of the community and supplying the schools with teachers during the winter months. The sisters were known as the Religious of St. Regis.

The hostel was an instant success. So many women flocked to it that the religious were kept busy day and night answering their needs. The hallways were crowded with mattresses to accommodate the crowds, and the pilgrims were often loud and boisterous. The novices, therefore, had no time to pray or study, and religious life suffered from the noise and the constant activity.

In Mother Therese's eyes this would never do if the sisters were to be religious, and not merely innkeepers. She suggested to Fr. Terme that they accept only those pilgrims who would agree to stay for at least three days and who would enter into some form of religious exercise—either a novena (nine days) or a triduum (three days). The results were startling: silence and prayer reigned.

Fr. Terme was presently to make a momentous discovery; he attended a retreat which was directed according to the Spiritual Exercises of St. Ignatius Loyola. Realizing the wonderful spiritual fruits to be harvested from these Exercises, he soon decided that the sisters should give the Exercises instead of the devotions they had been conducting. This decision was to set the direction for the future of the Congregation.

Unfortunately, Fr. Terme, the co-founder of the Congregation, died early. His loss was a terrible blow. Fr. Terme's thoughts, inspiration and direction had been invaluable to the fledgling community, and several sisters were even tempted to leave when he died. In his will he generously provided a financial foundation for the sisters, enabling them successfully to continue carrying out his plan for them. Nevertheless, his death heralded a long time of suffering for Mother Therese.

Shortly after Fr. Terme's death, the community was divided into two branches; some of the sisters continued their teaching apostolate as the Sisters of St. Regis, while the others were to continue with giving retreats. They would become known as the Society of Our Lady of the Retreat in the Cenacle, or simply the Religious of the Cenacle. This name recalled the time Our Lady spent in the Cenacle awaiting the coming of the Holy Spirit.

A period of time was now devoted to laying the foundations of the interior life and acquiring a good understanding of the Spiritual Exercises of St. Ignatius. In these endeavors various Jesuit priests guided the new Congregation and helped form its spirit in the spirit of St. Ignatius.

In the spring of 1837 Mother Therese made a special consecration of herself to Our Lady. She said to her heavenly Mother, "Accept the offering of all that I am and all that I have....May my love for you and my trust in your powerful protection increase...If you wish me to keep the title of superior it will be only a title, because I give up into your hands today the charge of superior. Whenever I have to perform any act of authority, I will ask your permission, since I have given you all....Obtain for me the grace to act always through supernatural motives, to be animated by the Spirit of Jesus Christ." During her upcoming years of suffering, Mother Therese would learn to the fullest that her offering had been accepted.

Through spite on the part of an assistant, false rumors began to circulate about Mother Therese's physical and mental health and about her business ability; these rumors undermined the sisters' trust in her. A new advisor replaced Mother Therese in the office of superior with a wealthy novice who was made superior after only one month in the novitiate; this woman was even designated "superior foundress" of the congregation. It would only be in the last years of her life that Mother Therese would be recognized as the real foundress.

The new superior had good intentions, but she did not understand religious life. Mother Therese had striven vigorously to maintain silence, recollection and absolute poverty. The new superior, however, relaxed the house rules; thinking poverty to be an evil, she even went so far as to borrow money to purchase nice things for the house. These policies worked havoc with religious observance and scandalized lay people who knew about it.

This superior was deposed after 11 months, after having caused the little community such great trials that Mother Therese felt they could not have stood it for any longer period. Yet despite these serious disorders, Mother Therese refused to say anything against her, even when summoned by the Jesuit Provincial to respond to rumors. She did not wish to fail in any way in the obligation of respect toward superiors. Thus the Provincial had to visit the convent and judge the situation for himself; this soon led to the deposition of this superior.

The next superior was practical, and she did much to build up the community. However, she assigned Mother Therese to hard manual labor in the garden and cellar, rather than the apostolic work of giving retreats, and she tried in every way possible to keep her away from the other sisters. This same superior dismissed three of the first members of the Congregation, for she felt that they were not suitable due to the fact that they were country women. For 13 years, in silence and submission, Mother Therese suffered this form of exile from the community she herself (with Fr. Terme) had founded.

After Mother Therese returned to the heart of her community and its work, she had a perfect opportunity to bewail her years of exile, or to recriminate against the superior who had treated her so badly. Instead, she practiced perfect charity. It was always her practice to say good things about those who caused harm.

Mother Therese was to spend many years at the Cenacle of Fourviere, serving as "Assistant," i.e., having charge of manual labor. An early record shows the great austerity practiced there in the first years: "The older Mothers (we speak of Mothers Therese and Josephine), accustomed as they were to work and to every sort of privation, gave to the little community an atmosphere of fervor, of regularity, which I recall with the greatest happiness. . . .The less desirable products of the garden were the only vegetables that came to our table; the better kind were reserved for the retreatants, or were sold."

Mother Therese also left a description of those trying times: "Wheat being so dear, we did not hesitate to gather up the remnants of black bread which the gardener did not wish to keep and which he threw alongside the convent wall. . . . At night and early morning one sole lamp was all the light the community had. It was placed in the corridor on which our cells opened; we had, therefore, to dress in semi-darkness. At recreation we would work by such a poor light that many of us have as a consequence impaired sight."

Mother Therese served briefly as Superior of the Paris community and then of the little community at Tournon. As Mother Superior she guided the sisters with goodness and great firmness. Her piety was vigorous, with a generous shouldering of the Cross and pursuit of mortification.

Various words of advice of Mother Therese have been preserved. For example, she said, "Great trials make great souls and fit them for the great things which God wishes to do through them." And: "Have confidence in God. The tree of the Cross bears fruit in every season and in every land. To it go always for the mercy of the good God; I always come away in peace. Let us say bravely and confidently: God is sufficient for me." And: "After all, the religious life is a sufficiently great grace even though one purchase it at the price of the most difficult of sacrifices."

Mother Therese's personality combined rustic wisdom, common sense, honesty, forthrightness and a keen sense of humor. She could be abrupt at times, yet she was keenly alive to the needs of others. The novices one day spoke of the uncomfortable kneeling benches; Mother Therese responded, "Then we no longer wish to mortify ourselves; we must find another way of going to Heaven!" For Mother Therese, everything was founded on the Cross.

On another occasion Mother Therese encountered a young sister carrying a large load of wood. She barred the way, forcing the sister to stop, then took part of the wood into her own arms. As she left she said, "Now make a fire that will last well, not one that will simply flame up."

Despite her emphasis on mortification and abnegation, Mother Therese found no place for sadness. She would say to the young religious, "We should never allow even one thought of sadness to enter the soul. Have we not within us Him who is the joy of Heaven!" And: "Believe me when I say that an obedient religious is a happy religious, because she makes of all her actions so many spiritual communions. . . ."

Mother Therese was confided with the task of welcoming back and caring for a member who had left the Cenacle during a distressing time of disorder and confusion in one of the houses. She attended the returning sister with great love and goodness, deeply sensitive to the wounds of heart and soul that needed to be healed.

The last 25 years of Mother Therese's life were a time of mystical graces and mystical sufferings. In 1859 she made a complete gift of herself to God. In 1864 she received an interior illumination on the Blood of the Lamb without stain flowing over every Catholic altar in the world, and she received an interior enlightenment that souls would not cooperate enough by prayer and penance. Mother Therese then received a revelation on the meaning of complete self-surrender to God—a revelation which she was unable to express in words. Self-surrender was a keynote of Mother Therese's spirituality. She exclaimed, "Oh! if one could understand in advance that sweetness and that peace which one tastes when there is no reserve with the good God! The surrendered soul has found Paradise on earth. . . ."

Mother Therese also received a vision in which the word "Goodness" was written on every creature in letters of gold, illuminating her on the truth that every created good has been communicated to creatures by the Infinite Goodness. This realization lit up her life like the sun and prepared her for the great sufferings which were to consume the last part of her life.

The last 10 or 12 years of Mother Therese's life were to be spent in a terrible mystical anguish of body and soul. Around 1875, moved by an interior grace, she had offered herself to Our Lord as a sacrificial victim. He accepted her offering, saying to her, "You shall be a victim for the holocaust." Day after day for years, but especially on Thursday evenings and on Fridays, she shared in Our Lord's Agony in the Garden of Gethsemane. She would spend hours weeping and sobbing in the tribune, located in a corner of the chapel near the altar—unaware, on account of her deafness, that others witnessed her agony. Over and over she would repeat to Our Lord the words, "Have pity on me!" When a newcomer went to inform the Mother Superior that someone in the chapel was suffering terribly, the Superior replied, "We can do nothing. It is Mother Therese, who suffers and weeps with Our Saviour. You are a newcomer here but you will hear that often, very often. Mother Therese weeps in the tribune. She is so deaf that she believes she cries noiselessly. We suffer with her."

Toward the end of her life the word spread among the houses of the Cenacle that Mother Therese had performed miracles. One noteworthy healing occurred when Mother Therese made a novena to the Blessed Mother to cure a paralyzed sister as a proof of the authenticity of her recent apparitions at Lourdes and La Salette— in which she (Mother Therese) had found it difficult to believe. On the last day of the novena the sick nun arose cured. It is said that Mother Therese doubted no more.

As Mother Therese grew older, her activity became increasingly limited and early in 1885 she was confined to her bed, patient with the pain, united to God in a state of great peace. As she lay motionless hour after hour, absorbed in prayer, she felt herself surrounded by mysterious spirits, moaning with intense suffering yet adoring God with an ineffable "reverence of which nothing on earth can give even a suggestion." She heard them intone verse after verse of the *Te Deum,* repeating the last verse at least 10 times, their voices filled with humility, ardor and confidence over-flowing with love. The mysterious spirits were souls in Purgatory.

Mother Therese repeatedly asked for prayers and Masses for the Poor Souls in Purgatory. She felt that her act of self-surrender had been accepted and was being used in some way to atone for sin.

When Mother Therese lay dying, she remained very still, her eyes closed, her hands folded over her crucifix. On September 26 at 4:15 p.m. she opened her eyes, gazed with joyful recognition at something near the foot of the bed, and then peacefully closed her eyes again. Her journey on this earth had ended.

At the canonization of St. Therese Couderc in 1970, Pope Paul VI spoke at length on her life. He especially praised her humility, her patience, her obedience—and most of all, her silence.

St. Therese Couderc, Foundress of the Religious of the Cenacle, yet a woman who led a very hidden life. In effect exiled from the community for many years, she was for a time assigned to perform hard manual labor. Her last decade of life (her 70's) was for her a time of terrible mystical suffering as a victim soul. Yet near the end of her life Mother Therese affirmed, "What does it matter if my bare and cut feet filled my sabots with blood; I would willingly begin my journey again, I have found God so completely."

23

SAINT VICENTA LOPEZ

Vicenta Maria Lopez y Vicuña
1847 - 1890
Spain
Died Age 43

Vicenta Lopez was an exceptionally gifted child; today she would probably be called a "child prodigy." In addition to being way above her peers in intelligence at an early age, Vicenta was also precocious with regard to the meaning of charity, the love of God and neighbor. At age seven she became a close friend and "soul mate" of her 46-year-old aunt; together the two would carry on a special apostolate for the servant girls of Madrid.

Vicenta Maria Lopez was born in the spring of 1847, the only surviving child of a titled lawyer and his noble wife. From an early age she was doted on by her parents and she attracted so much attention that it is a wonder she came through childhood unspoiled. At one point she did have temper tantrums, and one of her uncles said she was gluttonous, but very soon she was showing great spiritual maturity.

Her father started her formal education at the age of three, when she first began to read and learn Christian doctrine. At the age of six, Vicenta began to learn writing and arithmetic. For reading material, her father gave her the works of St. Teresa of Avila. At this time she began to gather the children of the poor and teach them their catechism. This early attraction to teaching stayed with her for the rest of her life.

It was in 1854 that Vicenta went with her parents to visit her Aunt Eulalia in Madrid. This 46-year-old aunt and the seven-year-old girl were to become fast friends, and it was on this trip that Vicenta first realized what her apostolate was to be.

Many young country girls flocked to Madrid in the mid-1800's to seek work as servants. They often arrived malnourished, dirty, frightened and homesick. Most were illiterate. While they looked for work, they lodged where they could and often fell in with bad company, thus falling from virtue and then becoming mired in lives of sin. Most of these girls arrived not trained for anything, and many had difficulty finding places.

Vicenta's Aunt Eulalia had already set up a special Christian care center for these girls; it was called the Casita. Vicenta became her helper in this work. Years later, Vicenta described the beginning of her vocation by saying, "The first time I visited the Casita and saw the young girls who were sheltered there, I said to myself, compelled by an impulse of spirit which was irresistible but at the same time pleasing and very like what I was then thinking: 'The care and the teaching of these poor little things shall always be my delight and my dearest occupation; and these little servant girls, without father and without support, shall all the days of my life be my special friends.' "

At the age of 10, Vicenta went to live with her aunt and uncle in Madrid in order to help with the work for the servant girls and to complete her own education. Her home town was too small to offer much opportunity for advanced education worthy of Vicenta's talents. Nothing could have pleased her more than this move, as she could now assist in the care of the servant girls—and she already considered her aunt as her "other mother." She was a good student and spent hours at her studies. In addition to the traditional subjects, she learned sewing, piano and a number of artistic skills such as making paper flowers.

Vicenta and her Aunt Eulalia had a very special spiritual relationship. In spite of the fact that Vicenta was a small child when her Aunt was in her late 40's, their mutual inclination to the things of God joined them in a spiritual friendship. This love lasted through the years, from the time when Vicenta as a child accompanied her middle-aged, married aunt on her works of charity; through the time when they both suffered the pain of the loss of Eulalia's husband and Vicenta's great friend; through the time when they lived together, mutually following a semblance of a religious rule; through the heartbreak of separation when Vicenta began living as a true religious while Eulalia, at age 68, could not follow that type of life—to Eulalia's death in 1877.

A sense of humor is always an asset, and Vicenta was not lacking in this department. As a child she enjoyed practical jokes. Once on a visit to the Visitation convent where one of her aunts was a nun, the sisters dressed Vicenta as a nun and made two visiting priests think she was a third order sister. Later, as an adult, she could even joke about a toothache. She wrote to one of her sisters, "I am doing well, but my molar is giving signs of life. I think that tomorrow we shall condemn it to death." Later, she wrote of the marvels of a painless extraction: "The pain came after the extraction of the forty reals [money] that the doctor took."

One burden that Vicenta had to carry all her short life was that of ill health. She had bouts of quartan fever, a malady similar to malaria. Later in her life, when even to live was an effort, Vicenta either minimized her troubles or did not mention her health at all. She was too busy in the service of others to bother about herself. At 15, she wrote to her mother, "Come and stay with us, and your ills will certainly mend. Imagination plays a large part in them, and here there are so many distractions that you will have no time to think." For Vicenta, "distractions" meant other people's troubles.

For girls of Vicenta's class in those days, a decision had to be made between marriage and religious life. There was no possibility for a profession, although with Vicenta's talents she could have made an excellent doctor, lawyer or teacher. Vicenta progressively came to the belief that she had a vocation to the religious life.

With Vicenta being of marriageable age, there were the usual speculation and matchmaking efforts among relatives. One attractive young man favored by her family had a lot of virtues to recommend him. Suspecting that Vicenta's preoccupation with prayer and her work of charity might lead her to turn the young man down, her parents arranged for a cousin to speak with Vicenta about him. After the cousin had extolled all his many virtues, Vicenta answered, "Auntie, I wouldn't marry a king, and I wouldn't marry a saint." After this, with the permission of her spiritual director, Vicenta made a private vow of perpetual chastity and of entering religious life. At this time she was 19 years old.

During this time, while Vicenta was pondering how to answer God's call and trying to decide in which particular order she should live her vocation, the work for the servant girls started by her aunt was also undergoing a transition. Eulalia had turned the work over to a religious order, and this resulted in a change in the original aim of this apostolate. Although the changes were in no way bad, Eulalia still wanted the apostolate to stay in line with the original aims she had planned for it. It was decided that to achieve these aims, the original house would be turned over to the religious order, and Eulalia and her brother would make a new beginning.

Vicenta was a most needed element in the work because she was the youngest and most active member of the team looking after the servant girls. She was accountant, secretary and the immediate guardian of the girls.

For some years Vicenta had divided her time between living with her aunt in Madrid and living at home with her parents. Now she felt that she was needed to stay with the work.

In 1868, when Vicenta returned to Madrid, she wanted to continue the work for the servant girls. She knew, however, that she had a religious vocation. Her family would have been happy had she chosen to become a Visitation nun. She wanted to follow the religious life she so ardently desired, yet she did not want to abandon this work of charity. In order to obtain divine guidance to solve her dilemma, Vicenta obtained permission to make the Exercises of St. Ignatius in the Visitation convent. Some notes that she made at this time, when she was 21, give a valuable insight into Vicenta's future actions and shed light on her sanctity.

She wrote, "I have not ceased to feel compelled to abandon myself wholly to God, bound hand and foot, willing to do what His divine Majesty shall want of me. Since God has created me, I am His property, and I belong to Him only. If Our Lord wishes to put me to work for His glory, I must make my nothingness my foundation, considering that if I have good desires it is because God gives them to me out of His infinite liberality; and I must work convinced that only God can do what has to be done, I being but the instrument whose cooperation He desires, and for that I have to do the work with zeal, as though its successful conclusion depended entirely on me."

After the exercises had been completed, Vicenta's Aunt Dominica, a Visitation nun, asked her niece what decision she had come to. Vicenta replied, "The girls have won."

For the time being, Vicenta planned that she and her aunt, along with one or two others, would live in the house for the girls, continue with their work and follow a rule similar to a religious rule.

Vicenta had, in a high degree, the gift of treating people as individual persons. She saw their true value before God. She respected and loved them and was eager to give them what they needed in order to make the most of themselves. She treated each girl as her own daughter.

Vicenta was a quick thinker, and more than once she put this ability to work in dealing with the girls and their problems. One of the girls fell in love with the son of a wealthy manufacturer. The parents of the young man were unhappy, thinking that their son had disgraced the family by falling in love with an orphan servant girl. Vicenta arranged an interview with the parents, and before they could begin their objections, she calmly demanded a dowry for the girl so that in case the boy should die and there were no children to take care of her, the girl might not have to go back into domestic service. The parents were dumbfounded. Then the objections began. But Vicenta lived up to her childhood nickname of "The Lawyer," presenting such good arguments in rebuttal that the parents were completely won over and the couple made a happy match.

Another time, a family brought their young daughter to the house, asking that she be sheltered and trained for domestic work while they themselves looked for work. The girl was dirty and unkempt. Without fanfare, Vicenta took the child to the attic, where she fixed a bath for her and gave her a new set of clothes so that no one would see her misery. Vicenta herself combed and fixed the child's hair. With such an introduction to charity, the girl was then ready to be open to the love of God.

Not all the girls, of course, were good or appreciative. Some left and went their own willful and dangerous way. But Vicenta loved these even more than the others, and she followed them with her prayers.

After a long period of self-doubt and after receiving much advice from her spiritual director, Vicenta and two other women adopted a religious habit on June 11, 1876 and began to live as religious, determined to found a new order in the Church. They took their vows in 1878.

In preparation for the beginning of their religious life, the three women made a three-day guided retreat. For Vicenta, this was a prelude to this new foundation she felt inspired to make. Her notes from this retreat give a clear indication of the spirit with which she was forming a new work for God. She wrote, "In these days I can receive light and find comfort. But I want nothing, O God, but to know Your will so that I may do it...Direct me in everything; I am Your handmaid. I thank You for having surrounded me with these poor little things, who can bring me to Heaven if I teach them to love You, if I separate them from the vanities of the world, which can bring them only bitterness. Give me, Lord, the means of consolidating and increasing this work, which ought to be so acceptable to Your Divine Heart; here You have me, do with me what You will."

From this small beginning, a healthy, thriving institute began to grow. As with every new order, it had its times of trials, but its progress was steady and others came to join in the work. Soon houses were opened in other cities, for Madrid had no monopoly on young girls in need of help and domestic training. The full name of the new Order was the Religious of Mary Immaculate for Domestic Service and the Protection of Youth.

In January of 1879 Vicenta began to exhibit the symptoms of the dreaded disease, tuberculosis. Because of her activity, her health seemed to fail completely, and rumors went around to the effect that should she die, the congregation would be left with no direction. Vicenta assured her sisters they need not worry about this. She said, "For all the fuss they are making, I shall not die until I am 43." She had 10 more years to live.

The decree of approbation for Vicenta's order was issued in April of 1888. The constitution of the Order stated its double purpose as sanctification of self and of others.

By 1890 Vicenta could no longer hide her sufferings. When it was physically possible, she continued her work, but by September she was too ill to move from her bed. As of December 14 her breathing was so painful that she could hardly speak.

On Christmas Eve the sisters came in turn to say farewell, and Vicenta spoke a little to them, begging them not to cancel any of the Christmas festivities planned for the girls, even if she should die.

She lived through Christmas Day. Then on the afternoon of December 26, she said, "My Jesus, mercy! Jesus, Mary and Joseph, be with me all three." Her head dropped gently and she died.

At the time of Vicenta's death there were five houses of the Religious of Mary Immaculate flourishing in Spain. Today the congregation carries on its apostolate in a number of countries, especially in Europe and Latin America. The sisters maintain residences for students and working girls and homes for orphaned and neglected children. They also operate training schools, home economics classes and night schools for working girls.

Vicenta Maria Lopez y Vicuña was canonized in 1975.

St. Vicenta Maria Lopez at age 12. An extraordinarily gifted child, at age 10 Vicenta began her life's apostolate of caring for the poor young country girls who flocked to Madrid looking for work as servants. At age seven, when visiting a Christian care center for these girls, Vicenta had realized irresistibly that this was her vocation.

A picture of St. Teresa of Avila drawn by Vicenta when she was a child. Vicenta began to read at age three; a few years later her father gave her the works of St. Teresa of Avila for reading material.

Vicenta at age 16. A couple of years later, Vicenta's relatives tried to arrange a good match for her, but Vicenta was attracted more and more
to the religious life. One day, after being told of a prospective groom's
many virtues, Vicenta responded by saying, "I wouldn't marry a king and
I wouldn't marry a saint." Her spiritual director then permitted her to
make a private vow of chastity. The *Spiritual Exercises* of St. Ignatius
which Vicenta made at age 21 shed further light on her vocation.

When Vicenta was about 29 years old, she and two other women adopted a religious habit, beginning a new order in the Church, the Religious of Mary Immaculate for Domestic Service and the Protection of Youth. Vicenta wrote a prayer in which she said, "I want nothing, O God, but to know Your will so that I may do it...I thank You for having surrounded me with these poor little things, who can bring me to Heaven if I teach them to love You, if I separate them from the vanities of the world, which can bring them only bitterness."

When Vicenta was about 33 years old her health seemed to fail from tuberculosis; it was feared that the fledgling congregation would soon be left leaderless. But Vicenta responded, "For all the fuss they are making, I shall not die until I am 43." She had 10 more years to live.

Facing Page: St. Vicenta Maria Lopez in death. She died on December 26, the day after Christmas, after saying, "My Jesus, mercy! Jesus, Mary and Joseph, be with me all three." At the time of her death there were five houses of her congregation flourishing in Spain.

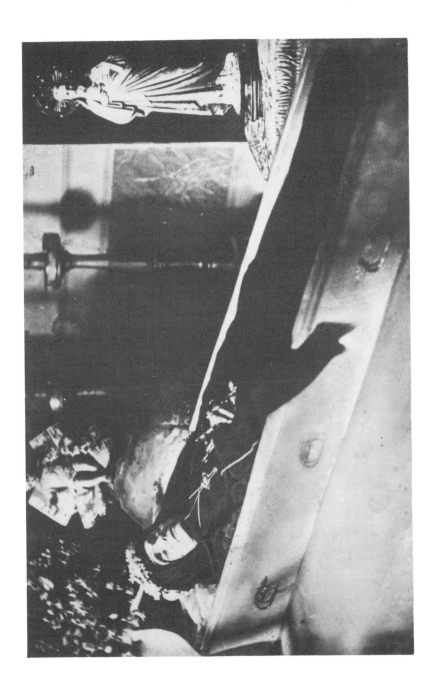

24

SAINT THERESE OF THE CHILD JESUS
The Little Flower

Saint Therese of the Child Jesus and the Holy Face, O.C.D.
Marie-Francoise Therese Martin
1873 - 1897
France
Died Age 24

"Jesus deigned to teach me this mystery. He set before me the book of nature. I understood how all the flowers He has created are beautiful, how the splendor of the rose and the whiteness of the lily do not take away the perfume of the little violet or the delightful simplicity of the daisy. I understood that if all the flowers wanted to be roses, nature would lose her springtime beauty, and the fields would no longer be decked out with little wildflowers.

"And so it is in the world of souls, Jesus' garden. He willed to create great souls comparable to lilies and roses, but He has created smaller ones and these must be content to be daisies or violets destined to give joy to God's glances when He looks down at His feet. *Perfection consists in doing His Will, in being what He wills us to be.*"

At the time of her death in 1897, no one would have suspected that scarcely 27 years later the life and heroic virtues of this unknown young Carmelite would be held up to the world as an example of the Gospel ideal of sanctity as a daily following of Christ without heroics or display. In the Bull of Canonization, Pope Pius XI expressed this beautifully when he stated that "Without going beyond the common order of things in her way of life, she followed out and fulfilled her vocation with such alacrity, generosity and constancy that she reached an heroic degree of virtue."

Shortly before her death, the consciousness of her mission became clear to Therese: "...I feel that my mission is soon to begin, to make others love God as I do, to teach others my little way. I want to spend my Heaven in doing good upon earth...After my death I will let fall a shower of roses. God would not inspire me with this desire to do good on earth after my death if He did not intend to realize it."

After her death, her sister obtained permission to put together and circulate Therese's writings instead of the customary circular obituary. The doctrine of these writings (not their literary merit) was startling in its simple return to Gospel precepts. The writings, titled *The Story of a Soul*, were originally sent to other Carmels. From there they were loaned to friends, passed around, and soon the Lisieux Carmel received requests for more copies.

Then reports of wonderful favors, cures and miracles began coming in. The Lisieux Carmel was deluged with requests for pictures and for relics. There was an increasing clamor for Therese's canonization.

Contrary to Therese's profound realism, there was much sentimentality spread by Therese's devotees. "We should never make any false currency in order to redeem souls," Therese had told her sister. The garish marketing of this saint, the plastic statues and insipid paintings of a beautiful nun with rose-strewn crucifix, shocked many who knew Therese the realist. Nonetheless, the life she lived so faithfully serves as an example both for the common man, and for those of refined taste and great education. Therese had said, "I saw that ALL vocations are summed up in LOVE, and LOVE is All in ALL." Neither the pious additions to her own words nor the enhancement of her portrait (both common practices of her time) can dim the light shed by this saint who truly lived the doctrine of sanctity and who has been called one of the greatest saints of all time.

Therese Martin was born at Alencon, France on January 2 of 1873, the last of nine children born to Louis and Zelie Martin. Louis was a watchmaker, and Zelie ran a small lace-making business from her home. Both the Martin parents had felt a call to a religious vocation, but this had been denied to them, so they brought up their family in a warm, loving and very religious atmosphere. The family was comfortably well-to-do.

Four of the older children had died in infancy or at an early age; when the baby Therese also became ill with an intestinal disorder, a doctor advised that she be taken immediately to a wet nurse if her mother wanted her to survive. With the good care and nursing of a farmer's wife, the baby grew fat and healthy, and when she came home for good at the age of 15 months, she was out of all danger. Although her mother described Therese in a pleasantly biased way as a "charming child," she also stated with candor that her daughter was at times a "little imp" who threw "frightful tantrums and banged her head against her wooden bed." Therese was inseparable from her sister Celine, the second youngest of the five Martin girls.

In 1876, the family received the shocking news that their strong and beloved mother was dying of incurable cancer of the breast. Courageously, she prepared her two eldest daughters to take her place. In the presence of her husband and older daughters, she passed to eternity when Therese was only four.

This painful loss initiated in Therese's life a 10-year period of shyness, oversensitiveness and many tears. She tried over and over to master herself, but her struggles seemed to be in vain.

The heartbroken Louis sold the business and retired with his children to a place in the country near his brother-in-law's home in Lisieux. This family, the Guerins, were to help with the practical aspects of raising the five Martin girls. The 54-year-old Louis and his youngest daughter, his "Little Queen," grew close, spending a great deal of time together daily fishing and exploring the countryside and the town. They often walked down to the nearby Carmelite monastery for a visit in the chapel.

Though she loved her father and her other sisters, it was her sister Pauline who for Therese replaced Zelie Martin. Pauline was the sister who taught her, scolded her, comforted her when she was ill, and in general loved her as a second mother. Therese had been a precocious child who had already begun to read at the age of three. Under Pauline's instruction, she learned more and more. Pauline prepared Therese for her first confession by emphasizing love and gratitude instead of sin or guilt, and Therese later wrote that she left the confessional "happy and light-hearted."

When Therese was eight and a half, she began school at the Benedictine Abbey. Two of her former teachers remembered, "She wasn't exactly pretty; her chin was a little large, but she had marvelous blonde hair and a touching air of innocence." Therese, serious and retiring, later remembered these school days as "the saddest years of my life."

On the first day of school the next year, Therese's "second mother," Pauline, entered Carmel. Therese took the separation badly and soon fell ill with an inexplicable malady that carried with it chills, fevers, convulsions, hallucinations and a great deal of crying. In spite of Pauline's letters full of love and encouragement, the illness continued for some time.

At one point her sister Marie, who was sitting with her in the sickroom, became so desperate over Therese's illness and hallucinations that she knelt before a statue of the Blessed Virgin and frantically begged for her sister's life; Therese joined Marie in fervent supplication. Marie then saw Therese "fix her gaze on the statue"; the child grew calm and began to cry quietly. The symptoms soon faded away. Later, Marie pressed Therese for details. The 10-year-old Therese said simply that the Virgin Mary had smiled at her. She had been cured.

The year after her illness Therese prepared for her First Communion. After the careful teaching of Marie, her preparation by studying the catechism, reading and re-reading Pauline's inspiring and love-filled letters, making hundreds of acts of virtue and aspirations, followed by a retreat for First Communicants, Therese received Jesus for the first time. It was a day of great grace. Therese said she experienced the Eucharist as a "fusion." "It was a kiss of love; I felt that I was loved, and I said, 'I love You and I give myself to You forever.' "

After this, Therese was troubled by scruples and self-doubt. She was treated as a sickly child, and was, in fact, lonely and overly sensitive. Finally, Therese quit school at the abbey and a private tutor was obtained for her.

When Therese's sister Marie announced her intention of leaving for Carmel, Therese already viewed life as only a time of suffering and separations. She would remind herself, "Life is your barque and not your home." At Marie's announcement Therese made a resolve to take no pleasure out of earth's attractions.

That Christmas, after Midnight Mass, Therese overheard her father remark with impatience that he was glad this would be the last year for the custom of filling Therese's shoes with Christmas gifts. Ordinarily Therese would have dissolved in tears, but on this night she felt a new inner strength. In order to make her father happy she behaved as if the custom gave her a great deal of pleasure. Therese said, "The work I had been unable to do in 10 years was done by Jesus in one instant." She had experienced what she called her "conversion"; to her it marked the return of the "strength of soul which I had lost at the age of four and a half." A new period of her life was now beginning.

In 1887, Therese read the *Imitation of Christ*. She felt that it had been written solely for her, and she determined to adopt the detachment from earthly things of which it spoke so highly. This and her other reading encouraged in Therese a growing inner life. Her scruples and self-doubts put aside, she grew taller and more mature. Her love for Jesus, nourished by daily sacrifices, grew daily. She knew God wanted her to spend her life for Him in Carmel, and she was eager to love Him there forever.

Soon Therese felt inspired with a great desire to save souls. Hearing about an unrepentant condemned criminal named Pranzini, she devoted her heart to obtaining his conversion, praying and making many sacrifices. On the day after his hanging Therese opened the newspaper to find that Pranzini had been unrepentant up until the moment before placing his head in the noose—then suddenly he had taken hold of the crucifix held out to him by the priest and kissed the wounds of Christ three times before he died. Therese felt a deep joy over the conversion of her "first child" of grace, and her desire to save souls grew and grew.

At 14, with all the strong will of her babyhood, Therese determined to enter Carmel. Although her oldest sister Pauline believed she had a vocation to the cloister, and her father touchingly gave his permission, there were more obstacles in the way. The Rule of Carmel allowed only those 16 and older to enter, so a dispensation was necessary; but the ecclesiastical superior refused to allow her entrance before she was 21. Therese appealed to the bishop, who offered no hope, only saying that he would speak with the canon.

Louis Martin had already planned a pilgrimage to Rome and obtained an audience with the Pope. Therese and Celine would accompany him. Therese planned to dare to speak to the Pope; in her determination she was certain that he could read her soul. If he agreed to her entrance into Carmel at age 15, the Bishop would have to consent.

Therese described the scene: "We passed in front of him in procession; each pilgrim knelt in turn, kissed the foot and hand of Leo XIII, received his blessing. . ." Then the announcement was made that no one was to speak to the Pope.

As Therese knelt in front of him and kissed his foot, he stretched out his hand for her to kiss his ring as everyone in the long line had done. Instead, she took his hand and blurted out her question:

"Most Holy Father, I have a great favor to ask of you...in honor of your Jubilee permit me to enter Carmel at the age of 15!"

The Pontiff was very kind, but he did not open the door of Carmel. He told Therese to follow the instructions of the proper authorities. When she reminded him that if he would say yes, everybody else would agree, he gazed at her steadily, and then said, "Go...go...you will enter if God wills it." The Swiss guards raised Therese to her feet and carried her in tears to the door.

Therese was left to pray and trust in God. At long last the desired permission came. Therese's entrance, however, was delayed until the Easter season; impatient Therese accepted the delay and learned a great lesson in patience. She entered the Lisieux Carmel in 1888, joining 26 other women in living the regulated monastic life.

For the next nine years, Therese lived the doctrine of sanctity without in any way going out of the ordinary as far as externals were concerned. She sought, and found, a means of going to Heaven that was "very short and very straight." As she explained, "We are living in an age of inventions and we no longer have to take the trouble of climbing stairs, for in the homes of the rich an elevator has replaced these very successfully. I wanted to find an elevator which would raise me to Jesus, for I am too small to climb the rough stairway to perfection..." Thus Therese devoted all her energies to loving God totally in absolutely everything she did. It was in a sense a simple program—but one requiring heroic faithfulness and constancy. Therese's vocation was above all to love, and she fulfilled it.

In the cloister, Therese would follow the Rule exactingly, obey her superiors, suffer from aridity of spirit, join wholeheartedly in recreation whether she felt like it or not, love her 26 sisters in religion despite differences and even clashes of temperament, pray, practice self-denial and renunciation and, all in all, live her "little way" of love of God in all things—often called the way of "spiritual childhood." Externally, she appeared simply as a good Carmelite should.

After Therese's clothing, she received the sad news that her father had become unwell and mentally ill. He was committed to a mental institution. The anguish she felt for her well-loved father was one of the greatest trials of these days. Again and again she was given the opportunity to practice real detachment from all things earthly, setting her sights on Heaven, the Christian's true home.

This detachment, especially from her father and her sisters, cost her dearly, but she persevered.

From the day of her entrance, Therese had practiced her little way of love of God in all things, through constant self-denial. When she served as novice mistress, she taught these ideas to her charges. She told them, "You know well enough that Our Lord does not look so much at the greatness of our actions, nor even at their difficulty, but at the love with which we do them." For Therese, to uncomplainingly answer a call which interrupted her, to be sociable when she preferred to be alone, to be kind and charitable in all things to those whom by nature she most preferred to stay away from, and to stay away and be detached from her two dear sisters that she would have preferred the company of—these were the gifts, and the only gifts, she could give. Her giving was constant.

In her childhood Therese had dreamed of being a great missionary and of becoming a martyr; these dreams deepened as she grew older. On the Feast of the Holy Trinity in 1895, when she was meditating on the mysterious refusal of men to give God the wholehearted love He desires above all else, she felt a sudden inspiration to offer herself as a victim of that love. She wrote an act of oblation which contained these words: "In order to live in a single act of perfect love, I offer myself as a holocaust to Your merciful love. . .and so let me be the martyr of Your love, O my God." It was after making this oblation that Therese had the only "mystical" experience of her religious life. Starting to make the Way of the Cross, she suddenly felt herself "wounded by a dart of flame" that seemed to envelop her whole being with indescribable sweetness. After this, her usual aridity of spirit returned. That her offer had been accepted was soon to be seen.

In April of 1896, Therese coughed up blood. The following summer, she developed a dry cough which was treated with various medicines. No one thought her illness was serious. But the piercing cold of the winter was too much for her, and she began to suffer increasing attacks of fever. At last, the community awakened to the seriousness of her condition. She was ordered by the doctor to refrain from all work, and she spent the month of June in a wheelchair, finishing her spiritual reminiscences at the urging of her sister Pauline and the prioress. By July, she was hemorrhaging often. The doctor had her moved to the infirmary and forbade all movement, but it was too late. The disease, tuberculosis, had riddled her lungs; she began having terrible attacks of suffocation, exhausting sweating spells, and was coughing up blood several times daily. Toward the end, she could breathe only with little cries of pain, and constant vomiting prevented her receiving Communion after the 19th of August.

Therese's spiritual trials during this time were more intense than the physical. She wrote, "God allowed my soul to be enveloped in complete darkness." It was only sheer faith and unflagging hope that carried her to the end. She had thirsted to save souls, and now God demanded that she live by faith alone. When everything else was gone, love alone remained. Once when her nurse found her awake after midnight, she explained that she could not sleep. The nurse asked what she said to God during the long, wakeful hours. Therese replied, "I do not say anything, Sister, I just love Him."

Ever a realist, in her illness Therese faced death squarely—and with joyful anticipation. She consoled her sisters in *their* fears. She made jokes about her condition and cheered those who came to help her.

In all of her discussions, her practical reality showed through. She was bothered by the flowery images of religion so common in her day. In particular, she disliked many of the romantic legends told about Mary. "We shouldn't say unlikely things or things we don't know anything about. Everything in their life [the Holy Family's] was done just as in our own." An unlikely saint, compared to the excessive sentimentality of her day, Therese knew and experienced all the unglamorous sufferings that someone in her state and her health would have been likely to. God allowed her to go through many interior sufferings. Her soul remained in inner darkness, she was empty of glowing feelings, she felt pain and revulsions. "Sanctity does not consist in saying beautiful things," she had once written. She told her sister, "I will have the right of doing stupid things up until my death if I am humble and if I remain little. Little children are not damned."

To the end, Therese remained faithful to her Little Way. On the day of her death, after choking in agony for over two hours, she asked a sister if death were coming. When the sister replied that it was, but that perhaps God willed that her agony be prolonged for a few hours, Therese replied, "Very well, I do not wish to suffer less." Looking at her crucifix, she gasped, "Oh, I love Him!

My God...I love...You." Then her head fell back, and with a
little sigh she died. She was 24 years old.

All four of Therese's sisters lived to see her raised to the honors
of the altar in 1925. They rejoiced with the countless others, well
over 60,000 at the canonization ceremony, who saw in Therese the
embodiment of a spirituality open to all Christians in any state
of life. Then in 1927, because of St. Therese's great desire to be
a missionary and her sufferings for souls, she was declared co-
patron of the missions (the other co-patron being St. Francis Xavier).

Today St. Therese's book of spiritual reminiscences, *The Story
of a Soul*, is famous all over the Catholic world. Moreover, Therese
has kept her promise to "let fall from Heaven a shower of roses,"
or graces. St. Therese of the Child Jesus is one of the best-loved
saints in the Church. Moreover, Pope St. Pius X called Therese
"the greatest saint of modern times."

Office Central de Lisieux

Therese (age 8) and her older sister, Celine, from whom she was inseparable. Therese was only four and a half when the girls' beloved mother passed to eternity. From then on, two elder sisters became the "second mothers" of these two younger sisters. Her mother's death affected Therese deeply and began a period of shyness and oversensitiveness for her that would last until she was 14 years old.

Therese at age 13. At this time Therese's mind was expanding through private lessons and much reading. Although she still found herself unable to refrain from shedding tears over minor things, her face nevertheless shows much sureness of purpose.

Office Central de Lisieux

Therese at age 15, a few days before entering Carmel. She had adopted this hairstyle some time previous in order to look older when asking the Bishop's permission to enter Carmel early. It had been only about a couple of years earlier that Therese received the great grace which she called her "conversion," a grace which freed her from the oversensitiveness and tearfulness she had struggled against in vain for 10 years and returned to her the strength of soul she had lost at the age of four and a half.

233

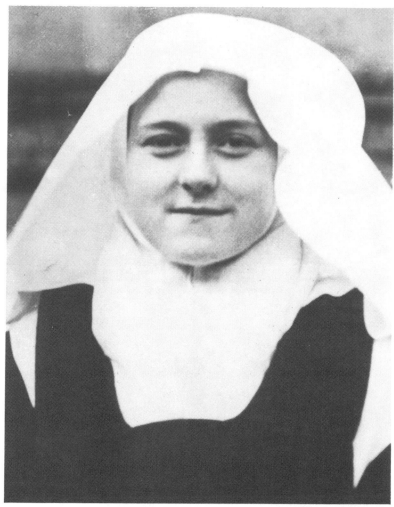

Office Central de Lisieux

Above: Therese wearing the white veil of a novice. In the convent she would spend the rest of her life following her heroic "little way" of love for God in all things.

Facing page: In the convent Therese lived each day with its constant little hidden sacrifices—opportunities for acts of great love of God. In her *Story of a Soul* Therese described how she kept silent in the laundry when a companion unknowingly used to splash her with dirty water; Therese refrained from even wiping her face. Therese is the fourth sister from the left, holding a laundry paddle in her right hand. To *her* left is her sister Celine, wearing a white veil.

235

Office Central de Lisieux

Above: Therese at age 23.

Facing page: Therese on a reclining chair (August 30, 1897) about five weeks before she died. Constant vomiting prevented her from receiving Communion after August 19. At this time Therese was enduring terrible darkness of soul, yet she continued to adhere to God with intense faith. On October 3 she would die gasping the words, "Oh, I love Him! My God...I love...You." Pope St. Pius X called Therese "the greatest saint of modern times."

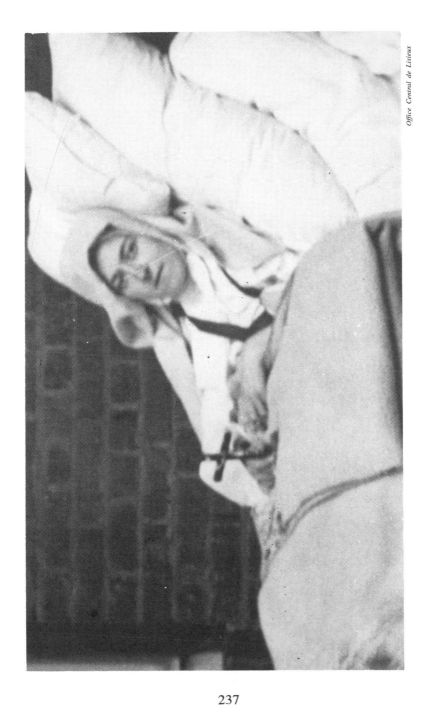

237

25

BLESSED MARIA ASSUNTA

Blessed Maria Assunta Pallotta, F.M.M.
Assunta Maria Liberata Pallotta
1878 - 1905
Italy - China
Died Age 26

Sister Assunta was the first non-martyr missionary sister to be beatified in the history of the Church. Moreover, although she went to the missions, she never taught catechism there or did other missionary work. Her life consisted rather of the everyday martyrdom available to anyone who aspires to sanctity.

Maria Assunta Pallotta was born on August 20, 1878 in the little town of Force, Italy. She was born at the home of her maternal grandparents, since her mother wished to be at her own parental home for the birth of her first child.

Assunta was baptized the day after she was born and was confirmed at the age of two. (Confirmation at that age was common in Italy at that time.) Assunta's father was a common laborer who was chronically out of work. Her mother often had a hard struggle to feed her children on the poor provisions of the family pantry. Thus, when Assunta became a Franciscan, she was already quite familiar with Lady Poverty.

The family grew to include three active younger brothers and, later, a younger sister. Assunta was the helpful older sister, and from an early age she learned to work for her daily bread.

At the age of eight this solemn little girl went to school to learn to read and write. By the time she was 11, her father had decided to leave home for a while to seek his fortune; Assunta, the dutiful older sister, helped her mother to keep house, raise the younger brothers and go out to work to help support the family. She carried cement and water to the brick masons. This was hard physical labor, but the strong, silent young girl was willing to help in order to meet the demands of the day. Besides, while she worked in silence, she had time to pray.

From the time she was a child Assunta was able to keep her own counsel and work amidst the ugliness of this world, praying and working, her heart set on a more beautiful world. Later in life, Assunta's smile and serenity would be two things noted about her, but as a child, solemnity was a keynote of her personality.

In the testimony for Assunta's beatification, a number of people remembered that as a child she was animated only when she was given the opportunity to teach others about religion. They recalled that she was always solemn and that she practiced penances far advanced for one her age. They noted that her rosary was always with her, and they remembered her joy at age 12 when she was allowed to make her First Communion.

Although Assunta's family was poor, she was filled with the spirit of Christian charity so pleasing to Our Lord. When giving testimony for Assunta's cause, her mother recalled, "Assunta knew how to minister to the needs of others in the spirit of charity; she assisted the sick poor by carrying water for one helpless old woman and aided a little friend by saying to me occasionally, 'Mother, put a little more water in the soup and a spoonful less on our plates, and prepare a portion for poor Marietta, who has nothing at home.' "

After Assunta had worked as the masons' assistant for some time, she went to work for a tailor. Although the work was still tiring and long, it was not as physically demanding. Here, too, she is remembered as being a solemn, quiet child. Few understood why, when other girls were laughing and visiting, Maria preferred to be at the foot of the tabernacle.

Often Assunta and the elderly tailor would return together in the evenings from a nearby village, and on the way they would pray the Rosary or recite other prayers. When they met a passer-by, the tailor would advise Assunta to lower her voice and not pray so loudly. With charming simplicity, she would reply, "Now is the time we should pray all the louder!" Assunta wanted to turn to God the thoughts of anyone who came across her path in life.

One year on the night before Ash Wednesday, Assunta attended a carnival dance with her mother and a childhood friend, Mary Fideli. Before the dance was over, Assunta asked her mother's permission to go home. The next day, Assunta asked Mary Fideli to go for a walk with her. Her friend saw that Assunta was troubled and asked her what was wrong. Assunta began to cry and sobbed to Mary Fideli, "Unless we become religious, we cannot save our souls—at least, I cannot..." She related that a young man at the dance had come up to her and said, "You are beautiful, Assunta, I would like to embrace you." This had caused Assunta much agony of soul.

As a young girl Assunta fasted often and practiced other mortifications. She was usually content with a little polenta (similar to cornmeal mush) seasoned with salt. Assunta would also put bricks, wood and iron in her bed, because of Jesus, "who had not a stone whereon to lay His head." With her confessor's consent, Assunta also wore a hairshirt with nails fastened into it.

In her late teens Assunta finally spoke of her desire to be a sister. As she was a child of poverty, there were two obstacles to Assunta's vocation. First, her family would have to make do without her income; moreover, she would have to find a convent willing to take a girl without a dowry. These two objections were overcome, and the parish priest made arrangements for Assunta to enter the Franciscan Missionaries of Mary. She left for Rome with a joyful heart.

As a postulant in the Roman motherhouse, Sister Assunta worked in the kitchen. There she was a model of humility and exact observance of the Rule.

On October 9, 1898 Assunta, clad in wedding apparel, approached the altar in the chapel of the motherhouse. When asked at one part of the ceremony if she knew the obligations of her future state, she answered in unison with the other postulants: "I know very well that a Franciscan Missionary of Mary is bound to offer herself as a victim of God for the Church and for the salvation of souls, to tend to perfection by the faithful observance of the constitutions of her institute, to strive to imitate Mary Immaculate in the virtues which she practiced on earth in union with her Divine Son." At her request, Assunta was allowed to keep her baptismal name. The celebrant intoned: "My daughter, you will no longer be called Assunta Maria Pallotta, but Sister Maria Assunta."

Assunta was sent to Grottaferrata to make her novitiate. There she was assigned to various farm tasks, such as the care of the animals and the harvesting of the olives. No matter how heavy the bundle of hay she had to carry, Sister Assunta always smiled.

Once one of the sisters met Sister Assunta buried under a burden of fodder, drenched with perspiration. When she asked why Assunta carried so much grass every day, the novice smilingly answered: "My animals are always hungry. They never have enough, but I don't mind. That gives me an extra bath, and it is quite refreshing. All for Jesus, little Sister."

Sister Mary Assunta expressed her appreciation of the life at Grottaferrata to one of the other sisters. She said, "One is very well cared for at Grottaferrata and the life is truly Franciscan; it is a real Paradise. Though they work in the fields, the solitude is a great incentive to recollection and prayer."

Once when Assunta and another novice were digging in the garden her companion remarked in a discouraged tone, "This charge is very hard and, to tell the truth, it is not pleasant." Assunta threw up her hands and exclaimed, "My Sister, we have come here to become saints!" Then, deeply impressed, she repeated the words, "We have come here to become saints."

Assunta had a most delicate conscience. The novice who slept in the bed next to her stated that she would sometimes hear Assunta weeping at night. When asked the reason, Assunta would reply, "I was weeping for my sins."

One day a fellow novice, who was undergoing a long-lasting temptation against her vocation, said to Assunta, "Do you know that I have decided to return to my family? Why don't you do the same, why remain here? At home we have at least our parents, who love us." Sister Assunta exclaimed in reply, "O Sister, that is a temptation of the devil! Try to overcome it at once. It is useless for you to invite me to follow you, for I have abandoned all the things of earth and I trust with the grace of God never to turn back for anything in the world." The other sister persevered and was professed at the same time as Assunta.

At the end of November a happy event was announced to the novices. Mother Mary of the Passion, the foundress of the institute, was coming for a visit. Assunta was full of joy, for she felt that she owed her happiness at belonging solely to God directly to Mother Mary of the Passion. At their meeting the saintly foundress spoke to Assunta with the same motherly care and interest which she showed each of her daughters. She asked her name and the news from her home. Then she told Assunta that the Marches, Assunta's home, was the land of saints, adding, "You must become a saint too." For Assunta, these words were as an official order.

One time, after a reading of the life of St. Gabriel of the Seven Sorrows, a lively conversation about sanctity ensued. Assunta's comment was, "If we really will it, I think we can all do it."

In 1900 Mother Mary of the Passion wrote to tell the novices of the martyrdom of seven of the sisters in Shan Si, China; these seven were the first martyrs, the Protomartyrs, of the Franciscan Missionaries of Mary. (See Chapter 24 of the first book of *Modern Saints*.) She closed her letter with an invitation to the sisters to strive for a greater love of Our Lord. Sister Assunta listened to these words and then determined that faithfulness and fidelity would be her way of immolation for the glory of God.

When her two years of novitiate were almost complete, Assunta developed a glandular inflammation which was causing her serious suffering. She became so ill that there was reason to think that she might have to leave the convent. Heartbroken, she begged God to allow her to die then and there rather than make her leave. Not only did she pray, but she begged others to pray for her. Her faith was rewarded, and she was admitted for profession in December of 1900.

After her profession Assunta returned to her farm work. Her mission was still the humble mission of good example. Her life was characterized by her practice of fraternal charity in a marked degree. All her sisters remember her self-sacrificing ways, her gentleness and her willing helpfulness.

Assunta loved all her sisters in religion without distinction and with genuine affection. Many instances of her help were recalled by the sisters when they gave testimony for her beatification. One sister recalled that when she had hurt her finger by accidentally sticking a pin into it, Assunta had carried her baskets of laundry for her and cut up her food at supper, as she could not do this herself. The cook recalled Assunta voluntarily carrying in stacks of wood, giving as an excuse that the cook would not have time to do this since she had so much other work. If work needed to be finished during the time set aside for recreation, Assunta was always the first to volunteer.

Sister Assunta lived in the presence of God. She would often say such things as, "For the love of God," or "All for Jesus," or "What God wills, as He wills, and may His Will be done," or "It would be better to die a thousand times than to offend Our Lord." On one occasion, to encourage a companion whose hands were cold when the two were picking olives in December, Assunta urged her to make as many acts of love of God as there were olives. It is said that the mystery of Our Lord's Passion thrilled her heart with its sadness and love. If she was troubled at the thought of having offended the Saviour, she would recall His mercy in dying for us and her serenity would immediately return.

Sister Assunta was extremely solicitous for the conversion of sinners. When some particular sinner was recommended to her prayers, she would pray with incredible fervor and employ penances, mortifications and the discipline, especially if the person was in danger of death; she exhorted her sisters to do the same. She often said, "Sinners are very numerous in the world, and how grateful we should be to God for having called us to the religious life. Pray for them!" When Sister Assunta's father failed to make his Easter duty one year, she grieved deeply. She was eager to offer herself for the conversion of infidels.

Sister Assunta was also very devoted to the Poor Souls in Purgatory. Every day she recited the "Eternal Rest" 100 times and she gained indulgences for the Poor Souls. One night, near the end of her life, Sister Assunta seemed to be seeing a vision; afterward she said to the sister taking care of her, "O Sister, if you only knew how necessary it is to be very faithful, for Purgatory is terrible for a religious."

Assunta practiced an exemplary obedience, never showing the slightest hesitation in obeying an order. She would often be heard to say words such as *"Si, Madre,"* "It is all the same," "Yes, yes." Often her sisters, knowing her to be so obliging, would pile additional work on her, but she was always glad to assist. A witness stated that Assunta would have thrown herself into the fire to obey.

Sister Assunta spent the next two years in Florence. For a time there she had the privilege of guarding the Blessed Sacrament by placing her cot at the door of the sacristy each night. One night, after Assunta had fallen into a deep and well-earned sleep, the sisters remembered that a traveling priest was coming to offer a very early Mass, before the rising bell. In order not to disturb Assunta, the superior and the sacristan simply picked up her cot and carried it off to the community room, sleeping nun and all. When Assunta awoke at the rising bell, she found the incident an amusing one to relate at recreation. At the end of the story, however, she begged the superior to put someone else at her post, saying, "What good am I there? Thieves could carry off the entire chapel, and I would sleep on. They could even carry off my bed with me in it and I would not know it!"

In January of 1904 Assunta wrote to her parents and spelled out for them what was to become, in truth, one of the main parts of her mission. She wrote, "I ask the Lord for the grace to make known to the world purity of intention—which consists in doing everything for the love of God, even the most ordinary actions." Little did she suspect that one day the world would call her "blessed" for her heroic purity of intention.

Sister Maria Assunta took her final vows in February of 1904. Following one of the beautiful customs of her order, at one part of the ceremony she was given a crown of thorns with the words, "Receive this crown...that thou mayest be worthy to participate in Christ's Passion on earth and His glory in Heaven."

Shortly afterwards, Sister Assunta received the joyful news that she was to be assigned to the missions in China, in the same province where the seven protomartyrs of the Order had died. Traveling through Rome, the sisters who were leaving for the missions received a special blessing from Pope Pius X. After a long and difficult journey—by boat, by foot, by train and by mule—the sturdy little band arrived at last in China.

Mission life was all that Sister Assunta had hoped for and dreamed of. Here she cooked, nursed, helped with the children and studied Chinese. Here she loved and served God in every way she could. In 1905 she wrote for herself a set of resolutions which began: "I came to the convent to become a saint. What good will it do to live long if I do not attain my goal?" The list ended with the resolve "To do all for the love of God." With her spiritual director's permission, Assunta later made a vow to do everything for the love of God.

Mother Symphorien, superior of the mission, recalled an incident which displays Assunta's spirit of extreme charity and humility. "At the slightest criticism, she would fall on her knees immediately and listen respectfully to whatever might be said. Then, thanking me, she would ask pardon, promising to do better, as she kissed the ground and returned to her work. It once happened that I admonished her severely for a fault which she had not committed, and learning some days later the name of the real culprit,

I sent for Sister Assunta to tell her my regret, and I asked why she had not explained the matter to me. 'Because there was nothing to excuse,' she replied with simplicity."

The winter months were extremely severe, and in February one of the children in the orphanage fell dangerously ill. The dread diagnosis of typhus was made. Soon a number of the community and many of the children were sick. Sister Assunta, young and strong, did all she could to help in the care of the stricken group. With total forgetfulness of self, she nursed the others; her fatigue was apparent in her face.

On March 19, just one year since she had left Italy, Sister Assunta herself was stricken with typhus. Her case was judged to be mild, and the doctor believed she would survive if she remained quiet and rested in bed. On March 25 she asked for Holy Viaticum and Extreme Unction, but the superior protested that Assunta was not very ill and would soon be well.

"No, Mother," she replied, "I shall die soon, and I would like to receive the Last Sacraments while I am fully conscious. It is a grace which I desire with all my heart."

It was felt best to accede to her request, so after her careful preparation and confession, the sisters came to her room. Assunta humbly asked their pardon for all the bad example and scandal she had given. Everyone was profoundly moved, as Sister Assunta had never given anything but good example. She responded to the prayers, received Holy Viaticum and renewed her vows.

There was a temporary improvement in Sister Assunta's condition; but when the superior teased her that she had been in too great a hurry to die, she replied with a smile, "You will see, Mother, I shall be with Jesus soon."

Then the fever rose and delirium set in. Sister Assunta begged repeatedly for Holy Communion, but she was unable to receive for she could not swallow. The words she repeated most during those long hours were the names of Jesus and Mary. Her desire for Communion was expressed in her last spoken word, *"Centi! Centi!"* (Chinese for Eucharist).

On the 7th of April the sisters gathered around the bed of the dying Assunta. The confessor of the community and five or six Chinese girls were also in the room. The prayers for the dying had been recited. All knew the end was near. Suddenly, those in the room began to notice a delightful fragrance which resembled a mixture of violets and incense. Both the superior and the confessor asked what the "perfume" was. There was no natural explanation. Quietly, the beautiful soul of Sister Assunta slipped away.

As he was leaving, the confessor told the superior that all should note down everything known about the little sister who had just passed from their midst.

That night Sister Assunta's body remained in the infirmary. The following morning a crowd of Chinese Christians invaded the mission compound, asking to experience the miracle. News of the fragrant odor had spread. For three days the mysterious perfume remained in the house, then it ceased on the day of her burial, April 9, at the hour at which she had died two evenings before.

The Chinese Christians began to ask Assunta for favors, and they became convinced that she had answered their requests.

Eight years after Assunta's death, the Community was transferred from Tong Eul Koo to Tai Yuan Foo, and the bishop wished that the body of Sister Assunta also be transferred. Disinterment revealed that the body was incorrupt. It remained in the chapel of the cemetery for a month without being affected.

In 1913 Pope Pius X said, "When I hear of the extraordinary, I am the most incredulous man in the world. But when I hear of sanctity expressed in the simple practice of virtue, as in the case of this little sister, I believe in that....the way to sanctity is not difficult. It is a thorny road, but easy...the cause should be introduced without delay."

In 1932, the decree of the heroic virtues of Sister Maria Assunta was read. She was beatified in 1954.

Bl. Maria Assunta, who was sent as a missionary to China and died there of typhus at age 26. A mysterious fragrance was noticed after her death; her body was found incorrupt when disinterred eight years after her death, and it remained in the chapel of the cemetery for a month without being affected.

Daughter of a poor Italian family, Assunta lived a life of great humility, obedience and gratitude for her religious vocation. When a fellow novice had tried to get Assunta to leave the convent with her, Assunta replied, "O Sister, that is a temptation of the devil! Try to overcome it at once. It is useless for you to invite me to follow you, for I have abandoned all the things of earth and I trust with the grace of God never to turn back for anything in the world."

248

26

BLESSED ELIZABETH OF THE TRINITY

Blessed Elizabeth of the Trinity, O.C.D.
Elizabeth Catez
1880 - 1906
France
Died Age 26

The grandfather and father of little Elizabeth Catez were soldiers, and she inherited from them a fiery temperament. In her early childhood she often had temper tantrums which seemed impossible to control. Her teacher mentioned that she had a "will of iron" and a "determination to have what she wants." The priest who prepared her for her First Communion told a friend, "With her temperament, Elizabeth Catez will be either a saint or a demon."

From the time of her first confession, Elizabeth turned her staunch determination to the battle against her hot-tempered and independent nature. Years later, she wrote, "We must fix our gaze on God. It requires an effort at first when we are boiling with anger, but gently, with patience and the help of grace, we conquer in the end." Her writing on this point was based on firsthand experience. She had conquered her temper so completely that she was known at home and in the society in which she moved as a gentle and gracious girl, who inspired those with whom she came in contact with peace and joy. She was attractive, intelligent and vivacious.

On Elizabeth's First Communion day, the Reverend Mother of the nearby Carmelite monastery explained to her that her name meant "House of God." This made a deep impression on Elizabeth.

Elizabeth worked very hard to overcome what she considered her two chief faults, anger and oversensitiveness. She also took care to keep herself from falling in love with the world. Elizabeth said, "The struggle was over by the time I was 18." By then her heart always turned spontaneously to God.

By the age of 14, Elizabeth had already decided that she wanted to become a Carmelite nun, but her mother would not hear of it.

Elizabeth's father had died when she was quite young, and she lived with her mother and her sister Marguerite. She tried to make them understand her call to Carmel by having a priest come and talk to them, but that only served to make Madame Catez more firm in her decision. So Elizabeth began to wait for God's direction.

This is not to imply that she stayed at home in glum silence. She was obedient to her mother's wishes and went everywhere. She joyously took part in the social life of her crowd, and received more than one offer of marriage. She entertained her friends with her skill at the piano. It was said, "No one interprets the great masters as she does." Many pleasant hours were spent in horseback riding, playing tennis, dancing and other social activities. During the summer holidays, the family left Dijon and took long trips. Elizabeth was able to see many parts of Europe. Yet amid all the fun and gaiety of her life, she still felt the call to Carmel.

In the midst of the social activities required by her mother, Elizabeth also maintained an ardent interior life. She practiced recollection, prayer, hidden penance and, above all, charity. She taught catechism to a group of "tough" children who worked in factories. She seemed to attract all children like a magnet.

When she was 18, Elizabeth spoke to a priest about a mysterious feeling she had of "being dwelt in." The priest explained that this was true, since the Holy Trinity dwelt in her soul through Baptism. The priest later wrote that during this conversation, "I saw her borne away as on a tidal wave." The doctrine of the indwelling of the Trinity in the Christian soul would become the very core of Elizabeth's spiritual life.

As her spiritual life deepened, she became more and more cherished by her family and friends. Yet Elizabeth's heart was steadfast, and her thoughts were ever with "Him." It became apparent even to her mother that this lovely child of hers belonged in the cloister. Finally, seeing that Elizabeth would not change her mind, her mother changed hers and allowed her daughter to follow her own heart as to her vocation. Joyfully, Elizabeth entered the Carmel at Dijon on August 2, 1902, at the age of 20. She received the name Elizabeth of the Trinity.

A true Carmelite spends herself all day in saving souls by means of prayer and silent immolation. Then, when evening comes, before taking her necessary sleep, she asks Mary to take her place, while she sleeps, in her work of intercession for poor sinners and to continue effectively the destruction of evil in the world. The first evening after Elizabeth entered the Carmel, the superior, Mother Germain, found her silent and recollected beside the great crucifix that stood in the garden. "What are you doing here, my child?" she asked.

"I have passed into the soul of my Christ," answered Elizabeth. "I want to make Him loved by the whole world. I love 'till I could die of love."

As a cloistered Carmelite, Sister Elizabeth of the Trinity spent her days doing the same things that her sisters in religion did. She prayed—for sinners, for those she knew and loved, for those she did not know, and especially for priests. She faithfully kept the Carmelite Rule—which included a great deal of silence and sacrifice. She even acted in plays during recreation periods and appreciated the good pies made by the monastery cook. No matter what she did, be it pleasant or painful, Elizabeth was very happy.

Elizabeth once said, "It seems to me that I have found my heaven on earth, for heaven is God and God is in my soul. On the day I understood that, everything became clear to me. . . ."

In Carmel, Sister Elizabeth moved rapidly toward the fulfillment of the special call which seemed to be hers— "to be a praise of glory to the Triune God," an idea suggested by St. Paul in his Epistles. This idea dominated Elizabeth's short religious life and she shared it in her writings. She referred to the Three Persons of the Blessed Trinity as "my Three." Theologians are amazed at the theological depths of Elizabeth's writings.

In the last part of her short life, Elizabeth began to call herself by another name—*'Laudem Gloriae.''* This means the "praise of Glory."

Elizabeth came to a profound realization that the spouse of Christ is called upon to be immolated with Him in the great work of Redemption. More and more she longed to spend herself in becoming to Christ "an additional humanity in which He may renew the whole of His mystery." She longed to suffer with Him for the "glory of His Father and for the needs of the Church." With the collapse of her health in March of 1906, and the terrible suffering that was hers until her death the next fall, Elizabeth was to realize her desire to the full. Her last wish was "to die not only as pure as an angel, but transformed into Jesus Crucified." She would suffer and die "with the dignity of a queen."

She wrote, "How happy I should be if my Master also desired that I should shed my blood for Him, but what I ask of Him especially is that martyrdom of love which consumed my holy Mother Teresa [of Avila] whom the Church proclaims Victim of Divine Love; and since the Truth has said the greatest proof of love is to give one's life for the one loved, I give Him mine, that He may do with it as He pleases. If I am not a martyr by blood, I wish to be one for love."

Before Elizabeth's death, the prioress of her Carmel had requested that she write down some of her thoughts. At night, when she could not sleep, Elizabeth obediently took up her notebook to write.

Much of her writing deals with the Divine Indwelling (through Sanctifying Grace). She wrote to remind us that in Baptism, the Holy Trinity comes to live within the soul of the person baptized. It was the ambition of Sister Elizabeth to tell everyone the secret of happiness and sanctity hidden in the depths of the soul by the Divine Indwelling.

Sister Elizabeth was admitted to the infirmary in March of 1906. One night, seeing a picture of Mary, she remembered a statue of Our Lady of Lourdes before which she had received many favors as a young girl. She asked her mother for the statue in order that she who had presided at her reception might also watch over her departure. From that time on, Elizabeth always called the statue *Janua Coeli*, or "Gate of Heaven."

Shortly before her death, Sister Elizabeth had been asked what her mission in Heaven would be. She replied, "In Heaven, I believe that my mission will be to draw souls to interior recollection, by helping them to renounce self in order to adhere to God in all simplicity and love; to maintain them in that profound interior silence which allows God to imprint Himself upon them and to transform them into Himself."

Sister Elizabeth of the Trinity died in November, 1906, after barely five years in Carmel. She was beatified November 25, 1984.

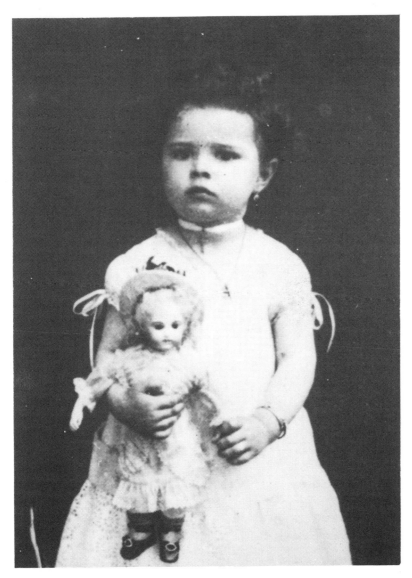

Bl. Elizabeth of the Trinity as a young child. The little girl often had temper tantrums. Her teacher said she had "a will of iron." Elizabeth's mother wisely guided her daughter, instructing her in self-conquest through love.

Elizabeth had great skill at the piano. People noticed that she had a genius for interpreting the great masters. She confided in a letter that her secret was to forget about the audience and imagine herself to be "alone with the Divine Master."

Elizabeth's widowed mother dreaded the separation from her beloved Elizabeth, who had a vocation to Carmel. Elizabeth knew from childhood that she wanted to become a nun and belong to God; at 14 she knew she was called to Carmel, but her mother would not give her up till she was 21. Elizabeth spent the intervening years in great love, reverence and obedience to her mother, actively taking part in the social life her mother wished for her—yet her heart was constantly with "Him."

255

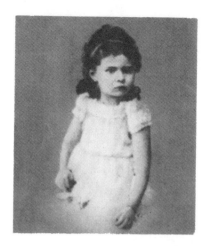

Elizabeth at ages three, eleven and twenty. Elizabeth struggled to overcome her impulsive nature and achieved many victories over herself in preparation for her First Communion. She also kept a close watch on her heart so as not to be caught up in the world. Gradually Elizabeth won this victory; she said, "The struggle was over by the time I was 18."

Sister Elizabeth of the Trinity, the Carmelite. Elizabeth's spiritual life was marked by a deep realization that the Three Divine Persons dwelt in her soul. She wrote, "It seems to me that I have found my heaven on earth, for heaven is God and God is in my soul. On the day I understood that, everything became clear to me."

257

Elizabeth had a special call "to be a praise of glory to the Triune God."
In the last part of her life she began to call herself *"Laudem Gloriae,"*
"the praise of Glory." She wanted to make the whole world love God.

In this picture Elizabeth's face seems to have become thinner; the picture may date from her last illness before she died at age 26. Elizabeth's health collapsed in the spring of 1906, and she went through many physical and spiritual sufferings in her last months, having offered herself to God as a holocaust. Her last wish was "to die not only as pure as an angel, but transformed into Jesus Crucified."

27

POPE SAINT PIUS X

Giuseppe Sarto
1835 - 1914
Italy
Died Age 79

A woman came to the Vatican to have an audience with Pope Pius X; she had brought her little son with her. As the mother spoke with the Holy Father, the little boy approached the Pontiff and put his hands on his knees, peering up into his face. Looking kindly at the child, Pius asked the mother his age. "He is four," she answered, "and in two or three years I hope he will receive his First Communion." The Pope looked earnestly at the little boy and asked him, "Whom do you receive in Holy Communion?" He answered promptly, "Jesus Christ."

"And who is Jesus Christ?"

"Jesus Christ is God."

The Pope turned to the mother and said, "Bring him to me tomorrow and I will give him Holy Communion myself."

Known as "the Pope of the Eucharist," Pius X was the one who lowered the age for First Communion from between 11 and 14 to the age of reason, around seven. Thus he made it possible for young children to receive Our Lord at a time when their hearts are still largely untouched by the distractions and dangers of this world.

Giuseppe Sarto was born on June 2, 1835 in Riese, a small village in Italy. He was the oldest of the eight surviving children of a postman and his seamstress wife. The Sartos were good, simple, pious peasant people who raised all their children to have the love of God in their hearts.

When he was barely 10, Giuseppe—or Bepi, as he was called—expressed his desire to become a priest. Financially, this would have been impossible, as the Sarto family was very poor, but the parish priest arranged for Giuseppe's schooling. In order to attend,

Giuseppe had to walk five miles into town each morning. He carried his shoes slung over his back so as to conserve the soles.

After four years Giuseppe applied to the seminary at Treviso, scoring extremely high marks on his entrance exams. Still his family simply could not afford the expense, so the pastor of Riese again took pity on the boy and obtained for him a scholarship to the seminary at Padua. He did very well at the seminary.

One day in 1852 Giuseppe knocked at the rectory door and, with tears in his eyes, requested leave to go home, as his father was sick. Permission was granted. After a short illness, Giuseppe's father died. In addition to the grief he felt at the loss of his father, Giuseppe realized that the family was now left with hardly any financial support. He offered to remain home to help his mother, but she valiantly refused his offer, telling him that God would provide. Giuseppe returned to the seminary and was ordained in 1858.

The young priest's first assignment was that of curate, or assistant pastor, of the village of Tombolo. There he began his ministry in a way that can serve as a model for all parish priests. Don Giuseppe went out to the homes of his parishioners, treating each person with love and respect. He comforted the sick and gave temporal aid to the poor whenever possible. Knowing well how it felt to be poor, he could not bear not to be able to help those in need. Because of this his silver watch—practically the only valuable thing he owned—went, more than once, to the pawnshop. When Don Giuseppe went to preach in a nearby parish, people would "ambush" him as he started back home with his stipend in his pocket; he sometimes returned with nothing. The pastor would protest, "It is not fair to your mother, Bepi; you should think of her." Bepi would reply, "God will provide for my mother; these poor souls were in greater need than she." Throughout his life the words "God will provide" were to be Giuseppe's watchword.

The pastor at Tombolo realized that a man with the talents of Giuseppe Sarto should not remain hidden in a small village. Through his recommendation and assistance Don Giuseppe was appointed as pastor of Salzano, one of the principal parishes of the diocese. Salzano was a parish of refined and high-class persons; they were at first appalled that the Bishop had assigned an unknown and ragged country priest to their illustrious parish. They even sent him a delegation in protest. The Bishop's calm reply was, "I am giving you the curate of Tombolo as parish priest; in this I am doing

Salzano a great favor." After Giuseppe's first Mass and sermon
the people were convinced. He promptly proved to be a saintly
pastor. They could always find him either with the poor, in the
confessional, or on his knees in front of the Blessed Sacrament.
When called to the dying he would drop everything, during the
day or in the middle of the night, and hurry out to prepare the
soul to meet God.

One of the things that distressed Don Giuseppe was the constant
swearing he heard among the men and boys. One thing that bothered
many of the men and boys was the inability to read and write.
Despite his heavy schedule Don Giuseppe offered to teach them.
Night classes were begun. When the pupils wished to do something to repay their priest, he answered, "Stop swearing and then
I shall be more than repaid."

In Salzano, as at Tombolo, Giuseppe went out to meet his flock,
not waiting for them to come to him. He tried to give them a
real understanding of the principles of Christian doctrine.

The teaching of catechism—to both children and adults—was always of primary importance to Giuseppe Sarto. He felt that if catechism instruction were neglected the faith of his people would
languish and die. His instructions were so well attended that a few
priests from neighboring parishes complained to the Bishop about
their own dwindling crowds. The Bishop replied, "Go thou and
do likewise."

Another innovation he brought to this parish was a school for
the training of a good choir and the establishment of a savings
bank to improve the economic conditions of the farmers. He also
tried to teach the farmers better agricultural methods. Don Giuseppe's
energy was boundless; he used to say, "Work is man's chief duty
on earth."

Giuseppe Sarto's favorites, here as everywhere he went, were the
poor. His sisters, who were his housekeepers, despaired of his constant charity; his policy of giving things away was as bad as before,
if not worse. Food, linen and clothes kept disappearing from the
rectory. Once his sister Rosa complained, "The meat for dinner
has disappeared from the pan!"

"The cat may have stolen it," suggested the pastor. Not to be
put off, Rosa asked if the cat were able to take the pan off the
fire. Giuseppe had to confess that he had taken the food to a poor
sick woman.

On another occasion Rosa got an old friend of the Sartos, Don Carlo, to assist in circumventing her brother's generosity. Giuseppe had just gotten a little money. His clothes were in sad shape, and a shirting merchant was planning to arrive on the morrow—but of course Giuseppe would insist that he had no need of his wares. When the merchant arrived Don Carlo was on hand to examine the fabric and then haggle over a fair price. He had the merchant cut off a nice length of material, then turned to Giuseppe and declared, "So many yards at such and such a price. Pay up, Don Giuseppe!" Giuseppe was disgusted—but he paid. Rosa was delighted; she told Don Carlo privately, "If you had not been here today, tomorrow there would have been neither money nor linen!"

In 1873 a terrible cholera epidemic struck Salzano. Throughout the epidemic Don Sarto acted like an angel of mercy, going on sick calls himself as he did not want his curates to be exposed to the disease. Some of the sick got the idea that the medicine prescribed by the doctors was intended to put them out of their misery; they would accept it only from the hand of Don Giuseppe. During this time Giuseppe was constantly on the go, coming close to exhaustion. Despite his strong constitution, he damaged his health and never fully regained his old vigor.

In 1875, at the age of 40, Don Giuseppe Sarto was appointed as chancellor of the diocese of Treviso and spiritual director (and later administrator) of the seminary. One of the tasks he took great care to perform was the instruction of little boys for First Communion. The vice rector begged him to leave this to someone with more time, but he replied, "It is my duty; am I not their spiritual father?"

At the seminary he took a special delight in helping those seminarians who were poor to afford their desire of attaining the priesthood. In the refectory, he was the life of the gathering. Laying aside his many cares and the big bundle of papers that accompanied him everywhere, he would tell amusing stories and begin interesting discussions, sometimes slyly teasing certain professors. During these times of recreation anyone who fell into heavy topics, e.g., by mentioning the word "logic," had to make up by telling a story.

Don Sarto's lifelong habit was to work much and sleep little, retiring after midnight and arising by four o'clock. At the seminary the occupant of the room next to his, Don Francesco, would sometimes hear his neighbor up late at night and would call out to him, "Go to bed, Monsignor. He works ill who works too long." Don Giuseppe would call back, "Quite true, quite true, Don Francesco. Put that into practice; go to bed and sleep well."

One morning in 1884 the Bishop of Treviso invited Don Sarto to come to the chapel and pray for God's assistance in a matter which concerned them both. After a short prayer, the Bishop handed Don Sarto a papal document dated September 16, 1884, notifying him that the Pope had appointed him Bishop of Mantua.

Back outside the chapel, the stunned priest replied that he was not fit for the job. He wept like a child. He even went so far as to write to Pope Leo XIII to set forth his own worthlessness and complete unsuitability for the job. The answer was direct: Obey. That settled it.

Shortly after his consecration Bishop Sarto showed his dear old mother his bishop's ring. She duly admired it, then in turn held out her hand with its plain gold wedding band, saying, "You would not have that ring if I did not have this one!"

As bishop, Don Giuseppe Sarto continued his policy of going out to his sheep. He announced a canonical visitation of all parishes, but asked that the pastors not give him a party or a dinner. Rather, he wanted them to welcome him in church, praying with their parishioners. He said, "That is the greatest honor they can do me. . . . I desire no useless pomp, but rather the salvation of souls."

The catechesis of children was one of the highest priorities of Bishop Sarto. He set up confraternities and schools, as well as teaching children himself to make sure they were properly instructed. He threatened with severe penalties those parents who would not let their children attend instructions. On this score the Bishop, so gentle toward the sorrowful and suffering, was stern and inflexible; the children's souls were at stake, he said, and he would not see their birthright withheld from them.

Bishop Sarto also took a great interest in Church music, requiring that it be decorous and religious, and that Gregorian chant should be used when possible. Later, as Cardinal of Venice, he was to ban from churches the use of string orchestras, drums, trumpets, tambourines, whistles and operatic-style music.

One of the pastors in the diocese had a reputation for being late to church every morning, which caused the faithful who wanted to go to confession before Mass to have to wait a long time. When making his pastoral visitation to this parish, the Bishop arrived unannounced, then entered the confessional and began hearing confessions. When the tardy priest arrived, Bishop Sarto explained that he did not want the poor people to have to wait too long, so he had come to help out.

On another occasion he instructed two priests to meet him in his parlor at 11 o'clock sharp. At the appointed hour the Bishop entered the room, dressed in coat and hat, and said to the priests, "Oh yes you were to come here this morning, but first I have to go to the Capuchin monastery. The carriage is waiting outside. Will you join me?" Of course the priests agreed. On arrival at the monastery, it was obvious that the Bishop was not expected. When the Father Guardian came to the parlor to ask what he could do for the Bishop, Bishop Sarto replied that he only wished a small favor. After inquiring whether the Capuchins had an available room and receiving an affirmative answer, he pointed to the two priests and said, "These two gentlemen have not made a retreat for more than five years and would like to spend a few days in seclusion in your monastery." Then with a friendly goodbye he left the two priests to make their retreat.

In 1893 Bishop Sarto was made Cardinal Patriarch of Venice. He had to borrow enough money to pay for the train ticket to Rome to receive the red hat. When he went afterward to visit his mother, she received him with joy, then, laughing, said, "But Bepi, you have turned all red!" Referring to his mother's advancing age, the Cardinal lovingly replied, "And you, Mother, you have turned all white."

At this time anticlericalism was strong in Italy, and the new Patriarch showed a political acumen that surprised many. He often settled bitter disputes between capital and labor. He encouraged the Catholic masses, who traditionally had stayed away from the polls, to vote and let their ideas be heard. Before and during the elections, he inaugurated a regular crusade of prayer throughout the diocese. Many good changes soon came about, proving, as the Cardinal had so often repeated, that the Church and state could very well live and work together peacefully. In political matters Cardinal Sarto's policy was to be extremely kind and bending with the person or persons involved, but absolutely uncompromising on Catholic principles.

The new Cardinal understood well the secularism that was turning souls from God. In his first pastoral letter he deplored the
fact that God was being driven out of learning, art, law, schools,
Christian marriage, the cottages of the poor and the palaces of
the rich. He said, "We must fight the great contemporary error,
the enthronement of man in the place of God. The solution of this,
as of all other problems, lies in the Church and the teaching of
the Gospel."

Cardinal Sarto preached not only by word but also by example,
and even with his new title and responsibilities he never thought
it beneath himself to do the simple work of the priesthood. He
would invite himself to a parish and sit for hours hearing confessions, and he would often assist a pastor with his Mass. A priest
friend was once astonished to find the Cardinal planning to serve
his Mass. "What!" exclaimed the Cardinal, smiling; "do you imagine that a prelate of my rank does not know how to serve Mass?
A fine idea you have of the princes of the Church!"

Here too Giuseppe Sarto insisted strongly on religious instructions for all ages. He knew that sermons often bore little fruit because preachers took for granted that their hearers were
well-instructed, when actually many, including those learned in secular sciences, were very ignorant of the truths of the Faith. He urged
priests to preach simply, emphasizing the basic doctrines.

As Cardinal, Giuseppe Sarto did not forget the poor. He visited
the sick and prisoners. It was said that the episcopal ring was pawned
more than once. The people loved him dearly and would say, "There
goes our dear patriarch, intent on some good. God bless him and
the mother who bore him."

In 1901 he led a crowd of 10,000 pilgrims to the top of Mount
Grappa to consecrate a shrine to the Blessed Virgin. He dressed,
as usual, in an ordinary black cassock. After the ceremony the
people flocked around and some began to shout, "Viva our patriarch!" With a shake of his head, the humble shepherd answered,
"Viva Our Lady." Don Giuseppe was deeply devoted to the Blessed
Virgin Mary; as pope he had a picture of Our Lady as an infant
placed over his bed.

Pope Leo XIII died in 1903, and the Cardinals from around the
world prepared to travel to Rome to vote for his successor. As Cardinal Sarto was leaving Venice, practically the whole city gathered
at the wharf. The people called out in unison, "Your Eminence,

come back soon!" Giuseppe Sarto answered, "Alive or dead, I'll return to my dear Venice, which I shall never forget!" (He would never return alive, though in 1959 his body was transferred to Venice for a month.)

When, after a number of votes, it became apparent that Cardinal Sarto might indeed be elected, he spoke to the assembled cardinals, stating with trembling voice that he was unworthy and unqualified, and begging the electors to forget him. As the American Cardinal Gibbons of Baltimore later related, this humble speech made the cardinals consider Cardinal Sarto all the more.

Monsignor Merry del Val, secretary of the conclave, was sent to Cardinal Sarto to ask whether he would still refuse if elected. The secretary found him in the Pauline Chapel, kneeling on the floor in front of a bench, his head between both hands. He was as white as a sheet and his eyes were filled with tears. He looked as if he were in agony. Cardinal Sarto still could not bring himself to accept the highest office in the Church. Later that day, however, he consented.

On the morning of August 4, 1903, the ballots were cast and an overwhelming majority named Cardinal Sarto as the next Supreme Pontiff of the Church. Some of the influential cardinals, including Cardinal Gibbons, called on him to obtain his official acceptance. He said, "The responsibility of the papacy is terribly frightening." This was said with real horror in his otherwise serene eyes. One cardinal replied that the responsibility of refusing to accept the lawful election would be worse, and when Cardinal Sarto further argued that as his health was weak he would pay for the acceptance with his life, the same forthright cardinal told him to apply Caiphas' words to himself: "It is expedient that one man should die for the people." After his acceptance, when asked his choice of name, he said, "Because the popes who in this century suffered most for the Church carried the name of Pius, I will take this name." From then on, he would be called Pope Pius X.

For more than three centuries, the popes had been elected from among the members of the Italian nobility or the upper classes. Now, a man of the common people had risen to the highest office in the Church, and the people loved him for it. There were many things he had to learn and to unlearn about his new status, and some things he changed. Although it was customary for the popes to eat alone, he changed this custom immediately. His white robes, which replaced his old familiar black cassock, caused some problems. His secretaries had to remind him that ink shows up more on white than on black and therefore he should not wipe off his pen on his sleeve.

The program of Pius' pontificate was "to renew all things in Christ"—a difficult task, but one which he worked at diligently. He had a particular interest in reverent and traditional church music, and he established a university in Rome for its study. He began the great legal work of the codification of canon law; this was finished under his successor, Benedict XV. In 1908 he brought about reorganization of the Roman congregations and tribunals, mitigated the rigorous fast and abstinence laws, and elevated a large number of saints and beati to the honors of the altar. Pius taught the laity to apply Christian principles to social problems, in order to bring all men under the rule of Our Lord Jesus Christ.

Pope Pius X called all the faithful to a better participation in the liturgy. It was this "Pope of the Eucharist" who, in the face of the Jansenism still floating around, encouraged all the faithful to receive Holy Communion frequently, even daily, since this Sacrament was intended by Christ to help the struggling, not as a reward reserved for the perfect. The required interior dispositions were the state of grace and a right intention. The Pope made a habit of inviting all the First Communicants of Rome to visit him in the Vatican, where he would instruct them and lovingly speak to them.

One of the great trials of Pope Pius X's reign was the growth of Modernism, which he called "the synthesis of all heresies." It was undermining the faith of many. In his famous encyclical *Pascendi* (1907), Pius clearly analyzed Modernism, showing how it is utterly irreconcilable with the Christian Faith and how it has its root in pride. Modernism denied the historical truths about Christ's life, reduced faith to an inner feeling and reinterpreted Catholic doctrines in a this-worldly sense, giving no real importance to religious authority. These ideas were passed off as simply a more progressive approach to Catholicism; whereas, they actually spelled the denial of all Christian truths. Priests and professors with modernist beliefs were passing as Catholics and thus corrupting the faith of others from "inside" the Church.

Following up his encyclical, Pius X required all priests to take an "Anti-Modernist Oath." This Pope with the great heart was inflexible when he had to defend the rights of God and protect souls.

Although there was a storm of protest from some over the Pope's "repressive" measures, faithful Catholics realized that the Pope had performed a lifesaving service for the Church. For the time, Modernism was largely to disappear, though it would break out again several decades later.

Pius took action to give substantial aid to the victims of a long list of disasters. It was said that he had "the greatest heart of any man alive." Often, people joked that he would be capable of selling the entire Vatican in order to help the poor. On one occasion when the Pope and his physician began a walk in the Vatican gardens, the doctor turned to lock the door—but the Pope told him not to trouble himself: "There's nothing in there anyway; I gave away the last penny this morning." More than once, through the Pope's blessing, people were miraculously cured of diseases which had baffled their doctors.

People who visited the Pope could sense his holiness, but if anyone referred to him as *Papa Santo*, "the holy Pope," he would quickly reply, "You err in one consonant: I am *Papa Sarto!*" When the priests at his former cathedral in Treviso wanted to erect a memorial stone to him, he told them rather to remember him in their Masses and prayers and to forget about "stoning" him. He himself lived as humbly as ever, often making a meal of a little cheese and a few nuts. When he first came to the Vatican he warned the two secretaries he had brought from Venice that if they used their new position to better their status in society he would have them dismissed at once. At the end of his life he said, "I was born poor, I have lived in poverty, and I shall end my days a poor man."

During the last part of his life, Pope Pius X felt an intense anxiety about the dangerous political developments he witnessed in the world. In the first months of 1914, when he heard how the bishops of Mexico had been driven out of the country, a profound sadness spread over his face—and his good-natured smile never returned.

The Pope had predicted that there would be a great war, and in 1914, when Archduke Francis Ferdinand and his wife were assassinated, he said, "This is the spark which will set the world afire." Suffering for all those who would be involved in the conflict, he said, "Oh that war, it is going to kill me!"

For several weeks in late summer Pius suffered from obstinate bronchitis, and in mid-August it was announced that he was ill.

Rather unexpectedly, on August 20, 1914, the great bell of St. Peter's tolled out *pro pontifice agonizzante*, "for a pope in agony"; at that signal, exposition of the Blessed Sacrament and special prayers began in all the patriarchal basilicas. Various Cardinals gathered at the Pope's bedside; some were in tears. The last words that Pius was able to speak were, "I resign myself completely." For several more hours he was unable to speak, but he blessed those who came to his bedside, clasping their proferred hands. Every so often he slowly made the Sign of the Cross on his brow and breast.

A little after 11:15 a.m. the Pope died peacefully. One prelate said, "The Holy Father has died of a broken heart."

Pope Pius X was canonized in 1954. He was the first canonized pope in 342 years.

Fr. Giuseppe Sarto as a young priest; he was ordained at age 23. Knowing well what it was like to be poor, the young curate more than once pawned his silver watch to obtain money for the needy. When called to the dying in the day or night he would drop everything and hurry out to prepare the soul to meet God. Parishioners knew that their priest could always be found either with the poor, in the confessional, or on his knees before the Blessed Sacrament.

271

Giuseppe Sarto as Bishop of Mantua, age 49. Throughout his entire cleri-cal life, even when he was Pope, Giuseppe gave catechism instruction. The usually gentle Bishop was stern and inflexible toward parents who would not let their children attend instructions: the children's souls were at stake, he said, and he would not see their birthright withheld from them.

Giuseppe Sarto as Cardinal Patriarch of Venice; he had to borrow the money to buy a train ticket to Rome to receive the red hat. The new Cardinal encouraged Catholics to let their voices be heard at the polls; bringing spiritual weapons to the political arena, he would organize a prayer crusade throughout the diocese before and during elections.

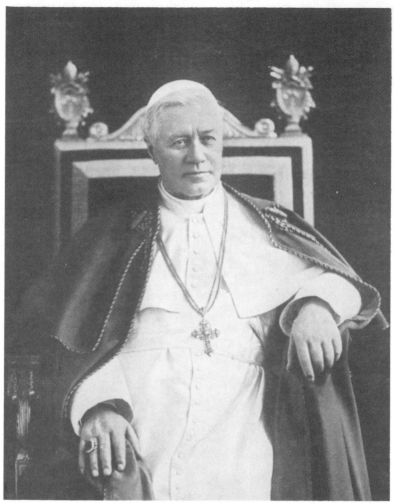

Giuseppe Sarto as Pope Pius X. He had pleaded with the Cardinals to elect someone else, but to no avail. Pope Pius X was to occupy the Chair of Peter from 1903-1914. The new Pope lowered the age for First Communion from 12 to 7, took strong measures against Modernism, and continued to give generously to those in need.

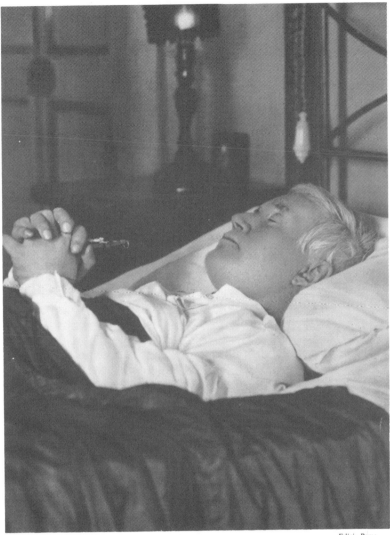

Pope St. Pius X in death. The country-boy-become-Pope had said, "I was born poor, I have lived in poverty, and I shall end my days a poor man." His last audible words were "I resign myself completely." One can well imagine the words Giuseppe Sarto must have heard as he entered eternity: "Well done, good and faithful servant."

28

BLESSED BROTHER MUCIAN
OF MALONNE

Blessed Brother Mucian of Malonne, F.S.C.
Louis Joseph Wiaux
1841 - 1917
Belgium
Died Age 75

What a misfortune it would be if sanctity were reserved alone to those who have extraordinary circumstances in their lives! The life of the humble Christian brother, Brother Mucian of Malonne, is a lesson that holiness does not necessarily require doing extraordinary things, but very often consists in doing ordinary daily tasks in an exact and faithful way.

Louis Joseph Wiaux was born on March 20, 1841 in the small village of Mellet, Belgium. He was one of six children of the local blacksmith and innkeeper. His father was a hearty block of a man who loved to swap yarns and tales with his customers; his mother ran the family inn and haberdashery. The parents brought up their children according to the precepts of their Catholic faith.

Although Louis was a bright pupil and a pious boy who loved to visit the church to pray, he was also a lively child who enjoyed the games he played with his companions. Louis was a leader, and he would often persuade a group of the village children to accompany him to the church to say the Rosary or make the Way of the Cross together. On the way to school, the children had to cross a narrow bridge over a small stream. If any of the children had been misbehaving, Louis would bar the way across the bridge until the culprit would promise to mend his ways. After primary school, as there was no nearby secondary school, Louis went to work in the forge with his father.

In 1855 the De La Salle Christian Brothers established a school in a nearby town. Fourteen-year-old Louis was fascinated by these brothers in the black robes and white rabats. At last he asked his parish priest if it would be possible for him to join them. The pastor spoke with Louis' parents and the superior of the brothers, and in April Louis was admitted to the novitiate in Namur.

At first the new way of life, run on strictly monastic principles, was strange to the young novice. Once he had such a bout of homesickness that he was tempted to run away. He persevered, however, and soon became one of the most fervent of the novices.

Three months after his entrance he received the habit and the name of Brother Mucian Marie. St. Mucian was a martyr of the early Church. The "Marie" was prophetic, for Brother Mucian Marie's life was to be marked by a firm and loving devotion to Our Lady. In one of his rare letters he wrote, "If you wish to find a short and easy path to intimate union with Our Lord, go through Mary. The more you love the Most Blessed Virgin, the more you will love her divine Son."

Brother Mucian's novice master insisted on an exact observance of the Rule. Brother Mucian never forgot this training; his devotion to the Rule was exemplary throughout his life. Pope Benedict XIV once remarked, "Find me a religious who has observed his Rule perfectly for the space of two years, and I shall canonize him without miracles." This Pope understood the difficulty of performing all one's actions according to plan. Brother Mucian understood also, and with heroic self-discipline followed the Rule exactly, giving his existence and his actions their maximum efficacy.

In 1859 Brother Mucian was sent to the teacher training college and boarding school, St. Berthuin's at Malonne. Here the 18-year-old was given charge of a group of unruly nine-year-olds. Brother Mucian was not a born disciplinarian, and he was far too gentle to manage these lively youngsters. His classroom was a shambles, and by April of 1860 it was obvious that as a teacher he was a failure. A chapter meeting was held to decide if it would not be more charitable to send him away, as there were such grave doubts as to whether he would ever be able to qualify for the life of a teaching brother. One of the senior brothers who taught art and music, Brother Maixentis, spoke up for Brother Mucian and asked to have him appointed as his assistant. Due to this, Brother Mucian was allowed to make his first vows.

Although he had no particular talent for either art or music, Brother Mucian considered it his job to do as he was told and began earnestly to attempt to learn. Following a timetable drawn up by Brother

Maixentis, he began to practice on the harmonium, the organ and a number of other instruments used in the school orchestra. Of these, the flute was his favorite, although he amazed both the staff and the students by playing the tuba.

Although he was hardly enthusiastic about his job of listening to the beginners, Brother Mucian displayed great patience. This, along with his gentleness, enabled him to get his pupils to progress with their studies. He became quite competent at the teaching of art, which he taught to both the boarders and to the young teachers in training.

Near the end of his life, one of the brothers noticed that at 9:00 each morning Brother Mucian went to the music room and set about practicing on the harmonium. This brother asked Brother Maixentis about this. After searching his memory, Brother Maixentis realized that he had told Brother Mucian to do this 50 years before—and had never rescinded his order!

Brother Mucian's day, like that of all the brothers, was quite full. He arose at 4:30 each morning and attended Mass at six. After supervising the pupils at study before breakfast, Brother Mucian spent the remainder of his day at a brisk pace—supervising the students, giving his music lessons, practicing and praying. Always praying.

The Rule of the Christian Brothers sets aside a goodly amount of time daily for prayer and spiritual exercises. In addition, Brother Mucian used all his spare time for prayer. He loved to visit one of the outdoor shrines or grottos on the campus or to slip away to the chapel to kneel in prayer before the Blessed Sacrament. The boys who did not know his name referred to him as "the brother who is always praying."

One of his former pupils relates that one day when he arrived for his music lesson, Brother Mucian was not there. After several minutes the boy went in search to the chapel, rightly guessing that he might find Brother Mucian there. Brother Mucian was kneeling, totally absorbed in prayer. The boy whispered that it was time for his lesson, but Brother Mucian seemed not to hear. After half an hour the boy again went up to the brother; he noticed that his face seemed all lit up, his eyes were closed, and he was completely motionless. At last the pupil gently shook his instructor; Brother Mucian looked up, sighed and followed the boy out, humbly begging his pardon for causing him to miss his lesson.

From 1875 to 1906, when his increasing infirmities caused his superior to relieve him of this duty, Brother Mucian was assigned to supervision. In a day school, the children go home after class and the brothers may relax or carry out their own occupations. In a boarding school, however, someone must constantly be watchful for hazards and dangers to both the souls and bodies of the young charges. Yet this service is often met with ingratitude. Brother Mucian never complained, nor did he ask to be relieved of this task, even when some of the other brothers took advantage of his charity and asked him to stand in for them. Brother Mucian never taught religion or exercised the regular teaching apostolate of the Christian Brothers, but he did carry out the apostolate of watchfulness and example. This was the Will of God for him.

A number of persons have related that when they would come upon Brother Mucian in prayer, they would often find him praying aloud, thinking he was alone. In his prayers he begged God's help and blessings on the faculty, the boys and many others. It is no wonder that as time passed, anyone in trouble went to Brother Mucian and begged his prayers. He prayed not only for those at Malonne, but also for those from far and near who came to seek his prayers.

Brother Mucian was truly a Marian soul. He loved to read books about Our Lady, and he used to say that the Hail Mary was the prayer that most pleased Our Lady since it recalled all her greatest prerogatives. During all his times of supervision, as he watched the boarders, his rosary was in his hand and he constantly murmured Ave Marias. Once he admitted that he had asked Our Lady to be always by his side, and he was conscious of her presence.

There are very few photographs of Brother Mucian. He was not photogenic and disliked having his picture taken. Once, near an archway over which there was a statue of Mary, someone asked Brother Mucian to allow himself to be photographed, telling him jokingly that he wanted a picture of the ugliest Brother in Malonne! Smiling, Brother Mucian agreed. In the picture, Brother Mucian has lifted his eyes to the statue of Mary, and it seems obvious that he has forgotten all about having his picture taken, intent on his prayer to Our Lady.

Brother Mucian had a great devotion to the practice of religious poverty. He once went to a newly appointed brother in charge of supplies and asked for a sheet of notepaper and an envelope, as he wished to write a letter. The supply brother attempted to give him an entire pad and a packet of envelopes, but Brother Mucian refused, saying, "Oh, please no! I would rather come each time I want some paper." When he had occasion to have to travel somewhere, he would hand in whatever cash was left over. Invariably, he would return all money except the exact cost of the ticket. He never spent anything on himself. Brother Mucian's idea was that each time he had to ask for something or some permission, he was making a positive act of poverty.

At the outbreak of World War I in 1914, Brother Mucian was 73 years old. In August the school complex was seized by the German forces to be used as a hospital: the 80 brothers and over 1,000 boarders were allowed the use of only a small section of the buildings.

The cold of the winters and the lack of proper food due to rationing began to tell on Brother Mucian and all the older brothers. Brother Mucian suffered from asthma and rheumatism, but he never failed to carry out his duties. In November of 1916 the house doctor found his heart so weak that he had him receive the Last Sacraments.

In January of 1917 Brother Mucian went to the music room to play, but his head fell down on his chest and his hands would not function. He was carried to the infirmary, where he grew weaker daily. On January 29 he was too weak to say his morning prayers aloud, although later he prayed a litany of the graces he had received in life, thanking God for each of them. On the morning of January 30th, as the rising bell rang, the infirmarian whispered to Brother Mucian the customary salutation of the Brothers: "Live Jesus in our hearts!" Brother Mucian had already passed from this life; he would answer the salutation in eternity.

Shortly after his death, people began to visit the grave of this holy brother to beg his intercession. Many extraordinary favors were reported. As more and more pilgrims came to his resting place, the brothers had his body reinterred in a more accessible spot near the parish church. In response to a steady stream of petitioners, the decision was made to open a cause for Brother Mucian's beatification.

Brother Mucian of Malonne was beatified by Pope Paul VI on October 30, 1977.

Bro. Mucian Marie of Malonne at age 23 in the habit of the Brothers of the Christian Schools. Bro. Mucian had come close to not being accepted into the Order because of his inability to keep order in class. He often performed the thankless task of supervising boarding students after school hours, even generously allowing other brothers to take advantage of him by asking him to stand in for them. Bro. Mucian's sanctity was forged over the space of 50 years of constant daily practice of "ordinary" virtues, especially poverty and obedience.

Bro. Mucian in recollection. Boys who did not know Bro. Mucian's name referred to him as "the brother who is always praying."

This is probably the photo which a fellow brother obtained by jokingly asking Bro. Mucian to pose for a picture of "the ugliest brother in Malonne." Rather than posing for the photograph, Bro. Mucian lifted his eyes to a statue of Our Lady. In one of his rare letters he had written, "If you wish to find a short and easy path to intimate union with Our Lord, go through Mary."

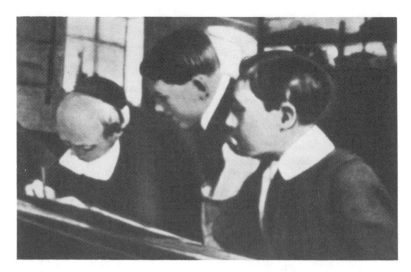

Bro. Mucian preparing his lesson and correcting the boys' sketches. Although he had no particular talent for art, by diligent persevering efforts he became quite competent at the teaching of art, displaying great patience and gentleness with his pupils.

Bro. Mucian at his morning greeting to Our Lady. Like the other brothers, he arose each morning at 4:30 and attended Mass at 6:00. Any spare time between school duties he spent praying.

Canonical identification of the remains of Bro. Mucian in 1938. After his death people began to visit his grave, and many extraordinary favors began to be reported. Bro. Mucian was beatified in 1977.

MOTHER MARIANNE OF MOLOKAI

Mother Marianne Cope, O.S.F.
Barbara Cope
1838 - 1918
Germany - U.S.A. - Kingdom of Hawaii
Died Age 80

"I am hungry for the work and I wish with all my heart to be one of the chosen ones whose privilege it will be to sacrifice themselves for the salvation of the souls of the poor islanders. I am not afraid of any disease; hence, it would be my greatest delight even to minister to the abandoned 'leper.'" So spoke Mother Marianne Cope, the second Provincial of the Sisters of St. Francis of Syracuse (New York).

She did indeed go to the lepers on Molokai and the other Hawaiian islands; she spent the rest of her life there in imitation of her holy founder, St. Francis, giving her all for the love of God.

Barbara Cope was born on January 23, 1838, in Heppenheim, Germany. She was the daughter of Peter Cope and his second wife. (The family name was originally Koob, but was Anglicized to Cope.) The family immigrated to Utica, New York when Barbara was less than two. Eventually there were seven brothers and sisters to share the home. Barbara probably received her First Holy Communion at St. John's Church and attended the parish school at St. Joseph's.

By 1855 the 17-year-old Barbara was the oldest child living at home with her parents. She apparently was drawn to the religious life from childhood, but at this time she felt she had to wait at home to help her parents. In the census of 1855 she is listed as a factory worker; she probably remained at this work until after her father's death.

In November of 1862 Barbara was invested in the Sisters of the Third Order of St. Francis in Syracuse, New York. She was 24 at the time. Professed with the name Marianne on November 19, 1863, she began her work as a sister in Assumption parish school there in Syracuse.

In a letter written to her nephew when she was 60, Marianne recalled, "When I was your age and younger my desire to retire from life in the world was very strong—but God did not will it—I was obliged to wait nine long years before it pleased God to open the convent gates to me."

From the beginning of her religious life Sister Marianne displayed an extremely practical skill in dealing with people and a capability for administrative responsibility. Thus she was given a number of administrative positions. She was elected superior of St. Joseph's Hospital in Syracuse in 1870. In 1877 she became the second Mother Provincial of her order, the post she was holding when the request came for volunteers to go to Hawaii.

In 1883 the Hawaiian government sought aid from Catholic religious orders of women to help care for the afflicted members of the Kingdom of Hawaii. An appeal was made to more than 50 religious communities before reaching the sisters of Syracuse. Mother Marianne invited Rev. Leonor Fouesnel, emissary of the Hawaiian government, to speak to the Sisters of St. Francis with his plea for volunteers in the Island's desperate situation, where leprosy had reached epidemic proportions. Thirty-six sisters from the young congregation generously volunteered for the mission; six were selected to go.

On October 22, 1883 Mother Marianne accompanied the six sisters from Syracuse, intending to return eventually to her own duties as leader of the community in Syracuse once the mission was well established. She never carried out this intention. Instead, she was to spend her life working among the lepers of Molokai for the remaining 35 years of her life.

Mother Marianne stayed at Honolulu for five years, where she managed the branch hospital. She also set up the first general hospital on the Island of Maui and opened a school for young girls. She assumed charge of the hospital in Honolulu and quickly turned it into a model facility.

When the government asked her to open a home for "unprotected women and girls" at Molokai in 1888, Mother Marianne responded as a true daughter of St. Francis. She did not merely accede to the request; she announced that the sisters *"cheerfully* will undertake the work." Throughout Mother Marianne's religious life, this Franciscan charism of joy permeated all of her actions. Her move to Molokai, the "settlement without law," was heroic indeed, for it was now perfectly clear that she would never go back to Syracuse.

Mother Marianne said, "I do not think of reward. I am working for God, and do so cheerfully. How many graces did He not shower down on me from my birth till now. Should I live a thousand years I could not in ever so small a degree thank Him for His gifts and blessings...I do not expect a high place in Heaven—I shall be thankful for a little corner where I may love God for all eternity."

In May of 1889, Mother Marianne wrote: "We visited the boys' establishment on November 28, 1888, and ever since that day, my heart has bled for them and I was anxious to help to put a little more sunshine into their dreary lives." "Our dear Father Damien died on the 15th of April. We visited him before he died, and standing at his bedside one could imagine the voice of God calling him to his reward—his was a grand and noble life of self-sacrifice; how closely he followed in the footsteps of our loving Saviour, living and dying for the poor outcasts. What more can a mortal do than give his life for his fellow creatures?"

With full knowledge that his time was coming soon, Father Damien had begged Mother Marianne to care for his boys.

Soon after Father Damien's death in 1889, Mother Marianne took charge of the refuge he had founded for homeless men and boys. Later, in 1894, she suggested that religious brothers be invited to take over the home and teach the boys skills in farming and carpentry. This suggestion was carried out.

Mother Marianne was an unassuming person and did not like to be singled out. She rarely talked about herself. Nonetheless, she was decorated by the King of Hawaii for her work among the islanders, and she was celebrated in a poem and in the letters of the famous author Robert Louis Stevenson.

In 1899, Robert Louis Stevenson wrote the following inspiring poem after seeing the work of Mother Marianne and her sisters:

> To see the infinite pity of this place,
> The mangled limb, the devastated face,
>   The innocent sufferers smiling at the rod,
> A fool were tempted to deny his God.
>
> He sees, and shrinks; but if he looks again,
> Lo, beauty springing from the breast of pain!
>   He marks the sisters on the painful shores,
> And even a fool is silent and adores.

In her work on Molokai, Mother Marianne was a model of Christian joy. From her emanated a spirit of cheerfulness and courage which was especially marked toward those most tempted to despair of God's care for them.

One of the sisters once asked Mother Marianne what she would do with her if she became a leper. Mother Marianne replied, "You will never be a leper. I know we are exposed, but God has called us for this work. If we are prudent and do our duty, He will protect us. . . . Remember, you will never be a leper, nor will any sister of our order." Not one sister from this order who has worked at Molokai has ever contracted leprosy, despite daily contact with people in the advanced stages of the disease.

Mother Marianne had to live her life in delicate health. Often she could hardly hold up her head because of headaches. But she refused to rest, although she advocated rest for others. Her strength of character gave her the necessary physical strength to do what was needed, including nursing, changing linens, dispensing medicine, etc. She took part in the roughest work such as washing, digging and planting.

Mother Marianne appreciated art and beauty. She assisted in making dresses for the leper girls and tied pretty bows of ribbon for their hair.

In order to give her patients a sense of pride, Mother Marianne was always finding work for them which they could enjoy. She potted up small plants which she then gave to the patients to plant at home, and she transformed the barren dirt around the hospital into a veritable garden. In her simplicity, she had a special appreciation for all the things of nature.

Mother Marianne studied the feelings of others, and her personality was tactful in the extreme. When she was obliged by duty to give a correction to one of the sisters, her eyes would fill with tears.

The changes brought about by the sisters at Molokai were remarkable. Sister Leopoldina, one of the original three sisters who made the move to Molokai, wrote how she had felt on first arriving there: "One could never imagine what a lonely, barren place it was. Not a tree nor a shrub in the whole settlement, only in the church yard there were a few poor little trees that were so bent and yellow by the continued sweep of the burning wind it would make one sad to look at them. It was the most sad and dreary place one could ever imagine. Now and then we came to poor little shanties, some of them partly broken down." Most of the unkempt hovels looked as sick as the sick who were within them. In those days, the lepers sent to the settlement could only expect to live for a few years at the most. Few patients had the will to do anything to improve their surroundings.

Mother Marianne revolutionized life on Molokai, bringing cleanliness, pride and even fun to the colony. People began to laugh.

Jean Sabate, a writer who visited the settlement in 1905, was so horrified by the sight of the physical ravages of leprosy that he told Mother Marianne, "It would be a mercy to put an end to such a hopeless and miserable life."

Gently, Mother Marianne expressed her philosophy to him, "God giveth life; He will take it away in His own good time. In the meantime it is our duty to make life as pleasant and as comfortable as possible for those of our fellow creatures whom God has chosen to afflict with this terrible disease."

At age 61 Mother Marianne became afflicted with lung hemorrhages. Suffering in silence, she never complained, but she could not hide the fact that her health was failing. She was faithful in her visitations of the convents on the other islands until 1899, when traveling became impossible for her. From that time on she corresponded frequently with the other sisters.

During her last illness Mother Marianne was afflicted with dropsy. The formerly frail and delicate woman became very large, with terribly swollen limbs which rendered her nearly helpless. But she preferred to sit up in her wheelchair, being with her sisters and the dear leper girls and working as long as possible.

After a long illness, she received Holy Viaticum on August 9, 1918 and prepared for death. She went to dinner with the sisters, and they put her back in bed about seven o'clock. She became semi-conscious about nine, then breathed her last shortly before 11 p.m. Mother Marianne died as she had lived, a peaceful, quiet, courageous and humble daughter of St. Francis of Assisi.

In August 1983, the Most Rev. Joseph A. Ferrario, Bishop of Honolulu, set up a tribunal to conclude the inquisitional, or research, state of Mother Marianne's cause. This tribunal is active, and favors through Mother Marianne's intercession are being sought in private prayer.

Above: Mother Marianne of Molokai, who spent her years from age 55 to her death at 80 caring for the lepers on Molokai and the other Hawaiian Islands. She promised the sisters of her order that none of them would ever contract leprosy. Mother Marianne brought a "woman's touch" to the formerly dismal shanty towns of Molokai where residents had little will to work on improving their surroundings for the few years they expected to live.

Facing page: Early patients at C. R. Bishop Home, Molokai.

293

30

SERVANTS OF GOD
FRANCISCO AND JACINTA MARTO

Francisco Marto	Jacinta Marto
1908 - 1919	1910 - 1920
Portugal	Portugal
Died Age 11	Died Age 10

On May 13 of 1917, the Blessed Virgin Mary appeared to three young shepherds in the village of Aljustrel in Fatima, Portugal. After promising to take them to Heaven, she asked, "Are you willing to offer yourselves to God and bear all the sufferings He wills to send you, as an act of reparation for the sins by which He is offended, and of supplication for the conversion of sinners?"

"Yes, we are willing," was their reply.

"Then you are going to have much to suffer, but the grace of God will be your comfort."

The three children agreed not to tell anyone about what they had seen. But that night, feeling unable to keep silent, seven-year-old Jacinta Marto told her mother the story of how she had seen a beautiful lady. Her nine-year-old brother, Francisco, confirmed his sister's story, as did their cousin Lucia dos Santos, age 10. The account was received by their families and later by ecclesiastical and civil authorities with skepticism and disbelief. But the Church has subsequently approved the apparitions of Fatima, declaring that they are of particular significance for these times.

The vision had been preceded by several visits of an angel, the Angel of Peace, who had knelt and bowed his head to the ground, teaching the children prayers of reparation. On his second visit he told the children, "Offer prayers and sacrifices constantly to the Most High." On his third visit, the Angel held a chalice; suspended above it was a Host. He made the children recite with him three times a prayer of reparation and of supplication for sinners. Then, giving the Host to Lucia and the Blood from the chalice to Francisco and Jacinta, he said, "Take and drink the Body and

Blood of Jesus Christ, horribly outraged by ungrateful men! Repair their crimes and console your God." Then he prostrated himself and recited the prayer three more times. Not realizing that he had received Communion, Francisco later said, "I felt that God was in me, but I didn't know how it was."

On the day of Our Lady's first apparition, the children had taken their flocks to the Cova da Iria, a rocky little knoll about a mile and a half from Fatima. There they tended the sheep and played games. Suddenly, a great wind arose and they were frightened by a flash of light. A brilliant white light moved toward them, stopping at last on top of a small holm oak tree. Within the light they saw a lady, more brilliant than the sun; she told them that she was from Heaven. She also told them to make sacrifices and to pray the Rosary every day for peace in the world, promising to return on the 13th of each month until the following October. At the apparitions of the Angel and of Our Lady, Francisco saw all the visions but did not hear them. Jacinta and Lucia both saw and heard them. Lucia alone spoke with Our Lady.

At each of the six apparitions the Blessed Virgin Mary was to ask for the daily Rosary. She repeatedly asked for prayer and penances for the conversion of sinners and in reparation to her Immaculate Heart.

In June, a small crowd accompanied the three shepherd children to the Cova. The people could see only a small white cloud atop the holm oak tree, but the children's actions began to convince some people of the miraculous events taking place.

In July, about 5,000 people attended. At this time Our Lady promised a great miracle for October 13. She said to the children, "Sacrifice yourselves for sinners, and say many times, especially whenever you make some sacrifice: 'O Jesus, it is for love of Thee, for the conversion of sinners, and in reparation for the sins committed against the Immaculate Heart of Mary.' " The Blessed Mother then showed the children a terrifying vision of Hell. She told them, "You have seen Hell, where the souls of poor sinners go. To save them, God wishes to establish in the world devotion to my Immaculate Heart." She promised that if her requests were granted, many souls would be saved and there would be peace—but otherwise "Russia will spread her errors throughout the world" and many sufferings and punishments would come upon the world. (The Russian Revolution was to take place in October of that year.)

The children suffered much from the skepticism and hostility of many people. In August, the anticlerical administrator of the district had the children arrested and placed in prison, and then he threatened to fry them in oil if they persisted in their story. The children steadfastly refused to deny the visions. Finally they were released.

They had spent August 13 in jail, but on August 19 they again saw the Blessed Mother. Looking very sad, she told them, "Pray, pray very much, and make sacrifices for sinners; for many souls go to Hell because there are none to sacrifice themselves and to pray for them."

On October 13 an estimated 70,000 people gathered at the Cova da Iria to see the promised miracle. A torrential rain had fallen all morning and the whole area was a sea of mud. At the appointed time, there was again a flash of light, and in a dazzling cloud of light, Our Lady appeared to the children. She requested that a chapel be built there to her honor, and she showed three scenes to the children: first, the Holy Family; second, Our Lord with the Mother of Sorrows beside Him; finally, Our Lady crowned as the Queen of Heaven, holding the Divine Child on her knee and extending the Carmelite scapular to the crowd.

Suddenly, Lucia cried out, "Look at the sun!" The rain had stopped abruptly and the sun seemed to spin about on its axis, then to descend toward the earth. Meanwhile, clouds, people, trees and other objects appeared to change colors constantly in the light of the sun. As the sun appeared to descend, many fell to their knees in terror, begging pardon for their sins. Then, suddenly, the downward course of the sun stopped, and it resumed its normal position. Those present discovered that their clothes were completely dry. Thousands of eyewitnesses have testified to the miraculous events of that day.

By the end of October 1918, scarcely a year later, both Francisco and Jacinta Marto had fallen ill, as predicted by Our Lady. Francisco died on April 4, 1919. Jacinta suffered a little longer, until February 20, 1920, when she, too, went to God.

The causes for beatification of the two little seers were introduced in 1949. The Church, however, does not hold persons up as examples simply for having been privileged to have something extraordinary happen to them. A process moves on examination and declaration of heroic virtue. Should the little shepherds of Fatima one day be accorded the full honors of the altar, they could be the first children non-martyrs to be canonized. Such an event would confirm the traditional teaching on the universal call to sanctity: all Christians, men and women, priests, religious and laity, rich and poor, adults, youths and children, are called to holiness.

* * *

Francisco and Jacinta were the last of 11 children of the Marto family. The family was poor and the children had to help with earning a living. At the time of the apparitions neither had learned to read (nor had Lucia).

Jacinta was endowed with a sweet and affectionate nature. She was also vivacious and somewhat capricious. Francisco, on the other hand, was quiet and submissive by nature. Jacinta loved dancing and playing games. She also wanted to win all the games she played, and would pout if she were the loser. Francisco preferred to play the flute while the others danced, and at games he never cared if he won.

The two children preferred to play with their cousin Lucia, and while at her house were often present at the catechism lessons that Lucia's mother gave her children and the other children of the neighborhood for whom she babysat. Even from this early age Jacinta had a great love for Our Lord. Once, when she had lost at a game of forfeits, Jacinta was told that her forfeit would be to give a hug and a kiss to one of her male cousins. She protested: "That, no, tell me to do some other thing. Why don't you tell me to go and kiss Our Lord over there." She pointed to a crucifix. "Very well," the winner said; "bring Him here and give Him three hugs and three kisses."

"To Our Lord, yes, I'll give as many as you like!" She ran and got the crucifix and kissed and embraced it with devotion. Then, looking attentively at the figure, she asked, "Why is Our Lord nailed to a cross like that?" When she heard the answer, she cried, saying, "I'll never sin again! I don't want Our Lord to suffer any more."

Francisco had a naturally calm temperament and was extremely good-natured. Once, he brought a handkerchief with a picture of Our Lady on it to show to Lucia and the other children. He was very proud of it, for a friend had brought it to him from the seaside.

It was passed from hand to hand and in a few minutes it disappeared.

The children looked for the handkerchief, and a little later Lucia found it in another small boy's pocket. This boy insisted that the handkerchief was his own, and that someone had brought him a handkerchief from the seaside also. To end the argument, Francisco said, "Let him have it. What does a handkerchief matter to me?"

Francisco liked animals. He once paid another boy two coins to free a bird he had caught. He would play with snakes and would pour milk into a hollow in the rock for them to drink.

Francisco liked to be alone to pray and offer sacrifices; he would even go off apart from Lucia and Jacinta when the three were with the sheep. When Our Lady promised to take Francisco to Heaven she had added, "But he must say many Rosaries." When Lucia and Jacinta told him this he exclaimed, "Oh, my dear Our Lady! I'll say as many Rosaries as you want!" From then on Francisco would often move off from the other two, and when they asked what he was doing he would hold up his rosary. "Don't you remember that Our Lady said I must pray many Rosaries?"

When the children were wondering what they could offer as a sacrifice, Francisco suggested giving their lunch to the sheep; this was quickly done. Jacinta soon gave up the dancing she had so loved. Francisco said he no longer wanted to sing songs after seeing the Angel and Our Lady. The little shepherds began to give their lunch to poor children every day, eating pine nuts and other things they could find in the pastures. They often made the sacrifice of doing without even a drink of water on those long hot days when they were parched with thirst.

As news of the apparitions spread there were many visitors who came questioning the children; this was a great trial for them. Often when they could see such visitors approaching they would take off and hide. Sometimes, however, there was no way to escape and the children had to console themselves with offering up the sacrifice. Francisco once said, referring to Our Lord, "I offer Him all the sacrifices I can think of. Sometimes I don't even run away from all those people, just in order to make sacrifices!"

One day Lucia found a rope, and the children cut it into three pieces so that all three could tie a piece around their waists as a mortification. Sometimes this was so painful that Jacinta could not keep back her tears, but when Lucia urged her to remove it, she answered, "No! I want to offer this sacrifice to Our Lord in reparation, and for the conversion of sinners." On September 13 Our Lady said to the three children, "God is pleased with your sacrifices, but He does not want you to sleep with the rope on; only wear it during the day."

Once Lucia asked Francisco, "Which do you like better, to console Our Lord or to convert sinners so that their souls won't go to Hell?" Francisco answered, "I'd rather console Our Lord. . . . I want first to console Our Lord and then convert the sinners so that they will not offend Him any more."

Francisco was also constantly occupied with thoughts of "the Hidden Jesus" in the tabernacle. Sometimes he would spend hours on his knees in church. Francisco would encourage the other two children in making sacrifices.

Francisco fell victim to the influenza epidemic which struck in autumn of 1918. After his first attack he recovered somewhat, but then relapsed in January. He suffered much, but still he always seemed joyful and contented.

He often said to Lucia, "Look! Go to the church and give my love to the Hidden Jesus. What hurts me most is that I cannot go there myself and stay awhile with the Hidden Jesus."

By the first of April, Francisco was so weak that he could hardly speak. His greatest desire was to make his First Communion, and he asked that Lucia come to see him. When she came he said, "I am going to confession. I am going to receive Holy Communion, and then I am going to die. I want you, Lucia, to tell me if you have ever seen me commit any sin. And I want Jacinta to tell me too."

Lucia recalled a few times Francisco had disobeyed his mother, running off to be with her or to hide when he had been told to stay home. Francisco said, "That's true." He sent Lucia to ask Jacinta the same question. Jacinta remembered a time when he and some other boys had thrown stones at each other; and once, a long time ago, he had stolen a tostao from his father to buy a hand organ.

"I've already confessed those sins, but I will confess them again. Perhaps it is for these sins of mine that Our Lord is so sad." Folding his hands he recited the prayer told to the children by Our Lady: "O my Jesus, forgive us our sins, save us from the fire of Hell; lead all souls to Heaven, especially those in most need of Thy mercy."

Francisco made his First Communion on the morning of April 3, 1919. He was radiant with joy, having received the Hidden Jesus into his heart. He died the next day.

Both Lucia and Jacinta missed Francisco terribly. Lucia said, "This grief was a thorn that pierced my heart for years to come." Jacinta would spend time lost in thought about Francisco, and her eyes would fill with tears when she spoke of him.

*   *   *

Jacinta's life was marked by constant concern over the "poor sinners" in danger of Hell. She often sat on the ground and thought about this, exclaiming out loud, "Oh, Hell! Hell! How sorry I am for the souls who go to Hell. And the people down there, burning alive, like wood in the fire!" Shuddering, she would recite the prayer taught by Our Lady: "O my Jesus, forgive us our sins. . ." Lucia said of Jacinta that "every penance and mortification was as nothing in her eyes if it could only prevent souls from going there." Jacinta urged Francisco to pray for souls, exclaiming, "So many go there! So many!" She would say, "Why doesn't Our Lady show Hell to sinners? If they saw it, they would not sin, so as to avoid going there!" "I'm so sorry for sinners! If only I could show them Hell!" Lucia told her not to be afraid, since she was going to Heaven. But Jacinta answered, "I want all those people to go there too!"

Jacinta fell ill with influenza shortly before Francisco became ill. Our Lady had let her know that she would be sent to two hospitals and that she would die all alone in the second one. This prospect filled her with great sorrow and fear. She clung to Lucia and sobbed, "I'll never see you again! Nor my mother nor my brothers, nor my father! I'll never see anyone ever again! And then I'll die all alone!" Jacinta often said, "O Jesus! Now You can convert many sinners, because this really is a big sacrifice!"

Many people came to see Jacinta in her sickroom at home because they sensed something supernatural in her presence. Women would bring their sewing to her bedside. If anyone spoke of sin, she would say, "Tell them not to do that, for it is a sin. They offend the Lord our God, and later they could be damned."

Before leaving for the hospital Jacinta would force herself to drink the milk and broth her mother wanted her to take, declining the grapes she would have preferred. She would also give up drinks of water even when she was very thirsty.

Jacinta once said to Lucia, "I so like to tell Jesus that I love Him! Many times, when I say it to Him, I seem to have a fire in my heart, but it doesn't burn me." She also said, "I so love the Immaculate Heart of Mary! It is the heart of our dear Mother in Heaven! Don't you love saying many times over, 'Sweet Heart of Mary, Immaculate Heart of Mary'? I love it so much, so very much."

One day Lucia gave Jacinta quite a nice holy card picture of Jesus. Jacinta thought it was "so ugly," in contrast to Our Lord, who was so beautiful. But she wanted it anyway; she said, "It is He just the same."

Jacinta told Lucia that she was suffering a lot but that she was offering everything for sinners and in reparation to the Immaculate Heart of Mary. "Oh, how much I love to suffer for love of them [Jesus and Mary], just to give them pleasure! They greatly love those who suffer for the conversion of sinners!"

Jacinta had an open wound and a drain in her chest; it had to be dressed daily. Painful as this was, Lucia says that she bore it "without complaint and without the least sign of irritation." A priest described how Jacinta looked: "a living skeleton, her arms nothing but bones, her face all eyes, her cheeks wasted away by fever."

As Our Lady had foretold, Jacinta was sent to two hospitals. At the second one, in Lisbon, she underwent an operation in which two of her ribs were removed. The surgery had to be performed with only local anaesthesia, since Jacinta was so weak. During the ordeal she repeated Our Lady's name over and over.

In Lisbon Jacinta had stayed for a time in an orphanage run by Mother Godinho. This sister recorded some of the sayings of little Jacinta during those days. They included the following: "More souls go to Hell because of sins of the flesh than for any other reason"; and "Many marriages are not good; they do not please Our Lord and are not of God!" and "People are lost because they do not think of the death of Our Lord and do not do penance"; and "If men only knew what eternity is, they would do everything in their power to change their lives."

On February 20 in the hospital, Jacinta called the nurse and asked for the Last Sacraments, saying she was about to die. The priest heard her confession and promised to bring her Holy Communion in the morning. Jacinta pleaded with him not to delay, telling him she would die that very night, but he did not feel that her end was so near. Jacinta did die that night, all alone, as Our Lady had foretold.

Sometime earlier Jacinta had summed up Lucia's mission in these words: "It will not be long now before I go to Heaven. You will remain here to make known that God wishes to establish in the world devotion to the Immaculate Heart of Mary. . . .Tell everybody that God grants us graces through the Immaculate Heart of Mary; that people are to ask her for them; and that the Heart of Jesus wants the Immaculate Heart of Mary to be venerated at His side. Tell them also to pray to the Immaculate Heart of Mary for peace, since God has entrusted it to her."

* * *

After Jacinta's death, Lucia was sent away to a boarding school by the bishop. Later, she became a Sister of St. Dorothy. Twenty-nine years after the apparitions, she was permitted to revisit Fatima before becoming cloistered as a Carmelite nun. She lives today in the cloister at Coimbra, Portugal.

It is to Lucia that we are indebted for much of our information on Francisco and Jacinta. Her *Memoirs* contain much information about them and are a precious document of the workings of grace in these two souls.

In 1989 the Holy See declared that Francisco and Jacinta Marto had practiced heroic virtue. This decree is the first major step toward canonization.

The three children who saw Our Lady at Fatima, Portugal in 1917: Jacinta, Lucia and Francisco. The children generously responded to and faithfully transmitted Our Lady's urgent warnings and requests for prayer (especially the daily Rosary), repentance, sacrifices and Eucharistic reparation. The Church has accepted the apparitions of Fatima as authentic.

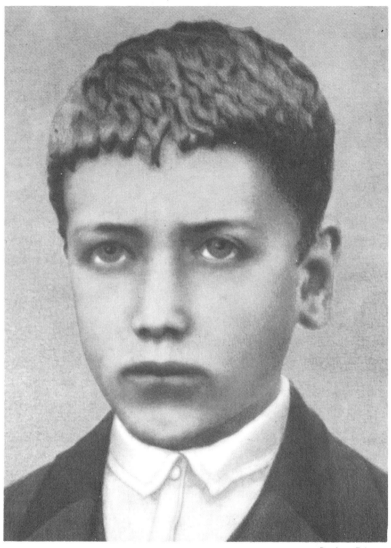

Francisco Marto, who was consumed with the idea of consoling Our Lord for the many sins committed. In her apparitions Our Lady had promised to take Francisco to Heaven, but she added that "first he must say many Rosaries." Francisco did just that; he died at age 11.

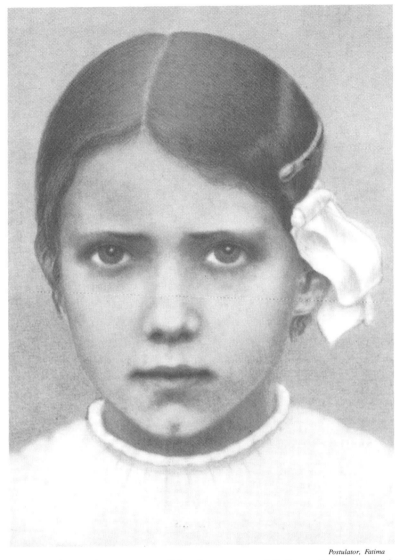

Jacinta Marto, the youngest of the three seers of Fatima. After Our Lady showed the children the vision of Hell, Jacinta was haunted by the thought of the many souls who go there. She constantly offered up prayers and sacrifices to save them. Jacinta died at age 10.

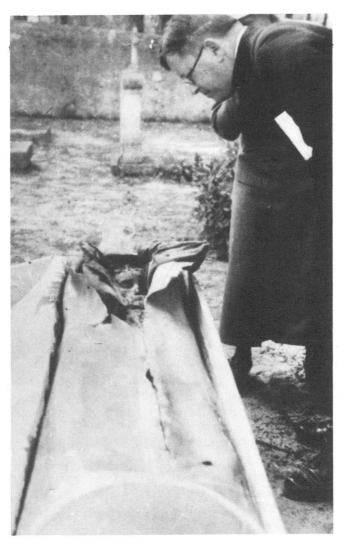

Above: Jacinta's body, found incorrupt upon exhumation in 1935. It was Lucia's loving response to receiving a photograph of Jacinta's body that prompted the Bishop to have her write down everything she could remember about Jacinta; this material is found in Lucia's Memoirs. Upon seeing the photo, Lucia had written to the Bishop, "I felt like removing the wrappings in order to see all of her...I was so enraptured! My joy at seeing the closest friend of my childhood again was so great...She was a child only in years..."

Preceding page: Jacinta, Lucia and Francisco.

31

BLESSED MARY THERESA LEDOCHOWSKA

Mary Theresa Ledochowska
1863 - 1922
Austria - Italy
Died Age 59

In the year 1898, in the midst of strong anti-Catholic feelings in Austria, Mary Theresa Ledochowska—a young woman with no business experience, no training in journalism and no financial backing—applied to the Austrian government for a license to set up an apostolic press center. Even her close friends advised her to drop the project. She was convinced, however, that religious publications would become the means of salvation for many souls on the continent of Africa. Remaining calm and resolute, using every human means as well as prayer, Mary Theresa applied three times for the needed permit. At last the concession was granted, and the power of the press began to contribute to the spread of the Faith.

Mary Theresa Ledochowska was born on April 29, 1863 in Loosdorf, Austria. She was the oldest child of Count Anthony Ledochowski and his second wife, who was also a member of the old nobility, Josephine von Salis-zizers. Mary Theresa had three older half-brothers and, later, eight younger brothers and sisters, of whom five lived past early childhood. Both parents were deeply religious. Count Anthony passed on to his daughter his artistic sense, power of organizing and mature sense of responsibility. He worked for the rights of religion and for the rights of farmers and the working classes; his little girl listened attentively to his conversations on politics and world events. "Mama Sefine" cared for each one of the children devotedly; with gentleness and patience she taught the children loyalty and self-control.

"Puffi," as Mary Theresa was called, was a precocious child. At the age of five she was already trying to write a play to surprise her parents. She preferred books to children's games. Drawing, painting, writing poetry and acting were other talents with which the young countess was well blessed. Until she was 10, Mary Theresa and her brothers and sisters studied at home with a tutor.

In 1873 the failure of a bank brought about financial reverses, and the family moved to St. Poelten, where they rented an apartment. Here the girls continued their education at the school of the Loretto Sisters. At school, even though she was the youngest in her class, "Puffi" was the leader of the group. She maintained first place in her studies, and her work was noted for its neatness and perfection. She graduated in 1877 with highest honors.

Following her schooling, young Mary Theresa was privileged to travel with her parents. An early friend noted that she was inclined to pride and self-assertion; however, there were spiritual depths in the young girl's character in spite of her pride, her presumption and her temper.

Mary Theresa brought much joy to others with the use she made of her many exceptional talents. She delighted in beautiful, expensive clothes; and while she kept up the practice of daily Mass, she also attended many entertainments and theatricals. Her mother encouraged her participation in these social events in order to prepare her for a happy marriage on her own social level.

At age 16 Mary Theresa traveled to visit her relatives in Poland. There she suffered a severe attack of typhus which kept her in bed for six weeks.

In 1882 Count Anthony bought an estate and moved his family to Poland, to a small town near Krakow. Mary Theresa assisted her father in the administration of the new estate, even though she was becoming more and more dissatisfied with worldliness. She helped him take care of the cultivation of the fields, plan the purchase and sale of the livestock, and supervise the workers. She learned to drive the horse-drawn carriage skillfully. Although such tasks were not what she was used to, she performed her duties conscientiously. In her spare time she captured the most beautiful scenes of the countryside with her brush and palette. For social life, the Countess took her daughters to Krakow, where they attended many functions with their cultured and wealthy friends and relatives. Mary Theresa began to look to higher things, however, and her mind was no longer fixed on Matrimony.

Mary Theresa's health had always been delicate, and in 1885 she came down with a high fever. With horror, the family learned that she had smallpox. Mary Theresa's mother nursed her daughter herself; when Mary Theresa's face became marked with dreadful scars, her mother ordered all mirrors removed, fearing her daughter's reaction. But one day Countess Ledochowska noticed a hand mirror on the table by the bed. With a gentle smile, Mary Theresa calmed her mother by telling her that she had known for some time that her face was permanently scarred. Countess Ledochowska was deeply moved by her daughter's courage—as well as gratified that Mary Theresa had triumphed over her proud nature. Later, Mary Theresa was even able to joke about it when a relative recoiled at the change in her once beautiful face.

About this time Count Anthony visited his daughter—and himself came down with smallpox. This, in addition to his asthma, caused his death in February of 1885. At about this time period Mary Theresa's brother Vladimir entered a seminary to become a Jesuit priest and her sister Julie left to join the Ursuline sisters in Krakow.

Soon Mary Theresa received a formal call to serve as a lady-in-waiting at the Court of Tuscany, the court of Grand Duke Ferdinand and Grand Duchess Alice. She assumed her duties at the Court in Salzburg in December of 1885. Shortly before leaving for court she wrote to her uncle, Cardinal Ledochowski, "I know well that the career which I now take up will be as trying and difficult as its exterior might be glamorous, but I take courage from the firm conviction that God will not deny me His assistance as long as I have good will and the earnest desire to remain His true servant." The young Countess already felt drawn to become solely God's.

Court life called for much adaptation. There were a number of duties and very little free time. At the same time, the Grand Duchess was a pious woman, and she attended Holy Mass nearly every day with her young lady-in-waiting. Here in the middle of the imperial residence Mary Theresa began to strive for perfection as if she were in a convent.

At court Mary Theresa gained much insight into the affairs of government, and she met important men and women of her time. This ease in meeting persons of rank would later be a help to her in her apostolate, as she would be able to interest people in her work and win their favor.

More and more, in spite of the travel and the glitter of her daily surroundings, Mary Theresa yearned for a higher way of life. She expressed herself thus: "There is a surging joy in my heart, a longing for something, I know not what. The happiest moments in life are tarnished by the knowledge that there is something more beautiful, which is unattainable. The heavenly Father reminds us constantly that there is a place prepared for us where our longings will be satisfied."

In 1886 two Franciscan Missionaries of Mary sought an audience with the Grand Duchess. Mary Theresa listened attentively to the narrative of these sisters. They spoke of the details of missionary life, with all its hardships, and of the eagerness of the natives to embrace Christianity. Mary Theresa envied the sisters, and she found that her own life seemed empty in comparison.

A year later the sisters came back, and Mary Theresa had a long visit with them. One of the sisters had herself been a lady-in-waiting at the Tuscan court. This sister, Mother Marie of St. Helene, told Mary Theresa about her present apostolate with the lepers in Madagascar. Mary Theresa was amazed at the heroism which had caused the sister to leave such a distinguished and comfortable post in order to labor in extreme poverty, caring for the outcasts of mankind.

Mary Theresa began to be drawn to such a life, but she held back because of doubts regarding her poor health. She waited and prayed for guidance. In 1888 she became professed in the Franciscan Third Order.

One day a non-Catholic friend handed Mary Theresa a pamphlet about Cardinal Lavigerie's crusade against slavery in Africa. In this pamphlet the Cardinal asked the women of London who had a talent for writing to use it in the service of his cause. Mary Theresa determined to use her talent for journalism to serve the missionary apostolate.

Mary Theresa continued to carry out her court duties faithfully, but her free hours were used for writing. She began by writing a drama about slavery entitled *Zaida, the Negro Girl*. She wrote to her uncle, Cardinal Ledochowski, in Rome, asking his blessing and his opinion. His reply encouraged her, and she began writing many articles and pamphlets.

Mary Theresa began an active correspondence with missionaries. A local editor made some pages available to her in each issue of his paper; she filled it with news of the missions and called the column "Echo from Africa."

Soon, in 1889, Mary Theresa was able to begin her own paper, also called *Echo from Africa*, filled with reports from the missions. She used the pseudonym "Africanus" because of her position at Court. The Grand Duchess was understanding; she followed with interest Mary Theresa's work for the anti-slavery movement.

In August of 1886 Mary Theresa went with their Imperial Highnesses to Lucerne. She learned that Cardinal Lavigerie was staying in the mountains nearby; having a brief break in her busy schedule, she climbed a steep mountain path to meet him. In this meeting she explained to him her missionary enterprises in Austria and Poland and presented him with a copy of her drama. When he asked about the author, Africanus, she explained that the author could not use her own name because of her social position. He gave her a penetrating look and then said, "Now kneel down that I may bless Africanus."

Mary Theresa continued publishing until the work of keeping up with the writing, as well as the recording and distributing to the missions of the money donations, became too much. At this time, 1891, she made a courageous decision: she petitioned Emperor Franz-Joseph for release from court. This was granted.

Many of Mary Theresa's friends and even her family disapproved of the talented Countess leaving such a secure position to chase after the folly of the Cross. But in May of 1891, at age 27, Mary Theresa took final leave of the Grand Duchess. The Duchess, along with a number of others at court, sincerely regretted Mary Theresa's departure and wished her well. In her diary Mary Theresa wrote, "Holy Communion offered for the new way of life. Very happy and serene...given up smoking."

To strengthen her health she went to take the water first at Woerishofen and then at Breitenfurth near Vienna. There she was walking in the garden one evening when a man sprang up as if from the ground, took hold of her and threw her down and tried to trample her. When she cried out to St. Aloysius for help, the man disappeared, while she ran to the convent. The grounds were searched but no trace of the man could be found. Owing to this incident Mary Theresa was ill for a long time, suffering from splitting headaches and swollen veins. She continued, however, to work.

Back in Salzburg, Mary Theresa retired to a home directed by the Sisters of Mercy where she could be undisturbed while writing and editing. She considered herself dedicated to God and spent long hours in the convent chapel. Soon the work became more and more demanding. A priest's housekeeper and a sacristan volunteered to help in the evenings, and Mary Theresa was finally obliged to employ a bookkeeper. Soon, though, she realized that she would have to organize on a broader basis.

A new plan suggested itself to the mission-minded Mary Theresa, and under the guidance of the Jesuit Provincial of Vienna she drew up the plan for founding a society of lay persons modeled after the Children of Mary. This pious association would be called the Sodality of St. Peter Claver for the African Missions.

In April of 1894, at age 31, Mary Theresa traveled to Rome to seek papal approval for the new Sodality; it received the blessing of Pope Leo XIII. On her way home, she enlisted her first member, Melanie von Ernst, a subscriber to the *Echo* who lived in Trent. Melanie joined Mary Theresa in Salzburg.

The foundress and her first companion lived joyfully in two rooms near Holy Trinity Church. Poverty, simplicity, prayer and work reigned. Mary Theresa began to add speaking engagements to her written work. In 1895 a young doctor's widow named Mary Jandl came to join the two auxiliary missionaries.

By then the little group had outgrown its cramped quarters, and Mary Theresa had to look for a house in the country. The three had already felt the need to transform the Sodality into a religious institute. In addition to finding a place big enough for their own new vocations, they needed a place where they could accept candidates for preliminary training who would then go as postulants to missionary congregations. When these young women transferred to mission houses they would be supplied with the necessary outfits. Farm management would be part of their training—an advantage for these candidates in their later apostolate in Africa.

At last a suitable place was found: a deserted paper mill near Lengfelden. This was purchased, and the property was named Maria Sorg in honor of Our Lady of Providence.

In August of 1897 three Franciscan Missionary Sisters of Mary arrived to help introduce the first members of the Sodality to religious life. They remained with the group for a year, after which they considered that the Foundress was able to continue the formation of her spiritual daughters herself. In September of 1897 Mary Theresa and Melanie von Ernst pronounced their final vows as religious during a Mass said by Prince Archbishop Haller. The new Order was devoted to promoting the missions in Africa and furnishing religious texts in African languages.

Novices came steadily to join the young foundation. The printing press at Maria Sorg hummed with activity, and the sisters were also busy in the garden, the fields and the stables. In addition to the newsletters, the sisters printed booklets, leaflets and religious texts in several languages—and in the African languages in particular. Loving hands set the type, printed the pages, proofread the books, bound the books and packed them for shipping to Africa. They were sent to the missions free of charge, with charitable donations covering the expenses.

The Institute was growing noticeably. Both educated young women and simple mission-minded girls from the city and country entered. Cardinal Sarto of Venice, later to become Pope St. Pius X, invited Mary Theresa to introduce her work in his diocese. He liked the work because it provided an opportunity for the poor to help, even with small offerings. He encouraged the Foundress to ask for the final approbation of Rome for the constitutions of her institute. This same Cardinal was to be the one who granted the approval, after being elevated to the Throne of Peter. Maria Theresa saw her work spread to several other countries, including the United States, at St. Louis, Missouri. There Cardinal Glennon became a supporter.

Mary Theresa's poor health continued to decline through the years, although her work did not flag. There were always new plans, new enterprises and new ideas to be put into practice. New houses were opened, and the "Directress General," as Mary Theresa was called, traveled extensively.

In 1902 the doctors diagnosed Mary Theresa as having tuberculosis. Her response was characteristic; she said, "The last journey may begin as He wants it and when He wants it."

Despite her weak constitution, the Foundress stayed busy with her apostolic work, a work which was gaining momentum. By speech and by the printed word, she wanted to tell all the faithful to become involved in the obligation of making the joyous message of the Gospel known to all peoples. Not all could go as missionaries, but all could and should support the missions with prayer, sacrifice and alms.

Mary Theresa was overjoyed when the constitutions of her institute, now called the Missionary Sisters of St. Peter Claver, received final approbation from Pope St. Pius X in 1910. The motto of the sisters is "The most divine of all divine things is to cooperate in the salvation of souls."

After a number of ailments, culminating in a severe bout of enteritis, the emaciated Foundress weighing only 62 pounds was at last forced to give up her ceaseless activity. Mary Theresa Ledochowska yielded up her soul to God on July 6, 1922. The Countess who had dared to exchange honor and riches for poverty and unceasing labor was called to her eternal reward.

Mary Theresa Ledochowska was beatified by Pope Paul VI in 1975.

Above: Countess Josephine Ledochowska and three of her children. Mary Theresa is on the right. On the left are Julia (Bl. Ursula) Ledochowska, also a future foundress, and Vladimir, who would become Superior General of the Jesuits.

Facing page: Five of the Ledochowska children. Mary Theresa is in the middle. To *her* right is Julia, and at her far left is Vladimir. Mary Theresa's childhood nickname was "Puffi"; a precocious child, at age five she was already trying to write a play to surprise her parents. Inclined to pride, temper and too much self-assertion, with her mother's guidance Mary Theresa strove to overcome these faults.

Mary Theresa at age 16. When she was 22 her face became permanently scarred by smallpox. Mary Theresa courageously accepted this fact, triumphing over her proud nature.

Mary Theresa as lady-in-waiting at the Court of Tuscany. Her life as a lady-in-waiting was very busy, but still Mary Theresa practiced prayer and sought perfection. Amidst the travel and outward glamour of her days Mary Theresa felt a longing for a higher life.

319

Mary Theresa began to get into a new apostolate by using her free time at court to write articles and pamphlets against slavery in Africa. She began corresponding with missionaries and started writing a column on mission news called "Echo from Africa," using the pen name "Africanus." Soon she began her own paper called *Echo from Africa*.

At age 27 Mary Theresa took leave of the court to pursue her budding vocation. In her diary she wrote, "Holy Communion offered for the new way of life. Very happy and serene...given up smoking."

Mary Theresa's work developed into a pious association which helped prepare missionaries for Africa and which translated books into African languages and sent them to the missions. The association would be called the Missionary Sisters of St. Peter Claver. Here Mary Theresa is shown with her first companion in the work, Melanie von Ernst. Cardinal Sarto, later to became Pope St. Pius X, encouraged the Foundress and invited her work into his diocese of Venice; he liked the work because it gave the poor an opportunity to help the missions, even with small offerings.

322

Mary Theresa's sister Julia, who became Bl. Ursula Ledochowska, Foundress of the Ursuline Sisters of the Sacred Heart.

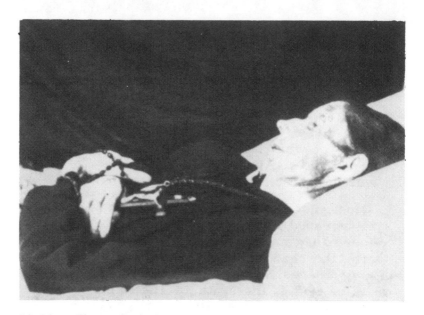

Bl. Mary Theresa Ledochowska in death. She passed to her reward at age 59, weighing less than 62 pounds. In her last moments a heavenly smile and an expression of indescribable joy transfigured Mary Theresa's face; the smile returned several times and was seen by all present. The motto of the Missionary Sisters of St. Peter Claver is "The most divine of all divine things is to cooperate in the salvation of souls."

32

SERVANT OF GOD
DOM COLUMBA MARMION

Servant of God Dom Columba Marmion, O.S.B.
Joseph Marmion
1858 - 1923
Ireland - Belgium
Died Age 64

Dom Columba Marmion was one of the greatest masters of the spiritual life in the 20th century. Within a few years, tens of thousands of his books in over 16 languages—plus braille—had been distributed. Even popes read them. Pointing one day to a copy of Dom Marmion's *Christ the Life of the Soul*, Pope Benedict XV said to an archbishop, "Read that; it is the pure doctrine of the Church." To Dom Marmion himself the Pope said of this book, "It is a great help to me in my spiritual life." Pope Pius XII was to state that Dom Columba Marmion's works were "outstanding in the accuracy of their doctrine, the clarity of their style, and the depth and richness of their thought."

People who had heard of Dom Columba's reputation for holiness and spiritual wisdom were often surprised, upon meeting him, to find so jovial a man. Laughter was one of the qualities most noted about the Irish Dom Columba Marmion, who had an unusually merry temperament. His joy went far deeper than temperament, however. "Joy is the echo of God's life in us," he wrote. Joy because of God's life in him was a hallmark of the life of this saintly abbot.

Joseph Marmion was born on April Fool's Day in 1858; he later joked, "I was born a genuine fool!" Although we have little written record of Joseph's early life, this does not seem to be a true statement, as he was a bright student in school.

Joseph was the son of an Irish father and a French mother. The Marmions' first two little sons had died, and the parents begged St. Joseph to obtain for them another boy. After the birth of another daughter, a son was born and was given the name Joseph.

His parents consecrated him to God on the day of his birth. From then on he was always considered to be destined for the priesthood and was always dressed in black.

Thus Joseph grew up in a large and pious family. He is remembered as a boy of quick intelligence, with a loveable and generous disposition. He had a somewhat thoughtful nature, and games such as cricket or football did not appeal to him. However, he did enjoy sea fishing.

Joseph began his education with the Augustinian Fathers at the College of St. Lawrence O'Toole; later, at the age of 10, he attended the Jesuit school at Belvedere College in Dublin. At 17 he entered the Holy Cross Seminary at Clonliffe College. Although he felt the call to the priestly life, he was of such a sensitive and home-loving nature that he had many moments of homesickness.

In the seminary Joseph was guided by a holy priest who instructed him in the ways of sanctity, emphasizing devotion to the sufferings of Christ. It was probably during this time that Joseph began his lifelong habit of daily making the Stations of the Cross. Joseph struggled constantly against small infidelities, concentrating especially on the practice of silence. He later said that he felt he had kept the rule of silence without one infraction for five or six years. Joseph underwent other interior struggles to repress his "overflowing fun" at inappropriate times.

During his seminary days Joseph received a special grace which was to influence him deeply for the rest of his life. One day as he was entering the study hall he received a supernatural illumination, "a light on the infinity of God." This lasted only an instant, but for the rest of his life it was "as it were always present" to him, and it was to mold the whole character of his spiritual life. Moreover, the future abbot's great reverence for God during Mass and the Divine Office was traceable—as he himself said—to this brief instant of divine illumination in his youth.

Joseph completed his studies in Rome, taking the gold medal for first place in his class, and was ordained there on June 16, 1881. On his way back to Ireland he visited a priest friend at the Benedictine Abbey of Maredsous, Belgium. The complete separation from the world, the liturgy, the constant prayer and total obedience he found in the monastery drew the young priest, who became convinced that this was where his true vocation lay. He promised the abbot that he would return to take the habit as soon as he could. But it was not to be quite so simple.

He had not counted on the opposition of his archbishop. The Archbishop wanted to keep this bright young priest in his diocese. Father Marmion spent a year as a curate at Dundrum and four years teaching philosophy at Clonliffe College before his repeated requests were heard. At last the Archbishop yielded. At the age of 28 Father Joseph Marmion left Ireland to enter the Benedictine monastery at Maredsous. The night before he left Ireland, a friend told him that he would not last at the monastery: "You will come back, I am sure of it; you will never be able to stand the life in the monastery."

Father Marmion did stay, but in the first months he often suffered in the new way of life. Everything was strange to the Irish priest— the country, the language, the quiet and the solemnity of the monks. Added to all of this, his novice master was unusually severe. When this same novice master later asked Father Marmion what was the most difficult thing he had had to put up with as a novice, Father Marmion answered truthfully, if not tactfully, "You, Reverend Father."

It was not that the monks were not kind to the novice, but his was a soul of an extremely sensitive nature. He was also undergoing interior darkness. Later he explained his feelings at that time: "For over 10 years, I felt a *strong desire* to become a monk; it was my dream, my ideal. As soon as I entered the monastery, all went dark; I felt as though I were suspended in space, deprived of all that I loved. This it is that gives merit to our cry of 'Lord, we have left all things and followed Thee.' " On one occasion Father Marmion went and threw himself down before the tabernacle, praying: "And yet, my Jesus, I know that You desire me here. And so I would rather let myself be hacked to pieces than leave the monastery."

Joseph's name in religion was Columba, after the great Irish monk saint.

Columba Marmion made his monastic profession in 1888; as a Benedictine monk his name would now be prefaced by the title of "Dom." On the day of his solemn profession three years later he would write in his diary, "I abandon all things and all inclinations, even the most holy, leaving the choice of my occupations entirely to obedience, sacrificing my tastes, and undertaking solemnly, if obedience should so require, to employ all the remainder of my life in actions which have no charm for me, and for which I may have a great repugnance." He well understood the mortification necessary that Christ might become the entire life of his soul.

After his profession Dom Columba became a lecturer and teacher to the young monks. He was noted for making even the most difficult ideas seem simple and easy to learn. For a time he had served as dean of discipline for the Benedictines' boys' school, but his imperfect French and his natural joviality made him less than suitable for this post.

About a year before his solemn profession in 1891 Dom Columba had begun the outside preaching which would become such a large part of his vocation. A local pastor had asked for a priest to preach. Dom Columba's French was not the best, but he was the only priest available, so the abbot gave him the assignment. Three days later the pastor was back at the abbey, testifying, "I never had such a preacher in my parish, no one who so much moved the people." This was the beginning of a remarkable career as a preacher and guide of souls.

Dom Columba's teaching was simple yet profound, bringing out in every facet of Catholicism the truth that Jesus Christ is the source, model and goal of the Christian life; the person of Jesus Christ is the source of all grace and supernatural action in souls. Dom Columba's teaching was steeped in the Holy Scriptures and the Sacred Liturgy. He received from the Holy Ghost many "lights" which he was able to convey to others.

Despite his fun-loving nature Dom Columba was moved by a truly supernatural spirit. Upon first meeting him a person would sometimes be surprised by his wit and joviality, but would soon realize that he was a man of God. Helping souls to find God was a constant desire of his life. He once wrote, "Every morning I consume Jesus Christ at the altar, to obtain the grace to let myself be eaten up each day by souls. May Jesus Christ be glorified by my destruction, as He is by His own sacrifice!" Cardinal Mercier, who had chosen Dom Columba as his spiritual director, said of him, "He makes you touch God."

In 1899 Dom Marmion went to Louvain as one of a group of monks to establish a new abbey. There he was elected prior. Rather than lecture about the correct method of doing things, Dom Columba preferred to use himself as an example; he wanted to master all the monastic customs perfectly so that the other monks could see how they were carried out. However, he admitted that he "trembled with fear" lest he "become like a signpost, showing the way to others and yet remaining stationary." Though he was not a professor at Louvain, he was highly valued there both as a theologian and as a spiritual director of priests. When he left, the rector said, "Louvain is losing her best theologian."

Dom Columba was a monk of great obedience, and he was also very mortified. Monks who happened to pass by his cell at the time appointed for taking the discipline stated that they heard him applying it vigorously.

Dom Columba always had a good sense of humor. He often told funny stories, yet his conversation and anecdotes always breathed the spirit of charity, humility and purity. Once he gave Benediction to a group of nuns whose singing was terrible. Afterward, their superior asked Dom Columba's opinion as to their performance of the chant. He could not lie, but he did not want to be unkind, so he replied, "Look here, my dear sister, there are some who sing so as to imitate the angels, and some who sing so as to put demons to flight."

In 1909 Dom Columba was recalled to Maredsous, where he was elected abbot. The position of abbot is one of great authority, and it lasts for life. For Dom Columba, this was to be a difficult position, as he was elected to succeed a born organizer and manager. In his humility Dom Columba was the first to admit that he lacked these qualifications. But he was wise enough to make up for this lack of skill by having wise advisors. Dom Columba could not be matched, however, in humility and love for the other monks. He was always happy when he could maintain peace and joy, and he always put mercy above justice.

During the beginning days of World War I, the German invaders of Belgium came to take the church bells and make them into bullets. Dom Marmion met a group of soldiers in the church, explaining that the bells belonged to God and that to take them would be a grave offense. Then he left the church. The soldiers left, too—without the bells.

Many of the monks left the Abbey to enlist in the defense of their country as chaplains or medical helpers. Abbot Marmion was chosen to lead a group of the young monks to Ireland, since not all of the monks could be supported at the Belgian abbey in time of war. While looking for a good place, he dressed as a civilian and tried to sneak into England without a passport. He was caught, and when all other explanations failed he told the inspectors, "I'm Irish and the Irish never need a passport—except for Hell, and it isn't there that I am wanting to go." He got across the border.

The Belgian monks were welcomed at the Benedictine Abbeys of Downside, Ramsgate and Caldey (on an island off the southwest coast of Wales); the last-named was a formerly Anglican monastery which Dom Columba had been instrumental in bringing into the Church in 1913. (Pope St. Pius X wrote to thank him for his charity in connection with this.) Dom Columba was also chosen (by Cardinal Mercier) to try to bring the Modernist George Tyrrell back to the Faith, but Dom Columba's letters to him unfortunately did not meet with the hoped-for response.

The war years were a great source of sadness to Dom Columba. In 1915 he wrote, "I have seldom suffered more *in every way* than for some time past. I feel we have to take our part in the general expiation, which is being offered to God's justice and sanctity. My soul, my body, my senses, God Himself, all things seem to combine to make me suffer." In all difficult situations Dom Columba turned to the words of St. John, "It is the Lord"; these words sustained him in obedience of heart to God's will in all things. His favorite devotion after the Mass and Office was the Stations of the Cross. He recommended the Stations to others and himself made them every day of the year except Easter Sunday.

Over the years Dom Columba's spiritual conferences had been bringing great good to many souls. He was able to present the most profound truths in a simple way and in a way that inspired people to interior action. He was able to make people see that the great Christian truths with abstract names like "Incarnation" and "Divine adoption" and "Blessed Trinity" should and can be the most important realities in the Christian's life—living realities that transform his whole being and all his actions. (One spiritual writer has dubbed Dom Marmion the "Doctor of Divine Adoption.") Of Dom Columba's writings it has been said: "Innumerable are the souls who are set at large and open out at contact with this doctrine of life, full of light and warmth, lofty and fruitful, generating action and reinforcing zeal."

A monk wrote down and organized Dom Columba's conferences, thus forming the book entitled *Christ the Life of the Soul*. *Christ the Life of the Soul* soon became a classic, as did Dom Columba's following books, including *Christ in His Mysteries* and *Christ the*

Ideal of the Monk. Dom Columba became one of the most famous spiritual writers of his day. With a mixture of humility and humor he explained that he had not really written his books: "I've simply let Our Lord and St. Paul do the talking, one of my monks has written down what I said, and someone has put my name underneath." Another time he wrote, "The reason of the success is that there is practically nothing in these works from me."

Dom Columba's spiritual conferences and writings were marked by a true "return to the sources." As one author has explained, "What souls really thirst for is Christ, and the great merit of Dom Marmion is that he gives them Christ." Dom Columba himself wrote, "For certain souls, the life of Christ Jesus is one subject of meditation among many others; this is not enough. Christ is not one of the means of spiritual life; He is *all* our spiritual life." Shortly after his solemn profession he had written to his abbot, "Now I see that the pearl of great price of which the Gospel speaks is Jesus Christ Himself." Dom Columba showed how all the aspects of the Catholic Faith take their meaning from the person of Our Lord. He showed how sanctity is *God's* work in the soul. Although Dom Columba's spiritual teaching is simpler and more focused on Jesus Christ than the teachings of some other Catholic spiritual writers, he was always quick to defend himself against the charge of innovation.

Dom Columba was instrumental in bringing about many remarkable conversions. One, mentioned earlier, was the conversion of the monks at the Anglican monastery of Caldey. Another was the conversion of a 37-year-old woman from a wealthy family who had left her husband and six children on account of the husband's infidelity. She had become an atheist, joined a Masonic society, and planned to die without religion. Feeling helpless because he had only a little over one day in which to work, Dom Columba begged God to work through him. A couple of interesting "coincidences," including a providential auto breakdown, came to his aid. The woman consented to confess to him; she then received Holy Communion with beautiful dispositions. Dom Columba's comment when telling this story was, "Such experiences confirm our faith."

Dom Columba manifested the gift of prophecy on several occasions, especially in predicting that certain persons would enter the religious life. In speaking with people he would often begin a spiritual discussion by saying, "Well, my child, how is your soul?" One nun said of him, "One felt him to be so close to God, and yet so close to oneself!" Dom Columba was also a great letter writer, both prolific and very sensitive. Although he did not believe in writing frequently—as he said, "The Holy Ghost alone can form souls"—there are in existence 1,700 of his letters.

The mercy of God was always in the forefront for Dom Columba; he wrote, "It is not our perfection which is to dazzle God, who is surrounded by myriads of angels. No, it is our misery, our wretchedness *avowed* which draws down His mercy. . .you are never dearer to God, never glorify Him more than when, in full realization of your misery and unworthiness, you gaze at His *infinite* goodness and cast yourself on His bosom, believing in faith that His mercy is *infinitely greater* than your *misery. . .*"

The war years, with their trials and physical hardships, took their toll on Dom Columba's health. As his health deteriorated, Dom Marmion found himself experiencing a tendency to sleepiness at inopportune moments. His sense of humor helped him to deal with this embarrassment.

Dom Columba had always been a special friend of the Carmelites at Louvain, and in January he was asked to visit a dying nun there. Although he was just recovering from a severe attack of influenza, he went to give the dying nun spiritual comfort. After his visit to her he gave a conference to the community. When he had gone, the sister said, "Father Columba is a saint—but he is going to die."

Dom Columba returned to his monastery and continued with his usual duties until he could do no more. Then, being confined to bed, he submitted like a good child to all that was prescribed for him. After receiving Extreme Unction he lay in his bed, praying constantly. Someone attempted to encourage him by reminding him that the many souls he had converted would now be praying for him—but he shook his head and said, *Deus meus, misericordia mea* ("My God, my mercy"). He often repeated a verse from the Magnificat: "He hath received Israel His servant, being mindful of His mercy." At one point he suddenly asked for holy water, which he then sprinkled in three directions; he then immediately became calm again.

Not long before he died, Dom Columba said, "I can say quite truly that for 12 years I have not let an hour pass without thinking about death."

After much suffering and with complete abandonment to the Divine Mercy, Dom Columba died on the evening of January 30, 1923, with the words of Psalm 58 on his lips: "My God, my mercy."

Both spiritual and temporal favors have been granted through the intercession of Dom Columba Marmion. The diocesan process toward his beatification was completed in 1961 and sent to Rome.

The Marmion family, with the future abbot in the center (standing). Joseph (later to be known as Dom Columba) was consecrated to God as an infant, and during his childhood and college years he was always dressed in black. Joseph's favorite companion and spiritual confidante was his youngest sister, Rosie (next to the father).

Young Joe Marmion and one of his sisters—probably Rosie. Assailed by fierce temptations against his vocation for days before entering the seminary, Joe almost did not show up on the evening of his farewell dinner. He finally arrived, over four hours late, in radiant happiness, with his doubts resolved. He later exclaimed to his sister, "Oh Rosie, how you must have been praying, and praying well!"

Joseph Marmion as a seminarian at Holy Cross Seminary, Clonliffe College. In the seminary Joseph was guided on the path of sanctity by a holy priest. On one occasion during vacation he learned that a certain poor old woman was threatened with legal action over a debt she could not pay. Joseph had been saving up little by little for a trip and he possessed the amount of the debt—but he did not want to give up his trip. However, after a night-long struggle he made up his mind, turning over his savings to the poor woman.

Dom Columba Marmion at age 30 in Rome, 1888, the year he made his monastic profession. His Archbishop in Ireland had finally allowed him to leave Ireland to enter the Benedictine Monastery of Maredsous, Belgium.

Around age 32 Dom Columba Marmion stumbled into the apostolate of preaching—a work which was to be a large part of his life. A local pastor needed a priest to preach, and Dom Columba was the only one available— so the Abbot gave him the job, despite his faulty French. Three days later the pastor was back at the Abbey, exclaiming, "I never had such a preacher in my parish, no one who so moved the people!"

338

Abbot Marmion in disguise, September, 1914. During World War I he was chosen to lead a group of monks to Ireland to find a place for them. Dressing as a civilian, he tried to sneak into England without a passport. He was caught, and when all other explanations failed he told the inspectors, "I'm Irish and the Irish never need a passport—except for Hell, and it isn't there that I'm wanting to go." He got across the border.

Dom Columba Marmion's heart was both jovial and full of spiritual wisdom. Pope Benedict XV once pointed to one of Dom Columba's books on his bookshelf and remarked to an archbishop, "Read that. It is the pure doctrine of the Church." To Dom Columba himself the same Pontiff said of this book, "It is a great help to me in my spiritual life."

Dom Columba Marmion would often begin a spiritual discussion with a person by saying, "Well, my child, how is your soul?" A nun once said of him, "One felt him to be so close to God, and yet so close to oneself." Despite his work of spiritual direction Dom Columba felt that "the Holy Ghost alone can form souls."

341

Dom Columba Marmion, one of the greatest spiritual writers of the 20th century. His *Christ the Life of the Soul* soon became a classic. Dom Columba commented, "The reason of the success is that there is practically nothing in these works from me."

33

SISTER JOSEFA MENENDEZ

Servant of God Sister Josefa Menendez, R.S.C.J.
Josefa Maria Menendez
1890 - 1923
Spain - France
Died Age 33

Eleven-year-old Josefa Menendez was on a short retreat in preparation for her First Holy Communion. One of the subjects of meditation was "Jesus, Spouse of Virgins." An earlier meditation on belonging entirely to Jesus had filled Josefa with joy but had also puzzled her; now here was the solution. Josefa later said, "Then and there I promised Our Lord ever to remain a virgin (I did not understand what it meant) that I might always remain entirely His." Then, delighting in the joyful thought of her upcoming First Communion, Josefa heard a voice which said, "Yes, little one, I want you to be all Mine." Long afterward she realized that this had been a call to the religious life.

On the day of her First Communion Josefa wrote out and made a promise of virginity to Jesus, asking Him to show her how to belong wholly to Him in the most perfect way possible. She was to keep the little paper of this promise until the day of her death.

When Josefa told the priest about the promise she had made, he explained that little girls should not make promises beyond that of being very good. Nevertheless, she did indeed enter the religious life, becoming at age 29 a sister in the Society of the Sacred Heart. She was to spend her four remaining years of life as a victim soul, receiving many visions and locutions from Our Lord.

Josefa was born on February 4, 1890 in Madrid, Spain. She was the oldest of four daughters of an artistically talented army officer. Her childhood was happy. By nature Josefa was both serious and vivacious; her father called her his "Little Empress."

Josefa was confirmed at age five and made her first confession at age seven. Her confessor guided her young soul, teaching her to meditate and to use ejaculatory prayer, so that she learned to be always aware of God's presence. The priest gave Josefa a little meditation book, by means of which she learned to ponder the truths of the Faith and make resolutions. She said, "I delighted in my little book, especially when it spoke to me of the Child Jesus or of the Passion. I found plenty to say to Our Lord and already I planned to devote myself to Him who possessed all my love."

One of Josefa's sisters said, "After Josefa's First Communion one may say that she ceased to be a child." Her piety, charity and spirit of sacrifice were evident; she was always sweet and cheerful.

Josefa took her position as the eldest daughter quite seriously. One time one of her sisters was sent to buy something, but forgot to pay for it. In terror she told Josefa—who comforted the frightened child and then went and paid the shop owner herself.

Josefa made regular visits to take care of a poor leprous woman, until her parents found out and forbade her to continue—to Josefa's great sorrow.

Josefa attended a school of arts and crafts where she learned needlework, at which she became expert. Later she and her sisters attended the free school of the Sacred Heart as day scholars. Then she was sent for training at a millinery establishment. There she suffered, sometimes to the point of tears, from the evil talk among the other girls; she said "I went through many perils, but God always protected me." She took strength and comfort from the belief that He meant her to be His own.

Suffering, so characteristic of Josefa's life, first began in 1907 with the death of her little sister, Carmencita. Josefa accepted suffering peacefully, and learned to suffer as she had learned to love— with her heart opened wide to sorrow and sacrifice.

Soon both of Josefa's parents became gravely ill; for a period of seven weeks their eldest daughter divided her attention between the invalids, the care of her sisters, and the many household duties. Medical care was costly, and soon the family savings were depleted, but the sisters of the Sacred Heart came to the aid of the family, as they did more than once.

Josefa did not have a sewing machine, so the superior of the Society of the Sacred Heart at Chamartin asked Josefa to purchase one for her (the Superior) and to use it for a while to see if it was a good machine. She then gave Josefa an order for thousands of scapulars for the Spanish soldiers. Then when Josefa finished the commission, the superior gave her the machine, telling her that making the scapulars had more than paid for it. Josefa was deeply touched by this generosity, and felt that it had come from the Sacred Heart of Jesus. From this time she desired to join the Sacred Heart sisters. But after the death of her father, Josefa's talent became the sole support of her family.

She longed to enter the religious life, but her family obligations and her mother's tears held her back. She organized a sewing workroom, where her talent, firmness and thoughtfulness made the place run smoothly.

At the age of 22, on the advice of her confessor, Josefa entered the Order of Marie Reparatrice. Gradually, however, she began to feel specially drawn to the Sacred Heart of Jesus and to wonder whether perhaps she had not yet found her true calling. Then, at the end of her postulancy, her mother begged her to return home; Josefa complied.

She resumed her sewing, but felt drawn to the Society of the Sacred Heart, which seemed to fulfill her every aspiration. She said, "Since childhood, my one prayer has been that 'I might dwell in the house of the Lord,' and the more I see of life outside, the greater is my longing to die if this wish of my heart cannot be granted."

In 1917 Josefa was accepted by the Sacred Heart sisters at Chamartin; her mother consented, but nevertheless shed so many tears at the last moment that Josefa's resolution was shaken, and she did not enter. Then she in turn wept. At age 29 she again applied, but was turned down. Superiors did not feel optimistic about a candidate who had hesitated so many times. Josefa felt devastated and begged Our Lord to accept her into the Society or let her die. He appeared to her, giving her the strength to continue suffering.

A couple of months later, in November of 1919, the superior of the Sacred Heart sisters at Chamartin asked Josefa if she felt equal to entering a French house of the Order, in Poitiers. Josefa did not hesitate. Her broken-hearted mother this time offered no opposition—and in order to avoid a painful scene, Josefa left home without saying good-bye. She would become a coadjutrix sister of the Order.

In the convent Josefa worked in the kitchen, swept the halls, did needlework and, in general, all the daily chores of the convent. The Sisters of the Sacred Heart undertake the work of educating children, and much of the needlework Josefa did consisted in making and mending uniforms and other clothes for the children.

To most of her sisters Josefa passed the four remaining years of her life unnoticed and hidden, simply and faithfully performing her obligations. She fit in well because she was a person of rare good sense and excellent judgment, someone who had acquired a breadth of understanding and kindness, capable and adaptable. After her death her sisters were asked to tell all they remembered of Josefa, but they were not able to say very much. They remembered her as dutiful and obedient, merry in recreation and willing to help when asked. Her life, as they saw it, was no more nor less than that expected from any good religious.

Josefa's superiors, however, knew that from her postulancy Josefa had received frequent mystical visits from the Sacred Heart, who had chosen her to be a victim of His justice and mercy and to spread the message of His boundless love for souls. Josefa also received visits from the Blessed Mother and from St. Madeleine Sophie Barat, the foundress of her order.

Our Lord showed Josefa that her mission was to suffer much to console His Heart and save souls from Hell—especially the souls of priests and religious. He told her, "The world does not know the mercy of My Heart. I intend to enlighten them through you....I want you to be the apostle of My love and mercy."

Explaining the value of this way of life, He said to her, "It is I who allow the souls I love to suffer. Suffering is necessary for all, but how much more for My chosen souls!...It purifies them, and I am thus able to make use of them to snatch many from hell fire." "The comfort given Me by one faithful soul compensates for the coldness and indifference of so many others."

Our Lady one day appeared to Josefa after she had performed a difficult act of obedience, saying to her, "As you overcame your repugnance through love, Heaven opened today to a soul whose salvation was in great peril. If you only knew how many souls can be saved by those little acts!" Our Lady also explained Jesus' plans to use Josefa as His messenger: "Jesus wishes His words to remain hidden as long as you live. After your death, they will be known from one end of the earth to the other, and in their light many souls will be saved through confidence and abandonment to the merciful Heart of Jesus."

Josefa's superiors were impressed by her simple and courageous obedience, her humble distrust of herself and her fear of an extraordinary spiritual path, and above all by her love of her vocation. These "ordinary" virtues indicated that her extraordinary experiences were authentic. Our Lord obliged Josefa to write down His words. But Our Lord told her to obey her superiors even in preference to Himself—and He Himself also obeyed them. Josefa's experiences and the words of Our Lord are recorded in the book entitled *The Way of Divine Love*. Cardinal Pacelli (later Pope Pius XII) wrote a letter of approbation for the first edition of the book.

As a postulant Josefa had experienced terrible temptations against her vocation. She fought them with the constant prayer, "My God, I love Thee." During this struggle one night she experienced one of those attacks of the devil from which she was to suffer for the rest of her life: a shower of violent blows fell on her through the night and the next morning until the Elevation of the Sacred Host at Mass, when they stopped abruptly. After five weeks of interior and exterior sufferings, Our Lord appeared to Josefa, making her "enter His Heart." This spiritual favor would be repeated at other times in Josefa's life.

Jesus often impressed upon Josefa the fact that He had chosen her for special favors not because of her merits but because of her misery and wretchedness: "I have selected you as one utterly useless and destitute, that none may attribute to any but Myself what I say, ask and do."

Jesus gave Josefa a desire for suffering. He often placed His Cross on her shoulders for hours or even for whole days and nights. He also entrusted her with His Crown of Thorns and its pain for long periods, and also made her feel the pain of His pierced side, as well as the pain of the nails in His hands and feet; every Friday He made her share His agony of heart and soul. One day He said, "Take My Cross, My Nails and Crown. I go in search of souls."

Josefa would suffer for specific souls who were in danger of Hell—particularly priests and nuns. Jesus would appear to her disfigured and agonizing, or with a thorn piercing His Heart, suffering from the sins of someone in grave danger of damnation. Then after days of terrible interior and exterior suffering by Josefa, He would appear to her beautiful and glorious, the soul in question having returned to Him.

Josefa also received visits from souls in Purgatory, confessing the sins that had led them there and begging for prayers.

God permitted the devil to afflict Josefa grievously. In addition to beating her with heavy blows, he would snatch Josefa away bodily in the very presence of her superiors; she would suddenly disappear and then after much searching would be found beneath heavy furniture or in some unfrequented spot. The devil also tormented her by fire; her superiors would see her clothes consumed and see marks of fire on her body, and the wounds would take a long time to heal. The devil would also appear to her in the form of a dog or a snake or in human form.

God also permitted that Josefa undergo the trial of being taken down to Hell, in order to save souls. This phenomenon is rare in the lives of the saints. Josefa would spend hours or even a whole night in Hell, enduring all the torments of Hell except hatred of God. She was obliged to write down her experiences; her descriptions of Hell, and of the cries of despair of the damned, are fear-inspiring. Josefa's body would seem to become lifeless during these journeys; after her return her clothes and body would give off a terrible odor like sulphur and putrid flesh. While in Hell she would feel that she was actually condemned there for all eternity; unable to love anymore, she was tormented by the memory of the closeness to Our Lord she had once known. In Hell Josefa realized the vast numbers of the lost. Each trip to Hell seemed to her to be her first one, although she was dragged there more than a hundred times. Josefa would experience unspeakable joy upon each return to find that she could still love God.

During one painful attack from the devil, Josefa suddenly heard the gnashing of teeth and a yell of rage; at that moment Our Lady appeared. She said to Josefa, "He may torment you, but he has no power to harm you. His fury is very great on account of the souls that escape him...souls are of such great worth...If you but knew the value of a soul...."

Jesus revealed to Josefa that His most intimate sorrow was the faithlessness of His chosen souls.

Our Lord said to Josefa, "How many souls are lost!" He also told her, "One faithful soul can repair and obtain mercy for many ungrateful ones." "Every soul can be instrumental in this sublime work....Nothing great is required, the smallest acts suffice: a step taken, a straw picked up, a glance restrained, a service rendered, a cordial smile...all these offered to Love are in reality of great profit to souls and draw down floods of grace on them."

In one mystical exchange Our Lord took Josefa's heart and replaced it with a burning spark from His own Heart. From then on she felt a fire of divine love in her heart; she felt such a desire to possess Jesus that it was "a veritable martyrdom to be still so far from Him." She was consumed with desire to love God and see Him loved.

One time when Josefa told Our Lord how worn out she was by weeks of pain, He answered, "I have no need of your strength, but I do need your surrender." He also told her, "There is one thing that you must do, Josefa: love, love, love!" Very frequently Josefa would renew her vows, thus giving herself again to Our Lord.

Jesus and Mary foretold clearly both the time and the circumstances in which Josefa would die. On August 7, 1922, Our Lord told her that it would be soon. He said that He would warn her a little beforehand so that the superiors could tell the Bishop everything.

In those last months Jesus required Josefa to overcome her timidity and three times to carry personal messages to the Bishop. Also, she traveled to Rome with a message for the Superior General of her order. Moreover, Jesus spoke to Josefa about her future mission in Heaven.

From the beginning of November, 1923, Josefa's physical suffering during the day, and principally by night, had been destroying her, while intolerable pains from an unknown cause increased in severity every Friday. Doctors were unable to make a diagnosis. Sometime earlier one doctor was surprised to learn that Josefa was only 33 years old. "She is worn out," was his comment.

On the afternoon of December 8 Josefa wrote farewell letters to her mother and sisters which, at her request, were sent only after her death. To her mother she wrote, "I am glad to die because I know it is the will of Him whom I love. Then, too, I long to see His face unveiled, and that is impossible here below. Do not be sad on my account, for death is the beginning of life, if we love and wait for His coming..."

On December 9 Josefa attended Mass for the last time. After Benediction that evening she gave in and went to the infirmary where she was to die. Still she was joyous, thoughtful of others, occupied with souls and forgetful of self.

Further examinations still produced no diagnosis, but on December 12 Josefa was given the Last Rites and made her Profession *in articulo mortis* ("at the moment of death"). For days she still lingered, in physical pain and for a time under diabolical influence or even possession. This trial consisted of several days of intense interior struggle, with the devil taking away her suffering and telling her she could get well if she refused the extraordinary divine paths God had called her to. A priest performed the rites of exorcism. A prayer to Our Lady of Sorrows and Josefa's act of total abandonment to the Sacred Heart of Jesus finally ended this trial and banished the devil from Josefa forever. In a moment her pain returned, the blessed pain with its great graces.

On the night of December 29 the infirmarian left briefly to go with the other sisters to community supper. This was the first time in almost three weeks that Josefa had been left completely alone. When the sister returned a few minutes later, Josefa was dead, a look of intense pain on her face.

But almost at once Josefa's face took on a look of serenity and peace; the house was filled with a sense of the supernatural and many graces were received. When the sisters came to clothe Josefa's body for burial they found it already clothed, although no one had entered the infirmary.

On the next morning, Sunday, December 30, the community was informed of the divine secret of the last four years, a secret that not one of the members had suspected. A letter from the Mother General of the Order said, "It is only just that they should be the first to receive the tidings of this grace."

In succeeding decades thousands were to learn about Josefa's mission through the book *The Way of Divine Love*. The diocesan work on a cause for Sister Josefa has been completed.

Josefa Menendez as a child. She was the oldest of four daughters; her father called her his "little Empress." Josefa made her first Confession at age seven and her First Communion at age 11. At the preparatory retreat for First Communion she promised Our Lord to remain always a virgin—though she did not know what this meant—in order that she might always remain entirely His.

Sister Josefa Menendez on the day of her vows. Josefa became a nun at age 29 and died at age 33; her life in the convent was a series of mystical conversations with and visions of Our Lord, who gave her many painful sufferings to endure as a victim soul to save other souls from Hell.

Sister Josefa suffered especially for the souls of priests and religious. Our Lord would mystically give Josefa His Cross, thorns and nails—and their pain—for periods of time in order that she might win back souls in grave danger of damnation. Josefa generously responded to Our Lord's requests, though she feared the extraordinary path God had chosen for her and would have wished for a more ordinary life.

During Josefa's four years in the religious life she sewed school uniforms, worked in the kitchen, swept the halls and did other daily chores. Josefa had good sense, was adaptable and fit in well; she was merry at recreation and willing to help others. Most of the sisters did not know about Josefa's extraordinary life as a victim soul until after her death.

34

FATHER LOUIS VARIARA

Father Louis Variara, S.D.B.
Louis Variara
1875 - 1923
Italy - Colombia
Died Age 48

Having founded a religious congregation composed of leper women, Father Variara wrote to these spiritual daughters, "The Cross is sweet because we carry it with Jesus." In keeping with the Salesian spirituality of happiness and activity, Father Variara created a joyful acceptance of the Cross among the people of the leper colony of Agua de Dios, Colombia, as well as among the sisters of this unique congregation.

As a boy Louis had had the providential good fortune of meeting St. John Bosco shortly before the Saint's death. In October of 1887 Louis' father, an elementary school teacher from Viarigi, had taken Louis to Valdocco to enroll him in Don Bosco's secondary school. Although Don Bosco watched the boys from his window, he was no longer able to be down among them as before.

But one day, the 13-year-old Louis finally got to see Don Bosco when he returned from a carriage ride. As the carriage drew up, the Oratory boys ran up to be close to their spiritual father. Louis was among them; he worked his way up as close as he could. Later he recalled, "Raising his eyes, Don Bosco looked hard at me. That was one of the happiest days of my life. I was certain that Don Bosco had discovered in my soul something that only God and he could know."

In 1891 Louis entered the Salesian novitiate, received the religious habit, and a year later became a Salesian. There he began his studies for the priesthood.

In April of 1894 Father Michael Unia, a Salesian who had for years worked among the lepers of Agua de Dios, came to Turin for a brief rest. He asked that one of the Salesians, preferably one with musical ability, return with him to help him bring "cheerful-ness" to his people. Nineteen-year-old Brother Louis Variara slipped a letter of petition under the statue of Our Lady Help of Christians. In his letter he asked the special favor of being sent to the lepers of Agua de Dios.

Against all hope Louis' request was granted; he became the first seminarian to be sent to work among the lepers.

After a tiresome trip, first across the ocean and then by riverboat and at last by mule, the inexperienced seminarian and the worn-out old priest finally arrived back in the tropical valley.

The leper colony had 2,000 people, 800 of whom were sick. Life in the colony was dull, monotonous and seemed hopeless.

Brother Louis began an oratory for the boys. He gave the older ones musical instruments and began to teach them. His superior wrote a report to Turin in which he said, "It makes you weep to see those poor boys spending most of the day blowing these instruments with what little breath they have." Brother Louis, un-afraid of putting his own lips on the mouthpieces where those of the leper boys had been a few seconds before, soon had the boys playing joyful tunes. Music and cheerfulness began to enliven the colony.

Brother Louis also began a drama club and organized youth groups, as well as a choir for boys and girls. And of course, he taught catechism, bringing the Good News of eternal life in Heaven. The whole atmosphere in the colony began to change. The lepers were beginning to experience a special kind of healing—the healing of hopefulness.

In the meantime, Brother Louis continued his studies for the priesthood; he was ordained in 1909. At his ordination one of the lepers said, "May you be blessed for the great efforts you have been making to sweeten the terrible cup of poison we have to drink."

The young priest wanted to open an orphanage for boys. He went to Bogota and preached from church pulpits a sermon directed to the children of Colombia. He asked that they each give one centavo for their less fortunate brothers and sisters. The money poured in, enough to buy the necessary land and to build the orphanage. Ob-stacles arose to delay construction: the work was stopped on ac-count of a bloody civil war and then by an outbreak of yellow fever. The two Salesians were worn out with overwork. At last, however, peace returned and the orphanage was built.

Some of the girls in the colony had clear signs of a religious vocation, but because they and/or their parents were lepers, they had no chance to dedicate their lives to God as religious. No community would accept them.

Father Louis thought of a simple plan. He would found a new congregation for them. These girls could take full advantage of their trying existence by making a generous offering of themselves to the Lord and by an active apostolate among the lepers. After thinking it over carefully, Father Louis acted. The first work of the congregation would be the care of the orphans.

The first seven aspirants in the new congregation, to be called the Daughters of the Sacred Hearts of Jesus and Mary, wrote to Father Michael Rua, then head of the Salesian Order. They asked to become affiliated with the Salesian Order and to keep Father Variara as their spiritual director. "We are stricken with leprosy, driven out of our homes, taken by force from our families, and now we see our most ardent desires being washed away. Father Variara knows the pain of body we endure and that deeper pain of soul, and he has shown us how to realize our dearest wishes in this place of suffering. It has become our paradise....Our aim will be to serve our fellow lepers. In our congregation, we will serve God, offering ourselves as willing victims of expiation under the protection of the Sacred Heart of Jesus and that of Mary Help of Christians . . . Father Variara cannot see why we should be deprived of religious life just because of our illness."

A storm of controversy arose over the plan. Many people considered it only the idea of a foolish and inexperienced young priest. Father Rua, however, understood and approved the plan.

The saintly Father Rua wrote these instructions to Father Variara: "Try to increase the numbers of your Sisters and always keep the religious authorities well-informed of everything. Your institution is a fine thing; it ought to go on and develop."

The first Daughters were all leprous women. Thus, they formed a unique community consecrated to suffering. Father Variara wrote them in 1920, "Your congregation was born of suffering and of contradiction."

Father Louis was moved, briefly, to a number of other posts. The young congregation still had great need of his help, but in obedience, he had to leave. He wrote the sisters, "The cross is sweet because we carry it with Jesus." At last he was sent to

Venezuela. His sisters missed him terribly and wrote to him regarding this. He replied, "Consider that if disease cuts you off from society, Jesus loves you more than others since more than others you suffer with Him. What, therefore, could you have to complain about if sickness does not separate you from God, but rather brings you closer to Him. What does the rest matter if Jesus loves you with a special love?"

The severe climate of Venezuela proved disastrous for Father Louis' health. Nephritis, uremia and other ills were diagnosed. In a state of extremely poor health Father Louis was taken to Cucuta, Colombia, to stay with a family who would take good care of him. However, it was too late; on February 1 of 1923, away from his beloved apostolate, he died.

Shortly before his death Father Louis had written, "I feel that the Lord is with me. I feel that He will stay with me and not leave me. I also feel He is with my daughters and wishes that of our hearts we make one, and lay it next to His divine Heart. In this way we will be united and happy."

In 1964 Pope Paul VI recognized the Daughters of the Sacred Hearts of Jesus and Mary as a congregation of pontifical right. The house of Agua de Dios still keeps its unique privilege of being open to leprosy-stricken candidates. Today, the Daughters have over 300 members, non-lepers as well as lepers. They work in leprosariums, hospitals and among the poorest of the poor.

A cause for the beatification of Father Louis Variara has been introduced. The decree approving his writings was issued December 19, 1963.

U.P. Opere Don Bosco, Torino/Omniafoto, Torino

Fr. Louis Variara, who began a congregation of leper sisters in the leper colony of Agua de Dios, Colombia. The sisters are known as the Daughters of the Sacred Hearts of Jesus and Mary. The sisters stated, "Fr. Variara knows the pain of body we endure, and that deeper pain of soul, and he has shown us how to realize our dearest wishes in this place of suffering. It has become our paradise..."

359

D.A.N., Roma Aurelio

Louis Variara with his band. He did not hesitate to put his own lips on the mouthpieces of the instruments where the mouths of the leper boys had been a few seconds before. At Louis' ordination one of the lepers told him, "May you be blessed for the great efforts you have been making to sweeten the terrible cup of poison we have to drink."

35

VENERABLE MATT TALBOT

Matthew Talbot
1856 - 1925
Ireland
Died Age 69

The young man wandered about the streets of Dublin, tormented by thirst and the horrible symptoms of alcohol withdrawal. He had tried to go to Holy Communion that morning, but he was convinced that he would lapse again into his old alcoholic state before the day ended and that he would break his "pledge." At last he collapsed outside the Jesuit church, where he lay prostrate, begging God to relieve his agony. Disgusted worshippers stepped around him as they entered the church; how shameful, they felt, for a drunk to be lying there. God, however, heard the prayer of this Irish laborer. Matt Talbot did not lapse back into the clutches of his craving for drink that day, or ever.

From his early teens until age 28 Matt's only aim in life had been liquor. But from that point forward, his only aim was God. His former drinking companions marveled; one of them commented simply, "Barney [Matt] is a changed man."

Matt Talbot was born on May 2, 1856, the second of 12 children born to Charles and Elizabeth Talbot. Charles was a scrappy laborer with a fondness for drink. Elizabeth occasionally went out to work as a charwoman to help meet expenses. Mrs. Talbot had a hard time trying to keep the peace within her rowdy family, but somehow she managed. She was noted for being a very hard-working woman. In Matt's early years he knew little security or stability, as the family moved frequently from one tenement home to another.

Matt took after his father in his slight stature. Although he was small, he was wiry. From his mother, Matt got his hard-working tenacity.

Compulsory school attendance was not in force, and Matt never attended any school regularly. When he was 11 he was given a general form of crash course in catechism and the basics of reading and writing. He spent one year at a Christian Brothers school, but was frequently absent: the brother marked him as a "mitcher."

At the age of 12 Matt got his first job; it was in a wine bottling store. It was at this age, too, that he came home drunk for the first time. The hiding he got from his father had little effect, and soon Matt came home drunk daily. All his time outside of work was spent in bars or in finagling the money to buy the liquor his body grew to crave more and more.

It was not only the atmosphere of this first job that led Matt to drink. In Ireland at that time there was an evil system whereby many of the laborers were paid their wages by cash or check on Saturdays at the local pubs—with the pub owner then feeling entitled to a large purchase for this service, especially if he had cashed a check. Workers who objected to this system often found themselves with no job at all.

From this first job Matt moved to a number of jobs, always as an unskilled laborer. After work, he drank. He is remembered as being generous with his drinking buddies, and if one had been out of work and did not have the price of his drink, Matt paid for him. If Matt and his friends were short, one would sometimes sneak a pickled pig's cheek from the barrel at the bar and sell it to get the cash to go back to the same bar and buy more drink. Matt always avoided doing the actual stealing when it was his turn, though he would help drink up the money obtained.

Once Matt and some of his buddies were drinking in a bar when an itinerant fiddler came into the bar to play. While the fiddler was not looking, the boys stole his fiddle and sold it for money for their liquor. Later the memory of this act weighed on Matt's conscience, and he spent a great length of time looking for the fiddler to return to him the price of the fiddle. When he was unable to do so after a number of years, he finally donated money to have Masses said for the fiddler.

On the job Matt was known as a good worker. He became an expert hodman. While he was working for one builder his foreman used to put him in front of the other workers to make them try to keep up with him. He fell away from the Sacraments for a couple of years, although he always attended Sunday Mass. He would not go to dances or card parties with his brothers or friends, preferring only and always to spend time drinking.

One fateful Saturday in 1884, Matt and two of his brothers had been out of work for a week and as a consequence were penniless. They decided to go to the public house where their friends and fellow workers would be coming to draw and drink their pay. After their own years of generosity, surely someone would stand the Talbots a drink.

Instead, their friends passed them by, and no one even asked them "if they had a mouth on them." Some even passed by on the other side of the street. After a bit, Matt's two brothers decided to stay a while longer, but Matt abruptly turned away, saying that he was going home. He determined to go "take the pledge."

Matt's mother was shocked to find him home early—and sober; when he told her of his proposed action she cautioned him: "Go, in God's name, but don't take it unless you are going to keep it." As he left, she prayed for him to have the strength to keep his resolve.

Matt went straight to Holy Cross College, where he found a priest, went to confession and took the pledge of abstinence from alcohol for three months. The next morning, Sunday, he went to Holy Communion. Many times Matt felt he would not be able to hold out for three months. But at the end of three months he renewed his pledge for a longer period, and within a year he took it for life. Matt was to keep his pledge for 41 years; he never touched alcohol again. Moreover, his family said they never heard him swear again. Matt wore two pins in his cuff to remind himself in this regard. A former drinking companion said of him, "He could never go easy—at anything."

The first three months were the worst. Matt turned to God for support and began new habits of life. He began the practice of going to confession once a week and of going to 5:00 a.m. Mass before work at 6:00 a.m. each day. If the church was not open yet he would kneel outside, even in the rain or mud. At the end of the work day he would take refuge in a distant church to get away from his drinking associations; he would stay there until it was time to go home to bed. Sometimes he would go from church to church making visits. Or, if he went home after work, he would make a visit on the way home, then spend the rest of the evening on his knees at home—until 10:00. He would spend hours in prayer. His sister reports that Matt would often eat his sparse supper on his knees.

Outwardly, except for his amazing sobriety, Matt appeared much the same. He was still the same undersized, wiry, hard-working man. A common laborer, used to heavy daily toil, Matt was used to carrying bricks and mortar or hard-to-balance heavy planks. Interiorly, however, Matt was a different person, a man intent on humbling and hiding himself, a man thinking of his soul and its progress, a worker faithful to both his spiritual and temporal employers.

Matt's mother and sisters noticed that he was subjecting himself to severe penances, but they kept silent about this. He began to fast, with a specific regimen for each day of the week. He never ate a full meal. At noon he often drank a mixture of tea and cocoa which he allowed to become tepid before he drank it, and on some days he ate a little meat. During Lent, and from Advent through St. Stephen's Day (December 26), in honor of the Infant Saviour, as well as during the month of June—in honor of the Sacred Heart— he ate only bread and his cocoa-tea mix, and sometimes a little fish. He fasted for a week before every major feast. Trying to persuade a co-worker to do more fasting, Matt said, "We do well to punish the body and not be studying the gut." Despite Matt's fasting he remained able to do his work.

Matt's bed was a wooden plank with a rough wood block for a pillow. This bed was hidden by a sheet and one thin blanket. He would sleep only about four hours per night. He also wore penitential chains around his body. Matt often referred to his past sins and said, "Where would I be only for God and His Blessed Mother?" His one celebration for the year was on Christmas morning. Then he would enjoy a steak which he would ask his sister to buy and cook for him. Later, when Matt's health broke down in his late sixties, he would eat what was recommended to him.

Matt gave most of his wages to his mother. He stayed living at home, except for a brief stay in a rented room. After his father's death Matt took care of his mother for the last 12 years of her life. At one point a young woman suggested to Matt that they get married. He told her he would pray about it, then after several days he told her that God wanted him to remain single. He remained single for the rest of his life. To someone who complained of being lonely, Matt replied, "How can anyone be lonely, with Our Lord in the Blessed Sacrament?"

Matt began to go for advice to Father James Walsh, a Jesuit, who started him on a program of reading spiritual works. Although he read only at a snail's pace and often had to copy out passages he did not understand, Matt began to read and understand more and more. He conquered discouragement and laboriously learned to read better. He felt irresistibly drawn to prayer and spiritual reading, which took the place of his former drinking companions.

Among Matt's collection of books, many of them marked up, were *The Book of Spiritual Instruction*, by Blosius; a book of the revelations of St. Gertrude; *A Life of St. Augustine*, by Moriarty; several Bibles; *The Sinner's Guide; Martyrs of the Coliseum; Life of St. Catherine of Siena*, by her confessor; *The Oath Against Modernism; Will Any Religion Do; Butler's Lives of the Fathers; Introduction to the Devout Life*, by St. Francis de Sales; *Spiritual Conferences* and *All for Jesus*, by Father Faber; and *Writings of St. Alphonsus Liguori.*

His sister had given him a book entitled *Hell Open to Christians*, which had aroused fear in him. In a Bible, Matt had marked the passage, "Unless you do penance you shall all likewise perish" (from *Luke* 13). Reading a life of St. Catherine of Siena, Matt was very impressed that Our Lord had called her "My own daughter Catherine."

A friend who used to converse with Matt about religious matters was impressed with Matt's shrewdness, clear-headedness, strong will and balance. This friend described Matt's ability to understand books beyond the grasp of an uneducated man: "The explanation seemed to me to lie in his clear, logical mind. He was convinced that if the truths of Revelation as regards the Incarnation and Redemption were accepted as true, there should be no limit to our service save the impossible. This view urged him on to his life of extreme penance and enabled him to persevere to the end."

Matt went back time after time to all of his old haunts and paid off debts that he had incurred in his drinking days. His name had long since been wiped off the slates in most cases, but he paid every penny that he could remember owing, or that someone would tell him he owed. He would go in, hand over the amount in an envelope, and hurry away.

The Talbot temper had troubled Matt for many years. When he recalled having spoken sharply to someone, he would return and beg pardon. If he found he had been wrong he would say, "You were right, I was wrong." He did not make excuses. He was very honest. Once when a neighbor's hen laid some eggs in his yard he returned them; the neighbor told him he should not have bothered but should have kept them. He replied, "No, they were not mine to keep." On another occasion, when a friend forgot to pay back some money, he went to collect it. He didn't care about the money, but he wanted the bargain kept.

As his spirituality advanced he became more and more quiet, and he avoided doing anything to mark himself out. He made a habit of keeping his eyes cast down all the time. Yet he was very popular with his fellow workers and people had a great respect for him. He was always good-humored and would join in the conversation.

Matt would speak up to men he knew if they used bad language. One time he made a little girl leave his yard for saying "O God!" after being warned about this on a previous visit. (This girl later became very saintly.) On other occasions Matt would silently lift his hat when he heard God's name taken in vain. Matt would talk to people about the things of Heaven. He would join in conversation about sports and other earthly things in order to be sociable but really had no interest in them.

Matt became a permanent employee of T. & C. Martin's, timber merchants and builders' suppliers. He worked in the section where timber was creosoted, and later in the saw mill section. Matt was glad of the transfer from the dirty creosote yard, as he always liked to be clean and tidy. A fellow worker suspected that this was due to the fact that he made visits to the Blessed Sacrament after work. Matt wore old clothes, often too big for him, but they were always very clean. There was nothing particularly striking in his appearance.

On breaks at work, Matt stood or knelt behind piles of timber and prayed. One man who knew that Matt did not like to be caught praying would cough or call to another man to signal that he was coming. Despite his differences from the other men Matt was not considered odd. He inspired respect.

A number of Matt's co-workers later gave testimony at the tribunal investigations for his cause. They remember that he was never obsequious to any man. Once he told his boss, "With all respect to you, sir, I never yet met a man I was afraid of." This man later said, "Matt would always tell you what he thought." Matt often said, "I have only one master, God Almighty." On one occasion he disobeyed an order that was against his conscience, even at the risk of getting fired. He said that "he had his soul's interests to consider first." On another occasion Matt apologized to a former foreman for some hot words he had spoken.

Matt's co-workers remembered that he got on well with his employers and at all times showed them respect. He was independent-minded and spoke out straight, was never behind schedule or late, and he took things quietly. As for his co-workers, they liked to work with him. He spoke little but enjoyed a good laugh, was affable and good company, and was always willing to help others. Though he avoided bad language in himself and others, Matt used a lot of slang. One expression he would use, in a jolly tone, when someone was trying to rush him was "Oh, get your hair cut!"

One friend of Matt who used to discuss religious books with him hesitated to smoke while with him, since Matt had given up tobacco. But Matt would insist; picking up a small white pebble which he carried around he would put it into his mouth and say, "I have this; now light up, John, and enjoy your smoke." Matt once told a friend that he had found it harder to give up tobacco than to give up drink.

Matt's charity was great. Among other things he often gave fellow workers the price of a pair of boots, and he would subscribe to every fund and charity in the yard. When two of his brothers died, he paid for their funerals. When asked to buy a ticket for anything, he would, but he would have to bring the money the next day as he didn't carry any with him. This habit arose because of a temptation he had experienced shortly after his conversion. Walking past a pub he had been seized by the desire for a drink. He walked up and down the street two or three times, then went in. But no one came to serve him. He waited a long time but still no one came, so he suddenly turned and walked out the door to a Catholic church a minute's walk away. He stayed there until it closed and resolved never to carry money with him in case the same temptation should come upon him again.

Whatever remained of Matt's wages, after paying his rent and buying the little food he needed, went to charity. An increase in wages just meant more money for charities. He helped his family and came to the aid of neighbors in distress, and he gave money for numerous charities. All the charity collectors knew Matt and received regular contributions from him. On one occasion a priest got permission to make a collection on payday at the yard where

Matt worked. The priest afterward told the foreman that he hesitated to accept Matt's donation as he had given "all he had about him."

A friend of Matt's, Raphael O'Callaghan, once asked him if he had ever had any remarkable spiritual experiences. He replied, "Only once." On further questioning he said that one night he had heard a voice urging him to pray for a fellow workman he had been trying to convert for a long time. The man died unexpectedly that night.

In the early 1900's, labor in Ireland was in a turmoil. Like most of the Irish workers, Matt was a union member. When the union went on strike, Matt did too. Trying to do the right thing, he read much Catholic material on social justice questions—on one occasion sending to America for a certain book—and he had a strong sense of justice.

Although Matt never spoke of or looked out for himself or his own rights, he was convinced that the workers were underpaid and were justified in seeking their own rights. Matt's strike pay went uncollected until some of the other workers discovered this and collected it for him. Matt used this money to help the strikers with young families. He seemed to sense which ones were in trouble and tactfully gave them money, as he put it, "to tide you over." During the major strike of 1913 Matt spent his time in church.

During the labor struggles and the later Irish uprising, Matt appeared oblivious to much of the world's activity. But after his death indications were found in his notes that his country and his fellow workers had been kept in his prayers.

In 1923 Matt fell ill and had to go to the hospital for a while. He was diagnosed as having heart trouble—tachycardia—and kidney ailments. He was a model patient, and he concealed his penances so well that he was thought of only as a gentle, good-natured, holy old man, though it was noticed that he spent much time in prayer. One of the sisters called Matt "Poor old Tach" in reference to his heart problem. When a young nursing sister was having trouble learning about the anatomical structure of the sternum and chest cavity, her superior told her to go and examine "poor Tach," because his ribs and breastbone were easily studied—"for of all the patients I ever saw, Matt Talbot is the one least covered with flesh."

For the next year and a half Matt was back at home, unable to work and badly off, as his health benefit was extremely small.

With difficulty, some friends got him to accept occasional help from the St. Vincent de Paul Society. One friend suggested that he go to an old folks home run by the Little Sisters of the Poor, but Matt explained that he would "rather be by myself," and anyway, "I'm shy." He had to modify his earlier habit of attending as many Masses as possible on Sunday. More than four decades of constant prayer and penance now separated the rowdy young drunkard from the Matt Talbot of 1925. Some knew him to be a man of prayer, but few knew of his penances.

In March of 1925 Matt went back to work about the yards, where the other workmen left him the lighter tasks. He didn't look well, and little change had been made in his regimen—except that in obedience to his doctor he took a little nourishment on Sunday mornings after attending his first Mass.

Trinity Sunday, June 7, was the hottest day of a heatwave that had hung on since the previous week. Matt set off on his usual Sunday rounds. When he returned home for his cocoa, a neighbor saw him and, thinking that he looked unwell, advised him to rest. But in a while Matt came down and, smiling, told his neighbor that he was going on to the 10 a.m. Mass in Dominick Street. He hurried off.

Within a few minutes of his goal, Matt stumbled and collapsed. Passersby came running, and a priest was fetched. No one knew who the stricken man was, and a Dominican Father gave the Last Rites, suspecting that he was dead. A doctor came and pronounced him dead, and an ambulance arrived to take the body away. Matt had no identification; only a rosary and a prayerbook were found in his pocket.

The body was taken to the Jervis Street Hospital, where the usual routine was followed and the corpse was undressed. Attendants found a heavy penitential chain wound around the body and a lighter chain on one arm; another, below one knee, was placed so that it must have caused pain when kneeling. The nurse in charge, Sister M. Ignatius, was sent for, and she left instructions that the chains were to be removed from the body and put into the coffin with the body after the inquest.

The next day Matt's sisters found that he was missing from his room, and eventually they learned what had happened. The verdict of the inquest was heart failure.

Matt had belonged to the Third Order of St. Francis, so his last garment was the brown Franciscan habit. The chains that the suddenness of his death had revealed were buried with him. Although a number of friends, relatives and co-workers attended the funeral, it was a poor man's funeral, the total cost not exceeding 10 pounds.

After Matt's death his reputation for holiness became widespread, and by 1931 the first inquiry into his life had begun. The decree on his virtues was issued October 3, 1975.

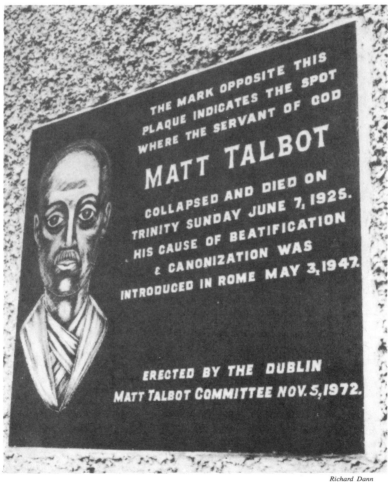

Richard Dann

Plaque on Granby Lane, Dublin, where Matt Talbot collapsed and died of heart failure on June 7, 1925. Penitential chains were found on his body after his death.

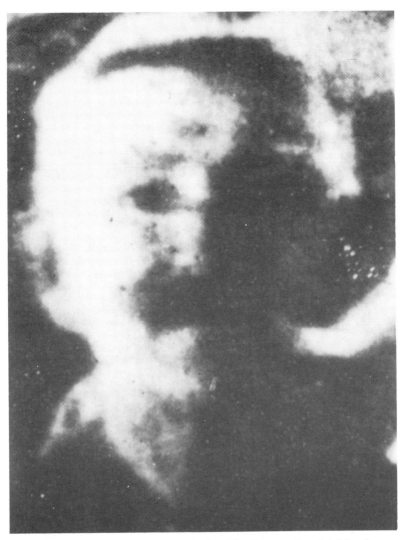

Ven. Matt Talbot, the saintly alcoholic. Matt's excessive drinking began when he was 12. One evening when he was 28 he went out and found a priest, went to Confession and "took the pledge" for three months. Many times he felt he would not be able to hold out for three months, but within the year he renewed the pledge for life, never touching alcohol again (41 more years). His resolve was maintained by a new life of much prayer, daily Mass, hard work and much penance. This is probably the only existing photograph of Matt Talbot; it was taken from a group shot and enhanced by computer.

36

BLESSED BARTOLO LONGO

Bartolo Longo
1841 - 1926
Italy
Died Age 85

Pompeii. The very name of this ancient city is a reminder of a place where artists and historians for years have found fertile fields of investigation into the beauties and intriguing mysteries of an ancient culture. *New Pompeii*. Although less familiar worldwide, this name stands for a mysterious beauty far greater than that of the old city beside which New Pompeii is built. New Pompeii exists as a monument to the love of God for all mankind as shown through Our Lady and her Rosary. An humble Catholic layman, Bartolo Longo, built this city where Mary could reign in queenly splendor and where a number of great corporal works of mercy are today carried on in her name.

Bartolo was born on February 11, 1841 in southern Italy, the son of a well-to-do physician. His mother was sweet-tempered and devout, and she taught her children the daily practice of saying the Rosary. From his father—who would die when Bartolo was only 10—the boy inherited a love for music and beauty. In later life he was a gifted orator, an eloquent prose writer and a talented musician. From his mother he learned to visit the poor, and he gained such a love for Our Lady that this devotion would one day lead him to the honors of the altar.

As a child Bartolo was lively and very intelligent. He was cordial and easy to get along with, although he had a fiery character. Later he described himself then as "a lively and impertinent imp, sometimes rather a rascal." At the age of six he began his education at a school run by the Scolopi priests. Later he studied law from a private tutor, but was obliged by law to complete his legal studies at the University of Naples.

At this time Naples University was a hotbed of rationalism and anticlericalism. Bartolo became involved in the political movements and esoteric cults so popular with the students, and finally became a spiritualist, searching for the "ultimate truth." He abandoned the religious practices of his childhood. As with many cults of today, extreme austerities and fasts were imposed by Bartolo's spiritualist regimen. His health was permanently damaged by these, and he became depressed and nervous. He seemed to hear the voice of his dead father calling him to return to God.

Bartolo visited his friend Professor Vincenzo Pepe, who was shocked at his appearance and exclaimed, "Do you want to die in an insane asylum and be damned forever?" Bartolo admitted his mental confusion, and Professor Pepe introduced him to a number of holy persons in Naples who could give him support and wise counsel.

Father Alberto Radente, a friend of the Professor, was a learned Dominican priest who subjected the young lawyer to a comprehensive review of theology. The doctrine of St. Thomas Aquinas was an important element in his conversion. After much study and prayer, Bartolo was received back to the Sacraments. On March 25, 1871 he was professed in the Third Order of St. Dominic and given the religious name of Fratel Rosario (Brother Rosary).

Never one to do things halfway, Bartolo made one last visit to a seance. Holding up a medal of Our Lady, he cried out: "I renounce spiritualism because it is nothing but a maze of error and falsehood!" He then went to student parties and cafes, denouncing spiritualism and proclaiming his faith in the Church. This was a bold step for a time when the Pope was a prisoner in the Vatican and religious orders were suppressed and expelled from their convents.

At this time Bartolo gave up his legal work and devoted himself to a number of charitable apostolates, working with several priests and the Ven. Catherine Volpicelli, Foundress of the Handmaids of the Sacred Heart. Bartolo was blessed in knowing many holy people—several of whom have been proposed for canonization. At this time he also worked with the wealthy Countess Marianna de Fusco, whom he was later to marry.

The wealthy, attractive and cultured Bartolo was an excellent marriage prospect. He rejected an offer from a baroness, but went so far as to promise to marry a wealthy and beautiful girl named Annina. But on the advice of spiritual directors, he decided against this marriage because he needed to be free in order to carry out apostolic works, something he had promised to do in expiation. Bartolo believed that possibly he should become a priest. In this idea he was discouraged by both his friends and his spiritual directors. He made a retreat to discern his true vocation and offered his life to God and Our Lady without reservation.

In 1872 Bartolo went to the valley of Pompeii with two armed escorts—the place was overrun with bandits—to handle some legal claims of land ownership for the Countess de Fusco. There he was shocked and filled with great pity by the ignorance, poverty and lack of religion among the peasants. The swampy locale had only a small, deteriorating church, which was under the care of an aging priest who rarely saw any of his hundred or so illiterate and impoverished parishioners. The people lived in the most abject poverty, and any religion they had was mixed together with superstitious practices. The adults did not even know their prayers, much less their catechism. He described the scene: "In the same dog-hole where the donkey, cow and pig were, not a few families passed their lives, lying and sleeping on the same dirty litter, father, mother and children . . ."

Bartolo's generous heart was touched. He heard a voice which said: "He who wishes to be saved, let him say the Rosary." Bartolo fell to his knees and promised: "Queen of the Rosary, I will not leave this place until I have witnessed the triumph of your holy Rosary."

Later, Bartolo wrote, "The modern Valley of Pompeii, consequently, lonely, sad and feared, and left by civil people, could well have been called the 'Unhappy Valley'. . .I therefore determined with a resolute spirit to promote with all my heart the devotion to the Rosary in this desolate valley where I happened to be because of a mysterious disposition of Providence.

"With the boldness of desperation, I lifted my face and hands to the sky, turning to the celestial Virgin: 'If it is true,' I cried, 'that you promised St. Dominic that whoever spreads the Rosary would be saved, I will be saved, because I will not leave Pompeii without having spread your Rosary!'. . .No one answered. . .a faraway echo of bells reached my ears and shocked me: the Angelus of noon was ringing. I knelt and articulated the prayer that in that hour a world of believers [would be] dedicated to Mary."

Now firmly convinced of what his vocation was to be, Bartolo made repeated trips to the Valley to teach the inhabitants how to pray the Rosary. He organized a Rosary feast, although the first attempt failed. Without giving up, he continued to visit the homes of each of the inhabitants, organizing another celebration with music, fireworks, races and even a lottery.

Bartolo and a brother named Friar Albert looked in vain in Naples for an image of Our Lady to be taken to Pompeii. Then one day a Dominican sister named Sister Concetta donated a large painting of Our Lady of the Rosary. Sister Concetta must have seen the hesitation of the two men, for the picture was dilapidated, wrinkled, soiled and torn. She advised them not to hesitate, though, predicting that the picture would work miracles. A wagoner agreed to convey the painting to the Valley along with his cargo—of manure!

At first, everyone who saw the picture was disappointed. The Countess commented, "It is so ugly that it must have been painted purposely to destroy devotion to Our Lady!" But an artist refurbished the unsightly canvas, and then ornamented it with diamonds donated by the faithful. A crown was placed on the head of Our Lady by the Countess, and in 1876 the painting was solemnly mounted on a throne of marble imported from Lourdes and placed on exposition. Bartolo commented, "There is something about that picture which impresses the soul, not by its artistic perfection, but by a mysterious charm which impels one to kneel and pray with tears." Our Lady had destined the picture to become the fount of many miracles and the center of one of the most famous shrines in the world.

A place for exposition of the picture was needed, so Bartolo sought permission of the diocesan bishop to erect a special altar for public veneration of the image. The bishop replied that Bartolo should build a church instead of an altar, and he pointed out the spot where the shrine should be built. He gave permission to solicit a penny a month from the faithful of the diocese, and he made a generous donation himself. Donations from wealthy friends of Bartolo and the Countess began to pour in, especially after Bartolo began to promote—in several languages—a book called *Devotion of the Fifteen Saturdays in Honor of the Fifteen Mysteries of the Rosary*. In 1876 the bishop laid the cornerstone of the chapel. In 1901 Pope Pius X would elevate the Shrine to the rank of a pontifical basilica.

When the picture was exposed, miracles began to take place and pilgrimages began. Among the first miracles recorded were the cure of Bartolo's dying mother, the restoration to health of a paralyzed Jesuit priest, and a miraculous cure which was accepted by the Holy See for the canonization of St. Margaret Mary Alacoque. Our Lady appeared to a dying girl in Naples, and besides curing her, promised special graces to all who make a Rosary novena of 54 days. By 1885, some 940 cures were reported at the Shrine. Favors were recorded with scrupulous accuracy in Bartolo's periodical, *The Rosary and the New Pompeii*, whose printings soon surpassed 100,000 copies. He also wrote *History of the Wonders of the Shrine of Pompeii*.

In 1884 Venerable Louis da Casoria gave his friend Bartolo a printing press. A talented writer, Bartolo began a publishing mission to tell about Pompeii and to encourage devotion. Later, Bartolo used the press in teaching a trade to some of the orphans he was caring for.

Few saints are exempt from suffering. Malicious rumors about the relationship between Bartolo and the Countess began to be spread. Were they really the models of purity that many thought they were? After so many years of working and traveling together, could their personal lives be a cause for scandal? Bartolo and the Countess took their problem to their friend Leo XIII, the great "Pope of the Rosary." The kindly Pope solved their difficulty in one sentence: "Lawyer, you are free; Countess, you are a widow; get married and no one can say anything against you." The marriage was celebrated on April 7, 1885. The Countess remarked, "We went to Rome good friends and returned good spouses." They remained good friends and co-workers until the Countess' death in 1924, when she passed away at the age of 88.

Around the growing sanctuary Bartolo Longo wanted to build a town of charity; its inhabitants were orphans of nature and "orphans" of the law. In 1887 Bartolo thought first of nature's orphan children. Then in 1892 he added the law's orphan boys, the sons of prisoners. Finally, in 1922, he began the care of the daughters of prisoners.

Bartolo was a zealous social worker. Beside the Pompeiian Basilica he erected a group of buildings dedicated to providing free service to the poor and destitute. This "New Pompeii" is popularly known as the City of Charity and the City of Mary, and it is maintained without government subsidy. There is an orphanage for girls and one for boys, as well as one for the homeless children of parents who are in prison.

In Bartolo's day many believed that children of convicts were themselves destined by heredity to become lawbreakers and immoral persons. Phrenology, or the study of a person's character from the shape of his head, was a popular pseudo-science. Bartolo had little use for these theories. He said, "Scientists! Don't take away Christ, who soothes the wounds of our souls. . . . If you come across an unfortunate boy—whose body has been transformed by the strains of misery and whose anomalous skull does not reveal an inborn atavistic deliquency but only the sad, deadly progress of rachitis [rickets] and scrofula [tuberculosis of the lymphatic glands, causing neck swellings]—have pity on him and not horror; think of assisting and not of imprisoning him; appeal to the doctor and not the magistrate."

Bartolo's plans for the education of all the orphan children consisted of two elements: "We will use two educational elements to educate a child brought up in misery and ignorance to honesty and uprightness: work and prayer." The unique Marian City includes a large printing press operated by orphan boys, a school of typography, a hospital, gymnasium, music school, vocational schools, post office, railroad station and housing for a large number of employees. Bartolo founded a congregation of Dominican Sisters, the Daughters of the Rosary, to provide for the education of the orphan girls and he engaged the Christian Brothers to teach the boys. All these works brought about a wonderful change in life at Pompeii.

In his educational projects Bartolo emphasized catechism instruction. He used to say, "People without catechism are people without religion."

In recent times the care of the aged has been considered, and following the direction of the Founder a home for them has been begun. To complete the Pompeiian family, there are a number of resident priests and monks to give spiritual assistance to the institutes and to the millions of pilgrims who come there.

Another of Bartolo's projects was a crusade of prayer to ask for the definition of the dogma of the Assumption of the Blessed Virgin Mary. He also petitioned many bishops to ask the Pope for this. The dogma would eventually be defined and proclaimed in 1950.

The phenomenal expansion of the Pompeiian complex could not

but arouse questions and comments about the Founder's management of such a large enterprise. Misunderstandings arose, and calumny and slander were spread. In his misery Bartolo cried: "I have sacrificed all that I had for the last 50 years for Our Lady, and now they call me a thief!" In the midst of these troubles, in 1904 Pope Pius X issued a decree separating the administration of the Sanctuary from the administration of the other works of the city. This was a heavy blow for Bartolo, and he was obliged to lay off many workers. Yet he bore the crushing humiliation with heroic resignation, as a last purification. Three months later, Pope Pius X became convinced of Bartolo's innocence and in effect revoked his earlier decree.

It was in 1906 that Bartolo Longo made his final detachment from his works, turning over them all, and even his own personal property, to the Holy See. (The property of the Sanctuary had already been handed over to Pope Leo XIII in 1894.) Then, obeying the command of Pope Pius X that he "must not die, you must work..." he loyally cooperated with the new head of administration and representatives of the Holy See to continue the work at Pompeii. He humbly stayed at the city as a simple employee.

Spiritually, Bartolo remained devoted to the Blessed Virgin Mary. He went to confession twice a week.

Bartolo remained at the Shrine until his death at the age of 85. During his last hours he lay quietly on his bed, praying the Rosary and blessing the orphans who came to keep him company. In his last will and testament he stated, "I wish to die a true Dominican tertiary in the arms of the Queen of the Rosary, with the assistance of my holy Father St. Dominic and of my mother St. Catherine of Siena." Bartolo's last words were, "My only desire is to see Mary, who has saved me and who will save me from the clutches of Satan."

Bartolo was buried beside the Countess in the crypt of the Basilica of Pompeii. On October 26, 1980, Pope John Paul II proclaimed him Blessed, calling him the "Man of Mary."

Tipografica Pompei S.p.A.

Bartolo Longo in his younger days. As a young man he had been involved in the political movements and esoteric cults so popular among the students. Upon his conversion at around age 30 he went around to his former haunts—student parties and cafes and even a seance—denouncing his previous spiritualism and proclaiming his faith in the Church.

At around age 31 Bartolo became acquainted with the area around the ancient city of Pompeii. The people there lived in the most abject poverty and filth: the adults did not even know their prayers, much less their catechism. One day, Bartolo was inspired to bring devotion to the Rosary to this desolate place. He fell to his knees and promised, "Queen of the Rosary, I will not leave this place until I have witnessed the triumph of your holy Rosary." Pompeii was to become a great Marian shrine; its famous picture of Our Lady is visible here.

The famous painting of Our Lady of the Rosary at the Shrine of Pompeii. The original picture was dilapidated, wrinkled, soiled and torn and was carted to the valley of Pompeii on a manure wagon. At first, everyone who saw the picture was disappointed. But it was destined to be the occasion of many miracles. It was refurbished and then ornamented with diamonds donated by the faithful. Here the picture is shown after its 1965 restoration.

Above: Bartolo Longo, founder of the shrine and modern city of Pompeii. Bartolo worked with the wealthy widow, Countess Mariana de Fusco, on his charitable projects. However, false malicious rumors began to circulate about their relationship. Bartolo and the Countess took their problem to Pope Leo XIII, who answered, "Lawyer, you are free; Countess, you are a widow; get married and no one can say anything against you." The marriage was celebrated on April 7, 1885. The Countess remarked, "We went to Rome good friends and returned good spouses."

Previous page: Bartolo opened an orphanage for boys and one for girls, as well as orphanages for homeless sons and homeless daughters of convicts; he became known as the "Father of Orphans." Bartolo's educational plan for the children consisted of two elements: work and prayer. He began a whole Marian City at Pompeii, with a school of typography, hospital, gymnasium, music school, vocational schools, post office, railroad station and housing for a large number of employees.

Bartolo with some of his orphan girls. Bartolo founded a congregation of Dominican Sisters, the Daughters of the Rosary, to provide for the education of the orphan girls, and he engaged the Christian Brothers to teach the boys. Bartolo emphasized catechism instruction. He used to say, "People without catechism are people without religion."

Toward the end of his life Bartolo became the victim of slander and misunderstanding, which eventually led to his turning over all the Pompeiian property, even his own personal property, to the Holy See. He humbly stayed on as a simple employee. Bartolo's last words were, "My only desire is to see Mary, who has saved me and who will save me from the clutches of Satan." Bartolo was buried in the Basilica of Pompeii, alongside his wife.

37

EVE LAVALLIERE

Sister Eve Marie of the Sacred Heart of Jesus (Third Order)
Eugenie-Marie-Pascaline Fenoglio
1866 - 1929
France
Died Age 63

"It is through suffering that we most resemble Jesus," wrote the penitent Eve Lavalliere, a member of the Third Order Secular of St. Francis.

At the end of her life, the suffering of this penitent was extreme. Once the toast of Paris as a famous actress, she had renounced her former life to live in reparation for her sins. Toward the end of her life, her face swelled beyond recognition. Her teeth fell out, and her mouth became a mass of swollen tissue. The doctor had to sew her eyelids together, without anaesthetic, to prevent her eyes from falling out of her head. As each of her once-beautiful features suffered attack, Eve thanked God: "I have sinned through these faculties, good Lord. Now I thank You for permitting me to expiate my sins through this suffering."

In a notebook, a short time before her death, Eve Lavalliere had written her own epitaph, "My Maker, have mercy." And to an acquaintance: "All suffering is an embrace of our dear Jesus." The priest said to her at the end, "God has pardoned you because you have loved much. Depart in peace, O liberated Christian soul."

"Eve Lavalliere" was the stage name of this woman who had begun life as Eugenie Fenoglio. The suffering of the sensitive soul of Eugenie began in childhood. Born in Toulon, France, on the Mediterranean Sea, she was the second child and only daughter of Emile and Albanie Fenoglio. Her father was a cutter and her mother a seamstress. Unfortunately, theirs was an unhappy marriage. Emile was a violent, alcoholic libertine who was given to jealous brooding and ungoverned rages. Often, Albanie would take the children and escape to the home of relatives until her husband sobered up and forgot his rage. Always, though, she would return. Eugenie's brother was the favored child, and from earliest childhood Eugenie faced the lack of love from her parents.

Eugenie was unhappy in school, and became known as a "bad girl." When she was 10, her family moved to Perpignan, and she entered a Catholic boarding school called Bon Secours. Here, away from the problems of her family life, she blossomed in the cheerful atmosphere. In recalling her childhood, Eugenie remembered a rare and beautiful peace on the day of her First Communion—a peace which she was not to feel again for many years.

At 12, Eugenie returned home. Again the family problems wore on her. She escaped into fantasy by creating and acting in original plays.

In 1883 Eugenie's mother, Albanie, left her husband and set up a household with her daughter. Albanie worked as a seamstress and Eugenie as a dressmaker. Her brother had joined the Navy.

On March 16, 1884 Emile wheedled permission to come for a visit, and Albanie prepared his favorite dinner. She felt he wanted a reconciliation and advised Eugenie to be nice to her father and make him feel at home. The dinner began in peace, and when some passing musicians passed by, Eugenie's father gave her some money to throw to them from the balcony. But suddenly the discussion in the house took a violent turn and Eugenie heard the sound of an explosion. When she ran inside, she saw her mother falling backwards with a face full of blood, and her father turned toward his daughter with a smoking revolver. Something stayed his shot at her, and he turned the gun on himself and shot himself in the temple. Eugenie's mother died three weeks after the fatal shooting.

The 18-year-old orphan lived for a time with relatives. She was unhappy and lonely, being constantly reminded that she was the daughter of a murderer. Thoughts of suicide began to plague her. One evening while she was staring at the deep waters of a stream in Nice, a gentleman passing by noticed her. He took her to supper and arranged a night's lodging. He then arranged for her to meet the director of a traveling theatrical group. From there she began her rise to stardom.

For three years, Eugenie traveled with the troupe learning the theatrical trade. Then, she became the mistress of the Marquis de la Valette. At last, she went to Paris to try to win fame. There, at 22, she met and fell in love with a promoter named Fernand

Samuel. He polished the rough diamond of her talent and soon she became one of the best comediennes in France. She had taken the stage name of Eve Lavalliere.

In 1895 Eve bore Samuel a daughter, Jeanne. Although Eve no longer practiced the Faith and Samuel practiced it only erratically, the couple had their daughter baptized.

Although Eve and Samuel were devoted to each other, Samuel was also devoted to several other women. Samuel was the only man Eve ever truly loved, although she had a number of affairs with other men. Constantly they provided her with money, furs and jewels.

By 1900 Eve had attained the stardom she so longed for. She was a great Parisian actress—witty, enigmatic, full of life. She became internationally famous and received homage from many kings and princes of Europe. From 1901-1917 she "reigned as indisputed queen of the light-comedy stage." The famous actress Sarah Bernhardt once said to her, "My dear, there are more talented actresses than you, but not one that can boast your creative gift." Eve had arrived.

Her success did not, however, make Eve happy. She confided to a friend, "I never enjoy myself anywhere. I always withdraw into myself wherever I am, except when I am on the stage." Fame, success and riches left Eve cold. She found no comfort in her relationships with men, nor in her daughter. Her daughter disliked her, and had been thoroughly spoiled by her father. Again, thoughts of suicide haunted Eve and she came close, on at least three occasions, to killing herself.

Samuel died in 1914. Eve hoped that relations with her daughter might improve. Instead they worsened. Her daughter had taken to wearing men's clothes and flaunted her female companions and perverse way of life in front of her mother.

During World War I, Eve performed many benefit shows for the French troops. She was nearly worn out with exhaustion. In 1917, she completed negotiations for an American tour which was to take place in the fall. She decided to spend the summer in the countryside, resting up for the tour. She rented a chateau in Chanceaux sur Choiselle. There, along with her servants and her companion, Leona, a Belgian war orphan, Eve planned to relax.

It happened that in this little French village Eve met Fr. Chasteigner, the village priest who was to be the instrument of her conversion and her return to the Faith. When Fr. Chasteigner noted that she had been in the village for two weeks yet had not gone to Mass, Eve responded, "Father, I have not been to Mass for years. And you have neither invited me nor given me your permission to come to your church."

"Mademoiselle, all—even sinners—are welcome in my church."

After a further conversation with Fr. Chasteigner, Eve experienced what she later called the decisive moment of her conversion. Later he gave her a copy of the *Life of Mary Magdalen* by Fr. Lacordaire. The book moved Eve, and grace touched her heart. She confessed and, in June of 1917, returned to the Sacraments of her childhood faith. She considered this her birth to real life, writing off her former years of life as years of death.

In the fall, Eve cancelled her American tour. Fr. Chasteigner advised her that she could be a good actress and a good Christian as well, but she was determined to retire and give up acting completely. Eve sold off her two apartments and their furnishings, giving much of the money to the poor. She wanted to join a Carmelite cloister, but although she tried several convents, she was refused by all. At first, Eve was angry with God for the rejections. Later, she realized that God was permitting her to experience a rejection like that suffered by Christ. In the loneliness which had plagued her all her life and which now helped to detach her from this world, Eve referred to herself as "Earth's eternal orphan."

Although Eve attempted to reconcile herself with her daughter, this did not work, and Jeanne even forced Eve to leave the chateau that had been willed to her by her father. Yet Eve forgave her daughter and continued to pray and work for her conversion. Jeanne would sometimes seem to be at the point of converting, but would then relapse into her former way of life.

For a time Eve lived near Lourdes, performing stern austerities like making the outdoor Stations of the Cross barefoot in the cold and rain. Such penances did not help her already delicate health. Eve suffered much from poor health and from the cold, especially after she had taken a vow of poverty, which meant she gave up many comforts. One time she took a train trip in a third class car, spending 18 hours on the hard seats. She explained how different it had been in her worldly days: "I didn't even know how to get myself a railway ticket; there was always a reserved compartment waiting for me, all decked out in flowers." But Eve did not regret her conversion. She told an acquaintance that despite all its hardships (including her physical and moral sufferings and times of darkness and depression), her new life brought her a happiness she had never known at any time before.

For about three years Eve had moved from place to place, always hoping that it might be God's will that she enter a convent, especially Carmel. But finally she realized this was not God's will for her. The Mother Superior at the last convent she applied to had been very impressed by her purity of heart and by her ability to love—"the only thing that matters in the Carmel" —but still the community felt the verdict must be negative, on account of Eve's poor health and her child, not to mention her notoriety.

In 1920, with the help of Fr. Chasteigner, Eve found a small home in Thuillieres where she and Leona finally settled. They called their new home Bethany. There Eve took an active role in her parish and in the same year she joined the Third Order Secular of St. Francis, taking the name Sister Eve Marie of the Sacred Heart of Jesus. Eve felt that she had received a great abundance of love from God. She tried every day to love Him like a little child, with abandonment to Him. Eve also concentrated on prayer and suffering to save souls.

From 1921 to 1924, Eve spent seven months each year in Tunisia, North Africa, as a member of a lay missionary nursing team. There her poor health and periods of depression continued to cause her much suffering. After she underwent a severe attack of African fever, the archbishop advised her not to return the next winter. He told her, "Mademoiselle, you are going to help this mission not by your deeds, but by your sufferings. Your task has just begun. Thanks to your sacrifices, this mission will prosper." As always, Eve accepted the will of God. Shortly before leaving for Africa, Eve had received what she considered a "great grace," the inspiration and courage to give up cosmetics and hair coloring; she threw them into the fire and then felt very happy and relieved at having given up one of her last attachments.

Back home again in 1924, Eve carried on a daily schedule, with Leona, of prayer, good works, much almsgiving, much illness, spiritual reading and meditation, seriously living out the practice of poverty, chastity and obedience as a Third Order member. She filled page after page of her notebook with her spiritual reflections, which read like the writings of the Saints. She seemed inflamed with love for God, and told a visitor that in her sufferings she was "so very happy." In fact, she told this visitor, "When people mention me to you, make it quite clear to them, all those who know me, that you have seen the happiest, indeed the most perfectly happy of women."

In August of 1928, Eve entered the last stations on her own personal way of the cross. She suffered from a bad case of peritonitis. She ran high fevers and was in constant pain. Her daughter came to assist Leona in caring for her. One evening when Jeanne was alone with Eve, she put a white powder on a knife blade under her mother's nose and asked her to sniff it to make her feel better. The powder made Eve relax and sleep well. For a number of days, Jeanne helped her mother's pain by giving her a dose of the powder. Being short on funds, Jeanne was trying to addict Eve to cocaine—and she did. She planned to sell her mother the cocaine once she was addicted. When the doctor found out what Jeanne had done, he personally ordered her out of the house. Unfortunately, Eve had built up such an addiction that he had to keep her on a maintenance dose of the drug until her death a year and a half later.

Eve's final agony was a long and difficult illness, which she accepted with joy. Her love for God was intense, and she had a great desire to suffer in reparation. Yet Eve still thought of others. She sent a gift to Father Chasteigner along with a message of her spiritual health. She prayed that her companion, Leona, would find a good Christian husband. (She did.) She spent hours in ardent prayer.

At the time of her death, journalists still puzzled over Eve's retirement and disappearance. The wildest motives had been discussed—that she had killed someone, that death threats made her life unsafe, that she was involved in espionage. Eve herself explained her motives in one of the notes in her spiritual notebook: "I thank You, O my God, that You have given me shelter beneath Your roof. Abandonment, love, trust—such is my motto." She further explained, "In this lost corner of Lorraine, far from the world, we will tarry for God's will in stillness and meditation."

Eve's passing from this earth was quiet, although there were several articles about her death in the press. Her body was accompanied by her friends and neighbors in a small funeral procession. Eve's body is buried near the small church in Thuillieres. Her soul has gone to meet the God she so ardently loved and served.

392

Above and facing page: Eve Lavalliere at the height of her fame. "Eve Lavalliere" was the stage name of Eugenie Fenoglio, famous Parisian actress of the early 20th century. Eve had risen to stardom after a tragic childhood. From 1901-1917 Eve Lavalliere "reigned as undisputed queen of the light-comedy stage" in Paris. She had a great power to fascinate, being witty, enigmatic and full of life. Many famous people and even members of European royalty paid her homage.

393

Eve's personal life was disordered. She had several affairs with wealthy men. Her most serious liaison was with a promoter and director, by whom she bore a daughter—who disliked her mother, pursued a perverse life and would cause her mother many trials, even purposely addicting her to cocaine at the end of her life.

In a little French village where she had gone to relax, grace was to touch the heart of the worldly French actress. Through the help of a good priest, Eve returned to the Sacraments of her childhood faith. She gave up acting immediately, leaving journalists to speculate over her disappearance from the stage. Eve saw her conversion as her birth to real life; she wrote off her former years as years of death. Henceforth she considered her real birthday to be the day on which, after much preparation and contrition, she had returned to Holy Communion.

395

Eve around the time of her conversion. Her restless heart had finally found God—and happiness. She would spend the rest of her life (12 years) in prayer, suffering and some mission work. Despite much physical and spiritual suffering, Eve told a visitor to tell his friends that he had seen "indeed, the most perfectly happy of women." Later, at the end of her life, Eve's once-beautiful face was attacked by illness and swellings; the doctor even had to sew her eyelids shut. Yet Eve thanked Our Lord for permitting her thus to expiate the sins she had committed through these faculties. Her motto was "Abandonment, love, trust."

38

CONCEPCION CABRERA DE ARMIDA
Conchita

Servant of God Maria Concepcion Cabrera de Armida
Maria Concepcion de Cabrera
1862 - 1937
Mexico
Died Age 74

Concepcion Cabrera de Armida—or Conchita, as she is usually called—was one of the most remarkable women in the Church in this century. Not a saint of the cloister, she fulfilled the roles of fiancee, wife, mother of nine children and widow. Yet she was also a great mystic who received volumes of deeply theological revelations from Our Lord, and she was instrumental in founding several religious institutes. Catholic authorities examining the case in Rome in 1913 were amazed at the extraordinary facts of Conchita's life.

In her 66-volume spiritual diary, Conchita has left a record of an especially favored soul who received extraordinary mystical graces from God. The central grace of her life was the mystical incarnation of Christ in her. But this does not at all conflict with the fact that she has also left the story of a real, warm, loving and faithful woman who constantly displayed all the virtues proper to her state of life, virtues which can and should constantly be imitated by all wives and mothers everywhere. In spite of her hidden penances and mortifications, the sadnesses and hurts she experienced, in spite of chronic illness, she was always able to follow this advice which she gave her daughter: Whatever God asks you to do, do it with a smile."

Concepcion Cabrera was born in San Luis Potosi, the seventh of 12 children of Octaviano de Cabrera and Clara Arias. When she was born, her mother was very ill and could not nurse her, so she was taken to a farm away from town to a wet nurse. Later, Conchita's mother told her that on the way to the farm, she was afraid to uncover the baby's face, fearing that she would open the blanket to find a dead child. Mauricia, Conchita's nurse, saved the baby's life, and Conchita loved her as a second mother. Both of her parents were devout Catholics, and her father daily presided over the recitation of the Rosary in the chapel at the hacienda. Often, Conchita assisted him in this if he had some urgent task that kept him away.

Conchita attended three schools. The first was at the home of some servants; later for a short time she attended a private school, and finally she went to a school run by the Sisters of Charity. When the Sisters were expelled from Mexico, Conchita's mother had tutors come to the house to teach the children some academics and music.

Conchita loved the piano, and as a young girl playing and singing were one of her greatest joys. Her mother taught the girls how to run the household, and by the age of 12 Conchita was assigned to take care of the expenditures of the house. At the hacienda she often milked the cows, kneaded the bread and prepared the meals. Her mother refused to allow any of her children to be idle, and on Sundays she took them to the hospitals to visit the sick and the dying. Conchita tells us that these visits to the hospital taught her not to be afraid of death and to help and assist the dying to die a happy and serene death.

Next to music, Conchita loved horses. When she was six, she got on a horse by herself. The horse was frightened and he reared and threw her off. But in spite of her tears, her father made her take a drink of water and then get back on the horse. From that time on she took delight in riding the most spirited of horses, which no one else could master.

In her diary Conchita tells us that from a very early age she was attracted to prayer and mortifications. When she learned to read, she read about the mortifications practiced by the saints and spent time trying to imagine how to imitate them. "Simplicity" is an adjective frequently used to describe Conchita; in her simplicity, Conchita believed that everyone loved prayer and penance. She was shocked when she learned this was not true.

Conchita grew rapidly and at an early age was taken to be much older than she was. By the age of 13 she was a beautiful young woman, and at a dance held in her home she was introduced to her future husband by one of her brothers. Although she did not like dances, it was the custom to go to them, and being an obedient daughter she always attended with her family. At another dance that same December, her future husband saw her again and she later confessed that she was embarrassed by his compliments. Conchita was such a pretty girl, with such a pleasant personality, that she had many suitors. At one time over twenty young men were courting her, though she felt like a bashful child and did not encourage their attentions.

At a dance in January, Pancho (Francisco Armida, Conchita's future husband) declared his love for her. He passionately told her that he would suffer greatly if she did not also love him. In her youth and innocence she felt a great disquiet, not having previously had any experience with this type of love. Her family rightly told her that she was too young; she and Pancho were engaged for nine years. She tells us in her diary that he was always correct and respectful and never took advantage of her simplicity. Conchita always tried to bring Pancho even closer to God. He sent her prayers and religious poems; she wrote and spoke to him about his religious duties and about love for the Blessed Virgin.

Conchita's betrothal never troubled her as an obstacle to her belonging to God. In spite of the fact that she often attended parties and the theater in order to see and be near Pancho, she never forgot God. She dreamed of Him as constantly as she could, and He drew her to Himself in an indescribable way. Conchita said to Our Lord, "Lord, I feel so unable to love You, so I want to get married. Give me many children so that they will love You better than I." At this time, she began wearing a haircloth belt underneath her party clothes, delighting in this penance for the sake of Jesus.

On the day of her formal engagement in 1884, Pancho gave her a golden bracelet which he fastened on her wrist. Conchita did not care for jewelry and at this time usually wore jewelry only when Pancho was around, taking it off immediately on his departure. But because of her love for him she did not take the bracelet off for years, though at the time it caused her considerable pain.

On the eve of her wedding, Conchita was given a beautiful white dress, pearl earrings, a cross studded with diamonds, some jewelry and a great number of gifts and clothes. Later, she offered part of the dress to the Virgin Mary, using the rest of it to decorate the prie-dieu for her future children's First Communion and pillows for the poor. The cross later became the stance of a monstrance. Conchita and Pancho were married November 8, 1884. At the wedding banquet, she asked him to do two things for her: to allow her to go to Communion every day, and never to be jealous. Pancho kept his promise about Communion so faithfully that he often stayed home with the children while she went to attend church, and during his final illness, when Conchita rarely left the room, he daily asked her if she had been to Communion.

Conchita and Pancho's first child was born in 1885. Conchita's ever-present sense of humor is shown in her comments about her difficulties in nursing him: "He did not want a wet nurse and so had to be fed donkey's milk, evidently the most like mine!"

This first son died when he was only six, and this was one of the first great sadnesses of Conchita's life.

In all her actions as a wife, Conchita was obedient to Pancho's wishes. She disliked intensely the dances, carnival parties and nights at the theatre that were part of her life, but she never objected to going; her prayer was that no one would be able to guess that she did not enjoy herself. She practiced complete self-mastery. Her simplicity and her charm attracted all who knew her. She constantly joked and laughed, and in all respects was a model wife, assisting Pancho in all the social customs required of her.

As a mother, before and after the death of her husband, Conchita was loving, firm and understanding of each of her children according to their temperaments and their needs. Although she was a mystically favored soul, each of her children has testified that at all times when she was around them, she was normal and never seemed any different from others.

Years after Conchita's death a theologian was questioning her grown children about their mother. Finally he concluded, "Your mama was a great saint and a great mystic." They answered, "Saint or mystic we do not know—but mother, the greatest mother that ever lived!"

In 1889, at the age of 27, Conchita made the first retreat she had ever made. She could not make a closed retreat because of her family obligations, so she came and went home each day. At this time, Conchita's outlook did not go beyond that of a woman living an ordinary life in her home; she did not suspect the extent of God's designs for her. God, however, chooses souls as He wills. One day, she clearly heard in the depths of her soul these words, which astonished her: "Your mission will be to save souls."

Conchita thought this message simply referred to her sacrifices as a wife and mother. She made some practical resolutions and redoubled her desire to love God.

More and more the love of Christ animated Conchita. She loved her husband and her family passionately, but within her great love for Christ.

Having from childhood seen the cattle on the haciendas being branded with the name of their owners, Conchita asked permission of her spiritual director to mark herself with the monogram of Christ. She later wrote, "By dint of many a plea, I got my director's permission to engrave the initials on the feast of the Holy Name of Jesus, January 14, 1894...I cut on my bosom in large letters: J.H.S. [for *Jesus Salvator Hominum*—"Jesus, Saviour of Men."] No sooner had I done this than I felt a supernatural force which threw me, face down, on the floor, my eyes filled with tears and a burning flame within my heart. Vehemently and zealously I then asked the Lord for the salvation of souls: Jesus, Saviour of souls, save them, save them! I remember nothing more. That was all I desired...The ardor of my soul far surpassed the burning sensation of my body and I experienced an ineffable joy of feeling I belonged wholly to Jesus, just as a branded animal to its owner."

Shortly after engraving the monogram, Conchita began to understand and develop the spirituality of the Cross. She learned more deeply the imitation of Christ which brought joy in suffering. Shortly after this, while she was praying in the Jesuit church in San Louis Potosi, the Holy Spirit appeared to her in a vision. A few days later, He appeared again in a vision of the Cross that has become the symbol of the Works of the Cross. The vision also included a Dove and a flaming heart encircled by thorns, with tiny crosses fastened within it.

The vision of this beautiful cross reappeared to Conchita a number of times, and she spoke of it to her spiritual director, who at first told her to disregard it; later he wrote her a letter which said, "You will save many a soul through the apostolate of the Cross." He did not realize that with these words he was designating the name for one of the "Works of the Cross," the spiritual works that would be founded under Conchita's inspiration, under the direction of Our Lord.

In her autobiography Conchita wrote, "As far as I was concerned, on reading this I only knew what I felt: this name must characterize the Work which the Lord began and of which I was now speaking." The Apostolate of the Cross is an organization whose members unite their sufferings with those of Christ in order to save souls. God chose this simple lay person, a young wife and mother, to make us be mindful of the mystery of the salvation of the world by the Cross.

In revelations from the Lord, Conchita was shown a vision of a congregation of contemplative nuns dedicated to a life of immolation of love; she was also told that a congregation of men would be made later, and that the message of the Cross was to be introduced to the whole Church in order to give glory to God. She was told that the Apostolate of the Cross is the work which continues and completes that of Our Lord's Heart, which was revealed to Blessed Margaret Mary, and that "the Cross" does not refer only to His external Cross.

Christ told Conchita, "This Cross is to be presented to the world to bring souls toward My Heart, pierced on that Cross. The essence of this Work consists in making known the interior sufferings of My Heart, which are ignored, and which constitute for Me a more painful Passion than that which My Body underwent on Calvary, on account of its intensity and its duration, mystically perpetuated in the Eucharist."

Our Lord revealed Himself to Conchita as Victim, Priest and Host. She wrote, "As for me, I am to model myself on Christ under two aspects which are identical: *Christ Priest* and *Christ Crucified*." Conchita's entire spiritual doctrine is marked by a sacerdotal, or priestly character. Our Lord lamented to Conchita the lack of fervor of some priests. He told her, "You are destined for the salvation of souls, most especially souls of priests."

Our Lord told Conchita, "I want you to be My host and have the intention, renewed as often as possible day and night, of offering yourself with Me on all the patens on earth. I want you, transformed in Me by suffering, by love and by the practice of all the virtues, to raise heavenward this cry of your soul in union with Me: 'This is My Body, This is My Blood.' Such is the end and essence of *My Works of the Cross:* a likeness of victims united to the great Victim, Myself, all pure, without the leaven of concupiscence. . .The Father, pleased, will receive this offering presented through the Holy Spirit, and the graces of Heaven will descend as rain on the earth."

Conchita was a prolific writer. At the insistence of her spiritual director, she kept a diary. This alone is 66 volumes. There were over 100 volumes submitted for the process of canonization. Conchita has written more than any other mystic in the church.

In spite of her mystical revelations and interior life of prayer, Conchita is not to be seen as a mystic with ecstatic eyes and strange behavior. Time and again her children have testified that there was nothing more natural than her external appearance. One point they stressed most of all is, "Even in church, we felt she was with us."

Conchita felt at ease in her home and in the circle of her family and friends. There she was the life of the party. She was fully aware that her place was above all with her children. Her daily life passed, as that of all mothers, in pain and joy. In spite of many illnesses, she did not let others see her suffering. Her home was filled with joy.

The Archbishop of Mexico was consulted and he ordered an examination of her life and writings. Conchita, as usual, was docile to the directives of the Church. In October 1900, she was examined by a number of theologians. They confirmed that her spirit was of God.

On September 1, 1901, Pancho died a good death, assisted by Conchita. Her own words express the tenderness of her love for her earthly husband of 17 years, the father of her children. "An interior presentiment of the night of the eleventh had made me know, without understanding why, the Lord was about to ask me to sacrifice my husband's life, something to which my soul was disposed, but which my fleshly heart refused and which I rejected. This sword pierced my soul, without any assuagement, without any consolation. I saw. . .moment by moment that my husband was losing his life. My heart is torn with pain. . .to the measure that I saw our separation approaching, the tenderness of my heart toward him took on more and more considerable proportions. I felt I had no longer head, nor faith, nor reason, but only a heart. I could but pray thus, 'May Your Will be done on earth as it is in Heaven!' But from that moment on, I felt the force of the Holy Spirit for accepting the terrible blow which. . .struck my heart and took away the father from my children. Four of my older children stood around his bed and saw him die. My God! What my heart felt. . .You alone, You alone know. I fell. . .down on my knees and made. . .the offering of perpetual chastity. . .Then with my eldest son, we laid him who was my companion in the coffin..."

In one of his last intimate conversations with Conchita, Pancho had told her he knew he was dying. She replied, "I have always tried to please you. If God calls you, I want to carry out your last wish. What do you desire of me?" He answered, "That you be wholly at God's disposal and at your children's."

The first days of her widowhood were terrible for Conchita, and the doctors thought she was going to die. The thought of her husband was with her constantly, and the sound of her children crying over their father pierced her soul. Her oldest child at this time was only 16. The young widow turned to Mary for strength and help in bringing up her eight "orphans."

It is about this time that Conchita met a priest named Father Felix Rougier who, along with her, was called by God to become the apostle of a renewal of the world by the Cross under the impulse of the Holy Spirit. Father Rougier was the one chosen to be the founder of the Missionaries of the Holy Spirit. He was able to give Conchita support and spiritual consolation in the death of her husband. Until the end of their lives, Father Felix and Conchita worked together for the founding and development of the Works of the Cross. They mutually sought each other's advice, carrying out mutual projects and speaking at length of God.

Without ever neglecting the duties of her state in life, Conchita found time to continue her apostolate of the Cross. She prayed, wrote and progressed further toward God. At the same time she considered that the duties of a mother were sacred ones and strove to carry them out perfectly.

When Conchita was about 44, she received the central grace of her life. Mystically, Christ was incarnated in her heart. Right after Conchita received this grace, God inspired her with the "Chain of Love," which was to raise up a spiritual elite wholly consecrated to God in the service of His Church.

Many Mexican bishops, learning of the Apostolate of the Cross and the contemplatives, wanted a foundation of "Priests of the Cross." They addressed a petition to Rome, basing their plea on the pastoral needs of Mexico. After consideration, Rome granted the permission, but then a telegram suspended the application of the rescript until an examination had been made into Conchita's private revelations.

Thus in 1913, by order of the Congregation for Religious, Conchita had to send to Rome nine volumes of her Life, volumes in which she revealed all the secrets of her soul and of her life to the supreme authority of the Church. Msgr. Ramon Ibarra decided to take Conchita to Rome for a direct examination. She took along her son Ignacio and her daughter Lupe. Before going to Rome, they made a tour of the Holy Land—which amazed and delighted all three. At Rome, in a private interview, Pope St. Pius X gave his approval and blessing for all the Works of the Cross. The name of the new congregation of priests, however, was changed to the Missionaries of the Holy Spirit.

Back in Mexico, Conchita was sewing one day when suddenly she heard a voice which said, "Pedrito is in the pool in the garden." She raced outside to find her youngest child floating in the pool, dead by accidental drowning. This was a great sorrow for Conchita.

Later, her son Pablo died in his mother's arms, a victim of typhoid fever. Only 18, he died a holy and religious death.

Of Conchita's other children, Manuel became a Jesuit priest. Until his death, he spent himself in the service of the Church as a missionary. In one of her many letters to him, Conchita had written, "Become a saint. Life is too short to stop along the road. No matter what path we take to seek God, it always passes by the Cross. . . Love it, for it is the main instrument of our salvation."

Concha, the oldest daughter, became a Contemplative of the Cross, joining the order inspired by her mother. She died in 1925 of tuberculosis.

Pancho was a businessman who, on the death of his father, had gone courageously to work to help his mother raise the other seven children. He founded and directed a typewriter company. Ignatio, Salvador and Lupe all married and raised families. All of Conchita's children—as well as her grandchildren, who called her "Mane"—loved her and enjoyed being around her. Their testimonials do not contain any reproach of their mother.

During the 1920's, there were a number of cruel persecutions of the Catholics in Mexico. Conchita constantly prayed for the priests, the religious and the Church in her country. Often she courageously hid priests, bishops and other religious in her own home.

In her last illness, Conchita was afflicted with bronchial pneumonia, erysipelas and uremia—as well as a feeling of desolation and despair. Conchita died a quiet and holy death on March 3, 1937.

The canonical opening of the process of beatification took place in Rome on September 19, 1959.

* * *

The five Works of the Cross inspired by Concepcion Cabrera de Armida are flourishing today and have not remained confined only to Mexico. Slowly, they are spreading, as predicted by Our Lord, to the far corners of the world. The Works are:

1. The Apostleship of the Cross, for Christians who desire to unite their own suffering and labors to those of Christ for the saving of souls.

2. The Religious of the Cross of the Sacred Heart of Jesus, contemplatives of perpetual adoration who offer their lives for the Church, especially for priests.

3. The Covenant of Love with the Sacred Heart of Jesus, for persons who in their own state of life commit themselves to seek perfection according to the spirituality of the Cross.

4. The Apostolic League, for priests and bishops who want to live in this spirituality and help other works of the Cross.

5. The Missionaries of the Holy Spirit, a clerical religious Congregation specially devoted to priestly works and dedicated to the spiritual direction of souls.

Conchita as a bride, age 22; she had met her future husband, Pancho, at age 13. From childhood Conchita had had a great love for prayer and penance. She told Our Lord, "Lord, I feel so unable to love You, so I want to get married. Give me many children so that they will love You better than I." Conchita was to have nine children. She loved Pancho and was a model wife and mother. Her simplicity and charm attracted all who knew her, and her home was filled with joy.

Conchita received many mystical graces and many revelations from Our Lord; she was inspired to carve the letters JHS (for *Jesus Hominum Salvator*—"Jesus, Saviour of men") on her chest. She wrote much; in fact, Conchita has written more than any other mystic in the Church; her diary consists of 66 volumes. Conchita was a victim soul. Our Lord told her, "You are destined for the salvation of souls, most especially souls of priests."

Under direction from Our Lord, Conchita was instrumental in the founding of five spiritual works; they would be known as the Works of the Cross. She was led to meet a priest named Fr. Felix Rougier, who labored with her for the establishing of the Works of the Cross.

A painting of Conchita's vision of the Cross. It became the symbol of the Works of the Cross.

After Conchita's death a theologian was questioning her grown children about their mother. He concluded, "Your mama was a great saint and a great mystic." They answered, "Saint or mystic we do not know—but mother, the greatest mother that ever lived!"

39

FATHER FELIX ROUGIER

Servant of God Father Felix of Jesus Rougier
Felix Benedicto Rougier
1859 - 1938
France - Mexico
Died Age 78

It was time for recreation at the Junior Seminary of Le Puy, France. The students were laughing and joking and enjoying their refreshments. That afternoon there was to be a visitor, a missionary bishop from Oceania.

Bishop Elloy, Vicar Apostolic of the Islands of Samoa in Polynesia, began speaking to the students about the life of a missionary. He was one of the priests of the Society of Mary, or Marist Priests. He spoke about the hardships of missionary life, and he eloquently pleaded for helpers in the mission to the poor lepers. He asked if there were one among the group who would have the bravery to go to these missions and who would raise his hand to volunteer. He asked for one who could look with compassion on these poor savages—men, women, and children—who were so ravaged by the awful disease.

An embarrassing silence fell on the group. No hand was raised. The silence lengthened. Then, the hand of a 19-year-old was held high. On the young man's face could be read the strength of his character—and his resolve. In a loud, clear voice, he spoke: "I wish to go, Father."

Who was this young man who was so generous? His name was Felix Rougier.

The next day the young man's spiritual director spoke with Felix and asked him to think about his resolution. He attempted to dissuade Felix from this idea. However, plans were made for Felix to terminate his studies in the humanities within a few weeks in order to enter the Marist novitiate. Repeatedly the spiritual director made objections, but the young man remained firm. Many years later, in remembering this incident, Father Felix said, "Inside of me there was an irresistible movement, and I determined in a second to go with this missionary bishop."

This act of generosity was the beginning of a grand vocation. From that moment Felix was haunted by a call to become a missionary. It turned out that God did not call him precisely to be a missionary on a small island of Oceania, and for years he was unsure how he would carry out the call. But after he was formed in the religious life by the Congregation of the Marist Fathers, Father Felix would eventually become, in Mexico, the founder of the Missionaries of the Holy Spirit and the founder of three other congregations; these would be founded on the spirituality of the Cross and would have as their goal union with the sacrifice of Jesus for the salvation of souls.

Felix Rougier was born on December 17, 1859 in Meilhaud, France—in the region known as Auvernes, where the people are known for their integrity, forthrightness and stubbornness. He was baptized the next day and given the name Felix Benedicto. Felix was the first child of Benedicto Rougier and Maria Louisa Olanier. Shortly after his Baptism his mother carried him to the church and placed him on an altar of the Blessed Virgin Mary, saying, "O Mary, my good Mother, I offer my son to you forever. From this day on he is not mine, he is yours. Please intercede for him before God and ask Him to make a missionary of my Felix. I will take him back home to care for and to educate him, but only for you and for God." Two more sons were born to the family.

The Rougiers were farmers. Both parents were pious. Maria Louisa had originally wanted to enter a convent, but acceded to the wishes of her family to marry. Her spiritual influence, however, affected all her family, and she was in all respects a model mother.

On one occasion Felix' mother asked him to pick some violets for the Blessed Mother's statue. He did so, then put them up to his face to smell them. His mother exclaimed, "Felix! What are you doing? I told you those flowers were for Our Lady. Throw those flowers away and go pick new ones. And do not smell them!"

Felix' father spent the last 27 years of his life living in a hermitage he had built on his property. When Felix was living in uncertainty for years over permission regarding his new religious order, his father assured him more than once, "The Pope will give that permission." And it finally was given.

On September 24, 1878, after obtaining his parents' blessing, Felix left for the Marist novitiate. His mother wrote in her diary, "O Mary, my favorite son is gone, my son and my friend. He left me for you. I give him to you with all my heart. . . .Take him to Jesus and make him a great apostle." Felix' mother had been praying since before his birth to be the mother of a priest. He said of her that she had a priestly heart.

At the novitiate Felix was known as one who enthusiastically followed all the rules of the novitiate. He was also known for his love of mortification and penance.

While in the novitiate Felix developed pains in his arm and hand. At last the doctors made the dreadful diagnosis—the hand would have to be amputated. This would mean the end of any thought of a priestly vocation.

However, Felix' mother was a Salesian cooperator, and she wrote to Don Bosco, begging him to cure her son's arm and hand in order that he might become a priest. Shortly thereafter, Felix was given a chance to visit with Don Bosco. The Saint received the young man kindly and talked with him a while about his life. Then Don Bosco asked Felix to kneel for his blessing. When Felix arose, his arm and hand were cured. A few days later Don Bosco said to Felix, "God will make you the shepherd of many souls."

Felix was ordained on September 24, 1887 in Lyons, France. From 1887 to 1895 he was a professor of Sacred Scripture in Barcelona, Spain. Thus he spent eight years teaching the Bible. The Scriptures touched Father Felix deeply; he felt the presence of the Holy Spirit when reading the Bible. To him the Bible was like the sea—ever the same but ever new. Father Felix said that the Bible is the book which teaches us to become saints, and that the two main characters in it are God and oneself. He saw a great need for better instruction on the Bible.

In Spain Father Felix also became director of an "Apostolic School" for young boys who might have a vocation to the priesthood but who were in danger of falling away from God if they went back to their families. Throughout his life Father Felix was to use this type of school as a means of fostering priestly vocations.

In 1895 Father Felix was sent to Colombia to open a grammar school and perhaps a seminary. His secret dream was to help prepare native priests. Whatever he was assigned to, he always obeyed with joy, seeing God's Will in his superiors' commands. He took great consolation from repeating, "My God, my God, my God!"

Colombia was a vastly different world for Father Felix—with its alligators, jungles, tropical birds, flowers, rains, mosquitos, 90° - 120° heat, and foods like potatoes, corn, yuccas and barbecued beef. Getting into the ways of the country, Father Felix became a good horseman, even learning to use a lariat; he donned a wide-brimmed straw hat and grew a long beard. Father Felix' attitude was that a priest should always treat each assignment as though it would last for the rest of his life, even though it might last only three days.

Teaching boys in Colombia, Father Felix recalled the axiom that when teaching a young man one should keep in mind his old age; Father Felix added: and his eternal life. He insisted that the boys participate in the Mass, since it is not a spectacle but a real act of redemption. He tried to inculcate three loves in his pupils: love for God, love for country, love for family. He believed strongly that the thermometer of the faith in a school or nation was the number of priestly and religious vocations. During this time in Colombia tensions were growing between the Church and the government, which would have preferred lay teachers to priests. Father Felix felt that education should be a wise mix of authority and love, understanding and discipline, sugar and the spur.

In hearing confessions Father Felix always tried to take the opportunity to give spiritual direction. He felt that many people were mediocre in the spiritual life because they had no one to listen to them, guide them and give them a little push. There was a saying among the Latin American people whenever they received a cross to carry: "God remembered me." With his great love for the Cross, Father Felix made this saying his own.

Eventually the tensions broke out openly in what was to be known as the Thousand Days War (1899-1903). The students were warned to leave the school; Father Felix and another priest went to the chapel and consumed the consecrated Hosts. During the fighting Father Felix was named a military chaplain; he preached to the soldiers, heard their confessions for hours on end and also brought them material aid.

Father Felix started an organization of young girls who felt they had a religious vocation; they were known as the Daughters of Mary. He also "imported" from France an organization known as the Bread of St. Anthony to encourage charity to the poor. To support this work he wrote and distributed a weekly bulletin—beginning his issues with stories to attract people's interest and then including little articles on liberal philosophies and other errors which were causing confusion among the people.

In the midst of the war a telegram came from the Marist superiors in France instructing Father Felix to go to Mexico City. There he became parish priest of Our Lady of Lourdes Church, where he was to serve from 1902-1904 as pastor to about 6,000 Catholics. He began visiting them right away to complete his *Liber Status Animarum* (spiritual census book). He made use of the parish bulletin to teach the people about God.

In Mexico Father Felix continued the Daughters of Mary and the Bread of St. Anthony and also began additional organizations: The Altar Boys and Choir Boys, who had sports and picnics but also talks about the liturgy and priesthood; The Angels, for young girls, which was also a way of getting their mothers to church; and a branch of the Apostolate of the Cross, an organization for lay people which had been approved by Pope Leo XIII to help people carry their crosses daily—for the salvation of other souls as well as in reparation for their own sins. As always Father Felix used schools and Catholic youth organizations to activate vocations to the priesthood and religious life.

On February 4, 1903 Father Felix had a providential encounter with a holy widow and mystic named Concepcion Cabrera de Armida, who is often referred to as "Conchita." From this first visit he was convinced of his vocation to collaborate with her in promoting various religious works known collectively as "The Works of the Cross." There were to be five of these Works, but at the time the only ones begun had been the Apostolate of the Cross and the Sisters of the Sacred Heart of Jesus. Father Felix was profoundly moved by this meeting; he felt that vast horizons had opened to him. He was confirmed in his favorable opinion of Conchita by the fact that her writings had been approved by bishops and the best theologians. Very soon he made a vow of suffering for the salvation of souls and of always trying to do the most perfect thing, sealing it with the holy Cross.

Soon Conchita told Father Felix that God wanted him to found a religious order for men; it would be called Priests of the Cross. This commission was to change the rest of Father Felix' life, opening up a phase difficult but very fruitful. He was willing to undertake the work, but he needed and wanted his superiors' permission.

The question of permission was to drag on for years. Conchita's revelations provided a large obstacle. But always, Father Felix' policy was obedience to his superiors, seeing in this the will of God.

After a year Father Felix traveled to Europe, where he faithfully rendered to his superiors an account of his surprising and unexpected meeting with Conchita. He told how he believed that God was calling him in a special way to found an order. But the Father General of the Marists judged otherwise, and made him stay in Europe. There Felix waited patiently for God's time.

For 10 years Father Felix was given teaching assignments in Europe. To fulfill his vow of suffering, he scourged himself each day 400 times until he bled. He wore a chain around his waist and slept on a plank. Like Conchita, he had used a blade and hot iron to mark his chest with the letters JHS (for *Jesus Hominum Salvator*—Jesus, Saviour of Men). The hardest thing for him during this time was to be doing nothing toward founding the Priests of the Cross. He said, "A child could put out the fire of the sun with his breath sooner than I can forget the 'Works of the Cross.' " But he accepted every setback, firmly convinced that God knew what He was about.

As he obediently carried out his teaching assignments, Father Felix tried to get his pupils to think more about their spiritual life; he had them keep a "spiritual calendar" for recording daily prayers, spiritual reading, aspirations and acts of self-denial. He felt that there was great generosity in young souls if someone would just show them the way. In fact, he felt that they surpassed him in generosity. Another apostolate Father Felix carried on at this time was writing spiritual letters; his congregation owns 25 thick volumes of them collected from all over the world after his death. During this time a persecution against Catholics was being waged in Mexico.

Finally, after petitions from several Bishops and Archbishops of Mexico, Pope Pius X allowed Father Felix to found the new congregation—though he was to call it the Missionaries of the Holy Spirit rather than the Priests of the Cross. Thus Father Felix returned to Mexico.

Upon disembarking at Vera Cruz on August 14, 1914, Father Felix met some Mexican bishops who, driven out by the persecution, were leaving on the same ship. They could not hide their amazement on seeing Father Felix coming in the other direction.

One of them, Bishop Orozco of Guadalajara, told him, "Humanly speaking, I feel that it is madness that you want to begin a work of this nature at this time; however, if God wants this work, go in peace, for in truth the nation is in agony." Father Felix courageously responded, "The Lord wants me to found His work during the agony of the nation."

On December 25, 1914 the congregation began, with just two novices, in a secret ceremony arranged to evade the revolutionaries. The Archbishop attended in civilian clothes, and the door of the chapel was locked during the ceremony.

From this time until the end of his life Father Felix worked with Conchita for the founding and development of the Works of the Cross. Conchita was to live until 1937, passing away just a few months before Father Felix himself died.

Despite his being the founder of the Missionaries of the Holy Spirit, for many years Father Felix was only "loaned," so to speak, to the new congregation. Time and again he wrote to and visited his superiors and the authorities in Rome, but again and again he was forbidden a dispensation from his vows in the Marist Society and permission to join the new order. In Rome there continued to be opposition to his calling. Despite support from at least 17 Mexican bishops, both Pope Pius X and Pope Benedict XV refused to allow him this. Finally, after 23 years of refusals, permission was granted by Pope Pius XI on February 9, 1926. Father Felix made his vows in the new congregation on February 28 with great emotion that now he was "a missionary forever."

The specific mission of the Missionaries of the Holy Spirit is to extend the reign of the Holy Spirit through the spirituality of the Cross, with an imitation of and incorporation into Jesus Christ, Priest and Victim. Thus this is a spirituality of the Mass. These priests and brothers work for the holiness of all, especially priests and those who profess the evangelical counsels. The characteristic works of the order are spiritual direction and a liturgical apostolate.

In 1919 Father Felix was also able to open the first Apostolic School in Mexico—like his other Apostolic Schools, a greenhouse for priestly vocations.

During this time he was instrumental in getting Mexico consecrated to the Holy Spirit; it was the first nation in the world to be so consecrated. Father Felix also persuaded 10 other bishops to send a petition to the Holy Father, asking him to consecrate the entire world to the Holy Spirit.

Since 1914 the revolutionary turmoil in Mexico had been causing difficulties for the Catholic Church. In 1926 General Calles proclaimed the "Calles law" against Catholic clergy, religious and institutions. Father Felix would have been subject to arrest on two or three grounds, as a foreign priest running a seminary and an Apostolic School, but by God's providence he remained at large. Things got so bad that, after consulting with Pope Pius XI, the Bishops of Mexico officially suspended all religious services in all the churches as of July 31, 1926. Mass continued to be offered in secret, however. When a two-million-signature petition was ignored by the Congress, the people undertook an economic boycott of the economy, then they gathered together an army of 30,000 volunteers. From 1926-1929, death, prison and exile were daily occurrences. Many priests were hung from trees and young men were stabbed to death for shouting *"Viva Cristo Rey!"* Statues of saints were used for target practice. Father Felix' name was on the list of most wanted priests; he tried to exercise normal caution, but would have been happy to be executed, feeling that such a death would provide a much better ending to his life than another few years of life.

There had been a priest shortage in Mexico before the persecutions, but since then it had grown vastly more serious. Twenty-six of the 45 Mexican dioceses were without priests. Father Felix estimated that 10,000 new priests were needed. During this time he opened a house in Rome for the Missionaries of the Holy Spirit.

Father Felix opened a retreat house for old or troubled priests who needed a place for rejuvenation. He told the priests to consider themselves totally at home: they were not to feel like guests, but like the owners of the house. The house was a wonderful blessing for many priests, and all left saying they planned to return. But in 1933 word was received that the secret police were coming. In three hours all the priests were gone. "The cage was left with no birds." The house was expropriated. Father Felix' response was, "God gave it. God took it away. Blessed be God."

In 1929 the revolutionary fighting came to an end but persecution of the Church continued. A law of 1931 allowed only 25 priests per 1 million Catholics. Any others who performed religious services had three choices: jail, exile or death. A law of 1935 closed all the Catholic schools in Mexico (60% - 80% of all schools).

In response to the teaching sisters' questions as to what they should do, Father Felix kept telling them to continually conjugate three verbs all at the same time: to pray, to forgive, and to hope.

A constant preoccupation of Father Felix was the need for priests; he considered this to be the number one problem in the Universal Church. He saw a chain: no priests because vocations were not helped to grow in young boys; and vocations not helped because of a lack of truly Catholic families where the call could be heard. He felt the solution was to give the parents an appreciation of the priesthood and religious life. He recalled the elements of his own childhood: "recreation, nuts, candies, animals, a soccer ball, but also a love for the priesthood. I received this love on my mother's lap. She had a priestly heart." Fostering vocations was the motive behind the "Apostolic Schools" that Father Felix was always striving to open.

Another dream of Father Felix was the conversion of the Jews. He began the National League for the Conversion of Jews. The tools were prayer, penance, visiting Jewish families and teaching the Faith. In nine months there were two conversions. Father Felix did not expect an avalanche of converts, and he took this modest harvest as proof that Jews could be converted.

Father Felix also founded three congregations for women. In January of 1924 the Daughters of the Holy Ghost was begun. These sisters work especially to promote priestly and religious vocations through contemplative prayer and through teaching. They are teachers and are currently located only in Mexico.

The Missionaries of Guadalupe (Missionary Guadalupanas) of the Holy Ghost were formed in 1930. These sisters bring Catholic instruction to those who need it, especially the poorest. Father Felix told them that first of all it was necessary for them to be saints, because they would be responsible for many souls. He said, "A thousand towns are waiting for them—first here in Mexico, then all over the world." These sisters are currently working in the United States, Puerto Rico, Mexico and Guatemala.

The last congregation founded by Father Felix is the Oblates of Jesus the Priest. These sisters pray and sacrifice themselves on behalf of priests, help promote priestly vocations and assist priests in their work. They do domestic work in seminaries in Mexico, the United States and Italy. This group was founded in 1935. To found these congregations Father Felix underwent many hardships and labors—he spent money, prayers and blood. He always said, "We have to suffer some for God."

Over the years Father Felix managed to write several books. Toward the beginning of his priestly life (1893) he published in Barcelona an archaeological study showing how science supports the doctrines of the Bible and proves the Mosaic authorship of its first five books. He also wrote *French in One Month; Treatise on Spiritual Direction; Conference on the Stars* (astronomy); *Mary: Her Life, Her Virtues, Her Cult;* and a pamphlet entitled *Manual for Devotion to the Holy Spirit.*

In September of 1937 Father Felix celebrated his golden anniversary as a priest. The Archbishop of Mexico presided, and many bishops, provincial superiors and priests took part. At the end of December Father Felix renewed an offering he had made to be a victim for the glory of God and for his congregation.

For the last two or three years of his life he was sick continually with problems of the heart and stomach: he suffered from insomnia and he was almost blind. He spent time in and out of surgeries, but also continued to exercise his priesthood in hiding and in disguise. He wrote, "I will go up to the altar of God, to God who gives joy to my youth."

Father Felix began to have internal hemorrhaging. The last three months of his life were spent in terrible suffering. He begged for prayers, and each time he regained consciousness he asked whether he had complained. From about the first of January he was unable to receive Holy Communion because of his constant vomiting. One of the religious commiserated with him. In reply, Father Felix reminded him, "All days I am permitted to receive the Cross." To the last, love of the Cross was at the center of his life.

Father Felix was given the Last Sacraments on the sixth of January. His final words were about his Heavenly Mother: "With her, everything. . .without her, nothing." During his final agony, Father Felix' eyes remained fixed on a small statue of Our Lady of Lourdes. On January 10 he passed to his final reward.

The opening of the canonical process for Father Felix' beatification took place in Rome in 1958.

Fr. Felix Rougier, a French priest who was to found the Missionaries of the Holy Spirit in Mexico. In his youth Fr. Felix had been told by St. John Bosco, "God will make you the shepherd of many souls." Fr. Felix felt that many people were mediocre in the spiritual life because they had no one to listen to them, guide them and give them a little push.

Facing page: Fr. Felix believed strongly that the thermometer of the faith in a school or nation was the number of priestly and religious vocations. He was always trying to begin "Apostolic Schools" to serve as greenhouses for priestly vocations. Here he is shown with some school pupils in Barcelona, Spain in 1905.

423

Félix de Jesús M.S.S.
S. Gen.

The latter part of Fr. Felix' life was taken up largely with his labors to establish the Works of the Cross in cooperation with Conchita Cabrera, widow and mystic (see chap. 38). In the midst of the revolutionary turmoil in Mexico he founded the Missionaries of the Holy Spirit, a society devoted to Jesus Christ, Priest and Victim. Fr. Felix was also instrumental in getting Mexico consecrated to the Holy Spirit.

40

EDEL QUINN

Servant of God Edel Mary Quinn
1907 - 1944
Ireland - Africa
Died Age 36

"Edel Quinn, envoy of the Legion of Mary to East Africa from 30th October, 1936 to 12th May, 1944, on which day she died at Nairobi. She fulfilled this mission with such devotedness and courage as to stir every heart and to leave the Legion of Mary and Africa itself forever in her debt. The Holy Father himself paid tribute to her great service to the Church. Of your goodness, therefore, will you give her generous remembrance in your prayers. R.I.P."

So reads the tribute inscribed beneath the white Celtic cross in Nairobi marking the grave of one of the Church's most ardent lay missionaries of modern times.

Edel Quinn was born in Greenane, near Kanturk, County Cork, Ireland, on September 14, 1907. Her father, Charles Quinn, was an official in the National Bank. Her mother, a housewife, was Louise Burk Browne. The name Edel was given to her by mistake at her Baptism. Her mother had intended to name her Adele, after one of her sisters. The priest, however, thought that she was being named Edel as a diminutive of edelweiss, a mountain flower.

When Edel was a child, her family moved to a number of provincial towns in Ireland due to transfers from the bank. During these years the family grew. Edel had three younger sisters and one younger brother. Finally, when she was 17, Edel's family settled in Dublin.

As a youngster Edel was always joyous and full of mischief. Once she got into trouble for trespassing in an orchard belonging to a local doctor. While chasing the young intruder, the doctor tripped and fell into a pool of water. Edel was reported at school and received a severe scolding.

Edel's zest for life increased daily. "Bubbling over with fun" is an apt description of her. She loved music, dancing and tennis. For a time she was captain of her school cricket team. She loved the holidays her family took by the seaside, and all forms of recreation appealed to her.

In spite of her constant gaiety, Edel is remembered from infancy for being completely unselfish and full of consideration for others. She became a daily communicant, and at her last school she is remembered for her efforts with the Sodality of Our Lady. Years later she told a priest that from the time she was a young girl she had prayed every day for three special graces: to love God with her whole heart, to make others love Him, and to die a martyr's death. By the time she finished school, she had made up her mind to be a nun in an enclosed order. For many years Edel cherished a longing for the cloister. But family circumstances, and then her own poor health, would prevent her from becoming a religious.

In 1924 Edel's father retired and her help was needed to educate her younger sisters and brother. After completing a course in a commercial college, Edel got a job as a secretary-typist. Her first employer, who later became a priest, said of her, "Angelic Edel Quinn was my private and confidential secretary in my Nassau St., Dublin offices for some time. . . .I left her in complete charge. I could see at once I had a treasure. My calling necessitated long absences from my offices. On my return. . .everything awaited me in perfect order." At home, Edel's father paid tribute to her wisdom by calling her "Granny!" She also had a delightful sense of humor.

Hearing of a young man who was in need of a secretary and who could pay Edel better, her first employer arranged for her to change work. After a year, the new employer, a young Frenchman, decided to secure the Dublin agency for Edel and to return to France. However, as he was about to depart, he realized that he had fallen very much in love with her and wanted to take her with him. He proposed marriage.

His tears flowed freely as she gently told him that marriage was out of the question for her because as soon as she had finished assisting her younger sisters and brother in obtaining their education, she planned to enter a Poor Clare convent. He left Ireland disconsolate. For a number of years the two kept up a correspondence. Her letters never gave him any hope that she was going to go back on her decision, but they do show that she was deeply interested in his welfare. The letters also show her desire for him to have a full appreciation of Catholic life. Eventually their correspondence died out; he married and began a family, naming his third child Edel in her memory. After Edel's death he wrote, "More than twenty years have passed away. In all that time the memory of Edel Quinn has not left me. . . . I know that she prayed much for me, and her petitions were heard. I owe her innumerable graces for myself and my family. I am conscious that her influence for good and against evil in my life has been immense and I thank her daily for it in my prayers."

The years of waiting for the cloister were difficult, but they brought Edel to the realization that, as she wrote to a friend, "God's Will is the only thing in the wide world that matters. Nothing else is worth considering—so prayer on that line is the business!" Although her work and her family responsibilities kept her busy, Edel began to live the interior life of a contemplative, with the Eucharist as the center of her days. At her Confirmation she took the name Eucharia Josephine, and this devotion to the Eucharist was evident not only in her actions but in her writings, too. In her private notes she wrote, "What a desolation life would be without the Eucharist. We want to be united to Him, to give ourselves to Him utterly. Our faith tells us He is in the Eucharist; let us seek Him there." Edel once said, "More than anything else I believe in the power of prayer." Her family members who went to later Masses on Sunday were sometimes embarrassed because Edel would attend the 7:00 and 8:00 Masses, go home for breakfast, then return for the 10:00, 11:00, 11:30 and 12:00 Masses, her head bowed, rapt in prayer.

When Edel was 19, she met a girl who was a member of the Legion of Mary. Edel had never heard of it and asked for more information. The Legion had been founded in Dublin only a few years previously by a civil servant named Frank Duff. Organized along Roman military lines—with the local unit being called a *praesidium*—and formed on St. Louis De Montfort's teaching on True Devotion to Mary, the Legion of Mary set out to provide spiritual help however and wherever needed. Its earliest and most spectacular successes were among the prostitutes who teemed in some of the city's most squalid tenements. The original members of the Legion braved threats and insults to win these girls back to God. The Legion would soon spread far and wide.

Soon Edel was accepted as a member. The praesidium which she joined met weekly. Its work included hospital visitation and home-to-home visits in a slum area. As one author has explained, "The Legionary is told that he or she must expect sour looks, the sting of insult and rebuff, ridicule and adverse criticism, weariness of body and spirit, pangs from failure and from base ingratitude, the bitter cold and blinding rain, dirt, vermin and evil smells, dark passages and sordid surroundings, the laying aside of pleasures, the taking on of the anxieties which come in plenty with the work, the anguish which the contemplation of irreligion and depravity brings to the sensitive soul, and sorrow from troubles wholeheartedly shared."

Edel gave herself generously to the active work of the Legion and assimilated its inner spirit in such a way as to become almost its living embodiment. She made and lived St. Louis De Montfort's consecration to Mary. Already Edel had a special devotion to Mary, and she had complete confidence that Our Lady would look after all of her concerns. Years later, when a priest asked Edel, "Did you ever refuse Our Lady anything," she answered, "No, I could never refuse Our Lady anything." Edel took a private vow of virginity, and at some point she took a vow of never refusing anything to Our Lady.

In addition to her regular Legion work, Edel would spend five evenings per week calling on lonely old ladies, bringing sunshine. Yet she once remarked to a friend, "I hate visiting, don't you!" Her kindness was based on love for God and was not the result of passing fancy.

After two years as an ordinary member of the Legion, Edel was appointed president of a praesidium engaged in rescue work among street girls in Dublin. Although she was 22 at the time, she looked much younger, and some of the members of the group did not believe that she would have the maturity and experience to lead them in their difficult and delicate work. They went so far as to protest to Headquarters, but the protest was ignored. Soon Edel had shown, by her great success, that she was capable of achieving all that was asked of her, and then more. Membership increased, and the work was very successful.

Soon after her 24th birthday Edel decided that the time had come when she was free to follow what she believed was her vocation.

All arrangements were made for her entry into the Poor Clare convent in Belfast. Shortly before the time for her entrance, however, a hemorrhage from the lungs led to the discovery that she was in an advanced stage of tuberculosis.

Thus at the beginning of 1932 Edel was taken to a sanatorium in County Wicklow, where the doctors gave her little hope of a cure. Her complete serenity amazed her friends. Remarks made by staff and patients at the sanatorium all mention the cheerfulness of her attitude and the uncomplaining nature of her acceptance of this cross. "She was the nicest girl who ever came here." ". . .She made everyone round her happy. She was never in a state of depression and would often laugh till the tears came. Her illness did not appear to weigh on her; she never spoke of it and never complained. One would have thought she was there on a holiday." "Her attitude was one of kindness and helpfulness to all. Anyone in trouble in the sanatorium would at once go to her for consolation."

Edel spent a year and a half in the sanatorium, and in the summer of 1933 decided to go home. She was worried about the expense to her family, and as there was no prospect of recovery she wanted to make better use of the short time left to her. Only years later did she realize that her presence at home could have infected other members of the family. She looked well, so people were deceived into thinking she had made some sort of recovery. After a short time she went back to work. She also resumed her work with the Legion and renewed her practice of daily Mass. She had little reserve of energy and tired easily, but she remained as friendly and cheerful as before.

In the spring of 1936 Edel got the idea of going to live in Britain, getting a job to support herself and giving all her spare time to spreading the Legion. Because of her poor health, the authorities at Headquarters were reluctant to give their consent—but promised to think it over. At the same time they had received appeals to send Legion envoys to South and East Africa. After much deliberation the frail young woman was offered one of these envoyships. Edel was thrilled and accepted on the spot, stating that this was the happiest day of her life.

During the official vote where this had to be confirmed by the concilium, one priest objected strenuously and suggested that it would be lunacy on the part of the Legion to send her—and suicide on her part to go. Her pleading won the day, however, and the vote passed unanimously. As the major preparation for her mission to Africa, Edel went on a pilgrimage to Lourdes with a large Legionary group. She was very tired, but devoted herself unsparingly to the invalids on the pilgrimage. She took part in all the functions at Lourdes, although she fainted at one ceremony.

On October 24, 1936 Edel left Ireland with the commission to establish the Legion of Mary over an area of about three quarters of a million square miles. Some who saw her off feared that, with her delicate health, she would not even survive the passage. Before leaving Edel had said to a friend, "I shall spend nine years in Africa and die there." She knew she would never come back to Ireland; she said to one of the Legionaries a short time before her day of departure, "Pray for me and keep joking as much as you can, so that I shall not break down."

Edel wrote to Frank Duff the following: "I only hope I do not fail the Legion when the work comes to be done. I am counting on all the prayers to counteract that danger. Whatever be the consequence, rejoice you had the courage to emulate Our Lord in His choice of weak things, in faith."

On November 23 Edel landed at Mombasa in Kenya. She was met by Bishop Heffernan, who had sent the appeal. On his advice she left by train for Nairobi, more than 300 miles away. There she contacted the clergy and some of the more prominent lay Catholics and explained her purpose of uniting Catholics of the different races and tribes in a single apostolic force under the leadership of the Blessed Virgin. With few exceptions, they told her the idea was utterly unrealistic. There was no question of trying to bring the diverse groups together; and with regard to the Africans, they would never accept or persevere in the Legion because of its strict discipline and insistence on regular apostolic work.

Edel's reply to this was, "The impossible has happened elsewhere—why not here? Let us give scope to grace and faith."

In spite of the general pessimism, Edel managed to get two branches of the Legion going within three weeks. One was made up of Europeans and Indians, and the other was all African. On April 4, 1937 the first Acies of the Legion in East Africa was held. This is an annual function at which Legionaries come together to renew their consecration to Our Lady, stating one by one: "I am all thine, my Queen and my Mother, and all I have is thine." At this event there were present African, European and Indian legionaries. This was the first occasion on which the different races had come together for a religious purpose, and it was an historic event for the Church in East Africa. Through Edel's faith and courage she had achieved what had been declared by so many to be impossible.

Edel's untiring efforts were spent not only in establishing the Legion and its spirituality and works, but in visiting and assisting the various groups to maintain their enthusiasm. From Nairobi she traveled from one mission to another, spending enough time in each to get the Legion established. Bit by bit she worked her way over the vast territories of Kenya, Uganda, Nyasaland and Tanganyika. Much of her journeying was done in trucks over rough roads. In spite of her frail constitution, Edel never complained about the bone-shaking trips. Sometimes she drove a battered old Ford that she nicknamed her "Rolls Royce." She went to places where no white woman had ever been seen. The Dublin authorities insisted that she not travel the jungles alone, so a Mohammedan drove her. Traveling gave Edel much time for prayer.

At the insistence of a spiritual director, Edel had begun keeping a sort of spiritual diary. Each year the heading was the motto she had chosen for herself: *"Amor vincit omnia* (Love overcomes all obstacles)." In Edel's life, fervent love, based on deep faith, overcame all obstacles. Her labors were crowned with success beyond all human expectation. Failures and disappointments occurred, of course, but she succeeded in establishing hundreds of praesidia over many vicariates.

Later, Bishop Heffernan told Cardinal Suenens: "After a year of Miss Quinn's work the atmosphere of my diocese had changed. Without any noise, she had brought a germ of life....One could feel the passing of grace. What she brought us was Catholic Action in all its purity...In her presence, questions of race and of social rank disappeared. Her coming among us was a direct and special favor from God for my vicariate. God's hand was visible there."

Edel once arrived back unexpectedly, at a convent where she was staying, after the nuns had gone to bed. Rather than awaken them she stretched out on the veranda and spent a bitterly cold night there, covered only by her thin blue coat. The nuns were upset, and tried to make her promise not to do such a thing again.

For two years Edel's health appeared to hold up. But at the end of 1938 she suffered a serious attack of malaria which left her greatly weakened. Once the crisis was over she was on the road again, but notes in her diary tell a tale: "Jaded out," "Utterly exhausted," "Spot of blood," "Mustn't let people see how tired I am." Her strong faith shines in these notes, too. "If one saw things truly, how one should be grateful and rejoice at every physical weakness, tiredness. . .These are our slight share in Christ's suffering and graces. We can never love too much; let us give utterly and not count the cost."

In January of 1940, at the urging of the bishop, Edel went to establish the Legion on the Island of Mauritius. This was one of the happiest periods of her mission, and when she was leaving she suddenly broke down in tears in front of one of her friends, saying, "Oh, my life is always like this. As soon as my work becomes really interesting and I have made real friends, I have to break away and face the unknown again." This remark was made when the two young women were near a church, so they went in and Edel spent some time before the Tabernacle. When they came out, she was as bright and cheerful as ever.

In September of 1940 Edel returned to Africa. Her health was failing rapidly. By the spring of 1941 her weight had dropped to 75 pounds, and she was in a constant fever. Even so, she refused to give up. "We have only this short life in which to prove our love. . . . Let us try to give utterly, in every way, without counting the cost, to be spent for Christ." Inevitably, she suffered a complete collapse while working in Nyasaland, and then spent over 18 months in various hospitals. There she continued her apostolate by correspondence, as well as by her prayers and sufferings. "If I cannot work, then I can suffer. My greatest joy is to suffer for the love of Our Lord."

In January of 1943, after a dreadful journey, the 35-year-old Edel returned to Nairobi. Her friends there were shocked at the change in her appearance. She was dreadfully thin, her hair was graying, and she looked years older. She was ready to go back to work, however, and gaily did so. She could no longer walk more than a few yards without becoming breathless and exhausted, yet she made some accomplishments. It was at this time that she established the Legion among the British troops stationed in Nairobi. Her main concern now was the visitation of her early foundations. She found most of them flourishing, with nearly all of the original members still faithful. Edel made several long tours; her life was to last one year more.

Early in 1944 Edel made a retreat as a preparation for her death. She spent a little time in Kilimanjaro, where, upon leaving, she told the bishop, "After this I am going on to Uganda and then I'm returning to Nairobi to die."

On April 11 Edel was met by a friend in Nairobi, and after a brief visit she was taken to her little room adjoining the Chapel of the Sisters of the Precious Blood. For the next month, she suffered greatly from frequent heart attacks. Then at about six o'clock in the evening of Friday, May 12, she became convulsed with a violent heart pain and lost consciousness. After a few minutes she came to and whispered to the superior who was standing by, "Mother, Mother, what is happening to me? Mother, I am very ill. What has happened to me? Is Jesus coming?" The superior told her that this time He was coming. Edel received Extreme Unction and the attack began again. After a few moments she died, with the Holy Name of Jesus on her lips.

A mere 14 years after her death, the Archbishop of Nairobi, Dr. McCarthy, announced that he was about to take the preliminary steps towards the introduction of Edel's cause for beatification. His Eminence Cardinal Suenens of Belgium wrote a definitive and moving account of her life and her work in Africa. The decree approving her writing was issued in 1973, and her cause is moving forward rapidly.

Edel Quinn at age four. She is remembered from infancy as being completely unselfish and as being full of consideration for others.

Edel at age 11. Years later she told a priest that from the time she was a young girl she had prayed every day for three special graces: to love God with her whole heart, to make others love Him, and to die a martyr's death. At home, Edel's father paid tribute to her wisdom by calling her "Granny." She also had a delightful sense of humor.

436

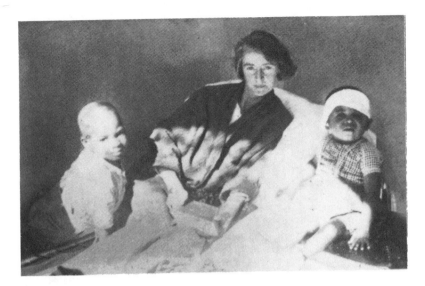

Left: Edel at age 28.

Above: Edel at the Dominican Nuns' Hospital, Umlamli, Aliwal North. When Edel was 19 she joined the Legion of Mary, which had recently been founded in Dublin by Frank Duff. Based on St. Louis De Montfort's *True Devotion to Mary,* the Legion set out to provide spiritual help however and wherever needed, with Legionaries often calling on people door to door. When Edel was 29 the Legion authorities offered to send her to East Africa. Edel was overjoyed and set off to spend the last years of her life establishing the Legion of Mary in many places over an area of about three quarters of a million square miles.

Edel with some little African children at the Benedictine Hospital in Nongoma, Zululand; also pictured is Ruby Roberts, who lavished care on the ailing Edel. Despite her frail condition Edel worked her way over Kenya, Uganda, Nyasaland and Tanganyika, being driven through the jungles over rough roads in a truck—or driving an old Ford she nicknamed her "Rolls Royce." She went to places where no white woman had ever been seen, pushing herself even though exhausted, setting up foundations of the Legion of Mary as she went. Edel died in Nairobi at age 36, with the name of Jesus on her lips.

— 41 —

VENERABLE JOSEPHINE BAKHITA

Venerable Mother Josephine Margaret Fortunata Bakhita
c.1869 - 1947
Southern Sudan - Italy
Died Age 78

"Madre Moretta" (Mother Negress) was dying. Having lived a long life, during which she had advanced from the most degrading slavery to the freedom of the children of God, the elderly black sister painfully but joyously awaited the call of God, her "Master," whom she loved with all her heart, all her soul and all her mind.

At last, on February 8, 1947, the humble African Canossian Sister closed her eyes to this earth. The people of the little town of Schio, close to the Italian Alps, mourned her passing. She had lived for many years in the convent there, and the people considered her their own. They erected a splendid marble monument over the grave of this sister who had so well lived the ideals of her order—humility in charity.

Bakhita was born in Southern Sudan, Central Africa, in approximately 1869. No one knows the exact date of her birth. She was stolen away from her family and her native home by Arab slave traders when she was about nine years old, out in a field looking for herbs. At that time the slave trade was flourishing in Africa. Bakhita had heard stories of slavery, and one of her older sisters had already been stolen by the traders. On being asked her name, the young girl remained silent. One of her Arab captors laughingly told her that this was all right, they would rename her Bakhita, "The Lucky One." At the time, of course, Bakhita considered herself far from lucky. She must have felt deep sorrow, along with apprehension for the future.

When Bakhita was first taken, she and another young girl made an escape attempt. They successfully eluded their first captors and ran off into the forest. There they were treed by a lion and spent the night in the tree, until the lion padded off to seek dinner else-

439

where. Unfortunately, their next encounter was with another slaver, and they were taken to the slave market of El Obeid. There the merchant himself took a fancy to Bakhita and gave her to his daughter. The little Sudanese girl became a lady's maid.

This first home was not a bad one. With her gentle and dignified disposition and her happy smile, Bakhita was popular and was well-treated for a while. One day, though, she accidentally broke a vase belonging to the merchant's son, who then beat her and demanded that his father get rid of her.

Bakhita's next owner was a Turkish officer and his family. The women of the household flogged Bakhita regularly and tattooed her by incision simply to gratify a whim of fashion. But Bakhita's life was to change for the better when her owner, traveling home on leave, decided to sell off his slaves in Khartoum.

Bakhita was bought by the Italian vice-consul. This kindly man treated her as well as a daughter and even tried to find out who her parents were so that he could send her back home. However, by this time Bakhita had even forgotten her original name, and his efforts were unsuccessful, so he took her back with him to Italy.

In Genoa, Bakhita and her kindly benefactor became friendly with a wealthy lady named Signora Michieli. The lady's small daughter became so fond of the young African that the vice-consul gave her over to their care. Thus at 14, Bakhita had yet another temporary home.

This family owned a hotel near the Red Sea, and the plan was that eventually Bakhita would be a waitress there. Although visits were made to the hotel, for the next six years Bakhita lived mainly at the family home near Venice, acting as a companion to the little girl.

Just as Bakhita was about to move to the hotel, the family steward made an unexpected request. He felt that as Bakhita had received no instruction in the Christian Faith, she should be allowed to stay in Italy long enough to learn something about it and then, if she wished, be baptized. The family agreed, and arrangements were made for Bakhita and the little girl, Mimmina, to board at the Venetian convent of the Daughters of Charity of Canossa.

Technically, Bakhita was a Moslem. Perhaps in the far past her people, the Daju, may have been Christian. In any case, Bakhita knew, from the moment she entered the convent, that at last she had come home to where she belonged. At the convent she learned to love the Master whom she had felt in her heart, even in times of most desolate abandonment. Her purity of heart was a fertile soil upon which the seed of the Gospel readily sprouted.

When Signora Michieli came to pick up the girls after 10 months, she received a shock. Gently but firmly, this African girl whom she still considered her property informed her that nothing short of physical force would ever make her leave the sisters.

The Mother Superior saw that this was a case for higher authority and called in the Cardinal Patriarch. Since civil law was also involved, he called in the King's Procurator. In the convent parlor these two high representatives of Church and State held court to decide the fate of the young African.

The hearing was heated on the part of the Signora, who demanded the return of her property.

Bakhita was invited to speak. Briefly she said: "I love the Signora dearly, and to part from Mimmina cuts me to the heart. But I shall not leave this place because I cannot risk losing God."

The Cardinal Patriarch had no doubts, but the final verdict rested with the Procurator. Since slavery was illegal under Italian law, he ruled that any slave was emancipated immediately upon touching Italian soil. Bakhita was a free woman.

On January 9, 1890 Bakhita was baptized by the Cardinal Patriarch, with a countess for a godmother and a large group of well-wishers eager to welcome her into the Church. It is said that Bakhita did not know how to express her joy but that her big, expressive, kind eyes sparkled, revealing her heart. From that day to the end of her life, Bakhita never ceased marveling that she was someone God loved, someone who was important in His eyes.

From the beginning, Bakhita had wanted to join the sisters, but it took a while for her to put her request to the Mother Superior. She did not know if she would be accepted, because of the color of her skin. The Mother Superior delightedly assured her that she would of course be welcomed.

Thus Bakhita became a Canossian sister. For the rest of her life she was totally happy in any task she was given. She always had a cheerful smile and a kind word for everyone. Bakhita, pure in heart, felt an ever-present sense of God's love. She said, "If I had known it when I was a slave, I would never have suffered so much."

Bakhita would have liked to return to Africa to help in the

conversion of her people. Instead, her superiors assigned her to travel the whole of Italy on lecture tours to gain support for the missions. She always ended her talks by saying: "Be good, love God, pray for the pagans." Many people turned out to hear her speeches. Later she said that although some might have thought these trips were pleasurable for her, she considered them a slow martyrdom. She gave of her best because she knew that this was the meaning of obedience—and she knew that her talks would help the people of Africa.

At the Canossian house of Schio, Bakhita worked first as a cook, then in charge of the linen, and finally as portress. There she was the friend of the poor, the little ones, the suffering and the abandoned. The people would even tell of miracles she had worked. Bakhita caressed the children by resting her hands very gently on the tops of their heads, since they were sometimes afraid of her because of her different color. She was often referred to as Mother Negress. She would spend over 50 years as a Canossian sister.

During the last four years of her life the once-healthy Bakhita fell prey to a number of afflictions, which slowly reduced her to helplessness. She also endured anguish of heart. Her greatest sorrow was the trouble she caused to others in caring for her. Those who came to her room to comfort her soon found their own spirits lifted by the ever-cheerful patient who preferred to joke about her own health. As her last, painful illness wasted her away, she said, "I'm all skin and bone—there'll be nothing left for the worms!" Until her death, her mind and her radiant personality remained unimpaired.

On February 8 of 1947 Bakhita, "the lucky one," rich in good works, went to meet "the Master."

Bakhita is said to have been "pure as an angel, meek as a lamb." The decree acknowledging her heroic virtue was issued on December 1, 1978. In the cathedral in Obeid, in Sudan, there is on the wall a painting of Mother Bakhita beside that of Our Lady, Queen of Africa.

Mother Josephine Bakhita, who as a young girl was stolen away from her home in Africa by slave traders, eventually ending up in Italy. She was sent to board with the Canossian Sisters, where she immediately felt she had come home to where she belonged. Bakhita embraced the Catholic Faith, being baptized at around age 21. She was "pure as an angel, meek as a lamb."

Bakhita herself became a Canossian sister. She was the friend of the poor, the little ones, the suffering and the abandoned. There were even stories that she had worked miracles. She was often called "Mother Negress." Mother Bakhita died in 1947, after 50 years of religious life.

42

ARTEMIDE ZATTI

Servant of God Brother Artemide Zatti
Artemide Gioacchine Desiderio Zatti
1880 - 1951
Italy - Argentina
Died Age 70

"The Patron of All the Poor" is an apt title for a humble Salesian lay brother who spent his life looking at Jesus crucified in the faces of the sick poor in Patagonia, Argentina. Incapable of saying "no" to anyone in need, Bro. Zatti often said, "The Providence of God is great, but He wants us to work hard to find what we need."

Artemide Zatti was born in Boretto, Italy on October 12, 1880. Baptized on the day of his birth, Artemide was the third of eight children of Louis and Albina Vecchi Zatti. The Zattis were farmers who raised their children with a sense of the value of work and a strong faith in God. The family was poor, so Artemide went to work at age nine. He arose at 3 a.m. daily to work in the fields. He received the startlingly low pay of about $1.25 per year, plus food. He attended school only until he was about 12, and continued working until he was about 16. At this age he had grown into a tall, gawky teenager, not physically handsome, and with very large feet, about a size 15. He was skinny and had already grown a mustache.

In 1897, at 17, Artemide and his family immigrated to Bahia Blanca, Argentina. His uncle was in charge of dealing with the Italian immigrants who were working in the fields there, and Artemide obtained work from him. He worked in the fields, sold produce in the market, and worked in a *fonda*, or low-class restaurant. He left his job in the *fonda* because he did not like the atmosphere. The entire town of Bahia Blanca was, at this time, anticlerical and Masonic, and the Zattis soon discovered that even some of their relatives had lost their religion.

The Zattis clung to their faith and attended the church run by the Salesian Order in Bahia Blanca. There Artemide began reading the life of St. John Bosco. Soon he determined to become a priest like Don Bosco, and he asked the pastor how he could realize this vocation. The priest informed the eager young man that it would be most difficult for him to become a priest due to his poor educational background. He counseled him, however, that with God nothing is impossible, and advised him to think about his vocation seriously before making up his mind because, as he said, "I do not want you to come home as a failure." At 19, Artemide entered the Salesian scholasticate at Bernal, near Buenos Aires, to prepare for the priesthood.

In spite of his diligence at his studies, the young man had great difficulty with Latin. His rudimentary education had not prepared him to cope scholastically with the necessary studies, especially since he had been away from academics for eight years. He wrote to his family about how happy he was, but he constantly confused his languages—Latin, Spanish and Italian, as well as his own native dialect.

The smiling, gawky young man studied heroically, and within two years was able to begin his postulancy and start his preparation for the novitiate. There was a priest there dying of tuberculosis, and Artemide volunteered to take care of him. Artemide himself soon contracted the disease. On the day of his scheduled investiture he was in bed with a high fever.

Because of the high humidity of Bernal, and because his disease was being very rough on him, his superiors wanted to send him home. Artemide, however, wanted to stay with the Salesians and persevere in his vocation. His doctors recommended the higher altitude of the mountains of the Andes. While he was waiting for the train to the Andes, he began coughing up blood and vomiting. Artemide traveled nearly 500 miles in a second class car, drastically ill and sitting on a hard wooden seat. At this point he felt a sense of failure, because he was certain that he could not be a priest. His mother was especially desperate with grief for her son. Artemide met a Salesian priest, Fr. Carlos, who advised him to go to Viedma in Patagonia instead of staying in the Andes.

Artemide was admitted to the seminary at Viedma. There in the frontier country of Patagonia, where many were studying for the missions, he met Fr. Evasio Garrone, an Italian priest who had been a male nurse in the Italian army. Fr. Garrone took the young man under his wing while he was there. He was able to see into the soul of young Artemide, and he saw his virtue and his great love for Jesus and Mary.

Fr. Garrone felt inspired to call young Artemide to the chapel, where he told him that if he would consecrate himself forever to the sick poor, Mary Help of Christians would restore his health. Artemide made this consecration, and within two years his health was restored. He became quite a vigorous man, and he set about dedicating all his life to the service of God as a lay brother, totally dedicated to the sick.

Artemide began work at the hospital named St. Joseph of the Mission in March of 1903; he persevered there until January of 1951, a month and a half before his death. By that time he was literally incapable of staying on his feet to fulfill his obligations. Here he spent 48 years of continuous dedication—with no vacations.

At first Artemide took care of the pharmacy of the hospital. He obtained a diploma through exams from the University of La Plata with the title of "Idoneo," or practitioner in pharmacy. This degree permitted him to practice medicine as long as there was not a pharmacist with a degree in town. When his protector and superior, Fr. Garrone, died, Artemide took his place as the head of the hospital.

In reality Artemide was not only the director, but also the administrator and a nurse. In this hospital, with its capacity of 70 beds, the patients who could pay would do so. Those who could not pay their bill paid only what they could afford, or nothing. The majority of the patients paid little or nothing. Thus Artemide had to find the money to support the hospital. In addition to working at the hospital, he pedaled his old bicycle to the poorest sections of the city in order to give his beloved poor vaccinations and other medical treatment.

In addition to his many hours of work each day, Artemide was always ready for night calls. He used to tell his patients, "In case of need, you have the obligation to call me, and I have the obligation of going to your aid." The word "no" was foreign to his vocabulary. In case of immediate need, the humble lay brother often gave up his own bed to a poor person.

In spite of his poor performance with the study of Latin and some of his other academic subjects, Bro. Zatti was blessed with a high intelligence and a quick memory. For this reason he learned well the art of healing and quickly became quite skilled. His patients were very devoted to him, and they would only go to a medical doctor on his advice. Many of his devoted patients called him "Don" Zatti, a title he rejected because he said it was meant only for those who were born rich and titled. He wanted his people to understand that he preferred to be only a common laborer, as they were.

In 1915 Bro. Zatti took an enforced five-day "vacation," as he called it. The town jailors used to send sick prisoners to him, and once he cured one of the inmates so well that that very day the man escaped. Because Bro. Zatti had been responsible for the custody of the man, the authorities took him to jail! A number of townspeople accompanied him to jail, singing hymns as the jailors towed him away.

In all of his work among the sick poor and the spiritually destitute, Don Zatti never failed to smile. He did his work without seeming to hurry, and he always kept his sense of humor. As the French would say, "A sad saint is a sad saint," and Bro. Zatti was the exact opposite of sad. He was too filled with the joy of God to keep a long face. In 30 years as administrator, he never refused anyone because of lack of ability to pay. Additionally, he used the most modern cures, even if they were more expensive.

The mode of Bro. Zatti's dress was a good barometer of the financial status of the hospital. When he rode his bicycle to work in his *guarda-polvo* (literally a "dust-protector," his white work jacket), everyone knew that he was going to work to administer treatment or medicine to someone. When he wore his black suit and tie, however, everyone knew that he was off on a begging trip. As he passed in this garb, the old ladies would say, "May God bless him and give him what he needs." By God's blessing, he always received what he needed. He would pedal to the homes of the rich ranchers, high government employees and businessmen. Very few were able to deny him what he asked. If the cash for a donation was not readily available, benefactors often loaned him the money or signed for him so that he could obtain bank loans. He was not only able to keep the hospital going, but twice he had to rebuild it when failure seemed imminent. It was necessary to renovate the hospital often, always adding new and more modern rooms and equipment. In spite of his cheerful smile, Bro. Zatti considered his begging trips the "Calvary" of his life.

No matter how much he was working, Bro. Zatti always found

time to keep up the religious practices required by his order. By 5:30 each morning he was already at meditation, and he often personally directed it. He served Mass with his eyes closed and his hands crossed over his chest, in a characteristic reverent attitude. In the evenings he attended spiritual readings with the other lay brothers; he was particularly attracted to reading Holy Scripture, with which he was very familiar, even in its Latin texts.

Bro. Zatti liked to sing religious songs, and he often sang while caring for the sick. Following a Salesian custom, he often gave little "good night" talks to those around him at night. Often he told stories about the lives of the Saints.

Artemide was devoted to the Rosary, and he said it while bicycling. To a surgeon who sometimes helped him, he said, "See, doctor, a machine will stop if you don't provide it with fuel. For me, the fuel is my prayer."

Bro. Zatti had a deep and abiding love for the Blessed Virgin Mary. He used to keep a lamp burning in the halls in her honor. When some people advised him to turn it off in the interest of saving money, he told them that it was necessary for the soul.

Following the custom of many religious orders, a religious reading preceded community meals. Stories about the Salesian missions, or about the Founder, St. John Bosco, touched Bro. Zatti deeply, and he often shed tears when these were the chosen readings. His love for the saintly founder was so great that he was chosen as a delegate of the brothers in Patagonia to attend St. John Bosco's canonization in Rome. At the ceremony he obtained a relic, a piece of the Saint's bone. He often touched it to his sick, especially the young.

Bro. Zatti's charity was outstanding. Often when poor patients left the hospital, the brothers would provide clothing for them. Artemide used to tell the man in charge of the clothing that he wanted to have something to "dress Jesus," and if the outfit provided was not suitable, he would ask, "Would you dress Jesus that way?"

Bro. Zatti had a particular love for the retarded and seriously afflicted young. In these as well as in all his sick poor, he saw the image of his crucified Jesus.

In 1950 Bro. Zatti fell from some stairs and was injured. He never recuperated from his accident, and soon it was discovered that he had developed cancer of the liver. Even in such a serious state, he did not lose his joyous sense of humor. Naturally, as in any liver disease, he began to jaundice, or turn yellow. Additionally, his features became fattened. Jokingly, he told people that he was "ripening like a cantaloupe." The doctors advised him to stay in bed, but he insisted on staying up. "Since my sickness cannot be cured, why should I waste the rest of my life?" he asked.

Bro. Zatti's consideration for others lasted through his last days. During his life he had filled out many death certificates. After his own death, the doctors discovered that he had already written out his own certificate, leaving blank only the lines for date, time and the signature of the doctor.

The entire town of Viedma manifested their love for this unassuming brother after his death. They erected a beautiful monument in his honor and named after him a new hospital opened by the Argentinian government. Additionally, one of the major commercial streets, a number of businesses, and an entire section of the town bear his name.

A cause for Bro. Artemide Zatti was introduced in 1979.

Artemide Zatti with his mother. Artemide was a Salesian lay brother who spent his life doing medical work. He had begun studies to become a priest, but this did not come about, due to health problems and his poor educational background. Artemide became director and administrator—as well as a nurse—at the 70-bed hospital called St. Joseph of the Mission in Viedma, Argentina.

451

Artemide saw in the sick poor the image of Jesus Crucified. Moreover, he was always ready for night calls. He would tell patients, "In case of need, you have the obligation to call me, and I have the obligation of going to your aid." In case of immediate need, he often gave up his bed to a poor person.

452

In addition to doing medical work, Artemide had to go in search of funds, for most of the patients could not pay. He would pedal his bicycle to the homes of rich ranchers, high government employees and businessmen. Despite his cheerful smile, Artemide considered these begging trips the "Calvary" of his life.

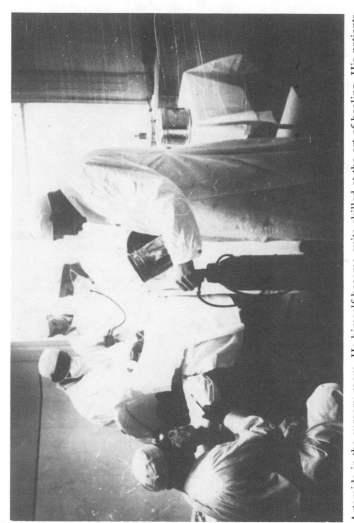

Artemide in the surgery room. He himself became quite skilled at the art of healing. His patients were devoted to him and would go to a medical doctor only on his advice.

454

Bro. Zatti was able to attend the canonization of St. John Bosco, to whom he was deeply devoted. He obtained a relic of the Saint, which he often touched to the sick. At the end of his life Artemide developed cancer of the liver, which caused his skin to turn yellow; moreover, his features became fattened. He joked that he was "ripening like a cantaloupe." Bro. Zatti died at age 70, after 48 years of continuous dedication to the sick.

43

BLESSED KATHARINE DREXEL

Blessed Mother Mary Katharine Drexel
Katharine Mary Drexel
1858 - 1955
United States
Died Age 97

Millions of dollars or eternal wealth—which is more valuable? Katharine Mary Drexel chose to be poor in order to gain great spiritual wealth, believing that her great fortune would be very well spent if used for God's poor among the black and Indian people of the United States. She considered the giving up of her wealth not a sacrifice, but a privilege.

Katharine Mary Drexel was born on November 26, 1858 in Philadelphia, the second daughter of Francis A. Drexel and his Quaker wife Hannah. A month after Katharine's birth, her mother died. In two years her father was remarried to Emma M. Bouvier, a devout Catholic. A third daughter, Louise, followed. Emma accepted Katharine and her sister Elizabeth as her own and brought up all three girls in a devout home with a strong religious sense and a generous spirit.

Francis Drexel, along with his brothers, shared ownership of a large, international banking empire. While Francis worked and made fortunes, Emma taught her children the value of responsible charity, and she prudently and wisely distributed Drexel funds to the poor and needy. This deeply religious couple believed that their wealth belonged to God, who had entrusted them with it to serve and aid the poor.

Emma, a well-educated and cultured woman, wanted her daughters to have the same benefits she had had. She sought out the best tutors and encouraged her children to receive a broad and complete education. Household duties, too, were a part of the girls' education. Emma taught them to cook, to sew and to trim their own hats. Additionally, the girls took turns with the management of the home. Emma taught her daughters to be unaffected, straightforward and fearless.

The family attended Mass together each morning, and in the evenings Francis entertained his family by playing the organ. Additionally, the family traveled extensively.

From Katharine's earliest childhood, a special devotion to the Blessed Sacrament is evident. In a charming letter which eight-year-old Katharine wrote to her mother, she mentions two desires. First, the unselfish and loving child begged her mother to allow her younger sister to have some bonbons as a Christmas treat. Mrs. Drexel did not approve of candy for children and years later Mother Katharine told her sisters at recreation that as a child she was only allowed to have candy once a year—at Christmas. Her second desire expressed in this and other childhood letters was to be allowed to make her First Communion. But since Katharine lived before the time of Pope Pius X, whose understanding of children and the special love of God for them made it possible for children to receive Communion from the age of reason, she was 11 years old before she was able to make her First Holy Communion.

At the time, Katharine said little of her first meeting with her Eucharistic God. However, years later in her retreat notes as a religious she made reference to her First Communion: "I remember my First Communion and my letter on that day. Jesus made me shed my tears because of His greatness in stooping to me. Truth made me feel the mite I was...."

In 1870, Mr. Drexel bought a beautiful country home for the family in Torresdale, Pennsylvania. The home was dedicated to St. Michael, whose statue was placed prominently above the entry.

There Mrs. Drexel proposed that Elizabeth and Katharine begin a Sunday School for the children of the men who worked at the farm. Fourteen-year-old Elizabeth taught the older children, and 12-year-old Katharine taught the younger ones. This Sunday School was held for many years, with 50 or more children attending. The two youthful teachers distributed prizes for attendance and for good lessons, and at Christmas they passed out useful gifts such as dresses and jackets; special treats such as cake and candies were given to all the children.

In 1879 Katharine made her debut into Philadelphia society, but the social whirl did not impress her. Although Katharine was a prolific letter writer, the only written mention she made of her debut was in a letter to Bishop O'Connor, her spiritual director. She wrote of her daily occupations during this time and mentions "attending a little party the other night, where I made my debut." She did not even write a complete sentence about this party which had been given in the grand style due the debut of a millionaire's daughter. Those who knew Katharine later as a religious testified that she never wanted to be the center of attention or in the limelight. This self-forgetfulness was perfected in her religious life, but it had been begun years earlier.

This period of Katharine's life was a study in contrasts. Outwardly, she lived the life expected of a person of her wealth. Following her debut, she and her sister Elizabeth were the center of a social whirl. Party followed party, and a great deal of matchmaking was arranged for the young society belles. Mr. Drexel kept a careful watch on his daughters, as he was afraid that some of their suitors might only be after their money. In a cleverly-worded letter to his daughters when they were vacationing at the seashore, he wrote, "I hope you are careful not to get into deep water either with the beaux or the surf."

In 1879 Emma fell ill with cancer, and Katherine nursed her tenderly. After three years of suffering, Emma died. Katharine's nursing brought home to her the fact that none of the family fortune could relieve Emma's pain or prevent her death.

Katharine reflected on the meaning of life, wealth, and her future. Although she felt a growing attraction to the religious life, and although she loved God very much, she was still uncertain about her vocation. She loved life, she was an attractive girl, and she had many suitors. Acting on the advice of her spiritual director, she wrote out on paper her reasons for and against entering religion. One of the things she wrote on the "for" side was "The attainment of perfection should be our chief employment in life. Our Lord has laid a price upon its acquirement when He says, 'If thou wilt be perfect, go sell what thou hast and give to the poor, and thou shalt have treasure in Heaven, and come follow Me...He that followeth Me walketh not in darkness.' How can I doubt that these words are true wisdom, and if true wisdom why not act upon them?" One of the reasons she gave against entering religion was "I do not know how I could bear the privations and poverty of the religious life. I have never been deprived of luxuries."

Not having come to a definite conclusion about her vocation after making her list, Katharine submitted both the list and the matter of her vocation to Bishop O'Connor. She wrote to him, telling him that she was in no hurry for his answer as the young man who had been courting her had proposed and she had turned him down. She humorously wrote that for the time being she felt her vocation was to be an old maid. A lengthy correspondence about Katharine's vocation ensued and was carried on over a matter of years. During Katharine's wait, Bishop O'Connor advised her to make an annual vow of chastity, which she did.

Two years after his wife's death, Francis died. The provisions of his will show his devotion to charity. He left one tenth of his estate for immediate distribution to charity, and the income from the remainder of his millions was to be divided equally between his daughters. At the time, the girls received approximately a thousand dollars a day from this income. Should his daughters die without leaving children, the rest of the estate would go to charity.

From the time of their father's death, the three Drexel sisters began supporting and encouraging a number of charitable works in the tradition of their parents. One of the first charitable enterprises they supported was the Catholic Indian missions. Katharine in particular was attracted to this apostolate.

In 1886 Katharine became ill. Doctors suggested a treatment at a health spa in Germany, so in company with her sisters she traveled to Europe. After her health was restored, Katharine and her sisters recruited European priests and nuns for the United States Indian missions.

In a church in Venice, the statue of the Madonna of San Marco seemed to come alive for Katharine for a moment, and she heard the words, "Freely have you received; freely give." Later, in a private interview with Pope Leo XIII, Katharine begged the Holy Father to send more missionaries to the Indians. The Pontiff suggested that Katharine herself become a missionary.

In the fall of 1887 the Drexel sisters visited the Indian missions in the Dakotas at the invitation of Fr. Stephen, one of the first missionaries who had appealed for their help. Katharine was appalled at the misery she witnessed, and she determined to take some action to help improve the lot of these native Americans.

On her return home, Katharine worked to set up systematic funding for the missionary effort from her own fortune. Within four years, she had built 13 mission schools in the Dakotas, Wyoming,

Montana, California, Oregon and New Mexico. In 20 years time, Katharine and her sisters would contribute more than a million and a half dollars toward the Catholic education of the Indians. But even these large donations, Katharine realized, were not enough. The United States government contributed funds, as did the French Society for the Propagation of the Faith. Still, the need was great. Katharine suggested to Bishop James O'Connor of Omaha that the U.S. Catholic hierarchy establish a bureau for "Colored and Indian Missions" to collect and disperse funds, and that a special collection be made each year for the missions on the Second Sunday of Lent. The bureau was established, and even today American Catholics respond generously on Mission Sunday.

Both of Katharine's sisters married. Wealthy, attractive and witty, Katharine had many suitors. However, she felt more and more drawn to the religious life. Her friend Bishop O'Connor at first counseled her that her health was not strong enough for the life of a religious, but finally agreed that her determination seemed firm. He then made a startling suggestion: "Why not found a new order for the Indian and Colored people?"

The responsibility of such a task frightened Katharine, but Bishop O'Connor overcame all of her objections. In a letter to him in 1889, she wrote, "The feast of St. Joseph brought me the grace to give the remainder of my life to the Indians and Colored, to enter fully and entirely into your view as to what is best for the salvation of the souls of these people."

In 1889 Katharine entered a postulant training program under the direction of the Sisters of Mercy of Pittsburgh. She embarked on her mission with a great sense of joy, with the love and blessing of her sisters, and accompanied by the publicity of hysterical newspaper headlines such as: "Miss Drexel Enters a Catholic Convent— Gives Up Seven Million!"

Katharine was received into the novitiate in 1889. No bride ever looked more beautiful or radiant than Katharine did on the morning of November 7, 1889 as she entered the chapel of the Sisters of Mercy in a white wedding gown trimmed with orange blossoms. She wore diamond rings on her fingers and a diamond necklace. Eight little girls in white satin dresses and white silk veils followed her. The sisters and Katharine's close relatives and friends watched Katharine leave the chapel in her bridal array and return shortly afterward in the habit and white veil of a sister. Archbishop Ryan of Philadelphia, who had presided at the reception, later said, ". . .she knelt before the illumined altar of the God of all races of men and offered her great fortune, her life, her love, her hopes, that until the grave shall receive her, all she possesses now or shall possess in the future may belong to God and to the Indian and Colored races. She hopes that other Christian maidens may unite with her and thus inaugurate the great work of reparation and help to render it perpetual."

In 1890 Katharine lost both her younger sister, who died in childbirth, and her spiritual helper, Bishop O'Connor. Philadelphia's Archbishop Patrick J. Ryan stepped in and, consoling her in the loss of her spiritual director, offered his assistance in order for her to go on with her mission. She poured out her heart to him. Katharine was worried about being able to begin such a grand enterprise, and his encouragement gave her new hope.

In February of 1891, Katharine Drexel professed her vows as the first Sister of the Blessed Sacrament for Indians and Colored People. In addition to making a vow of poverty, chastity and obedience, she made a fourth: "To be the mother and servant of the Indian and Negro races according to the rule of the Sisters of the Blessed Sacrament, and not to undertake any work which would lead to the neglect or abandonment of the Indian and Colored races."

Immediately after her profession Sr. Katharine opened a novitiate for the Sisters of the Blessed Sacrament. She had purchased property in Cornwells Heights, near Philadelphia, and began building a novitiate. As the building was not completed, the first group of novices and postulants lived for a time at the Drexel's summer home in nearby Torresdale. The Sisters of Mercy loaned their novice mistress for a year, and a Philadelphia Jesuit, Fr. Scully, came to give monthly conferences and to be the sisters' spiritual director. By the end of the first year there were 21 members of the little community. The sisters began their work with the establishment of Holy Providence School, a boarding school for poor children.

Archbishop Ryan kept careful watch and direction over the eager young band. At last, he allowed a pioneer group of sisters to open a boarding school at St. Catherine's Mission in Santa Fe, New Mexico.

All three of the Drexel sisters—Elizabeth, until her death, and Louise and Katharine for the rest of their lives—shared a common concern for the black race. Elizabeth had already established St.

Francis Industrial School in Eddington, Pennsylvania, an interracial trade school for orphan boys. Louise established St. Emma's Industrial and Agricultural Institute for young black men in Richmond, Virginia. Both schools were staffed by the Christian Brothers. Nearby at Rock Castle, Virginia, Katharine established St. Francis de Sales School for black girls.

The three sisters had an extensive knowledge of European educational methods, and they applied them to their educational institutions. Katharine, like her sisters, wanted the best educational and social opportunities for the poor and underprivileged. The Drexel sisters firmly believed that quality education of the young was the way for these peoples to become leaders and to attain fully their rights and dignities as children of God and citizens of the land they loved.

Katharine wanted to bring each of these children to the recognition of the position they could hold as children of God. She recognized in the Indian and Colored missions a field of souls ripe for harvest for her Divine Lover. Katharine recognized in each of these Indian and black children a unique personality to be brought into the loving arms of God. She felt a duty to each of them to help them grow and be all that they were capable of being.

Racial prejudice and opposition to Katharine and her sisters was not lacking. Serenely, they persevered in their task. Mother Katharine took such rejections with patience, often comparing their rejection to that of the Holy Family at Bethlehem or to that of Our Lord in His own mission.

Throughout the South, the sisters established a system of Catholic schools for black children. By 1942 these foundations covered 13 states and included 30 convents, 40 mission centers and 23 rural schools. Fifteen thousand children and unnumbered adults were under the care of the Sisters of the Blessed Sacrament. Thousands of dollars annually went to the support of small parishes. Overall, by this time, over $11,000,000 had been used to further the education of black people.

St. Frances Cabrini advised Mother Katharine to take to Rome, for approval, the rule which had been developed for the Sisters of the Blessed Sacrament. Pope St. Pius X granted preliminary approval in 1907.

On her return Katharine was elected superior general, and the community continued to grow, opening new missions in Boston,

New York, Chicago, Columbus and Cincinnati. Yet she always tried to work without fanfare, saying often, "It is better to do things quietly." She herself would wear her habit until it was almost threadbare.

In 1912 Mother Katharine contracted typhoid fever while visiting the New Mexico missions. When death seemed imminent, she remarked with her usual sense of humor, "As this is certainly not according to my plans, it must be God's will." Exhaustion and other complications compounded the problem and caused her to return to the motherhouse for an extended rest. She recovered fully, however, and soon was back at work. She made another European visit to obtain final approval of her rule and to find vocations for the American missions.

In 1915 Mother Katharine established Xavier University in New Orleans, the first U.S. Catholic institution of higher learning for blacks. By 1925 the school had received its charter as a college of liberal arts and sciences, and by 1932 it had reached university status. (The school became integrated in 1954.)

In 1935, during an extended visitation of the Western missions, Katharine suffered a severe heart attack. Her doctors advised her to retire as superior. She followed their advice and appointed a new superior. Gratefully, she moved to the Cornwells Heights Convent infirmary, where for 20 years she would spend her days and nights in prayer. Daily, she bore her illness gracefully.

Mother Katharine wrote, "I fear suffering, but not if it is dealt out by the God of Mercy, Who will not make me bear what is above my strength." She continued, "My dying is eternal life with Christ. To the extent which I comprehend Christ in faith, to the same extent I shall embrace Him in love." Mother Katharine was often seen kissing a picture of the Sacred Heart.

More and more Mother Katharine united herself with her Lord in the contemplative manner she had so desired as a young woman. She wrote, "The shadows of my life grow long. And so He speaks with me... He abides in my house—the house of His publican. It is as if all glory were nothing to Him, and I alone were all His care. We speak together, I listen—and thus a lifetime passes. Then comes a moment—who can tell what happens? It is as though a veil were rent and my eyes opened. A radiance not of earth surrounds Him. It is the moment of my passing hence. Blessed death approaches—that death which never corrupts the converse of the soul with God, but which lets fall all earthly sufferings, all mists and veils of faith, and shows us face to face our long desired Guest and Sovereign Master—Jesus."

On March 3, 1955, with the community chaplain, her doctor and the sisters kneeling in prayer, Mother Katharine calmly and peacefully slipped away. She had helped more missions than can be numbered, and given away her millions for their support. Greater than these gifts, she had given herself, and willingly she gave back to God the life He had given to her. At her death there were more than 600 Sisters of the Blessed Sacrament.

Nine years after her peaceful death, His Eminence John Cardinal Krol opened her cause for beatification and asked that all existing documents, correspondence, notes and testimonial evidence on Mother Katharine Drexel be gathered and sent to Rome for consideration of the nature and extent of her sanctity. The decree introducing her cause was published in 1979. Katharine Drexel was beatified in Rome in November of 1988.

Blessed Katharine Drexel at age 18. Katharine was the daughter of a Philadelphia millionaire.

Upon the advice of two American bishops Katharine began the Sisters of the Blessed Sacrament for Indians and Colored People. She recognized in the Indian and Colored Missions a field of souls ripe for harvest for her Divine Lover. Throughout the South she worked to establish Catholic convents, mission centers and schools for black children.

465

Due to illness, Mother Katharine Drexel spent the last 20 years of her life in prayer and suffering. She wrote, "I fear suffering, but not if it is dealt out by the God of Mercy, Who will not make me bear what is above my strength." Mother Katharine Drexel died in 1955.

44

FATHER MATEO CRAWLEY - BOEVEY

Father Mateo Edward Crawley-Boevey, SS.CC.
Mateo Edward Crawley-Boevey
1875 - 1960
Peru—Chile
Died Age 84

In 1906 a dream came true for a young Peruvian priest. With the help of a wealthy benefactress, he built a school of law as part of the Sacred Hearts College. His dream came true in May—and in August it was shattered.

A huge earthquake made a ruin of the school. The priest was tempted to ask God, "Why did You let this happen?" Instead, he made an act of blind faith in the infinite wisdom of God. Later he realized that had it not been for this earthquake, he might never have become the "globe-trotter of the Sacred Heart."

Mateo Edward Crawley-Boevey was born on November 18, 1875 in Arequipa, Peru; as a child he was called Edward. His father was an English banker who had been sent by his bank to Peru, where he met and married Maria Murga, a daughter of a justice of the Supreme Court of Peru, and a strong Catholic. Although Edward's father converted from his Anglican faith, he did not become a practicing Catholic until shortly before his death. He was, however, an extremely intelligent and just man who was to encourage his son in his desire for the priesthood.

When Edward's father was recalled to England, the family prepared to go. At the last moment, however, baby Edward developed a terrible stomachache which the doctor feared would cause him great trouble on the long trip. As it turned out, he remained in Peru for a number of years with his grandfather, who greatly influenced the boy in his religious and moral formation.

After the parents' return to Peru, the family was transferred again, in 1884, to Valparaiso, Chile. Edward was sent to the school conducted by the Fathers of the Sacred Hearts of Jesus and Mary, the Sacred Hearts College.

When young Edward said that he wanted to become a priest, his father visited the superior to find out what the priests and brothers of the Sacred Hearts had as their main purpose. On his return home he told his son that their main goal was "to become a saint" and that therefore Edward had his permission to join them. He cautioned his son, however, that if he had not made up his mind to pursue that goal wholeheartedly, he had better stay at home. Edward found his vocation with the Fathers of the Sacred Hearts and was ordained in 1898.

Young Fr. Mateo realized that although his order was a missionary one, "charity begins at home." He felt the need of strengthening the faith and knowledge of both the upper and the lower classes. He instituted a course of law for the former and established a social center for the latter.

In 1900 the social center of Santiago instituted by Fr. Mateo set the following goals: 1. Make the royalty of Jesus Christ known and loved, 2. Make reparation for public offenses against Him, and 3. Bring Jesus the Redeemer into contact with the entire family. In this program lay the beginning of the crusade of Enthronement of the Sacred Heart of Jesus.

With the help of a wealthy benefactress, a Mrs. Edwards, the young priest succeeded in building a school of law as a part of the Sacred Hearts College. He himself taught several courses in it. It was dedicated in May, 1906; at last this dream had come true.

But sometimes dreams turn into nightmares. As alluded to above, one quiet, sunny day in August of 1906, Fr. Mateo was with a group of fellow priests at recreation in the courtyard of the college. The bell had just rung to end recreation, and as the priests began to enter the building the earth began to tremble beneath their feet. They threw themselves to the ground, expecting at any moment to be crushed. None of the religious lost his life, although the death toll in the city ran high. The college buildings, however, were a scene of almost total destruction.

One of the few things in the entire college which was not damaged by the earthquake was a large oil painting of the Sacred Heart. It was found hanging at a crazy angle from a beam, covered with dust but unharmed. This picture had been painted by an outstanding Ecuadorian artist by order of President Gabriel Garcia Morena and had been used for the solemn consecration of Ecuador to the Sacred Heart in 1873. In this picture the universal kingship of the

Sacred Heart is symbolized by the sceptre and the globe. Upon looking closely a person will see, close to the Heart of the Saviour, the little country of Ecuador being inflamed with a ray of light and fire from the loving heart of Jesus.

After President Moreno was assassinated, a revolution broke out. Twice, attempts were made to burn the Sacred Heart painting, but providentially it was saved by members of Moreno's family. It was given for safekeeping to a Father of the Sacred Hearts from Chile who took it to the provincial in Valparaiso.

Years later, young Fr. Mateo had been helping the provincial arrange his archives when, going through a trunk, he found a rolled-up canvas, the Sacred Heart picture. The picture seemed to symbolize everything he was working for—the recognition of the sovereign rights of Jesus the King, ruling over every phase of society by the power of His love, through His Heart. When Fr. Mateo asked the superior about the history of the picture, he was fascinated by the story. He asked if he might have the picture, and permission was granted.

Fr. Mateo had the painting framed and installed in the place of honor in the new law school, where it remained until the earthquake. After this it went back to Valparaiso, Chile and stayed there until recent years, when it was returned to its native land, where it is preserved in a magnificent shrine in Quito. Today, reproductions of this picture are found throughout the world, thanks to Fr. Mateo.

Because of the banking background of his family, Fr. Mateo headed the distribution of relief funds after the earthquake. Because of his efforts for the injured and homeless victims, Fr. Mateo's health—always rather precarious—eventually failed. He went to Europe on the advice of his doctor.

After a number of stops Fr. Mateo visited Paray-le-Monial, where the Sacred Heart had appeared to St. Margaret Mary. There he was cured. In Paray, Fr. Mateo was inspired with a unique plan to spread devotion to the Sacred Heart. He then traveled to Rome. In Rome he first mentioned the plan to Cardinal Vives, a friend of the Crawley-Boevey family. The Cardinal was enthusiastic, and he urged Fr. Mateo to submit the plan to Pope Pius X.

Fr. Mateo's plan was to establish the social reign of the Sacred Heart by getting families to enthrone the Sacred Heart as the head of their households. In an audience with the Holy Father, he asked for permission to preach this message everywhere.

"No, my son," came the answer. He continued, "You ask for permission and I say no. I do not *permit* you, I *command* you to give your life for this work..."

These words seemed like a command from Heaven to Fr. Mateo. He returned to Paray-le-Monial, and there, in the sanctuary of the apparitions, he implored guidance and begged for the health necessary to carry out his mission. At this time he received an extraordinary grace. He saw clearly the method of the work he was to do. "I understood what Our Lord desired of me. That same evening I resolved upon a plan to conquer the whole world for the love of the Heart of Jesus—home after home, family after family." He understood that the devotion to the Sacred Heart, hitherto limited for the most part to churches, was to be brought into the family circle, and that the family was to carry out all of Our Lord's requests in the home itself in order to benefit from His marvelous promises.

Fr. Mateo began his campaign in Chile. Accompanied by the parish priest, Fr. Mateo would go from home to home, "enthroning" the Sacred Heart by putting up a picture or statue of the Sacred Heart of Jesus in a place of honor and performing a simple ceremony naming Him the Lord of the home. Our Lord had promised St. Margaret Mary that He would bless any place where an image of His Heart was exposed and honored. Enthronement also involves the consecration of the family to the Heart of Jesus. The family dedicates itself to Our Lord, its rightful Head. This consecration is a covenant in which the family members promise to be obedient to the will of the Lord; it is like a collective renewal of the baptismal promises made by each member of the family.

The results were startling. Family after family returned to a fervent and ardent practice of their faith. Conversions abounded. Word of the work began to spread rapidly, and in April of 1913 the Bishops of Chile requested indulgences for the ceremony of the Enthronement. The petition was quickly granted by Pope Pius X, and in 1915 these indulgences were extended to the entire world by Pope Benedict XV.

To further the crusade Fr. Mateo got together a group of young boys and girls to be his "secretaries." They copied hundreds of letters, often in languages which they did not understand, and sent them all over the world to make the work of the Enthronement of the Sacred Heart of Jesus better known.

People all over the world began enthroning the Sacred Heart in their homes, and sometimes even in their cities and nations. They did this out of love for the Sacred Heart—but not all people loved Jesus. In 1936 in Spain a firing squad of Communists "executed" a prominent outdoor statue of the Sacred Heart. After the firing, they dynamited the statue.

Fr. Mateo traveled all over the world preaching the message of the Enthronement of the Sacred Heart. It would be impossible to give a detailed account of the seemingly endless whirlwind campaigns of this apostle of the Sacred Heart. He traveled all over Europe, and by 1935 had worked his way to the Orient. Later he traveled to the United States and Canada.

From 1907 to 1960 Fr. Mateo traveled, preached and wrote unceasingly. He was fluent in five languages and spoke to over 100,000 priests and countless religious and lay persons. He also converted hundreds of notorious sinners. At the Vatican it was said, "No one since the time of St. Francis Xavier has done more for the Church than Fr. Mateo." It is also said that during his long apostolic career Fr. Mateo worked many spiritual miracles, as well as some physical ones.

Today, Fr. Mateo's work is carried on in many nations. In the United States, literature on the Sacred Heart Enthronement is available from the National Enthronement Center in Fairhaven, Massachusetts.

Fr. Mateo came to the United States in 1940, where he stayed and preached throughout the country for four years. During this time he suffered greatly from diabetes, sometimes being so weak that he could hardly begin the opening conferences of his retreats. One of the highlights of his stay in this country was the solemn consecration of the Chicago Archdiocese to the Sacred Heart before a crowd of over 125,000 in 1943.

Father Mateo had a great appreciation for the value of the Holy Mass. At a talk given in Arizona he said, "Do you know what I am preaching everywhere? I am preaching: *Pay the ransom of souls* with the *Chalice*, with the *Chalice*. The greatest means of converting souls is *one more Mass*, one more Mass during the week, and, with sacrifice, two or three more Masses; if possible, *daily Mass*, to pay for the eternal salvation of souls so dear to you. That is the great thing—the Chalice filled with the Precious Blood."

He spoke of the great value of the Mass in converting sinners. "You are asking for a miracle; I approve. But I tell you that you must pay the ransom for the conversions you make. You have a right to ask for such miracles. Do you know what a conversion is? It is the resurrection of a soul. It is far greater to see the resurrection of a soul than the resurrection of a corpse. Oh, one more Mass! Please—one more Mass! Pay the ransom with the Chalice. One more Mass! If you have anyone at home sick, or dying, oh, pay the ransom with the Chalice—one more Mass!"

Fr. Mateo went on to tell of how his Anglican father had been converted at age 58, weeping tears of joy at his first Confession and First Communion. Fr. Mateo explained that his mother had been the instrument of God in this conversion: "How did she succeed? Speaking generally, you know that husbands do not like sermons at home. Then how did she convert my father? She never missed Mass, her daily Mass, except when sick and dying, and even then the priest came to give her Holy Communion.

"When I left home for school in the morning, she was already back from church—and we were 11 children. She knew her first duty was to the home, to attend to her family; and yet in spite of that she found time to go every morning to Holy Mass and to receive Holy Communion. She paid the ransom...I venerate my mother. She died in 1935, when I was preaching in Japan. She is saying, as I am saying, that it is the Chalice, the *Chalice*, the *Chalice!*"

In 1944 Fr. Mateo left the United States to begin what proved to be his last apostolic tour. Finally his health failed, and in 1946 he was hospitalized. Taking advantage of a privilege granted him years before, that of offering Holy Mass seated, he was able to enjoy the consolation of daily Mass except when he was too weak even to sit at the altar. In 1948, in a hospital room, he celebrated the Golden Jubilee of his priesthood.

In spite of a number of major heart attacks which almost put an end to his work, Fr. Mateo rejoiced in being able to end his days in what he called his "Cloister of the Divine Will." From his hospital room there flowed from his prolific pen letters, articles and even a book.

In February of 1956 he was flown back to Valparaiso, Chile where, despite his failing health, he carried on an intensive writing apostolate until his death on May 4, 1960.

The body of Fr. Mateo is buried near the main altar in the Church of the Sacred Hearts, the church where he first preached his Enthronement Crusade. A cause for Fr. Mateo's beatification is in the beginning stages. Any favors gained through his intercession should be reported to the Men of the Sacred Hearts, Abbeville, Louisiana.

Fr. Mateo Crawley-Boevey, who was inspired at Paray-le-Monial with the idea of a unique way to spread devotion to the Sacred Heart—the Enthronement of the Sacred Heart in the home. When he went to Rome to ask Pope St. Pius X for permission to spread this devotion everywhere, the Pontiff replied, "No, my son." Then he continued, "You ask for permission and I say no. I do not *permit* you, I *command* you to give your life for this work." This picture was taken while Fr. Mateo was preaching in Spain in 1917, age 42.

Fr. Mateo wanted "to conquer the whole world for the love of the Heart of Jesus—home after home, family after family." He began his crusade in Chile, then traveled to many corners of the globe. He traveled, preached and wrote unceasingly from 1907-1960, spreading devotion to the Sacred Heart. He spoke to over 100,000 priests and many more religious and lay persons, converting hundreds of notorious sinners. At the Vatican it was said, "No one since the time of St. Francis Xavier has done more for the Church than Fr. Mateo."

Fr. Mateo had a great appreciation for the value of the Mass in converting sinners and saving souls. He would urge, "Pay the ransom with the chalice!" He credited his father's conversion at age 58 to his mother, who had gone to Mass and Holy Communion daily, despite the fact that she had 11 children. She had "paid the ransom" for her husband's soul.

Communist firing squad "executing" a national monument to the Sacred Heart of Jesus in Spain in 1936. After the firing, they dynamited the statue.

45

THERESE NEUMANN

Therese Neumann
1898 - 1962
Germany
Died Age 64

"I resigned myself to the will of God because the duty of every Christian is to accept the cross which the Saviour sends. It would be a sin to strive against the will of God. I did not accept the cross because of the cross, but in devotion to the Cross of the Saviour. . . My pains by themselves are of no avail to save souls, but only when united with the pains of Our Lord. If it were possible, I would willingly accept sufferings in Heaven in order to bring more souls to the Saviour." These words were spoken by Therese Neumann describing her role as victim soul.

Possibly the most controversial stigmatic and mystic of our age, Therese Neumann has been credited with the sacred stigmata, the ability to live on no food other than Holy Communion, and a number of other mystical phenomena such as visions, special vicarious sufferings, knowledge of hearts and bilocation. She also had mystical experiences involving the Blessed Sacrament, her Guardian Angel, and the Poor Souls in Purgatory.

Properly and prudently, the Catholic Church has refused to recognize visions, apparitions and other mystical phenomena as proofs of the holiness of a soul. The deciding factor is the favored person's personal conduct and application. Thus, the main question is whether or not Therese Neumann followed Christ by practicing virtue to an heroic degree. In this light only can the wealth of charismatic phenomena in her life have any power to convince. If one day Therese Neumann is numbered among the officially proclaimed "Blessed" or "Saints" of the Church, it will not be just because of the mystical phenomena which she experienced. It will be because of her faith, love of God, willingness to serve others, and her heroic acceptance of the will of God for her, including the physical and spiritual sufferings she endured.

Therese Neumann was born on Good Friday, April 8, 1898, in the small Bavarian town of Konnersreuth. She was the first of 10 living children of Ferdinand and Anna Neumann. Her father was a tailor and had a small farm. All of the family members worked hard on the small farm to earn their daily bread. Therese was often called by the nickname "Resl."

Therese was intelligent, industrious and pious. She received a solid education, and her final report card in 1914 showed that her over-all grade was very good.

At age 14 Therese worked as a hired laborer for a Mr. Martin Neumann. Later, two of her sisters joined her there. They managed his household and ran an inn. Therese was the largest and strongest of the sisters, so she ploughed and kept the fields and did much labor that would normally have been delegated to a man. This was due, in part, to the fact that most of the men were involved in World War I.

When she was 15 Therese dreamed of becoming a missionary to the colored missions in Africa as soon as her brothers and sisters were grown up enough so that they would no longer need her at home. She had already made plans to enter the Missionary Sisters of St. Benedict at Tutzing. With her father's permission, she was saving a part of her wages for her dowry.

In 1918 a fire broke out at a neighboring farm. As one of the strongest hands in the neighborhood, Therese took her position on some bales of hay and lifted full buckets of water up over her head to another person who poured them over the walls of a shed threatened by the flames. Here she had an accident in which she dislocated her spine.

The dislocation of her spine caused a partial and then a complete paralysis, and Therese became bedridden in her parents' home. The medical treatments, which were the best her family could afford, did not help. Then in 1919, at the age of 21, she became totally blind. For seven years Therese matured spiritually in patient suffering and sickness.

Earlier, her father had given her a little picture of St. Therese of Lisieux, and Therese developed a strong devotion to this saint, the Little Flower of Jesus. A number of the miraculous cures that Therese would experience are directly attributable to the Little Flower. In each instance Therese dreamed of or heard a voice telling her what was happening. First she was cured of her blindness. She was also cured of bedsores, an infected foot, her paralysis and appendicitis.

Therese told her confessor, Fr. Naber, that she had seen a beautiful light and that a voice came out of the light asking her if she wanted to be cured. She answered that whatever God wished was what she herself wanted. With her childlike simplicity, Therese told the voice that she wanted anything and everything that comes from God—flowers and birds, or any suffering He might send. Then the voice told her that she would be able to walk again, but that she would still have very much and very long to suffer. "Only through suffering can you best work out your desire and your vocation to be a victim, and thereby help the work of the priests. Through suffering you will gain more souls than through the most brilliant sermons."

In 1925, for the first time since her accident in 1918, Therese was able to go to church. During her days of suffering she had learned how to find meaning in suffering. Since she could not be of any service to the human community by her activity, she hoped, by offering up her sufferings, to be a useful member of the Mystical Body of Christ.

From 1922 on, Therese began to have no feelings of hunger or thirst, developing instead a certain repugnance to food. From about 1927 until the end of her life, a period of 35 years, she lived without taking any food or drink except daily Holy Communion. The Host would remain undissolved within her for 24 hours, giving her strength until her next Communion. Therese was always cheerful and affable, even in the midst of her greatest sufferings. She remarked that she dared not be otherwise, when she knew that the Blessed Saviour was present within her.

On March 4, 1926 Therese experienced for the first time a vision of Christ kneeling in the Garden of Olives. She heard Him praying, and suddenly He seemed to look at her. At the same moment she felt such a sharp pain in the region of her heart that she thought she was going to die. Blood began streaming down from the spot and she kept on bleeding until noon on Friday. This vision and others began to recur, and gradually Therese received all of the stigmata associated with the Passion of Our Lord—the marks of the nails in the hands and feet, the scourging, the crown of thorns. Additionally, she bled from her eyes and sometimes sweated blood.

These "Passion ecstasies," in which Therese relived Our Lord's sufferings on Good Friday, would occur on about half the Fridays of the year—several hundred times in all. The estimated loss of blood from one Passion ecstasy varied between two and three liters.

Later, Therese was examined medically, as were her stigmata. The blood was analyzed, and every scientific test possible was made to rule out trickery or natural causes. She ate only the Eucharist during the two-week test. The fact is that the mystical phenomena experienced by Therese Neumann defy all known explanations.

The stigmata were not the only charisms which Therese experienced. She could recognize relics, and she knew when the Blessed Sacrament was present. She could also recognize priests even if they hid the fact of their priesthood. Therese read the hearts of many of her visitors, and many left her presence renewed in heart and spirit. Special sufferings for both the living and the dead occupied a great part of her time.

Therese also experienced many visions on the lives of the Saints and events in the Bible, coordinated with the liturgical feast for the day. She would see souls in Purgatory on All Souls Day and many saints on All Saints Day. Often she would see the same event over and over again from year to year. Sometimes Therese would receive miraculous Holy Communion, the Host appearing on her tongue all by itself. The Host would also disappear without any motion of swallowing by Therese.

The news of the mystical happenings at Konnersreuth spread worldwide, and a storm of sensationalism broke loose. Public interest grew. Some people were attracted because of the needs of their souls; many came out of mere curiosity. But many of the curious were moved enough to go to church, pray and receive the Sacraments, undergoing conversion if need be. This became one of the missionary lessons of Konnersreuth—a strengthening of faith and confidence in God. This seemed to make up for all the many difficulties and self-denials that Fr. Naber and the members of Therese's family had to endure to make the crowds of visitors welcome. Therese's natural desire to avoid sensational curiosity-seekers must have cost her greatly in terms of patience and humility. She was very gracious to the crowds of visitors, and was a very charming person.

Therese loved flowers and animals, particularly birds. She was given a pony and cart, and also quite a few exotic birds as gifts;

these were a real delight for her. Therese also greatly enjoyed work outdoors on her parents' farm.

In agreement with her father, Therese consented to a medical observation and documentation. Her attitude was: "Saviour, You have started things here; You can also bring them to the conclusion You desire; we leave it all to You."

In a letter to a professor friend, Therese once mentioned a little of the way she felt about all the controversy and push for scientific examinations. "Since I am convinced that you have a clear picture and a good grasp of what our dear Saviour has been working through me, His miserable servant, I will write to you about what is closest to my heart and what causes me such pain, since it does not please our dear Saviour, not in the least. . . .You know very well that I never like to hear a whole lot about real smart people. . .who want to explain everything in terms of human reason and do not even stop to think that our dear Saviour is superior to them. I always think that true science and knowledge are supposed to lead to our dear God, but the contrary is usually the case. . . .it is a question of God's grace and our own cooperation and good will. I do not know how these people who keep torturing me, like the doctors, can have such a poor grasp of the fact that God can do more things than they can understand. . .Let us pray and beg our Saviour to forgive everyone whose arrogance makes them oppose whatever our dear Saviour is trying to accomplish; they really don't know what they are doing."

In another letter she wrote: "If only He [God] will keep giving me the strength I need, then I'll be glad to take everything He sends. Then if the Church people or some outsiders like to think that I'm nothing but a fake, well, that's all right too. . . .Sometimes, when things are really hard, I like to think: if it didn't hurt it wouldn't be a sacrifice."

During World War II there was a request for another clinical observation of Therese. This time her father refused. Too much had been spoken of the "experiments" of the Third Reich, and her father feared for her life. Although there is no proof that anything harmful would have happened to her, the clinical examination would not have been made under the requirements which her father had requested, primarily that of allowing her mother or one of her sisters to be present at all times. It is probably best that this request was not acceded to.

On April 20, 1945 American soldiers occupied Konnersreuth after the city had been shelled by the Nazi SS and the Americans. During the firing Therese and 30 of her relatives, mainly nieces and nephews, were hiding in a temporary shelter her father had built. The shack over the dugout began to burn. Therese saw this and hurried to lift out the children. She escaped with only singed hair and clothing. About a fourth of the homes in town burned, but after the American soldiers entered the town, Therese and her family were able to return to their home. The soldiers expressed their sincere sorrow for what had just happened in the town.

In the following days Therese cared for the wounded and helped to ease the state of emergency in the village. Many of the American soldiers visited her.

Therese took an active interest in the needs of the Church. After the war she was instrumental in obtaining some property at Fockenfeld for a seminary for late vocations. After the death of Therese's parents and two members of her family, Fr. Naber and his housekeeper moved into the family barn and stable buildings, which had been made into living quarters for him.

Therese's last active project was to attempt to raise the funds for a convent of perpetual adoration in her diocese. She gave the project a good start, and an energetic benefactor completed it after her death.

Therese had long suffered from angina pectoris. On September 15, 1962, just after she arose and was dressing, she suffered the heart attack that caused her death. Although the local doctor gave her an injection and heart massage, she experienced terrible pain and had to be sat up in her bed and propped up on a pile of cushions. In this position on Tuesday, September 18, she was taken into her sister Mary's arms and died, without being able to say a single word of farewell. She had received Holy Communion and asked for a little water that morning. This was the first time in years she had asked for water with Communion.

After Therese's death she was laid out in her parents' room, and a glass window was put into the door. From Tuesday until Saturday, from early morning until midnight, thousands of pilgrims passed her body. On Saturday the funeral Mass took place in the parish church, and toward the end of the services the casket was closed. Three doctors all substantiated the fact that despite four days of lying in state, there was no trace of decomposition and no perceptible odor. One estimate is that there were more than 10,000 pilgrims present at her funeral.

Although an official cause for beatification has not yet been opened, the Episcopal See of Regensburg has been conducting diocesan investigations into Therese Neumann's life and has received numerous petitions to open the cause for beatification. These are based on the conviction of many people that Therese Neumann was blessed by God with an extraordinary degree of grace and that she lived an heroic life in the practice of her religion in faithfulness to "the Saviour."

Therese Neumann as a young woman in the early years after receiving
the stigmata. Deeply devoted to St. Therese the little Flower, Therese Neumann had been cured through St. Therese of blindness and paralysis that
had caused her to be bedridden for years. From at least 1927 until the
end of her life (35 years), Therese lived without food or drink except
the Eucharistic Host, which she received daily.

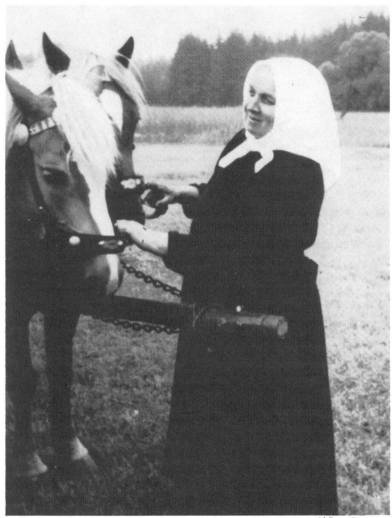

Adalbert Albert Vogl

Above: Therese was a very cheerful person. She loved animals and enjoyed working outdoors on her parents' farm. Therese had the remarkable gift of being able to recognize relics. She could also tell when the Blessed Sacrament was present, and she could recognize priests even if they hid their priesthood.

Facing page: In 1926 Therese received the stigmata, the wounds of Christ. For many years she suffered the Passion of Christ on certain Fridays, experiencing the scourging, the crowning with thorns and the piercing of the nails, while bleeding profusely from her eyes and wounds.

486

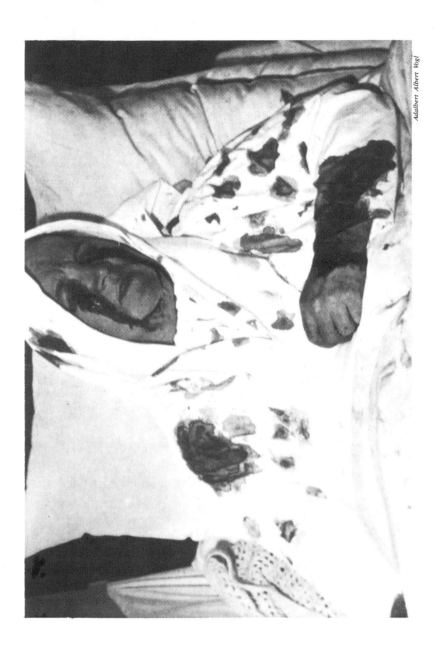

487

Therese saw many visions of Biblical events—and of the lives of the saints on their feast days. Moreover, on All Saints Day she would see saints, and on All Souls Day she would see souls in Purgatory. Many thousands of persons came to the Neumann home over the years; these included a large number of GIs during World War II. Therese was a gracious hostess to the many visitors.

Facing page: Therese Neumann in death, 1962. She died of a heart attack at age 64. Therese's body was laid out from Tuesday through Saturday, while thousands of people came to pay their last respects to this Bavarian peasant woman who had borne the wounds of Christ.

SOURCES BY CHAPTER

The individual bibliographical entries in this book consist of publications and names of correspondents who gave information or leads to information. American archivists' addresses are listed in the *Official Catholic Directory*, a copy of which is on file in the chancery office of each diocese.

1. SAINT ELIZABETH SETON
    Publications
    Dirvin, Joseph I., C.M. *Blessed Elizabeth Ann Seton.* New York: archives, 1963.
    Dirvin, Joseph I., C.M. *Mrs. Seton: Foundress of the American Sisters of Charity.* New York: Farrar, Straus and Giroux, 1962.
    Melville, Annabelle. *Elizabeth Bayley Seton.* New York: Charles Scribner's Sons, 1976.
    Correspondence
    Sister John Mary, D.C., archivist; Emmitsburg, Maryland.

2. SAINT JOAN ANTIDA THOURET
    Publications
    Kempf, Rev. Constantine, S.J. *The Holiness of the Church in the Nineteenth Century: Saintly Men and Women of Our Own Times.* Translated from the German by Rev. Francis Breyman, S.J. New York: Benziger Brothers, 1916.
    Trochu, Francis. *Saint Jeanne Antide Thouret.* London: Sands & Co., 1966.
    Various pamphlets and archival materials.
    Correspondence
    Sister M. Pia Panfili; Rome, Italy.
    Sister Marie Sophia Tevarotto, S.C.S.J.A., secretary to the Provincial; Milwaukee, Wis.

3. BLESSED MAGDALEN OF CANOSSA
    Publications
    Mother Agnes, F.d.C.C. *Blazing the Trail.* Parkway, England: Hazell Watson and Viney Ltd., 1963.
    Kempf, Rev. Constantine, S.J. *The Holiness of the Church in the Nineteenth Century.* New York: Benziger Brothers, 1916.
    Various pamphlet materials.

491

Correspondence
> Sister Filomena Annoni, F.d.C.C., Superior General of the Canossian Sisters; Rome, Italy.

4. SAINT ANDREW KIM AND COMPANIONS
Publications
> *The Catholic Church in Korea.* Seoul, Korea: The Bicentennial Episcopal Commission, 1984.
>
> Egan, Rev. Thomas R., M.M. "Brief Look at the Church in Korea." Seoul: *Korea Pastoral Exchange*, Jan. - Feb., 1983.
>
> *Franciscan Missionaries of Mary Communication.* Providence. Vol. 7, No. 2, winter, 1985.
>
> Latourette, Kenneth Scott. "Andrew Kim Ordained in 1845." Seoul: *The Korea Times*, April 26, 1984.
>
> Latourette, Kenneth Scott. "Christianity Began with Tragedy." Seoul: *The Korea Times*, April 25, 1984.
>
> "The Martyr Saints of Korea." Houston: *Texas Catholic Herald*, August 10, 1984.
>
> "103 Martyrs Canonized by Pope in South Korea." Houston: *The Houston Post*, May 7, 1984.
>
> "103 Saints Created on Korean Church's Happiest Day." Houston: *Texas Catholic Herald*, May 11, 1984.

Correspondence
> Sister Anne Dundin, F.M.M.; Pusan, Korea.
> Sister Rosemarie Higgins, F.M.M.; Providence, R.I.

5. SAINT VINCENT MARY STRAMBI
Publications
> Gioacchino della Sacra Famiglia, P., C.P.S. *Vincenzo Maria Strambi.* Rome: Postulazione dei Padri Passionisti, 1950.
>
> Grashoff, Raphael, C.P. *I'll Not Be a Traitor.* St. Meinrad, Indiana: The Grail, 1950.
>
> Kempf, Rev. Constantine, S.J. *The Holiness of the Church in the 19th Century.* New York: Benziger, 1916.
>
> Schamoni, Wilhelm. *Das Wahre Gesicht der Heiligen.* Stein am Rhein: Christiana-Verlag, 1966.

Correspondence
> P. Enzo Annibali, C.P., Archivist General of the Passionist Order; Rome, Italy.
>
> Mother Mary Joseph, C.P., Superior; Passionist Nuns, Ellisville, Mo.

6. SAINT VINCENT PALLOTTI
Publications

Cruz, Joan Carroll. *The Incorruptibles*. Rockford: TAN Books and Publishers, Inc., 1977.

Herbert, Lady Mary E. *Venerable Vincent Pallotti: Apostle and Mystic*. Rev. and enlarged by Rev. Nicholas Wilwers. Milwaukee: Pallottine Fathers, 1942.

Kempf, Rev. Constantine, S.J. *The Holiness of the Church in the Nineteenth Century*. New York: Benziger, 1916.

Wilwers, Rev. Nicholas M. *The Story of Vincent Pallotti*. Techny, Ill.: Divine Word Publications, 1954.

Pamphlets.

Correspondence

Sister M. Edwina, S.A.C., Pallottine Sisters; Huntington, W. Va.

Bro. Louis E. Rojas, S.A.C., National Pallottine Mission Office; Baltimore, Md.

Fr. Josef Vikoler, S.A.C., archivist; Rome, Italy.

7. MOTHER THEODORE GUERIN
Publications

Burton, Katherine. *Faith Is the Substance*. St. Louis: B. Herder Book Co., 1959.

Eleanon, Sister Joseph, S.P. *Call to Courage*. Notre Dame: Dujarie Press, 1969.

Correspondence

Sister Eugenia Logan, historian, Sisters of Providence; St. Mary-of-the-Woods, Indiana.

8. SAINT JOHN VIANNEY (THE CURÉ OF ARS)
Publications

Cruz, Joan Carroll. *The Incorruptibles*. Rockford, Ill.: TAN Books and Publishers, Inc., 1977.

Fourrey, Rt. Rev. René, Bishop of Belley (text) and René Perrin (pictures); captions by Jean Servel, O.N.I.; trans. by Mary Ruth Bethel. *The Curé D'Ars: A Pictorial Biography*. New York: P.J. Kenedy & Sons, 1959. (Translation of *Le Cure d'Ars*, Éditions du Chalet, Lyons, 1958).

O'Brien, Fr. Bartholomew J. *The Curé of Ars: Patron Saint of Parish Priests*. Rockford, Ill: TAN Books and Publishers, Inc., 1987.

Trochu, Abbé Francis. *The Curé d'Ars*. Trans. by Dom Ernest Graf, O.S.B. London: Burns Oates and Washbourne, 1927. Reprint by TAN Books and Publishers, Inc., Rockford, 1977.

Correspondence

> Soeur Madeleine, religeuse de S. Joseph; Margasin de l'Oeuvre, Ars.

9. VENERABLE PAULINE JARICOT

Publications

> Burton, Katherine. *Difficult Star: The Story of Pauline Jaricot.* London: Longmans, Green and Co., 1947.
>
> Dollen, Father Charles. *Charity without Frontiers.* Collegeville, Minn.: The Liturgical Press, 1972.
>
> Hanley, Boniface, O.F.M. "She Persevered to the End." *The Anthonian,* Paterson, N.J.: Vol. 54, 2nd quarter, 1980.
>
> Neill, Thomas P., Ph.D. *They Lived the Faith: Great Lay Leaders of Modern Times.* Milwaukee: The Bruce Publishing Company, 1951.

Correspondence

> Father Mario Arroyo, Society for the Propagation of the Faith; Houston, Texas.
>
> Msgr. William J. McCormack, National Director, Society for the Propagation of the Faith; New York, N.Y.

10. SAINT JOSEPH CAFASSO

Publications

> Bianco, Enzo, S.D.B. & Maraldi, Assunta, F.M.A. *First Centenary of Don Bosco's Missions.* Rome: SDB Publishers, 1975.
>
> Bosco, St. John. *St. Joseph Cafasso, Priest of the Gallows.* Rockford, Ill.: TAN Books and Publishers, Inc., 1983.
>
> Kempf, Rev. Constantine, S.J. *The Holiness of the Church in the Nineteenth Century.* New York: Benziger Brothers, 1916.

11. SAINT MADELEINE SOPHIE BARAT

Publications

> Bascom, Marion, R.S.C.J. *Rose Philippine Duchesne.* New York: Manhattanville College. (undated.)
>
> Cruz, Joan Carroll. *The Incorruptibles.* Rockford: TAN Books and Publishers, Inc., 1977.
>
> Kempf, Rev. Constantine, S.J. *The Holiness of the Church in the Nineteenth Century.* New York: Benziger Brothers, 1916.
>
> Lovasik, Rev. Lawrence G., S.V.D. *Picture Book of Saints.* New York: Catholic Book Publishing Co., 1970.
>
> Monahan, Maud. *Saint Madeleine Sophie: Foundress of the Society of the Sacred Heart—1779 to 1865.* London: Longmans, Green and Co., 1925.
>
> Pamphlet materials.

12. SAINT EUPHRASIA PELLETIER

Publications

Bernoville, Gaetan. *Saint Mary Euphrasia Pelletier*. Dublin: Clonmore and Reynolds, Ltd., 1959.

Boardman, Anne Cawley. *Good Shepherd's Fold: A Biography of St. Mary Euphrasia Pelletier, R.G.S.* New York: Harper & Brothers Publishers, 1955.

Dent, Barbara. *Saint Euphrasia Pelletier*. St. Louis: B. Herder Book Co., 1962.

"A Harvester of Souls." *Tabernacle and Purgatory*, March, 1944.

A Harvester of Souls. Clyde, Mo.: Tabernacle and Purgatory Press, 1961.

Sister Mary of Our Lady of the Angels, R.G.S. *The Little White Shepherdess*. Chicago: J. S. Paluch Co., Inc., 1950.

Correspondence

Sister Mary Angela, Communications Director; Suore Buon Pastore, Rome.

Sister Marie Francis, R.G.S., Provincial Secretary; Jamaica, N.Y.

Betty Holmes, secretary, Provincial Convent of the Good Shepherd; St. Louis, Mo.

Sister Mary Komas, R.G.S.; Cincinatti, Ohio.

13. FATHER JOHN JOSEPH LATASTE

Publications

Collected Writings of Father Jean Joseph Lataste, O.P. Translated.

Father Lataste and Bethany. Mimeographed by the Sisters of Bethany, 1983.

Pamphlet materials.

Correspondence

Sister Mary of Christ, Dominican Sisters of Bethany; Millis, Mass.

Sister Renata of Jesus, Dominican Sisters of Bethany; Millis, Mass.

14. BLESSED MARY OF PROVIDENCE

Publications

Buehrle, Marie C. *I Am on Fire*. Milwaukee: Bruce Publishing Co., 1963.

Rene-Bazin, Marie. *A Witness of the Invisible*. London: Catholic Truth Society, 1958.

Correspondence

Sister Marie Dion, H.H.S.; Chicago, Ill.

15. SAINT CATHERINE LABOURÉ

Publications

Cruz, Joan Carroll. *The Incorruptibles*. Rockford, Ill.: TAN Books & Publishers, Inc., 1977.

Dirvin, Joseph I., C.M. *Saint Catherine Labouré of the Miraculous Medal*. Rockford, Illinois: TAN Books and Publishers, Inc., 1984.

Husslein, Joseph, S.J. *Heroines of Christ*. Milwaukee: Bruce Publishing Co., 1949.

Laurentin, R. and P. Roche, C.M. *Catherine Labouré et la Medaille Miraculeuse: Documents Authentique*. Paris: Congregation de la Mission, Filles de la Charité, Dessain et Tolra, 1976.

Lovasik, Rev. Lawrence, S.V.D. *Picture Book of Saints*. New York: Catholic Book Publishing Co., 1970.

The Saint of Silence and the Message of Our Lady. Paris: Daughters of Charity, 1968.

Correspondence

Central Association of the Miraculous Medal; Germantown, Philadelphia, Pa.

Sister Regina M. Triche, D.C.; Paris, France.

16. BLESSED MARIA OF JESUS CRUCIFIED

Publications

Icone de la Bienheureuse Mariam de Jesus Crucifie. Rome, 1983.

Rossi, Hans. *Ein Regenbogen über dem Heiligen Land*. Freiburg, Germany: Kanisius Verlag, 1983.

Servitium Informativum Carmelitanum, Vol. XVI, 1983, no. 6. Rome.

Solenne Proclamazione della Prima Beata della Terra Santa. Rome, Nov., 1983.

Pamphlet materials.

Correspondence

Carmelite Sisters; Alhambra, California.

Discalced Carmelite nuns; Danvers, Mass.

Sister Mary Eileen, O.C.D.; Baltimore, Md.

Mrs. Karin Fuller, translator.

Sister Miriam of Jesus, O.C.D.; Eugene, Ore.

Rev. Howard Rafferty, O. Carm., Director, Aylesford; Darien, Ill.

Father Simeon of the Holy Trinity, O.C.D., Postulator General; Rome, Italy.

Sister Theresa, O.C.D.; Roxbury, Mass.

17. CORNELIA CONNELLY

Publications

Cornelia Connelly Special Issue. *The Pylon.* Society of the Holy Child Jesus. Vol. XXIX, No. 3, 1968.

Eleanor, Mother Mary, S.H.C.J. *Mother Cornelia Connelly. Pylon* Supplement No. 1, Rome, 1960.

God Alone: An Anthology of the Spiritual Writings of Cornelia Connelly. London: Burns and Oates, 1959.

Hanley, Boniface, O.F.M. "The Grace to Know Your Will." *The Anthonian.* Paterson, New Jersey: St. Anthony's Guild, 1983.

Member of the Society, A. *The Life of Cornelia Connelly, 1809-1879, Foundress of the Society of the Holy Child Jesus.* London: Longmans, Green and Co., 1922.

Molinari, Paolo, S.J. "Commitment to Love: A Reply to Cornelia Connelly's Critics." *Homiletic and Pastoral Review*, New York, October, 1963.

Smith, Sheila Kaye. *Quartet in Heaven.* New York: Harper and Bros., 1952.

Therese, Mother Marie, S.H.C.J. *Cornelia Connelly.* Westminster, Md.: The Newman Press, 1963.

Walsh, James, S.J. "The Vocation of Cornelia Connelly." *The Month*, London, 1959.

Whatmore, Leonard A. "Cornelia Connelly: Gold in the Fire." *Homiletic and Pastoral Review,* New York, February, 1963.

Correspondence

Sister Mary Cletus, S.H.C.J., The Cornelia Connelly Guild; Drexel Hill, Pa.

Sister Helen Logan, S.H.C.J., Rosemont College; Rosemont, Pa.

Sister Caritas McCarthy, S.H.C.J., Director of Studies, Society of the Holy Child Jesus; Rome, Italy.

18. BLESSED JEANNE JUGAN

Publications

Jeanne Jugan. Chicago, Ill.: Little Sisters of the Poor.

Hanley, Father Boniface, O.F.M. "The Grace of Asking." *The Anthonian,* Vol. 56, 1982.

Milcent, Paul. *Jeanne Jugan, Foundress of the Little Sisters of the Poor.*

Milcent, Paul. *Jeanne Jugan: Humble, so as to Love More.* London: Darton, Longman and Todd, 1980.

Serenity. Special Centennial Issue. Little Sisters of the Poor. Summer 1979, No. 26.

Serenity. Little Sisters of the Poor. Autumn 1979, No. 27.

Correspondence
> Sister Mary Bernadette, l.s.p.; Baltimore, Md.
> Sister Mary Richard, l.s.p.; Baltimore, Md.

19. SAINT MARY JOSEPH ROSSELLO

Publications
> Burton, Katherine. *Wheat for This Planting*. Milwaukee: Bruce, 1960.
>
> *Golden Jubilee, Province of Newfield, N.J.* Newfield: Daughters of Our Lady of Mercy, 1969.
>
> "Turn Down a Legacy, and Become a Saint." *Key to Happiness*, New York, 1968 (11-12).

Correspondence
> Daughters of Mercy; Newfield, N.J.

20. BLESSED PAULINE VON MALLINCKRODT

Publications
> Blankenburg, Sister Mary Angela. *Pauline von Mallinckrodt*. Trans., Sister Agnes Schmittdiel. Wilmette, Ill.: Maria Immaculata, 1972 (unpublished mimeographed work).
>
> Burton, Katherine. *Whom Love Impels*. New York: P. J. Kenedy & Sons, 1952.
>
> von Mallinckrodt, Pauline. *Pauline von Mallinckrodt Tells Her Story*. Mendham, N.J.: Sisters of Christian Charity, 1973. (English translation from the German original.)

Correspondence
> Sister Mary Thecla, S.C.C., archivist, Sisters of Christian Charity; Wilmette, Ill.

21. SAINT PAULA FRASSINETTI

Publications
> Cruz, Joan Carroll. *The Incorruptibles*. Rockford, Ill.: TAN Books and Publishers, Inc., 1977.
>
> *A Life according to the Sacred Heart of Jesus*. New York: Sisters of St. Dorothy, 1949.
>
> *Paola*. Taunton, Mass.: Sisters of St. Dorothy, 1958.
>
> A Sister of St. Dorothy. *A Great Servant of God*. Grasmere, N.Y.: Sisters of St. Dorothy, 1951.
>
> *Ven. Mother Paola Frassinetti*. Rome: Sisters of St. Dorothy, 1922.

Correspondence
> Sister M. Fraga, S.S.D.; Taunton, Mass.

22. SAINT THERESE COUDERC

Publications

Encounter through the Cenacle. Fall, 1970.

Paul VI, Pope. "Canonization Address for Saint Therese Couderc." May, 1970.

Perroy, Rev. Henry, S.J. *A Great and Humble Soul: Mother Therese Couderc, Foundress of the Society of Our Lady of the Retreat in the Cenacle (1805-1885).* Transl. Rev. John J. Burke, C.S.P., S.T.D. New York: The Paulist Press, 1933.

Surles, Sister Eileen, r.c. *Saint Therese Couderc.* Milan: Editrice Ancora Milano, 1970.

Women of the Cenacle. Milwaukee: Convent of Our Lady of the Cenacle, 1952.

Correspondence

Sister Ellen Frawley, r.c.; Rochester, N.Y.

Sister Quinn; Houston, Texas.

23. SAINT VICENTA LOPEZ

Publications

En El Sexagesimo Aniversario de su Muerte es Exaltada a la Gloria de la Beatificacion. February, 1950. (Beatification pamphlet.)

Lawson, Rev. William, S.J. *All You Need Is Love.* Langley Bucks, England: St. Paul Publications, 1969.

Correspondence

Sister Mary Agnes Chevalier, R.M.I., Superior Provincial; San Antonio, Texas.

Sister Maria Herminia de Jesus, R.M.I., archivist; Rome, Italy.

24. SAINT THERESE OF THE CHILD JESUS

Publications

Beevers, John. *Saint Therese the Little Flower: The Making of a Saint.* Rockford, Ill.: TAN Books & Publishers, Inc., 1976.

O'Connor, Patricia. *Therese of Lisieux.* Huntington, Indiana: Our Sunday Visitor Press, 1983.

Office Central de Lisieux. *Visage de Therese de Lisieux.* 2 Vols. Lisieux: Office Central de Lisieux, 1961.

St. Therese of Lisieux. *The Story of a Soul: The Autobiography of St. Therese of Lisieux.* Transl. by John Clark, O.C.D. Washington, D.C.: ICS Publications, 1976.

St. Therese of the Child Jesus. Clyde, Mo.: Benedictine Convent of Perpetual Adoration, 1964.

Therese. Reno: Carmel of Reno, 1984.

Correspondence

> Sister Helen Theresa, C.S.J.; Pasadena, California.
> Mother Mary John, O.C.D., Carmelite Monastery; Traverse City, Mich.
> Sister Michael, O.C.D., Carmelite Monastery; Reno, Nevada.

25. BLESSED MARIA ASSUNTA

Publications

> Cruz, Joan Carroll. *The Incorruptibles*. Rockford: TAN Books and Publishers, Inc., 1977.
> Salotti, Rev. Charles. *Sister Mary Assunta*. N. Providence, R.I.: Franciscan Missionaries of Mary, 1931.
> *The Theme Song of Assunta*. Compiled by One of Her Sisters. North Providence, Rhode Island: Franciscan Missionaries of Mary, 1956.

Correspondence

> Sister Rosemarie Higgins, F.M.M.; North Providence, R.I.
> Sister Agnes Willmann, F.M.M.; New York.

26. BLESSED ELIZABETH OF THE TRINITY

Publications

> *Cause de Beatification et de canonisation de la Servante de Dieu Elizabeth de la Trinite*. Dijon: Jobard, 1931.
> *Une Louange de Gloire*. Louvain pamphlet.
> Meulemeester, Maur de, C.Ss.R. *O Mon Dieu, Trinite que j'adore*. Louvain: S. Alphonse, 1959.
> Philipon, M.M., O.P. *The Spiritual Doctrine of Sister Elizabeth of the Trinity*. Westminster, Md.: Newman Bookshop, 1931.
> *The Praise of Glory: Reminiscences of Sister Elizabeth of the Trinity, A Carmelite Nun of Dijon, 1901-1906*. Translated from the 5th French edition by the Benedictines of Stanbrook. Westminster, Md.: The Newman Press, 1962.

Correspondence

> P. Simeone delle S. Famiglia, O.C.D., Postulator General of the Carmelite Order.
> Sisters, Carmel of Dijon; Dijon, France.
> Sisters, Carmel of Reno; Reno, Nevada.

27. POPE SAINT PIUS X

Publications

> Bazin, Rene. *Pius X*. London: B. Herder Book Co., 1928.
> Dal-Gal, Fr. Hieronymo. *Pius X: The Life-Story of the Beatus*. Transl. and adapted by Thomas F. Murray, M.A. Dublin: M. H. Gill and Son Ltd., 1954.

Forbes, F. A. *Pope St. Pius X.* Originally published 1918. New and revised edition: London: Burns Oates & Washbourne Ltd., 1954; reprinted by TAN Books and Publishers, Inc., Rockford, Illinois, 1987.

Giordani, Igino. *Pius X, A Country Priest.* Milwaukee: Bruce, 1954.

Lovasik, Rev. Lawrence, S.V.D. *Picture Book of Saints.* New York: Catholic Book Publishing Co., 1970.

Smit, Most Rev. Jan Olav, D.D. *St. Pius X, Pope.* Boston: St. Paul Editions, 1965.

Thornton, Francis. *The Burning Flame: The Life of Pope Pius X.* New York: Benziger, 1952.

Von Matt, Leonard, and Nello Vian. *St. Pius X: A Pictorial Biography.* Chicago: Henry Regnery Company, 1955. Trans. by Sebastian Bullough, O.P. from orig. German ed. published by NZN Buchverlag, Zürich.

28. BLESSED BROTHER MUCIAN OF MALONNE

Publications

Brother Mutien of Malonne. Malonne: Christian Brothers, 1948.

The Christian Brothers Today. Vol. 8, No. 4, Nov. 1977.

Holiness a Sign of Life. Rome: Tricentenario Lasalliano, 1981.

O'Toole, Brother Lawrence, F.S.C. *Brother Mucian of Malonne.* Rome: De La Salle Brothers, 1977.

Correspondence

Brother Hilary Gilmartin, F.S.C., Director of Public Relations, Christian Brothers Conference; Romeoville, Ill.

Brother Luigi Morell, F.S.C., Postulator General; Rome.

Brother John H. Mulhern, F.S.C., archivist; Rome.

29. MOTHER MARIANNE OF MOLOKAI

Publications

Hanley, Sister Mary Laurence. *Mother Marianne of Molokai, Missionary to the Lepers.* Syracuse, N.Y.: Sisters of St. Francis of Syracuse, 1977.

Newspapers and pamphlet materials.

Correspondence

Sister Mary Laurence Hanley, Directress of the Cause; Syracuse, N.Y.

John J. Scanlan, Bishop of Honolulu; Honolulu, Hawaii.

30. FRANCISCO AND JACINTA MARTO

Publications

Johnston, Francis. *Fatima: The Great Sign.* Rockford, Ill.: TAN Books and Publishers, Inc., 1980.

Kondor, Father Louis, S.V.D., ed. *Fatima in Lucia's Own Words* (Lucia's Memoirs). Transl. by Dominican Nuns of Perpetual Rosary of the Monastery of Pius XII, Fatima. Fatima: Postulation Centre, 1976.

McGrath, Msgr. William C. "Fatima" in *A Woman Clothed with the Sun: Eight Great Appearances of Our Lady.* Edited by John J. Delaney. New York: Doubleday Image, 1961.

Our Lady of Fatima's Peace Plan from Heaven. Rockford, Illinois: TAN Books and Publishers, Inc., 1983.

Pamphlet materials, including issues of the bulletin for the causes of beatification of Francisco and Jacinta.

Correspondence

Father Louis Kondor, S.V.D., Postulator; Fatima, Portugal.

31. BLESSED MARY THERESA LEDOCHOWSKA

Publications

Walzer, Sister Mary Theresa, S.S.P.C. *Two Open Hands Ready to Give: The Life and Works of Blessed Mary Theresa Ledochowska.* St. Paul: Missionary Sisters of St. Peter Claver, 1978.

Correspondence

Father Richard Flores; Ft. Worth, Texas.

Missionary Sisters of St. Peter Claver; Chesterfield, Mo.

32. DOM COLUMBA MARMION

Publications

"Abbot Marmion." *The Word Magazine.* April, 1958.

Delforge, Thomas, Monk of Maredsous. *Columba Marmion: Servant of God.* Transl. by Richard L. Stewart. St. Louis: B. Herder Book Co., 1965.

Marmion, Dom Columba. *The Structure of God's Plan*, being the first part of *Christ the Life of the Soul.* Transl. by a Nun of Tyburn Convent. St. Louis: B. Herder Book Co., 1962.

Marmion, Dom Columba. *A Thought a Day from Abbot Marmion.* St. Meinrad, Ind.: Abbey Press, 1964.

Monks of Marmion Abbey. *Abbot Columba Marmion.* Benet Lake, Wis.: Our Faith Press, 1958.

Thibaut, Dom Raymund, O.S.B. *Dom Columba Marmion: A Master of the Spiritual Life.* St. Meinrad, Indiana: Grail Publications, 1938.

Correspondence

Rev. Alcuin Deck, O.S.B., Vice Postulator, Marmion Abbey; Aurora, Ill.

Rev. Gisbert Ghysens, O.S.B., Vice Postulator, Abbaye de Maredsous; Belgium.

33. SISTER JOSEFA MENENDEZ

Publications

Keyes, Louise, R.S.C.J. *Learn of Me*. Alumnae of the Sacred Heart.

Menendez, Sister Josefa. *The Way of Divine Love*. Westminster: Newman Press, 1961. Reprinted by TAN Books and Publishers, Inc., 1972.

Pamphlet-style materials.

Correspondence

Sister Julia Hurley, R.S.C.J.; Washington, D.C.

Sister M. Monrozier, R.S.C.J., archivist; Montpellier, France.

34. FATHER LOUIS VARIARA

Publications

First Centenary of Don Bosco's Missions. Rome: S.D.B. Publishers, 1977.

The Salesian Bulletin. New Rochelle, N.Y.: Salesians of St. John Bosco, Jan.-Feb. 1981, Vol. 35, No. 1.

Correspondence

Father Dominic Britschu, Secretary General of the Salesians; Rome, Italy.

Brother Robert Dias, S.D.B.; Rome, Italy.

35. VENERABLE MATT TALBOT

Publications

Dolan, Albert H., O. Carm. *Matt Talbot, Alcoholic: The Story of a Slave to Alcohol Who Became a Comrade of Christ's*. Chicago: The Carmelite Press, 1947.

Dolan, Rev. Albert, O. Carm. *We Knew Matt Talbot*. Chicago: Carmelite Press, 1948.

Knowles, Leo. *Candidates for Sainthood*. St. Paul: Carillon Books, 1978.

Purcell, Mary. *The Making of Matt Talbot*. Dublin: Irish Messenger Office, 1972.

Purcell, Mary. *Matt Talbot and His Times*. Revised edition. Chicago: Franciscan Herald Press, 1977.

Correspondence

Rev. Morgan Costellow, Vice Postulator; Dublin, Ireland.

36. BLESSED BARTOLO LONGO
Publications

Caggiano, Pietro. *L'av ventura cattolica.* Naples: Azienda Autonoma di Cura Soggiorno e Turismo, 1981.

Ladame, Abbe Jean. *Blessed Bartolo Longo (1841-1926).* Chulmleigh, Devon, England: Augustine Publishing Co., 1988.

Pompei Citta' Mariana. Prof. Lo Piccolo Don Salvatore. Plurigraph Narni-Terni, 1974.

Rubba, John C., O.P. *Blessed Bartolo Longo.* Providence: Providence College, 1981.

Pamphlet material from the Shrine.

Correspondence

Mons. Pietro Caggiano, administrator, Pontifical Sanctuary of Pompei.

Rev. Guglielmo Esposito, O.P., Curia Generalizia of the Dominicans; Rome.

Rev. John Rubba, O.P.; Providence, R.I.

37. EVE LAVALLIERE
Publications

Hanley, Father Boniface. "Because of Her Great Love." *The Anthonian.* Vol. 54, 1980.

McReavy, Fr. L. L., M.A. *Eve Lavalliere: A Modern Magdalen* (1866-1929). St. Louis: B. Herder Book Company, 1934.

Correspondence

Father Salvator Fink, O.F.M., St. Anthony's Guild; Paterson, N.J.

Father Boniface Hanley, O.F.M., *The Anthonian;* Paterson, N.J.

38. CONCEPCION CABRERA DE ARMIDA ("CONCHITA")
Publications

Cabrera de Armida, Concepcion. *Con Dios Cada Dia.* Mexico City: Ideal, 1979.

Labarthe, Ma. Guadalupe, R.C.S.C.J., ed. *Fui bautigada con el nombre de Maria de la Concepcion.* Mexico City: Concar, A.C.

Navarro, Ignacio, M.S.S. *Concepcion Cabrera de Armida.* Mexico City: Concar, A.C., 1976.

Philipon, M.M., O.P. *Conchita: A Mother's Spiritual Diary.* Transl. by Aloysius J. Owen, S.J. New York: Alba House, 1978. [This work was the main source for this chapter.]

Sierra, Maria Louisa. *Esposa, Madre y Apostol.* Madrid: Cause, 1978.

Trevino, J. G., M.Sp.S. *Concepcion Cabrera de Armida.* Mexico City: Editorial la Cruz, 1973.

Correspondence

Chuck Angelica; Houston, Texas.

Luis Diaz Borunda, M.Sp.S.; Mexico City, Mexico.

M. del Carmen Velasco, secretary, Concar, A.C.; Mexico City, Mexico.

39. FATHER FELIX ROUGIER

Publications

Borunda, Luis Diaz, M.Sp.S. *Como un Patriarca.* Mexico: Misioneros del Espiritu Santo, 1979.

Borunda, Luis Diaz, M.Sp.S. *La Synaxis Eucharistica.* Mexico: Misioneros del Espiritu Santo, 1980.

Borunda, Luis Diaz, M.Sp.S. *Felix de Jesus Rougier un Llamado una Respuesta.* Mexico: Misioneros del Espiritu Santo, 1980.

Padilla, Jesus M. *Sacerdote de Dios.* Mexico: Misioneros del Espiritu Santo, 1979.

Padilla, Jesus. *El Padre Felix Rougier.* Mexico: La Crus.

    I. Preparandolo para su mision—1973.

    II. Seis años en Colombia—1964.

    III. El Fundador—1964.

    IV. Fecundidad espiritual.

Peñalosa, Msgr. Joaquin Antonio. *My Name Is "Felix de Jesus."* Trans. by Fr. Roberto Gonzalez C., M.Sp.S. and Bro. Lorenzo Miranda, M.Sp.S. Unpublished manuscript.

Trevino, J. G., M.Sp.S. *Felix of Jesus.* Mexico, 1953.

Correspondence

Luis Diaz Borunda, M.Sp.S., Vice Postulator; Mexico City, Mexico.

Brother David Tejada, F.S.C., translator; Santa Fe, New Mexico.

40. EDEL QUINN

Publications

Duff, Frank. *Edel Quinn.* Dublin: Cahill Printers, 1960.

Hanley, Fr. Boniface, O.F.M. *Edel Quinn: A Mind of Her Own.* Paterson, N.J.: St. Anthony Guild, 1975.

Knowles, Leo. *Candidates for Sainthood.* St. Paul: Carillon Books, 1978.

McAuliffe, Marius, O.F.M. *Envoy to Africa: The Interior Life of Edel Quinn.* Chicago: Franciscan Herald Press, 1975.

Moynihan, Anselm, O.P. *Edel Quinn.* Cork: The Dominican Bureau.

Peffley, Mary. *Woman of Faith.* Norristown, Pa.: Balance House Publications, 1974.

Suenens, Leon-Joseph Cardinal. *Edel Quinn.* Bruges, Belgium:

Desclee de Brouwer et Cie, 1952.
Correspondence
Rev. Timothy Collins, Sect. Archbishop's House; Dublin, Ireland.
James P. Cummins, Officer-in-Charge, Concilium Legionis Mariae; Dublin, Ireland.
Leo Knowles; England.
Angela Place, Catholic Press and Information Office; Dublin, Ireland.

41. VENERABLE JOSEPHINE BAKHITA
Publications
Knowles, Leo. *Candidates for Sainthood.* St. Paul: Carillon Books, 1978.
Pamphlet materials.
Correspondence
Sister Filomena Annoni, F.d.c.c., Superior General of the Canossian Sisters.

42. ARTEMIDE ZATTI
Publications
Blanco, Jose, S.D.B., translator. *Coadjutor Salesiano Artemides Zatti.* Bahia Blanca: Salesians of St. Francis Xavier, 1980.
Entraigas, Raul A. *El Pariente de todos los Pobres.* Buenos Aires: Editorial Don Bosco, 1960.
Testimony of Father Feliciano Lopez, director of the Community of Salesian Brothers of Viedma, who knew the Servant of God during his last years. Bahia Blanca: La Piedad, 1976.
Articles for introducing the cause of the Servant of God.
Pamphlets and newspaper materials.
Correspondence
P. Italo Martin, S.D.B., Vice Postulator; Viedma, Argentina.

43. BLESSED KATHARINE DREXEL
Publications
Duffy, Sister Consuela Marie, S.B.S. *Katharine Drexel.* Cornwells Heights, Pa.: Mother Katharine Drexel Guild, 1977.
Hanley, Boniface. "A Philadelphia Story." *The Anthonian,* Vol. 58, 1st quarter, 1984.
"The Peacemaker." Sisters of the Blessed Sacrament. Autumn 1979 and Winter 1980 issues.
Tarry, Ellen. *Katharine Drexel: Friend of the Neglected.* New York: Farrar, Straus and Giroux, Vision Books, 1958.
Various pamphlet-style materials and newspaper articles.

Correspondence
> Sister M. Thomasita, S.B.S., Director, Mother M. Katharine Guild;
> Cornwells Heights, Pa.

44. FATHER MATEO CRAWLEY - BOEVEY, SS.CC.
Publications
> Larkin, Father Francis, SS.CC. *Enthronement of the Sacred Heart.*
> Pulaski, Wis.: Franciscan Publishers, 1970.
> Pamphlet materials.

Correspondence
> Rev. Francis Larkin, SS.CC., National Director; Fairhaven, Mass.

45. THERESE NEUMANN
Publications
> Carty, Rev. Charles M. *Who Is Teresa Neumann?* Rockford, Ill.:
> TAN Books and Publishers, Inc., 1974.
> Pamphlet materials.
> Steiner, Johannes. *Therese Neumann.* New York: Alba House, 1967.
> Vogl, Adalbert Albert. *Therese Neumann: Mystic and Stigmatist*
> *(1898-1962).* Rockford, Ill.: TAN Books and Publishers, Inc.,
> 1987.

GENERAL SOURCES
AND SELECTED BIBLIOGRAPHY

Publications

Antonelli, Franciscus, O.F.M. *De Inquisitione Medico-Legali Super Miraculis in Causis Beatificationis et Canonizationis.* Roma: Antonianum, 1962.

Attwater, Donald. *A Dictionary of Saints.* New York: P. J. Kenedy & Sons, 1958.

Attwater, Donald. *Martyrs.* New York: Sheed & Ward, 1957.

Blaher, Damian Joseph, O.F.M. *The Ordinary Processes in Causes of Beatification and Canonization.* Washington, D.C.: Catholic University of America Press, 1949.

Butler, Rev. Alban. *The Lives of the Fathers, Martyrs and Other Principal Saints.* 4 Vols. Chicago: The Catholic Press, 1961.

Delaney, John J., and Tobin, James. *Dictionary of Catholic Biography.* Garden City, N.J.: Doubleday, 1961.

Farmer, David Hugh. *The Oxford Dictionary of Saints.* Oxford: Clarendon Press, 1978.

Foy, Felician A., O.F.M., ed. *The Catholic Almanac.* Huntington, Ind.: Our Sunday Visitor, various editions.

Habig, Rev. Marion, O.F.M. *Saints of the Americas.* Huntington, Ind.: Our Sunday Visitor, 1974.

Holweck, Rt. Rev. F. G. *A Biographical Dictionary of the Saints.* St. Louis: B. Herder, 1924. Reprinted by Gale Research Co., Detroit, 1969.

Index ac Status Causarum Beatificationis Servorum Dei et Canonizationis Beatorum. Roma: Sacra Congregatio Pro Causis Sanctorum, 1962 and 1975 editions.

Official Catholic Directory. New York: P. J. Kenedy & Sons, 1978.

Paul VI, Pope. "Sanctitas Clarior." Apostolic Letter of March 19, 1969 on reorganizing procedures in causes for beatification and canonization. Washington, D.C.: U.S. Catholic Conference, 1969.

"Sacra Rituum Congregatio." *Acta Apostolicae Sedis,* 61 (1969).

Schamoni, Wilhelm. *The Face of the Saints.* London: Sheed & Ward, 1948.

Schamoni, Wilhelm. *Das Wahre Gesicht der Heiligen.* Stein am Rhein, Germany: Christiana-Verlag, 1966.

Correspondence

Rev. F. Beaudoin, Archivist, Sacred Congregation for the Causes of Saints; Vatican City.

508

ALPHABETICAL LIST
OF SAINTS IN THIS VOLUME
(By surname where commonly used)

If you have enjoyed this book, consider making your next selection from among the following . . .

Prices guaranteed through June 30, 1994.

Prices guaranteed through June 30, 1994.

Prices guaranteed through June 30, 1994.

At your bookdealer or direct from the publisher.
Prices guaranteed through June 30, 1994.

NOTES

NOTES

NOTES

NOTES